THE LIPAN APACHES

☽

Lipan man with hair-pipe breastplate (1852).
Friedrich Richard Petri, Center for American History,
UT-Austin, di_04093.

The Lipan Apaches

People of Wind and Lightning

THOMAS A. BRITTEN

UNIVERSITY OF NEW MEXICO PRESS   ALBUQUERQUE

© 2009 by the University of New Mexico Press
All rights reserved. Published 2009
Printed in the United States of America
14 13 12 11 10 09   1 2 3 4 5 6

Library of Congress Cataloging-in-Publication Data

Britten, Thomas A. (Thomas Anthony), 1964–
   The Lipan apaches : people of wind and lightning /
Thomas A. Britten.
         p. cm.
   Includes bibliographical references and index.
      ISBN 978-0-8263-4586-8 (hardcover : alk. paper)
1. Lipan Indians—Historiography.
2. Lipan Indians—Ethnic identity.
3. Lipan Indians—Social life and customs.
I. Title.
      E99.L5B75 2009
      976.4004'9725—dc22

                        2008043132

❧

Book design and type composition by Kathleen Sparkes.
This book was designed using Minion Pro OTF 11/14, 26P.
Display type is also Minion.

To my wonderful children

Zachary, Reuben, Gabriel,

Asa, Lydia, and Emily

CONTENTS

~

ILLUSTRATIONS
AND MAPS

Note on Illustrations

Friedrich Richard Petri (1824–1857) completed his sketches and watercolor paintings of Texas Indians in the 1850s. According to anthropologist William W. Newcomb, in his 1978 book *German Artist on the Texas Frontier*, a close examination of the historical evidence (i.e., clothing, ornamentation, weaponry, and Petri's known haunts) "supports the conclusion that some of the Plains Indians Petri portrayed were Lipans and reinforces the belief that all of them probably were. It does not rule out the possibility that some of the Plains Indians depicted were Comanches" (142–43).

Note on Maps

All maps created by Matthew A. Crawford.

PREFACE

☾

AS THE SOLDIERS AND CITIZENS of the *presidio* San Antonio de Béxar and the nearby *villa* of San Fernando de Valero celebrated New Year's Day, 1733, an exhausted Texas governor Don Juan Antonio Bustillo y Ceballos recuperated from his recent six-week campaign against bands of hostile Indians (*indios bárbaros*). For months, small bands of mounted warriors had been stealing his soldiers' horses, frightening settlers, and attacking the slow-moving mule trains that trudged back and forth between San Antonio and northern Coahuila, carrying supplies and messages to the lonesome and isolated inhabitants of New Spain's northern frontier. The threat that these raiders posed to His Majesty's ambitious plans to extend Spain's reach beyond the Rio Grande had prompted Bustillo to assemble a force of over two hundred soldiers and friendly Indian auxiliaries to track them to their *rancherías* located far to the north on the San Sabá and San Gabriel rivers. The Indian raiders, whom the Spaniards identified as "Apaches, Lipans, Ysandis, and Chentis," had given Bustillo's army a tough fight before dispersing in the face of musket and cannon fire, and the governor—a veteran Indian fighter—felt fortunate that Spanish casualties had been light. Besides recapturing several hundred horses, the Spaniards brought back thirty Apache prisoners, all women and children, with whom Bustillo hoped to leverage his demands that the Indians cease their hostilities. On January 4, the governor sent two of the women home, bearing invitations for their chiefs to visit San Antonio to discuss peace. Three tense weeks passed before the Spaniards saw smoke in the distance, the signal that the Indians had arrived to parlay. A few days later, one of the women, escorted by three warriors, informed the governor that several chiefs were indeed interested in opening a new chapter in their relationship with the Spaniards. Remaining cautiously optimistic, Bustillo treated the four visitors as honored guests, and after a brief stay, they disappeared once again into the wilderness, promising to return within two moons.[1]

In a demonstration of friendship and goodwill, the Spaniards allowed small groups of Apache traders to enter and leave San Antonio with relative freedom while they awaited the arrival of the chiefs. The Indians brought piles of beautifully tanned bison and deer hides to exchange for tobacco, coffee, corn, sugar, and assorted trinkets. Toward the end of March, a group of four Apaches, having completed their business, made their way out of town accompanied by a three-soldier escort. Once they reached the outskirts of the settlement, however, a large contingent of Apache warriors rode up, surrounded the bewildered soldiers, and captured two of them. What the two men endured next at the hands of their captors must have been ghastly. Witnesses testified that they discovered the remains of the two Spaniards shortly after their abduction. The Apaches had pierced their bodies repeatedly with arrows and lances, and in some places stripped the flesh away from their bones. The gruesome incident sparked panic and despair in San Antonio, where only days earlier, settlers had clung to the hope that peace was at hand. Franciscan missionaries labored to restrain their Indian neophytes from fleeing into the wilderness for safety, while soldiers petitioned to have their families removed beyond the Rio Grande and out of harm's way.[2]

The Apaches responsible for this atrocity were relative newcomers to south Texas, but the Europeans did not understand their precise identity and organization at the time. Within a decade, however, there probably was not a Spanish official in Texas unacquainted with these tenacious warriors, whose distant ancestors had inhabited the mountains and boreal forests of Alaska and northwestern Canada. Though few in number, and scattered in small, autonomous bands, the Apaches exerted an important influence on the development of the American Southwest. The easternmost group, the Lipan Apaches, made especially significant contributions in Texas—one might even say they played a lead role—during much of the sixteenth and seventeenth centuries. In the eighteenth and nineteenth centuries, the Lipans' role changed, but they remained crucial players in the pageant of Texas history, right up to the twentieth century. One need only peruse the correspondence of soldiers, missionaries, and settlers on the south Texas frontier to grasp the terror, frustration, amazement, and admiration that most felt when it came to their dealings with the Lipans. During the Spaniards' century-long tenure in Texas (from the first decade of the eighteenth century through the first decade of the nineteenth century), they considered the Lipans as the single greatest Indian threat to the development of New Spain's northern frontier. During the remainder of the nineteenth century, frontier officials representing the interests of Mexico, Texas, and the United States also devoted considerable time, manpower, and treasure to address the "Lipan problem." Oddly, except for Thomas Schilz's brief history *The Lipan Apaches of Texas*, there have been no comprehensive studies undertaken of Lipan tribal history and culture.[3]

The fundamental aim of this book, consequently, is straightforward. I seek to provide a wide-ranging study of the Lipan Apaches that focuses on their history, culture, and their relationships with an astonishingly wide range of Indian and non-Indian peoples. The Lipans—like all Apaches—were an adaptable people, and significant cultural changes coincided with the various migrations and pressures that they faced throughout their history. Like any human community, the Lipans possessed qualities and characteristics that were admirable and praiseworthy, as well as some that were lamentable and troubling. I have tried to maintain a balanced approach, neither romanticizing the good nor excoriating the bad. In the process of this effort, I argue that the peoples that coalesced over time to become Lipan Apaches exercised a disproportionately strong influence in Texas for nearly four centuries— roughly from 1500 to 1900—particularly in the period stretching from 1600 to 1880.

In an attempt to provide as comprehensive a history as possible, I have marched (and at times stumbled) my way through a maze of fascinating, stimulating, but often contradictory scholarship that has accumulated over many years and from a variety of disciplines. Reconciling and synthesizing this scholarly bird's nest of conflicting theories, hypotheses, and speculation has been a challenge. Providing something approaching a consensus view or a synthesis is particularly difficult given the wide disparity of viewpoints, while offering even a precursory historiographical summary is equally impractical due to the sheer volume of scholarship. Take, for example, the word "Lipan." John Upton Terrell writes that "almost all names by which Plains Apache groups and bands are designated were initially given them by Spaniards and are either corruptions of Athapaskan words, Spanish idiom, or reflective of some Apache characteristic or custom."[4] Added to these Spanish names and corruptions are an even larger number of appellations that native peoples applied to the Lipan Apaches (including what the Lipans called themselves) and the Spanish corruptions of *these* names. Writing in the late nineteenth century, anthropologists Frederick W. Hodge and James Mooney maintained that the Lipans called themselves the *Ná-izhan* (meaning "ours" or "our kind"). Hodge argued that the name "Lipan" was probably based on the Spanish or Indian corruption of the Athapaskan appellation *Ipa-n'de* ("Ipa" being the personal name of a great warrior or chief, and "n'de" meaning "people"), while Mooney suggested that the word came from a Spanish corruption of a name belonging to some other tribe altogether.[5] In the 1970s, Albert H. Schroeder concluded that the Lipans called themselves the Sejines, but were also known as Cipaynes, Chilipaines, and Canecy, the latter word a corruption of the Caddoan name for the Apaches.[6] A generation later, Daniel Castro Romero Jr., the chairman of the Lipan Apache Band of Texas, Inc., declared that the word Lipan means "warriors of the mountains," but that they called themselves the Tindi.[7]

Scholarly debate is even more voluminous and contradictory about a score of other pertinent issues: Where did the ancestral Lipan Apaches come from? Why and how did they end up in Texas? When did various unnamed bands of Southern Athapaskans and other Indian peoples coalesce and become "Lipans"? Which Indian groups (each possessing a plethora of Spanish and Indian names) should be included as Lipans? Should we classify the Lipan Apaches as Plains Indians? Southwest Indians? Both? Neither? Or something in between? Did the Spanish, Mexican, Texan, and American governments treat the Lipan Apaches as they did other Texas Indians, or did the Lipans constitute a "special case"? I have done my best to address each of these questions as thoroughly as the evidence allows, but my conclusions certainly will not be the last word.

Throughout the book, I have tried to keep the focus on the Lipan Apaches rather than on the Spanish, Mexican, Texan, and American officials on whose reports and correspondence I rely heavily. Each chapter begins with a story from Lipan Apache oral tradition that relates in one way or another to that particular era in Lipan history. A key theme that runs through practically every chapter is how the Lipans responded to the various crises and pressures that seemed to follow them wherever they went. Social scientists sometimes say that they can learn a lot about people by observing how they react under pressure and bear the strain and emotional weight of stress and adversity. I have attempted to apply this observation to the Lipans—particularly worthy "test subjects," given that so much of their history in the eighteenth and nineteenth centuries was stress-filled. Where useful and necessary, I have provided historical context, and have endeavored to keep explanations of peripheral issues brief. At times, the balance may seem to weigh too heavily on the side of policy concerns, and the Lipan voice becomes muted. This is certainly not to imply that the Lipans were passive spectators of events. Instead, it illuminates perhaps the historian's greatest shortcoming in piecing together a tribal history when virtually all the written evidence comes from only one side of the equation. The best we can do to achieve any semblance of balance is to ask ourselves, "What might the Lipans have thought about this issue? How would they have responded given what we know about their culture and worldview? What do their responses tell us about them?" My answers to these critical questions, while based on extensive research, are at best educated guesses. I hope that they generate new inquiries and research into the history and culture of the Lipan Apaches and other "eastern Apache" groups, and that this study will provide a useful starting point for such pursuits.

INTRODUCTION

☾

LIPAN APACHE ORAL TRADITION indicates that Killer-of-Enemies—their primary deity and culture hero—was responsible for creating both the deer and the horse. At the beginning, Deer was lying down and Killer-of-Enemies lifted him up, but Deer just stood there. Killer-of-Enemies wanted the animal to walk, but the animal did not know just how to do it. So Killer-of-Enemies got the little whirlwinds to come, one from each direction. They entered the deer at four places. After that, Deer was able to walk. In the same way, Killer-of-Enemies created the horse. The whirlwinds came from four directions and entered the horse at four different points: one entered at the flank, one under the shoulder, and one at the hip on either side. Then the horse began to breathe and move when the winds came through it, though before it could not.[1]

☾

THE LIPAN APACHES and other Southern Athapaskans deemed wind and lightning as essential to the animation of all living creatures.[2] Life began when wind and lightning entered the body, and ended when the lightning burned out and the wind abated. On a different level, wind and lightning are powerful metaphors for the Lipan Apaches as a people. Wind brings change and moves in response to various atmospheric pressures, while lightning is fast-moving and a source of breathtaking energy and power. The Lipans likewise moved in response to various pressures and brought important changes to the environment around them. Like lightning, they moved quickly and were capable of unleashing surprisingly potent bursts of energy to accomplish their objectives. Just as wind and lightning are powerful, unpredictable, uncontrollable, and potentially dangerous and destructive forces, so too were the Lipan Apaches—at least from the perspective of the Indian and non-Indian peoples that struggled with them for control over territory and resources. Ironically, the Lipans geared much of their social organization and religious expression toward overcoming, or at least controlling, the various seen and unseen forces and dangers that beset their world. A brief summary of Lipan material and social culture, therefore, is an appropriate starting point for students of Lipan Apache history.

By virtually all accounts, the Lipans were physically impressive. Men were tall and well proportioned and kept their faces free of hair—no beards or mustaches, and they even plucked their eyelashes and eyebrows. Warriors pierced their ears in as many as six to eight places and wore at least one earring in each ear made of shells, feathers, or small rodent skins. The left side of a Lipan man's face was apparently his "good side," since they cut their hair off even with their left ear while allowing the hair on their right side to grow long. Men usually folded and tied their hair with string so that it hung only to the shoulders, or they braided it and wrapped the ends in fur or buckskin. Some Lipans decorated their heads with white clay, leaves, trinkets, or tufts of feathers. They painted their faces and upper bodies, especially in preparation for battle, and etched tattoos into their skin with black and red clay pigments. Frederick Law Olmstead, who met the prominent Lipan chief Cuelgas de Castro in the mid-1850s, was no doubt astonished when the latter rode up on a mule. The chief was dressed in buckskin decorated with beadwork and wore a wreath of fresh oak leaves on his head. He had plucked his eyebrows and eyelashes, sported heavy brass rings in his ears, and had a vermillion streak painted across his face.[3]

Lipan women were generally shorter than their male counterparts and wore their hair long—either loose, or in a single braid down the back. They too painted their faces and perforated their ears, wearing various handcrafted earrings and necklaces of mountain-laurel beads or shells. A small bag of crushed mint attached to a necklace served as perfume.

Contemporaries commented on the comeliness of Lipan women. José María Sánchez remarked in 1828 that Lipan maidens were "as a general rule, good-looking," while Englishman William Bollaert commented that Lipan women were "noted for their prettiness and good figures." On this account, he speculated, the Comanches "have often made war upon the Lipans so as to become possessors of their women."[4]

The Lipans were excellent tanners, and their clothing was clean and well crafted. While manufactured primarily for utility, Lipan clothing also evinced a strong concern for aesthetics that allowed a degree of individualism and self-expression. The summer clothing of Lipan men consisted of a breechcloth, moccasins, and sometimes buckskin leggings or trousers. When dressed in a breechcloth, men might suspend pouches made of mountain-lion skin, powder horns, knives, or whistles from their waists. Women wore a two-piece dress of tanned deerskins. Sometimes the upper part was a complete doeskin with a hole cut in the center, which they wore like a poncho. For decorative purposes, women left the dewclaws on the legs, and the tail (with the hair still on) they allowed to hang down the back. More common, however, were deerskin blouses decorated with fringes, paint, shells, or beads. Elijah Hicks, a Cherokee delegate to a large gathering of Indians for treaty discussions in 1846, commented that Lipan women dressed in buckskin capes, petticoats, and bootees, all elegantly fringed and which "would be a rich dress anywhere."[5]

The proto-Lipan Apaches of the sixteenth and early seventeenth centuries inhabited the flat, grassy plains of the Texas Panhandle, where they hunted bison—massive herbivores whose flesh, bones, entrails, and hides provided practically all that was required for the band's survival. The Lipans' acquisition of the horse, which probably occurred sometime in the early-to-mid-seventeenth century, allowed them to expand their hunting range, and altered some of the communal hunting techniques that they had employed while on foot. Lipan warriors on horseback, seeking to acquire prestige, status, and respect in the eyes of their people, now had powerful incentives and new opportunities to conduct raids on their neighbors, expanding the potential size and reach of the battlefield so that no group's geographic isolation could shield them from attack. Horses also came to represent wealth and stature among Plains Indian peoples, and individuals and groups judged one another

Lipan girl with melon (circa 1853).
Lipans were renowned for their beautifully made clothing. The mother of this little girl would not allow her to pose for this watercolor until she donned the blue and white beaded belt. Friedrich Richard Petri, Center for American History, UT-Austin, di_04092.

by the size and quality of their horse herds. Horses permitted Lipan bands to move quicker and to take more of their belongings with them, but horses did not immediately end their use of dogs as beasts of burden. The French trader and explorer Bénard de La Harpe, who visited a Lipan Apache encampment between 1710 and 1720, noted that bands with horses still utilized dogs to transport robes and tipi poles. Rather than totally replacing traditional plains culture traits, therefore, the horse broadened and intensified those already in place, evolving to become the essential vehicle of transportation, medium of exchange, and regulator of economic values and social status for Plains Indian peoples.[6]

Even after their acquisition of the horse, Lipan bands spent much of their time in pursuit of bison. Like other Plains hunters, the Lipans believed that huge herds of buffalo and other game animals originated in a "country" under the ground or inside mountains, and that every spring they swarmed up out of great cave-like openings in the earth that were located somewhere in the "Llano Estacado" of Texas. In general, bison herds drifted south to winter in the canyon bottoms of the south Texas Panhandle, so the Lipans may actually have, on occasion, witnessed them emerging up onto the plains in the spring. Nevertheless, the migratory patterns of bison herds were usually unpredictable and erratic, and experienced hunters understood that the timing of the previous year's bison migration was no guarantee about the upcoming one. The Lipans were mindful of all this, and over the course of several generations, developed migration patterns of their own. In the spring, after the women had sown crops and gathered a variety of wild plants, nuts, and seeds, several bands joined in a large hunting expedition. They returned home in the summer to harvest their invariably meager crops, and in the fall set out again on another hunt to procure meat for the winter. During the eighteenth century, after the Comanches had displaced them as masters of the Panhandle Plains, the Lipans sought buffalo on the San Sabá and upper Colorado rivers in the Edwards Plateau region of central Texas. In the nineteenth century, however, the Lipans sought bison along the lower Nueces and Guadalupe rivers southeast of San Antonio, a region at the southernmost edge of the bison migration.[7]

While bison were the most important large-game animal to the Lipan Apaches, it was by no means their only source of meat. Deer and pronghorn antelope were also critical components of Lipan diets, and

Lipan hunters employed an assortment of tricks and devices to harvest these fleet-footed animals. Masks, decoys, game calls, head nooses, and blinds were all common tools for hunters in pursuit of deer. When small groups of hunters stalked antelopes on the open plains, they used head masks and crept up as close to the herd as they could get. Should large numbers of mounted hunters be available, however, they employed the surround, which, if successful, could decimate an entire herd. Antelope hunting was apparently one of the few occasions where men allowed women to participate in the actual pursuit and killing of game (rabbit hunting being another exception). This may have been a result of practicality, as numbers were critical to the success of hunts that employed surrounds. A greater number of participants meant hunters could target a larger area, or that they could make the surround itself less permeable. Either way, more hunters enhanced the chances of success.[8]

Lipan hunters also sought bears and peccaries (*javelinas* or wild pigs), the latter of which were common across much of Texas. Hunters either shot these feisty creatures with bows and arrows or, if close enough, clubbed them over the back with big sticks. When large game was scarce, Lipan hunters turned to smaller animals such as rabbits, porcupines, quails, turkeys, doves, prairie dogs, squirrels, and rats. They took rabbits in surrounds, clubbing or shooting the bewildered animals as they sought to escape. Rodents were flooded out of their burrows, or pulled out of the ground via notched or forked sticks. The Lipans baited dead animals with horsehair snares to catch turkey vultures—not to eat, but to extract wing and tail feathers for arrows. They caught and ate turtles, tortoises, grasshoppers, river mussels, and, on occasion, fish—which they trapped in the shallows or shot with arrows.[9]

Lipan boys learned about hunting from early childhood. When a boy had attained proficiency with a bow and arrow and learned how to set traps and build blinds, he was ready for his first hunt. His grandfather usually accompanied the novice on this important venture, both to give instructions and to perform a ceremony over the boy's first kill. Essential to the young hunter's training was his recognition of, and adherence to, elaborate and complex rules regarding the compact that existed between hunters, and between man and animal. A successful hunter, for instance, shared his kill with comrades who had not been as fortunate. Hunters also took great care processing the animal's carcass.

The Lipans believed that deer, for example, withheld their favors from those who failed to treat their flesh and hides with conventional respect. With the wind as their messenger, deer were always aware of the position of the hunter and surrendered themselves only to those who showed due respect for the rules and observances of the hunt.[10]

There were certain animals that Lipans, for religious, cultural, or simply culinary reasons, refused to eat, although scholars disagree about precisely which animals should be included on the list of taboo foods. In a series of interviews conducted in 1940 with a seventy-five-year-old Lipan woman named Stella La Paz, anthropologist Edward W. Gifford recorded that wildcats (or bobcats), wolves, coyotes, eagles, hawks, and turkey vultures were animals that the Lipans would never eat. Frank Buckelew maintained that the Lipans despised ducks and other waterfowl as well. The Lipan Apaches, unlike some Plains peoples, were not dog eaters either—perhaps because of the canines' greater utility as pack animals and family pets, or due to their close resemblance to wolves or coyotes. Scholars also disagree about whether Lipans ate horses. Most Plains Indian groups abhorred the idea of eating horseflesh, and as a result held the horse-eating Apaches in contempt. Anthropologist Andrée Sjoberg maintains that the Lipans were horse-eaters, but horsemeat was not a preferred or staple food. When bison were abundant, after all, the Lipans needed horses to conduct hunts and carry tipi poles and covers. Juan Antonio Padilla, a Spanish *presidial* commander who had firsthand experience with the Lipans, offers some clarification on the matter in his 1820 observation that the Lipans ate horsemeat, but only when they had to.[11]

By the mid-eighteenth century, the Lipans were probably becoming beef-eaters, either because they were disinclined to venture into enemy territory to hunt bison, or due to convenience. By the mid-nineteenth century, they were tending large herds of cattle that they had secured in raids on both Indian and non-Indian settlements, through natural increase, or through the capture of wild cattle. Possessing large herds of cattle (and horses) forced some Lipan bands to practice a form of pastoral nomadism, shifting their camps from place to place to seek better pasturage for their livestock. According to Frank Buckelew, the Lipans developed a unique method of securing meat when they needed it— what might be termed an informal "drive-in"! When the band needed meat, the warriors rode out and drove the herd into the village, where they singled out and slaughtered several head. Afterwards, they drove the herd back out to pasture. The women then began the arduous task of preparing the slaughtered animals. While the excitement, danger, and organization of these "drive-ins" certainly lagged behind the hunting of bison, the Lipans must have appreciated the efficiencies inherent in simply driving their food supply right to their very doorstep.[12]

Besides cooking and preparing meals, Lipan women contributed significant supplements to their families' food supply. Some bands attempted planting corn on occasion, but beyond inserting the seeds into the ground, the Lipans did little in the way of preparing the soil, clearing away brush, weeding, or fertilizing. If the patch was near a stream or other water source (river bottoms were prime locations), and if time permitted, they might attempt to dig a crude irrigation ditch to water the crop. Nevertheless, their nomadic lifestyle and frequent relocations prohibited them from relying too heavily on farming, and only a few families bothered to try. As Stella La Paz explained, "The Jicarilla could farm because they stayed in one place. But the Lipan were different. They went all over. They never stayed in one place. They kept roaming around almost all the time and couldn't stay around and take care of crops." Lipan elder Antonio Apache concurred. The Lipans, he recalled, "used to go off and hunt, or gather other foods, or hunt the buffalo or the antelope, and then come back for the harvest. They had no means of keeping wild animals out of the corn. They did not care much about it. If nothing bothered [the corn patch] before they came back, they would have a little corn. But they didn't depend on it."[13]

The Lipans' somewhat half-hearted efforts at farming may have developed as a defensive response against the repeated raids of their numerous enemies. Being tied down to a particular place to tend their crops provided their enemies with a critical advantage of launching surprise attacks, since they knew when and where their Lipan adversaries would be at certain times of the year.[14] Frank Buckelew recollected how the Lipans with whom he was living in the 1860s had apparently forgotten how to farm. One day, some elderly Lipan women led him down to a river bottom and, after showing him a small bundle of seed corn, asked how large an area would be necessary to sow the corn. Buckelew paced off a small plot for them, and with their help, began clearing it of brush and debris. The women soon grew weary of the activity, however, and planted their corn in a much smaller patch. "I never saw our crop any more," Buckelew later recalled, "as the tribe soon moved away."[15]

While agriculture did not rank very high on the Lipans' list of critical food resources, the gathering of wild plant foods most certainly did. While living in south and south-central Texas in the eighteenth and nineteenth centuries, Lipan mothers and daughters gathered a wide variety of edible plants, nuts, berries, and tubers that were rich in vitamins, starch, and carbohydrates, frequently tipping the balance between their families' survival and starvation. Some of the plants carried the added benefit of possessing medicinal qualities that a skilled practitioner could harness to treat a wide range of maladies. Among the most important wild plants that Lipan women harvested were the sotol (*Dasylirion wheeleri*) and various types of cacti and agaves. The sotol (or Desert Spoon) was in some respects the "bison" of the plant world for the Lipans. Consisting of hundreds of three-foot-long green ribbons emanating from a central core (or bulb), the plants resemble a bright green porcupine. In early summer, the sotol plant produces a long, slender flower stalk that can grow up to twelve feet high, making it a simple matter to find them. Akin to the buffalo, the Lipans used virtually every part of the plant. The stalks, for example, made an excellent building material to construct lean-tos, sweat lodges, or travois. When split open, the stalks produced a sweet syrup or honey that the Lipans used as an additive to various foods and drinks. When the stalk was young and tender, the Lipans slow-roasted them by constructing a wooden frame above a fire and then leaning the sotol stalks against the frame and slowly turning them. Women then peeled away the burnt outer skin and ate the rest. They used the long, grassy ribbons, meanwhile, as bedding, as a roofing material, and even as cigarette wrappers. The most important part of the plant, however, was the bulb, which they slow-roasted in earthen ovens. After several days of cooking, they uncovered the earthen crock-pot, removed the bulbs, and then spread them out in the sun to dry. When perfectly dry, the women placed them inside rock or log mortars and pounded them with large wooden pestles until the concoction resembled white flour. After mixing the sotol flour with water, the women fashioned small cakes or loaves and baked them in the ashes and embers of a fire.[16]

The Lipans also utilized various species of cacti. The fruit (or tuna) of the prickly pear cactus and the pitahaya cactus (*Acanthocereus tetragonus*) were eaten fresh or dried, as was the fruit of the small and large barrel cactus (*Ferocactus wislizenii*). Women cooked the stems, stalks, and "hearts" of agave, and the "heads" of mescal plants in underground kilns (like sotol); these were eaten or pounded into flour to make bread. They boiled young blooms of the agave plant and extracted the sweet syrup. In an emergency, one could crush and chew the leaves as a temporary source of water. Various species of yucca (*Yucca baccata, Yucca elata, Yucca schotti, Yucca angustissima*), another member of the agave family, provided the Lipans with "fruit" that they could eat raw or after they had cooked the plant in coals and allowed it to dry. The root and trunk of the plant provided bathers with soap and shampoo, while the fibers from Schott's yucca (*Yucca schotti* or Spanish bayonet), when twisted together, made fine rope, baskets, or sandals. Lipans consumed the stalks from the narrow-leaf yucca like sotol stalks and boiled their blossoms in a soup with wild onions.[17]

Lipan women also made efficient use of several types of shrubs and other wild plants. The small red berries of the sumac plant could be consumed, and when mashed up provided an effective poultice for various skin irritations. The roots of the osha plant, when mixed with tobacco and boiled in water, provided a cure for colds and headaches, while smoldering osha plants cleared up nose infections. The okra-shaped pod of the devil's claw was also edible, most commonly added to meat and onion concoctions. In marshy areas along lakes and river bottoms, the Lipans harvested tule (cattail) shoot tips, stem bases, and flower spikes. Cattail pollen, collected from the upper (smaller) part of the flower spike, is rich in protein, and women added it to flour mixtures or used it to thicken soup. Its primary usage among the Lipans, however, was for certain ceremonies. Wild fruits and berries such as plums, cherries, strawberries, raspberries, gooseberries, persimmons, and grapes, when in season, would have also provided a welcome variety at mealtime.[18]

The actual dwellings of Lipan families fell into one of two categories: hide tents (or *tipis*) or brush shelters (*wickiups*). Lipan tipis were composed of a framework of three stout foundation poles with additional light poles—the heavier ends placed in a circle on the ground, with the lighter, thinner ends tied together at the top with rawhide. Women took bison hides dressed on both sides, and occasionally bear skins, and threw them over this framework, leaving a smoke hole at the top and a small entryway facing east. Large tipis could house a family of ten or more, while smaller ones accommodated only three or four individuals. The second type of dwelling, the wickiup, consisted of several slender poles (again either sotol or yucca stalks) that were bent over or arched to form a rough half circle. Women plastered over the cracks and crevices between the poles with mud to keep out the wind, or filled them in with grass, bark, or branches. Otherwise, hides thrown over the top and sides provided cover. Why some bands opted for tipis while others chose wickiups is unclear. The Lipans based their decision on the weather, on the number of days they intended to stay in a certain place, on the availability of building materials on hand, and perhaps on family tradition. Occasionally, both wickiups and tipis provided shelter in the same encampment. When the band decided to move to a new location, they abandoned the wickiups, but the women dismantled the tipis and packed them on the backs of horses or dogs until they reached their new encampment, where they would immediately get busy setting them up again.[19]

The Lipans enjoyed music and fashioned a variety of instruments from the resources at hand. They constructed drums, for instance, by stretching deer or bison hide around a wooden frame or across the mouth of a bowl, and made rattles out of gourds, bison horns, or by stringing together disc-shaped bones or hooves. Wind instruments included eagle-bone whistles, turkey-bone whistles, and flageolets with reeds made of cane. The Lipans believed that flutes possessed special "love magic," but to blow on them without actually knowing how to play them could cause windstorms to occur. Some Lipans also played a musical bow, by either plucking the bowstring or rubbing the string of a second bow across that of the first, akin to playing a violin. Lipan fiddlers constructed their instruments from hollowed-out mescal stalks, using horsehair strings, and painted them blue, green, or red. The bows were made of wood with horsehair.[20]

The Lipans also enjoyed games. Both men and women played "shinny," which was a cross between football and field hockey. Participants played shinny with a buckskin ball and curved sticks on a field about 150 yards long. The object was to get the ball through goals located at either end of the field. It was apparently a rough game, with much shoving and tussling. Therefore, while men and women played the game, they never played together. Hoop and pole, another popular men's game, involved one participant rolling a small hoop along the ground that had been carpeted with pine needles or grass so that the hoop rolled smoothly. Just as it was about to fall over, the two contestants would attempt to throw a long, notched pole through the hoop's center. The person getting the most notches within the hoop scored. Not only did men forbid women from playing this sport, they considered it taboo for females to approach the field or to handle the equipment. The Lipans also loved games of chance and often wagered on the outcome. The moccasin game, for example, involved two teams that buried all but the tops of four moccasins. Each team would then hide a bone in one of them, raising a blanket beforehand to hide their selection. When the first team lowered the blanket, a member of the opposing team came forward with stick in hand to strike the moccasin containing the bone. If he guessed correctly, it was his team's turn to hide the bone. Should he guess incorrectly, the opposing team won points and continued to hide the bone until the first team made a correct guess on the first attempt. The Lipans were also fond of various dice games, and were renowned card players.[21]

Given the nomadic nature of Lipan existence, it seems difficult to imagine how families were able to pack an entire household and move to a new locale at often a moment's notice. "They raise the camp with unimaginable speed when they detect superior enemy forces in the vicinity," noted one Spanish official, and "choosing the most difficult and punishing terrain, they made their migration like wild animals through the most impenetrable wilderness."[22] The task of packing and loading fell on the women, who, through long experience and repetition, made quick decisions regarding what to take and what to leave behind. Items that had required much labor to produce, such as tanned hides, utensils, and perhaps some of the special household goods mentioned above, would make the trip; items that could be readily found or reproduced at the new location (such as wickiups, lean-tos, and bedding), or that were too heavy or unwieldy to carry (such as mortars and pestles) were more often than not left behind. At river crossings, the Lipans constructed rafts and bullboats to transport women and small children and their belongings safely across.[23]

Violence and warfare played a crucial role in Lipan Apache history and culture. Material and sociocultural factors that at times precipitated violence include competition over critical resources (bison herds, fertile soils, water, wood, pasturage, holy places), defense of homeland or territory, and a variety of economic issues such as gaining access to (or control over) commerce, high-status trade items (e.g., European weaponry, alcohol, and manufactured goods), and other valuable commodities (such as horses and enemy captives). Besides these material concerns, one might add group ethnocentrism and religious or ideological traditions as sociocultural issues that contributed to Lipan violence and warfare. The psychological motivations that help explain why individual Lipan warriors were willing to commit acts of violence and engage in warfare include their desire for status, prestige, respect, and social mobility. Raiding and warfare also provided opportunities for individuals to exact revenge and as an outlet for stress and frustration.[24]

The Lipans' instruments of war included bows and arrows, lances (which may have been as long as ten feet or more and required two hands to throw), pikes, spears, war clubs, slings, hatchets, knives, and sticks. Lipan warriors carried circular shields constructed from layers of dried bison or cowhide stretched around a wooden frame. They cut two slits into either side, through which they inserted buckskin straps so that the warrior could wear it on his forearm, thereby shielding his body from arrows and bullets. Rifle shots, unless they hit dead center, usually glanced off these surprisingly durable devices. Warriors painted their shields with images (such as the moon, stars, serpents, and turtles) that added supernatural protection. During the seventeenth and early eighteenth centuries, warriors wore protective leather armor constructed of layers of bison hide that they had glued or sewn together, and they fitted their horses in similar gear, although they abandoned these accessories with the introduction of firearms.[25]

Most Lipan engagements were small-scale episodes involving war parties of twenty or fewer participants. Campaigns were also generally brief, given the fact that the Lipans were unable (due to ammunition and food shortages, or because their families were nearby) to sustain active combat or continual maneuvering. Warfare was also seasonal, as warriors had to transition to hunting during annual bison harvests—although the congregation of several bands at this time provided opportunities for larger campaigns to be conducted. Nevertheless, large war parties were uncommon—frequent raids, ambushes, and skirmishes were the norm. Raiding operations conducted for horses, captives, or food and supplies were relatively commonplace occurrences that satisfied the varied cultural, social, and psychological needs of warriors.

The most frequent and effective Lipan tactic was the raid, often followed up with an ambush of the pursuers. If the opposing force was small and the Apaches enjoyed a numerical advantage, a favorite battle formation was to advance in a crescent-shaped line, with ends thrown forward to outflank and surround the enemy as rapidly as possible. In September 1731, for example, a small group of Apaches stole some horses from the presidial herd at San Antonio, and the Spanish commander sent five men in immediate pursuit. When the commander and a couple of squads of Spanish soldiers rode out to help, they found their men engaged in a fight for their lives with at least forty Indians. As the Spaniards rode into battle, an estimated five hundred Apaches came out from their hiding places and encircled the soldiers, who hastily dismounted to make a last stand at the foot of a tree. The Apaches pressed the attack for a while, and then, much to the Spaniards' astonishment, they began to flee—perhaps worried that additional reinforcement might come from the presidio, or possibly content with keeping the horses they had stolen. At any rate, this clever luring of a small group of Spanish troops into ambush accomplished all that the Indians had hoped for, leaving fifteen enemy casualties.[26]

The observations of Colonel Manuel Antonio Cordero y Bustamante provide important insight into the detailed preparations required to conduct a raid. According to Cordero, once a band had decided to launch an offensive expedition and selected leaders, the Apaches found safe shelter for their families and then set out in small groups toward the target. The leader dispatched one group to a location well suited for an ambush, and sent the others ahead to lure away the enemy by stealing some cattle or horses. Communicating with one another via smoke signals, waving buckskin, or through verbal animal calls, the Apaches coordinated their actions. At the given moment, warriors seized the herd; the victims gave pursuit, and when they entered the ambush site, the Apaches "attack[ed] them suddenly, making a bloody butchery." The Apaches then proceeded on, leaving in place a rear-guard with fast mounts. "If the news from the rearguard makes it evident that inferior forces are pursuing them, they await in a pass and commit a second massacre, repeating this trick as often as their good fortune and the lack of skill of their opponents make it possible."[27] Thus, the Apache raids and ambushes required extensive preplanning, knowledge of the terrain, good timing, communication, and flexible leadership that was willing to make quick decisions as circumstances merited.

The Lipans frequently employed tactics aimed at catching their enemies at vulnerable moments, when warriors could inflict maximum damage without taking significant casualties themselves. From the perspective of Spanish authorities, the Lipan tactics made use of "treachery" and "deceit"—innate character flaws the Spaniards believed were common among all Indians. Teodoro de Croix, the commandant-general of the Interior Provinces of New Spain from 1776 to 1783, expressed astonishment when a Lipan leader proposed in the early 1780s that the Spaniards ally with the Lipans in a ruse aimed at the Mescaleros. According to Croix, the Indian leader suggested that the Spaniards "treacherously pretend" to have declared war on the Lipans. Spanish authorities would then alert the Mescaleros that they were at war with a mutual enemy and suggest an alliance. After the Spaniards had made peace with the Mescaleros and invited them to celebrate their new relationship in an open and exposed spot, the Mescaleros could "be attacked and exterminated by Spanish and Lipan arms."[28]

Where Lipan weakness seemed likely to lead to defeat, they thought nothing of employing abject submission, approaching the Spaniards with humble requests for peace, conversion, and a place where they might take up the hoe and settle into a quiet, peaceful coexistence. Frequently, the Spanish, either exhausted by combat, in dire financial straits, or hopeful of Apache sincerity in such declarations, convinced themselves that their enemy would in fact accept reduction. Periods of peace, however, lasted only as long as the Spaniards were prepared to enforce it. Because frontier officials never seemed to possess an adequate "peacekeeping" force, the Lipans returned to their old habits of rustling livestock and attacking poorly defended settlements, and the litany of violent incidents and robberies brought Spanish officials to a state of complete frustration.[29]

As we have seen, the belief systems and social culture of the Lipan Apaches—like that of any group of people—were diverse, multifaceted, and complex. They provided the essential psychological grounding and motivation for their material culture, warfare, diplomacy, and a host of other human behaviors and activities. The Lipans' conception of the supernatural power that permeated their universe, and the necessity of harnessing this force for their benefit, dominated their individual and collective well-being. Lipans understood that in order for the power to become effective, it had to "work through" humankind. Its method of doing this was to use animals, plants, natural forces, and inanimate objects as "channels" through which to communicate with people. The Lipans' only hope of understanding this communication and acquiring supernatural assistance was by observing a bewildering array of ritual procedures, rules, and personal revelations, often under the guidance of elders, shamans, or other learned individuals.[30]

In Apachean religious ideology, deities were personifications of natural forces. The elements of the natural world did not assume their present forms until the great emergence, when the various individuals of the underworld ascended to the surface and transformed into their present shapes and state of being. The earth to which they ascended, Lipans believe, was a female, and those who lived upon her body were her children. The sun and moon also traveled for a time with the people of the emergence as they marched around the earth in search of a home. The Lipans attributed male characteristics to the sun, which they personified as Killer-of-Enemies, the Lipan Apache's most important culture hero.[31] They conceived of the moon as a woman, whom they associated with Changing Woman, the culture heroine and mother of Killer-of-Enemies.[32] Before they left the people of the emergence, Killer-of-Enemies and Changing Woman promised that they would always keep moving in the heavens, guiding and watching over those with whom they had journeyed. The sun in particular was a model of industry and virtue, never tiring of telling earthlings to get up when he did. During the summer, the sun travels closer to the earth, while in the winter he is more distant. Consequently, winter was the most dangerous time for Lipans as well as the most inclement of seasons.[33]

In the Lipan worldview, animals and plants possessed human sensibilities and could be befriended or angered, trusted or feared. According to one oral tradition, a Lipan woman found shelter from the Comanches after beseeching prairie dogs for sanctuary. They allowed her to come down into their burrow, fed her, and provided gramma grass to keep her warm. When the coast was clear, the prairie dogs gave her provisions for the trip back to her people. Often what appeared to be an animal might actually be the alternative form of some divine being who controlled the means to gain wealth, prestige, hunting prowess, courage, and a host of other important personal attributes. The Lipans associated the cow-bird, for example, with the capture and taming of wild horses; owls and ravens were portents of death, sorcery, and witchcraft. Crickets were linked with love magic, and coyotes with trickery and buffoonery. To some Apache groups, trees were a source of supernatural power, and the particular tree from which (or under which) one gained his supernatural experience (or vision) was considered special and might be singled out and named in songs. Other trees, however, were bewitched, and people feared that those who ate their fruits would suffer from poisoning.[34]

Thus, in some respects, the Lipan universe was small and intimate, filled with animate and inanimate objects endowed with consciousness and human characteristics that bound the wind, rocks, plants, animals, and people into a close personal relationship. On the other hand, the Lipan belief that all things on earth were once alive—and could be so again—magnified their importance. The feelings, attitudes, and place of all things—great and small, animate and inanimate—always had to be considered, for to the very end of his days the Lipan did not know which animal, insect, plant, or rock might aid him, and which might be instrumental in his destruction.[35]

A powerful consciousness of the evils and dangers that beset humanity exercised a profound influence on Lipan behavior and thought processes. As anthropologist Morris E. Opler has observed, "The great majority of Apachean rites are events born of crisis and fear. They are held because of sickness, contact with unclean animals, the contamination of death, and the assaults of ghosts, enemies, and witches."[36] The Lipan Apaches spent much of their time and energy, consequently, trying to protect themselves from these numerous and recurring hazards. "The foundation-stone of the Apache religion," John G. Bourke noted in an essay published in 1891, "is fear: fear of the unseen, the unknown, the unknowable." They were among the most obstinate and warlike people in the Southwest, he maintained; yet in their dealings with the invisible world, the Apaches fell "prey to puer-ile apprehensions" and were "enslaved by [their] superstitions."[37] Writing over half a century after John Bourke, Opler declared that the recognition of evil and danger was "woven into the very fabric" of sacred legend and the Lipan worldview. No sooner had the Lipans emerged from the underworld and settled down, for instance, than they encountered threats from monstrous buffaloes, owls, antelopes, and eagles. Their culture hero Killer-of-Enemies had to vanquish them before the earth was inhabitable for humans. As time passed, new problems and dangers emerged that the Lipans associated with ghosts, bad dreams, water monsters, and a host of other fiendish beings that served as scapegoats for the general insecurities they felt but could not directly control. The Lipans attributed sickness and misfortune both to the malicious activities of witches and sorcerers, and to personal misconduct or carelessness. Seeing, smelling, or touching certain animals (e.g., owls, snakes, coyotes) could cause illness, and even crossing the trail of one of these creatures or resting where one had lain could have dire results. The Lipans had a vivid appreciation of more explicit and observable dangers too, and a constant uneasiness about them. The likelihood of injury or death as a consequence of horseback rides, target practice, raiding, or at the hands of their various human enemies contributed further to their general sense of tension and anxiety.[38]

In the face of these seen and unseen dangers, the Lipans trained themselves and their children to overcome them—or at least meet them head-on. They took the view that from the very beginning of their existence, life had been a series of hazards and dangers to meet and overcome. The Lipans expressed their determination to conquer fear and weakness in various ceremonial contexts, since they believed that supernatural forces favored those who were not easily intimidated. In visions, when people who sought a ceremony entered the "power homes" of supernaturals, fearsome animals and obstacles usually barred the way. Only those who showed no fear or doubt at this time, however, gained power and the right to conduct special ceremonies. Peyote tested its adherents severely in this manner. Some people, when they first chewed peyote, saw frightening visions. If they became alarmed and fled the place of the meeting in a panic, the unpleasant episodes they envisioned would occur. The proper course for men was to remain seated and to force the unpleasant visions aside, and to continue chewing peyote until apparitions that were more desirable appeared.[39]

The Lipans' struggle against evil and danger required ceaseless vigilance and an acknowledgment that maintaining the status quo was perhaps the most they could hope for. To keep on even terms with both men and supernaturals, the Lipans had to ensure that they kept breaches of faith and conduct at a minimum, while they sought to rally beings and forces—both great and small—to their cause. In exchange for their assistance, these beings and forces demanded reciprocity from the Lipans. Buffalo, for example, insisted that hunters observe certain rules and rituals before he allowed people to use his flesh and hide, while horses gave faithful service in exchange for gentle treatment and well-maintained saddles and blankets. Even plant life demanded respect. Care providers took the unused part of plants gathered for medicinal purposes and put them back in the ground, while plants that gave of their roots required respectful handling of their leaves in return.[40]

While not perfectionists, the Lipans strove nonetheless to exhibit certain character traits and personal attributes that would please (or at least not anger) the supernatural forces in the world and secure themselves places of respect among their people. Truthfulness, wisdom, attention to etiquette, cheerfulness, piety, and modesty among women evoked commendation, but there were three critical virtues set apart from the others: industry, generosity, and bravery.[41]

The sun was the symbol of the need for industry. When human beings first appeared on the earth, the Sun ordered them to arise early in the morning just as he did. Elders stressed the importance of doing something useful at as early an age as possible, and they took care to channel children's play in the direction of adult work patterns. Mothers encouraged their daughters to "play camp," carry wood, and fetch water, for example, while boys were pushed to run races, practice constructing bows and arrows, and to hunt rabbits, squirrels, and other small game. A young Lipan woman with bad work habits, despite her beauty, had a hard time finding suitors. Even though men might be attracted to her, their relatives would oppose a union with a lazy girl. Likewise, a slothful young man was likely to receive a negative answer from the family of the girl he sought to marry.[42]

Generosity was another attribute that the Lipans encouraged and held in high esteem. Men who returned from raids or war with captured horses or supplies expected to give practically everything away, particularly to the poor and needy. Successful hunters, likewise, were bound to share their harvest with their companions, as well as with any person in camp who requested food. Those who took meat from the hunter usually exercised moderation, however, for they knew that their hungry brethren would subject them to similar demands when their hunting fortunes improved. If neighbors required assistance, parents and grandparents urged their children to volunteer aid; when sickness or injury struck nearby, parents sent their daughters to the family of the afflicted to carry water and wood, and their sons to tend to their horses. It was a Lipan rule that a friendly visitor should never go away hungry, even if the host had to slaughter a horse to supply the meat.[43]

Bravery was also one of the outstanding virtues of the Lipan Apaches. Killer-of-Enemies was a warrior and raider extraordinaire who established a cult of bravery among the Lipans. To be called a coward, a "crow," or a "woman," or to face charges of shirking one's duty and avoiding danger, were intolerable provocations. As an example of how a true Lipan man should act, the elders told a story about a small group of Lipan warriors who had their horses stolen by a superior number of enemies. Because of their greater number, the enemy felt perfectly secure and moved eastward at a leisurely pace. This act of wanton disrespect infuriated the Lipans, who exclaimed, "These people think we are cowards. Let's show them. Let's follow them and fight. Let's die bravely."[44]

Shamans played a central role in the ceremonial life of the Lipan Apaches, and it was their solemn responsibility to ensure that their people conducted various ceremonies and rituals in accordance with the examples set by the ancients. A person became a shaman by having supernatural experiences, and by convincing his often skeptical brethren that the experiences were authentic. Thus, a successful shaman needed strong oratorical skills to accompany his powers of divination. Shamanistic rites were conducted for a variety of purposes: to cure the sick, help locate and obtain game, bless a new dwelling, bring misfortune to the enemy, foretell of an enemy's approach, find lost objects, and control the weather. Supplicants made remuneration to the shaman through ceremonial gifts (tobacco, pollen, abalone shells), along with more tangible items such as food or clothing. Shamans also engaged in curative rites and frequently made use of medicinal herbs. They burned and boiled sagebrush leaves, which Lipans considered "purifying," and soaked the leaves in water to make an extremely bitter tea used as a tonic to prevent illness, or as a cure for colds and upset stomachs. Tobacco was also a staple in virtually every Lipan ceremony and ritual. Tobacco or sage smoke was essential in driving away evil spirits and in helping supplicants to contact supernaturals. Tobacco poultices, meanwhile, relieved swollen joints, rheumatism, skin infections, and toothaches. Rituals and ceremonies, to be effective, had to be performed perfectly. If the power was misused, the supernaturals were liable to punish the original holder. Hence, shamans would not usually risk transferring their power until late in life, and only to people they could trust to conduct themselves appropriately.[45]

Many anthropologists credit the Lipans as the tribe responsible for bringing peyote to the tribes of the United States. They argue that the Lipans probably learned about peyote from the Carrizos—a Coahuiltecan tribe that once inhabited the peyote-rich region along the upper Rio Grande border between Texas and Mexico.[46] Evidence of ritualistic peyote use among the Lipans is evident in a folk tale that speaks of four Lipan men who decided to hold a peyote meeting. After erecting a tipi, the men took a large woven basket and filled it with fresh, dry peyote buttons. They entered the tipi, and for the next four days and nights ate the peyote while sitting around a small fire. The Peyote People heard about the meeting and sent a representative disguised as an old man with a cane to find out what the four men were doing. Upon arriving, Old Man Peyote hit one of the participants over the head with the cane and took his spirit back to the Peyote People. The remaining three men—upon seeing their friend slumped over unconscious and fearing that he was dead—became frightened. The old man assured them that if they remained for four days and four nights, he would restore their friend to them. On the morning of the fourth day, as promised, Old Man Peyote returned their friend to them. The Lipans rejoiced at their reunion, and afterward they smoked and prayed, washed their hands and faces, and ate a meal.[47]

Lipan Apache sociopolitical organization centered on the extended domestic family, with matrilocal residence. Each nuclear family had a separate dwelling, but several families ordinarily formed a cluster of homes occupied by persons related by blood and marriage. The women were lifetime members of this social group, while the men entered it via marriage. A respected elder of the group acted as its representative, and the extended family was usually associated with his name. Several extended families that resided in the same general area and jointly exploited its resources constituted what Morris E. Opler terms "local groups." Made up of parents, unmarried sons, daughters, and sons-in-law, these family-based local groups tended to remain together. A collection of local groups composed a band, which could consist of anywhere from forty-five to three hundred men, women, and children, although most bands fell somewhere in the ninety to one hundred person range. According to Lipan oral tradition, fourteen distinct Lipan bands existed during the eighteenth and nineteenth centuries. The size and composition of bands were flexible and fluctuated over time. Members of a particular band could leave and join another, and often did so to escape intraband conflicts or punishment. Band members were often, but not necessarily, united through kinship ties. Unlike the Navajos and Western Apaches, the Lipans did not possess larger social groupings such as clans or phratries. Necessarily spread out over a large area, Lipan bands avoided large concentrations of population that would too rapidly deplete essential resources. On special occasions or in emergencies, several bands might temporarily encamp near one another and join forces. Despite their frequent movements within a given territory, the Lipans developed a strong attachment to their homeland and a deep affection for it. Although some bands and local groups manifested long-term preferences for particular localities, the need for mobility and the recognition that all Lipans possessed equal rights to resources precluded any one group from "possessing" a particular region.[48]

The Lipan Apaches were one people, but not politically united or universally governed. Men of influence, rather than wielders of power, exercised leadership at the band level, and adult males usually selected chiefs (or "captains") informally. Leaders formulated opinions and decisions based on consensus and by understanding the various needs and desires of their people. They had to be skilled speakers and diplomats to exhort and persuade others that their decisions were wise. Leaders did not have to be great warriors or particularly bellicose, nor did they require the possession of supernatural power. Rather, leaders were usually mature and experienced men, somewhat aloof and detached in their demeanor to avoid charges of favoritism, observant and aware of tensions within the band, and exemplars of the moral order. Chiefs were usually not particularly wealthy individuals, as the demands on their generosity were always great. A leader would have to be a good diplomat to solve intraband quarrels and to protect the interests of his people when dealing with outsiders. His decisions were not mandates, however, but expressions of the general will, and individuals who disagreed could always pack their belongings and join a new band more to their liking. Lipan bands replaced chiefs who made consistently bad decisions, but they did this informally and without fanfare. Leadership was not hereditary, but the sons of chiefs, having watched and learned from their fathers' example, would have been familiar with what the job required and therefore been in a favorable position to assume leadership.[49]

Kinship ties and their requisite set of strict and demanding social obligations and sanctions bound together members of extended families. The Lipans practiced matrilocal residence, requiring a new husband to join his wife's household. Marriage also obligated a man to perform certain duties for his in-laws, who often watched carefully to ensure that their new son-in-law was not slacking. As the wife's brothers left the extended family when they grew to manhood and married, the protection and subsistence for the family fell to the husbands of daughters, and the son-in-law obligation sought to ensure the smooth functioning and productive capacity of the extended domestic family. During the first few years of marriage, the least desirable and more precarious tasks of the encampment fell to the son-in-law. The bride's parents might ask their son-in-law to break dangerous horses, to ride out to identify approaching visitors, to round up horses that were grazing at a distance, or to sleep on the edge of the encampment. Unsatisfactory performance in any of these tasks could lead to harsh criticism and even banishment. On the other hand, once a son-in-law proved his worth, his in-laws could become invaluable allies. If a woman threatened to divorce a hard-working husband, her kin often sided with the husband. The Lipan family was slow to reject an in-law who was considerate, useful, and a good provider. Even when a man's wife died, his familial obligation still bound him to serve his in-laws until they released him. Normally they would provide another wife for him, either a sister of his deceased wife (sororate) or her cousin. In that way, parents were able to retain the services of productive sons-in law. If there was no close female relative available, or if the family so desired, they could release him back to his

Lipan warrior and his wife.
*Illustration by Hal M. Story
from* The Indians of Texas:
From Prehistoric to Modern
Times, *by William W.
Newcomb Jr.* © 1961, renewed
1989. *By permission of the
University of Texas Press.*

original band. At times, a widower secured his release through purchase
or barter—a string of ponies for instance. The widespread custom of
marrying a deceased's sister was an extremely effective social mecha-
nism that ensured a family's economic well-being in the event of the
provider's sudden departure. Remarrying too quickly, or without the
consent of former in-laws, could have serious consequences. A man who
remarried without permission could have his horses confiscated, and in
some instance be subject to physical assault. The woman who dared to
marry him could also be subject to violent reprisals.[50]

Scholars remain divided on the issue of whether the Lipans practiced
polygamy. Antonio Cordero writes, "Polygamy is widespread in [the
Apache] nation, and every man has as many women as he can support,"

while Englishman William Bollaert noted in 1850 that "polygamy is permitted amongst the Lipans, but few have more than one [wife]." Andrée Sjoberg, meanwhile, maintains that Lipan men could have more than one wife, although the practice was "limited to the chiefs and most outstanding warriors." Others argue that the Lipans did not practice polygamy—Morris Opler going so far as to say that the Lipans were the only Apaches who did not observe the practice.[51] It seems unlikely that many Lipan men would have been able to care adequately for households with more than one wife, given the matrilocal residence that Lipan couples observed—not to mention fulfilling the affinal obligations to various sets of in-laws—unless, of course, a man married sisters. While some bands may have practiced polygamy earlier in their history (e.g., during the heyday of the bison-hide trade in the seventeenth and eighteenth centuries, when additional wives or captives were needed to tan hides), the restrictions imposed by a life on the run inevitably brought changes to their social customs, and monogamy may have become the norm for most Lipan families.[52]

One of the most important rites of passage for Lipan youth was receiving their first haircut. When a child was born, new parents sought out an elder to cut their newborn's soft hair with a flint knife. Failure to do this, parents feared, would result in their child's development of a very low forehead. When the child was two years old, they cut the hair again—always in springtime when the sumac began to bloom. An elder first painted the toddler's head with dark red paint and then put a little pollen—symbolic of life—on the top. For little boys, the elder left tufts of hair at five places—one on top, one over each ear, one in front, and one in back. The family then gathered up the cut hair into a bundle and put it up in a yucca bush. The Lipans repeated the process for four consecutive years in hopes that the child would grow up to have a happy life and good luck.[53]

A second important ceremony for Lipan youth was the girls' puberty ritual, a joyous and festive occasion that at times brought together entire bands from a particular area. This was an event when well-wishers gathered to congratulate parents on bringing their daughter safely to maturity, although the daughter remained at the center of attention. During the four-day ritual, the Lipans referred to the girl as "Changing Woman," and considered her to possess certain healing powers. Small children were brought forward to have their bodies pressed against her so that they might grow strong and straight. Preparations for the rite began as much as a year before the girl's first menses, as food and other paraphernalia were gathered and stored for the big event. Mothers painstakingly crafted a special ceremonial deerskin garment for their daughters, while other family members constructed a sacred shelter in which celebrants chanted and sung sacred songs. The lead singer, who through close observation and practice had learned the various songs connected to the ritual, also enjoyed a place of honor, supervising construction of the sacred shelter and serving as the overall master of ceremonies. Elaborately costumed masked dancers, meanwhile, representing mountain-dwelling supernaturals called the Hactci, performed for boisterous onlookers each evening.[54]

The girls' puberty rite notwithstanding, the Lipan Apaches held a paradoxical attitude in regard to women. On the one hand, men viewed women as morally and physically weaker than themselves, especially susceptible to contaminating influences, and the source of various types of contamination. Nevertheless, men insisted that women be treated with respect and esteem, and acknowledged them as important contributors to the social, economic, and religious life of the band. From the Lipan perspective, women were no match for the greater strength and physical toughness of males. While men swam across rivers, for example, women and children rode across on bullboats. Women's dependence and weakness also discouraged men from taking them on the warpath, where their perceived tendency toward excitability and panic would only make things harder for warriors. Men also alleged that women suffered from particular sensitivities to illness or evil influence. Women were to avoid passing through an anthill, for example, because an ant sting was likely to cause them to develop a high fever. While the Lipans considered it hazardous for anyone to handle eagle, crow, or raven feathers, they believed that the danger was more pronounced for females. The perceived weakness of the woman extended to the moral sphere as well. All traditional stories of unfaithfulness and perversion have women as the primary instigators.[55]

Men also viewed women as the purveyors of contamination. A menstruating woman had to refrain from touching a man's hair lest she cause it to fall out, and females were expected to keep their distance from curing rites, for their presence only made the patient's condition worse. Men barred women from sweat baths, meanwhile, since convalescent males made ill by contact with menstrual blood were the most common bathers. Lipan social strictures also prevented women from playing the musical bow and constructing flutes, and they could not approach the area where men were playing the hoop-and-pole game, nor wear clothes made of skins smoked during the tanning process. There were a host of additional taboos concerning women touching their husband's weapons, which it was feared undermined their accuracy and lethality.[56]

In spite of the disabilities and restrictions to which Lipan men subjected their women, females enjoyed much equality, and certain advantages too. Matrilocal residence ensured women a degree of security, since the home, the household equipment, and her personal effects belonged to her and were inviolate. Living close to family also helped shield women from abusive or violent husbands. If a man was mistreating his wife, her father and unmarried brothers could intervene and perhaps send the errant husband away. Fathers welcomed the birth of girls, understanding that daughters brought strong young men into the family. Like men, women could obtain supernatural power and perform certain ceremonies. The ceremony performed over a new tipi was entirely in the hands of women, and it was an old woman who selected, blessed, and marked the poles, and sanctified the beds and fire pit. Women enjoyed their own games (e.g., the stave game), and while men could watch it, few men availed themselves of the opportunity since most men considered the game effete. Women could take an active part in rabbit surrounds and antelope hunts, and a true gentleman did not overtake a woman who was pursuing an antelope or kill the animal for himself. At war and scalp dances, only women could utter a formalized call signifying applause, and elderly women whose relatives had indicated that they were joining a war party could join in and dance among the men. After a successful raid, warriors turned the prisoners over to the women who had lost family members in the fight. The women made the decision about whether to adopt the prisoners, or to torture and kill them.[57]

As has been noted, Lipan men and women were particularly sensitive to the presence of the various evils and dangers that threatened their life on earth, and existence itself was a challenge to the forces of death. Consequently, living a long, full, and satisfying life was an important and brave goal. Lipan ceremonialism was largely an effort to preserve or protect life, and most of the ceremonies, rituals, and prayers that they performed were to ward off sickness and disaster and to promote longevity. The elderly, having successfully combated death for a number of years, enjoyed the admiration of their people, and the Lipans believed the old folks could transfer their ability to live a long life to the young. Nor did the Lipans fear an aged person who was near death. In fact, they sought a blessing from the dying elder in hopes of prolonging their own life. Many Lipan parents sought out elders to perform the first moccasins ceremony, to bless dwellings, to give names to newborns, and to roll the first cigarettes for boys wishing to join their inaugural raiding party. Grandparents were the primary disciplinarians and reprimanded wayward youths through verbal rebukes, threats, and storytelling. Because of the elders' broad experience and spiritual toughness, grieving families often sought them out to prepare and bury the dead.[58]

The Lipan death complex, like so many of their other cultural expressions, was protective in nature—done as much to preserve and defend the living as to honor and appease the dead. Just as life began when lightning and wind entered the body, it ended when the lightning burned out and the wind abated. Thus, the Lipan refer to death by the phrase "he burned down"—like a candle or a wick. At death, they believed, a person's soul traveled to the rim of the underworld, where it slid down a steep decline into the place from which people had emerged at the beginning of time. A mountain divided the underworld into two sections. The northern section was a dark and gloomy place where witches and other evil inhabitants ate lizards, toads, and snakes. The southern section was a happy place where the good people lived a life of ease, participating in many of the activities they had enjoyed in life. Some stories suggest that juniper trees lined the entrance to the underworld and the trail leading below. Body parts hung from their branches. As the deceased passed by the trees on their way below, the owners reclaimed their missing body parts and entered the underworld whole and restored once more.[59]

The Lipans gave great care to the preparation and burial of the dead. Because of their fear of ghosts and anything associated with death, they disposed of the body as quickly as they could make proper arrangements— at times on the very day that the death occurred. The family usually requested the services of elders, since the Lipans considered the young and inexperienced as susceptible to disorders or maladies associated with contact with the dead. The old man or woman in charge prepared the body and dressed him in his best clothing and jewelry. At the gravesite, the funeral party dug a shallow trench and placed all the personal possessions of the deceased into it. When possible, they placed the body in the crevice of a mountain with the head facing toward the east, and the person in charge placed sage in the form of a cross at the head and feet, telling the dead person that he must go away peacefully and must not look back or bother his surviving relatives in any way. These warnings were particularly important when the deceased had died in the prime of life—when their aims were unfulfilled and they were still struggling for recognition, affection, status, and favor. If they died dissatisfied and vengeful, their ghosts would invoke great fear.[60]

Ghosts manifested their presence in the sounds of animals (owls or coyotes), whistling, or strange tapping. During the days immediately following burial, when the spirit of the deceased lingered near the gravesite, some people might complain of "ghost sickness," a malady whose symptoms included fainting, unconsciousness, delirium, and bad dreams. After the burial, the deceased's horse was killed at the grave, usually with an arrow shot into its throat. The burial party then returned to camp by a different route from which it came. To use the same path would invite the ghost or some other evil spirit to follow. After returning, the members of the burial party would wash and purify themselves with yucca suds and discard the clothes they had been wearing. Relatives who had not been involved in the burial ceremony expressed their bereavement in various ways. They destroyed the possessions of the dead not buried with him—clothes, weapons, eating utensils; they even burned the tipi in which the deceased had lived. The immediate family then moved camp, always in the opposite direction from the fresh grave. If this were not done, they feared, the ghost of the dead might come back to bother them. All neighbors of the immediate family would usually follow suit, hoping to create an unbridgeable gap between themselves and the newly deceased. Anyone who sought to linger near the gravesite would be open to suspicion, for only witches harbored such desires.[61]

Mourners ripped off their good clothes and donned old ones as a mark of grief. Both men and women cut their hair, placing it among growing plants in some open, deserted spot. The relatives might request that the shaman sprinkle them with pollen or ashes, while at night they burned sage and bathed themselves in its smoke to ward off evil spirits. Before retiring, they sprinkled ashes at the head of the bed to discourage visits from ghosts. To think or dream about ghosts or the dead was dangerous, as it drew their attention. To counter such thoughts, relatives and friends often visited the immediate family to tell stories and jokes to cheer them up and get their minds off their troubles. In the days following a burial, any mention of the dead was discouraged, and the Lipans considered speaking the name of the deceased a very serious and dangerous breach. They believed particularly malevolent individuals returned from the dead as owls so they could persecute those who did them harm in life. The Lipans, consequently, were scared of hooting owls and discouraged whistling at night for fear of attracting owls' attention.[62]

As discussed earlier in this chapter, marriage and the familial obligations that accompanied it bound families together into important social and economic units. Ironically, the Lipans did not celebrate marital unions with elaborate ceremonies, and took very little public notice of such events. Organizing a raiding expedition or a curing rite, for example, were occasions of far more ceremonial activity than was a marriage. To understand why the founding of a new family did not merit special notice, we need only to consider Lipan death practices. Contrary to modern Judeo-Christian traditions of cherishing the memory of loved ones who have died so that they will, in some respects, "always be with us," the Lipans suppressed the memory of the dead; there could be little pride in ancestry or lineage. Furthermore, Lipan family members destroyed the belongings of their deceased loved ones, so there was no familial property to inherit or defend. "Loyalty was to the present and the living," Opler writes. "There was no historicizing of the family, no sense of the family over time, no need to bind a new family unit to a tradition."[63]

The Lipans, like most any other people, were prone to accept new ideas or traits that would ease their way of life, save time and energy, and/or provide instant stimulation and satisfaction. Such a willingness to adapt to their immediate circumstances or surroundings led to substitutions in—not alterations of—their basic cultural patterns. But the long-range implications of their various cultural adaptations were consequential, to say the least. As one psychologist has noted, adapting to cultural change is like "having the rug pulled from under one's feet—one does not know whether to fall forwards or backwards or to either side to catch a hold. But no sooner does one regain composure than something else happens. More than the change itself, it is this rapidity of change that is most unsettling and stressful."[64] As the Lipans migrated from mountains to plains to the arid expanses of south Texas and northern Mexico, they struggled to maintain a semblance of cultural continuity. Cherished Lipan values such as bravery, generosity, fortitude, and industry remained a bedrock of security amidst a sea of often bewildering and complex challenges. As time passed and their numerous Indian and non-Indian enemies pressed them on all sides, Lipan men and women suffered from a diminished control over their lives, from a discontinuity for which they were unprepared, and from a bewilderment that resulted from having to sift through the painful alternatives that life's circumstances offered them. As we will see, the Lipan Apaches of the mid-to-late nineteenth century were a people quite unlike their forebears of the eighteenth century. While clinging to their cherished values and traditions, new behaviors and aspirations emerged that must have been painful to a people who had once dominated the southern plains.[65]

To conclude our discussion of Lipan Apache culture, a final question deserves consideration: Can we properly regard the Lipan Apaches as "Plains Indians"? As "Southwestern Indians"? Or as something in between? The Lipans and the Kiowa Apaches were the only Southern Athapaskans to reside permanently on the plains and become dependent on bison for a considerable part of their diet. This dependence helps explain their nomadic lifestyle, their utilization of tipis and load-bearing dogs, and the increasingly important role that women played as food processors, tanners, clothes makers, and manufacturers of tools, utensils, and receptacles. The Lipans' acquisition of horses in the seventeenth century only heightened this dependence on bison, and further solidified their decision to remain as nomads on the Plains. The Lipans traveled exclusively by land, and performed river-crossings via bullboat or crude raft. They were renowned tanners, but not terribly proficient in weaving, basket making, or pottery—handicrafts that were difficult for nomadic peoples to develop fully. They constructed circular shields made of dried bison hide stretched over a wooden frame and wore fringed shirts. On occasion, they decorated both the shields and clothing with painted designs. The Lipans and Kiowa Apaches were the only Southern Athapaskans to adopt the Plains Indian attitude that considered counting *coup* on a fallen enemy a meritorious act.[66]

Although the Lipans never adopted the elaborate ceremonial organization and religious life typical of many Plains Indian peoples, they shared virtually all of the external features of Plains culture.[67] Not until after the Comanches displaced them from the Texas Panhandle in the early eighteenth century did the Lipans stray from this lifestyle. No longer full-time plains residents, the Lipans ceased being "Plains Indians" as they adapted to their new environment in south Texas and located new food sources, building materials, and so forth. Consequently, the Lipan diet grew more diverse, with increasing emphasis placed on the acquisition of smaller game animals as well as wild plants. Wickiups constructed of sotol stalks, leaves, and brush emerged as common alternatives to tipis, while the role of women grew even more crucial to family economies as evidenced by their expanded duties locating, harvesting, and preparing hundreds of plant-based food and medicinal items. Thus, the Lipan movement from the Texas Panhandle to the hill country and arid coastal plain of south-central Texas parallels their abandonment of a strictly Plains culture complex. In its place, a new system evolved— a hybrid of sorts—that blended Plains culture traits, such as nomadic bison hunting, with new ones, such as the acquisition of smaller game species; gathering plants, nuts, and seeds; trading; and desultory farming activities. Further nudging the Lipans from a Plains orientation was their association with (and at times assimilation of) Indian peoples with very different traditions (such as Coahuiltecans, Pueblos, and Jumanos), not to mention Spanish and French missionaries, soldiers, and traders. All these groups introduced the Lipans to new foods, clothing, tools, weapons, technologies, and ideas that they tailored in varying degrees to their needs and desires, continuing a tradition of adaptation and cultural reinvention that had persisted for centuries.

CHAPTER ONE

The Genesis of the Lipan Apaches

Down in the lower world, at the beginning, there was no light; there was only darkness. The beings that inhabited the lower world held a council and discussed if there was another world above them. They decided to investigate. They sent the Wind upward and he came to the surface of the earth and found it covered with water. He rolled back the water like a curtain, and land appeared. The beings of the lower world then sent Crow and Beaver up to investigate what lay above them. But Crow forgot about his mission, spending his time picking the eyes out of the dead fish left stranded when dry land appeared. Beaver, meanwhile, busied himself swimming from stream to stream and building dams. The beings of the lower world grew impatient awaiting the return of Crow and Beaver, so they sent Badger to the surface. He was faithful to the beings below, and returned to the lower world to report that there was dry land on the earth above them.[1]

The beings of the lower world then sent four men to the surface to prepare it for occupation. With the help of Mirage, the men made the hills, mountains, and arroyos, as well as springs and rivers. When all was ready, the beings of the lower world ascended the path that led to the surface and began to occupy the land. They moved around the earth clockwise, all the while looking for a place to live. Leading them on the journey were the Sun and the Moon. As the former occupants of the lower world grew tired and stopped along the way, they became animals, trees, birds, grass, and rocks, and they communicated with one other since they all spoke the same language. The juniper people stopped, for example, and became juniper trees, and the turquoise beads they had been wearing became juniper berries; the oak people stopped next, and the black beads they had been wearing became acorns. Other beings of the emergence became People, and as they marched around the earth, they stopped and settled at various locations. Once they had stopped, they developed their own languages and cultures, becoming unique Indian Nations. The very last groups to stop their journey around the earth and find a home were the ancestors of the Tonkawas and the Lipan Apaches. The Sun and Moon kept walking, however, promising never to stop circling the earth.[2]

❨

THE LIPANS' BELIEF that they were among the last groups to end their journey around the earth is a testament to the importance that they attach to qualities such as endurance, tenacity, and strength. These important character traits, among others, would prove critical for Lipan survival during much of their history. But where exactly did their journey around the world end? Where was their original place of birth? The Lipan creation story is similar to that of the Pueblos and the Navajos, indicating a possible Southwestern influence, but its allusions to Crow, Beaver, water, and fish point to a northern origin.[3] Besides their creation story, Lipan oral tradition suggests that their homeland was some place to the north and west, and if one takes those admittedly vague directions to their geographic limit, northwestern Canada and Alaska appear appropriate places to begin an inquiry into Lipan Apache origins.

The Lipans' distant ancestors, whom anthropologists believe constituted one branch of a much larger language family known as the Na-Dene family (or phylum),[4] traversed the Bering Strait at some point between 7000 and 5000 B.C. and settled over a broad area in subarctic Alaska and northwestern Canada.[5] It was a rugged, wild country of mountains, hills, plateaus, streams, and innumerable lakes, with vast stretches of muskeg—a spongy, greenish-brown swampland that is all but impassible in summer. Deciduous forests of spruce, balsam fir, and birch gave shelter to woodland caribou, muskoxen, deer, elk, black bear, grizzly bear, and moose, as well as to smaller mammals such as beavers, muskrats, woodchucks, porcupines, and snowshoe rabbits. Glacial lakes, rivers, and streams, meanwhile, contained ample stocks of grayling, whitefish, trout, and pike, while rivers with mouths on the Pacific Coast would have abounded with seasonal runs of salmon. Migratory waterfowl was also plentiful. Flocks of ducks, geese, cranes, swans, and loons nested near lakes and rivers, while owls and eagles flew overhead in search of their next meal. Population fluctuations, however, were commonplace among these animal species, a response to climatic changes, the normal succession of forest stages, and other natural phenomena such as forest fires, blizzards, and volcanic activity. Winters were long and piercingly cold, while summers were short and intense, with swarms of mosquitoes and black flies making life miserable for man and beast alike. Similar to other prehistoric immigrants from Asia, the Na-Dene people were nomadic hunters who probably concentrated the bulk of their time and energy securing food and shelter for their families. Caribou and salmon, in particular, were vital staples for a people constantly on the move in a harsh and often inhospitable environment.[6]

The Na-Dene language phylum includes four branches: the Eyak, Tlingit, and possibly the Haida language families (all of which are single languages spoken along the coastline of western Canada and southern Alaska), and the Athapaskan family of languages, which are spread out over the interior of Alaska and western Canada (Northern Athapaskan), along the Pacific Coast of Oregon and California (Pacific Coast or Western Athapaskan), and in the American Southwest (Southern Athapaskan).[7] Of these four branches, the Athapaskan branch deserves special attention, as all Apachean peoples—the Lipan Apaches no exception—are Athapaskan speakers.[8]

The prehistoric Athapaskans were hunters who depended on a wide variety of foods for their survival. As mentioned earlier, the population of various animal species underwent periodic fluctuations in response to climatic and faunal cycles, and starvation was common among early Athapaskan groups.[9] To combat overreliance on specific species of game animals and fish, therefore, Athapaskans supplemented their diet with edible fruits, nuts, acorns, seeds, shrubs, bark, and sap. Even so, caribou (*Rangifer tarandus*) were by far the most important food staple for peoples residing in Alaska and northwestern Canada. By one account, an Athapaskan family of four would have required 250 caribou per year to meet all dietary and domestic requirements, including food for their dogs. Besides consuming the meat, internal organs, stomach contents, and the fat of the animal, Athapaskans used the skins to manufacture clothing, footgear, tents, sleeping bags, mattresses, house covers, and various types of blankets and bags. The long guard hairs on hides were excellent insulators that made them ideal for use in winter clothing. Athapaskan artisans transformed bones and antlers into tools and utensils, while women boiled bones and then split them open to extract the protein-rich marrow.[10]

A typical Athapaskan family probably belonged to a small autonomous band that moved quickly and frequently to exploit food supplies (like the caribou) that were mobile or seasonal and unevenly distributed over a wide area. That being the case, affiliations with a centralized or coordinated political organization would have been unlikely, although some bands may have gathered periodically for seasonal and collective hunts, or during the annual salmon run. Except for Arctic drainage groups (such as the Dogrib, Slave, Beaver, Hare, and Chipewyan) most Northern Athapaskans developed a matrilineal principle of descent and matrilocal residence, an anomaly of sorts since anthropologists usually associate hunting-and-gathering societies with bilateral recognition of kinship ties and patrilocal residence.[11] Anthropologist Richard Perry offers three explanations that might account for the Athapaskans' peculiar adaptation: (1) Matrilocal residence and matrilineal descent diffused from other societies, such as the socially stratified peoples of the Pacific Coast who were known to have strong matrilineal descent groups. (2) The proto-Athapaskans may have brought these organizational features with them from Asia. (3) Athapaskan matrilineality and matrilocal residence may have developed autonomously in the western Subarctic because of particular local factors. Chief among these would have been the Athapaskans' residence in the mountainous ecosystem of the subarctic cordillera, where they established relatively stable base camps from which hunters carried out prolonged food quests. Such circumstances generally brought about a high degree of male absenteeism, leaving women, children, and other nonhunting individuals at the base camp. This situation, in turn, led to the cohabitation of closely related women—mothers, daughters, and sisters—and their children. Such an assembly was conducive to the adoption of a matrilineal system of kinship that defined the bonds between individuals based on relationships through women. Once established, matrilocal residence functioned as an effective device to enhance sporadic, cooperative hunting activities among male relatives dispersed over a broad region.[12]

The nomadic hunting economy and social fragmentation that characterized early Athapaskan life remained relatively constant for several centuries, but for reasons that remain unclear, Athapaskan peoples began to drift away from their homeland in Alaska and northwestern Canada. One explanation is that a significant shift in the migratory patterns of caribou herds forced the Athapaskans to seek new hunting grounds. Climatic changes most certainly influenced the movement of animals and, by extension, the behavior of Athapaskan hunters. Years of higher than normal rainfall or snow would have encouraged grass growth and swelled the size of caribou herds, thereby permitting hunters and their families to remain more or less in the same area. Periods of drought, on the other hand, would have forced herds of caribou or deer to wander far and wide for forage, luring bands of hungry Athapaskans farther and farther from their ancestral homeland. Richard Perry has reasoned that a period of falling temperatures beginning around 1500 B.C. may have driven Canadian caribou herds south to areas with better forage potential, and that Athapaskan hunters who derived the bulk of their subsistence from the animal had little choice but to follow. Around 0 A.D., however, there was a warming trend that led to retreating snow and ice, permitting the caribou to drift back north to their original ranges, once again with Athapaskan hunters following close behind. But not all of them followed the caribou herds north. Some bands—perhaps those not as dependent on caribou for their livelihood—remained farther south. As time passed, the distance between Athapaskan groups increased, and social contiguity was lost.[13]

A second possible explanation for the Athapaskan dispersion centers on volcanic activity in southeastern Alaska—in either the Wrangell or St. Elias mountain chains. Northern Athapaskan oral traditions contain stories of "exploding mountains" that produced fires, smoke, and floods, causing the people to scatter in different directions. Scientists who have studied the so-called "White River ash fall" believe that around 20 to 100 A.D. there was a significant volcanic eruption that spewed noxious gas and ash over a large swath of southern Alaska and central Yukon. A second, larger eruption rocked the Athapaskan world circa 750 A.D. This latter eruption apparently emanated from the same volcano and deposited a layer of ash over an area covering an estimated 130,000 square miles. Just how much damage this inflicted on the region's ecosystem is unknown, and uncertainty remains about how long plant and animal life may have taken to recover. If the White River ash fall led to some type of wildlife catastrophe in Alaska and the Yukon, that very likely could have triggered a substantial Athapaskan exodus from their original homeland.[14]

Before we examine where the Athapaskans went and which routes they took to get there, a quick word is in order to address the question "How were they able to move to unfamiliar areas and still manage to sustain themselves?" Virtually all anthropologists agree that the proto-Athapaskans were a mobile, agile, and readily adaptable people. After all, they had to be if they were to base their survival on the occasionally fickle bounty of Mother Nature. When life got tough for certain bands, as it invariably did from time to time, their social adaptability, decentralized political organization, and flexible systems of kinship reckoning enabled them to merge with (or break away from) other bands, or to move to new areas that had not yet been exploited. Nevertheless, adaptability and flexibility were not their only advantages. The Athapaskans' utilization of the bow and arrow from a very early date played a significant role in at least the initial stages of their expansion. Bows and arrows held distinct advantages over spears and dart throwers, such as increased range, velocity, and accuracy. Such improvements enhanced hunters' abilities to bring home food to their people, which in turn boosted their status and prestige. Groups confronted by hostile neighbors armed with bows and arrows, meanwhile, had little choice but to adopt their use—or perish. Evidently used in the Arctic as far back as 3000 B.C., the bow and arrow slowly diffused southward. By 1500 B.C., hunters in the Canadian Subarctic possessed them, but it was not until around 200 A.D. that people on the northern plains of Saskatchewan and Alberta acquired the bow. At this point, the dissemination of bow-and-arrow technology accelerated, and within a few centuries, it became the weapon of choice among inhabitants of the central and southern plains. Several scholars have suggested correlations between Athapaskan migrants and the earliest appearance of arrow points on the northern plains, and linguists can point to words for "bow" and "arrow" that reconstruct to proto-Athapaskan. If the Athapaskans were in fact some of the earliest archers in the Americas, they would have made distinctively efficient hunters and dangerous enemies.[15]

Having occupied the southern portion of Alaska and northwestern Canada for several centuries, groups of Athapaskan hunters, perhaps because of climatic changes, receding glaciers, volcanic activity, or fluctuations in caribou herds, began a slow but steady migration outward beginning around 100 to 200 A.D. The movement was not a sudden mass exodus, but a slow, steady trickle of families, extended families, and bands over several centuries. At certain critical junctures, the dispersion accelerated—such as in the aftermath of the volcanic eruptions in the mid-eighth century. At other times, the pace of dispersion slackened, perhaps during periods when game fluctuations veered in a positive direction. Some groups drifted west, moving deeper into Alaska or southwest along the Pacific Coast; other bands headed east through the Mackenzie River drainage, eventually pushing all the way to Hudson Bay. Still others journeyed south into British Columbia, or southeast onto the plains of Alberta and Saskatchewan. By approximately 500 to 1000 A.D., there were increasingly clear divisions among the Athapaskans. The northern (or Canadian-Alaskan) group continued to occupy the original homeland in the subarctic interior of Alaska and western Canada. These widely dispersed peoples developed over twenty Athapaskan languages and regional dialects whose correlation with one another continues to intrigue linguists.[16]

The group known as the Pacific Coast or Western Athapaskans began arriving in Oregon and northern California around 700 to 900 A.D. Sedentary hunter-gatherers, the Pacific Coast Athapaskans adopted several of the technological innovations (particularly food-getting equipment) and cultural conventions of other Pacific Coast tribes, such as patrilineal descent, an emphasis on social rank and group stratification, large cedar-plank dwellings, art forms of carved wood, and potlatches (ceremonial feasts). They hunted marine mammals such as the sea lion (or "ocean deer") as well as inland game, caught salmon, and harvested acorns and various plant foods for their subsistence.[17]

The third migration, that of the Southern Athapaskans—the ancestors of the Apachean peoples of the American Southwest—could have taken a variety of paths to reach Arizona, New Mexico, and Texas. By virtually all accounts, the movement of Athapaskans south out of Canada onto the northwestern plains occurred piecemeal, with small groups of nomadic hunters serving as the vanguard. The rugged geography that they encountered along the way rivaled that of their old haunts in Alaska, the Yukon, and British Columbia. Mountain ranges, intermountain basins, major rivers, high-altitude plateaus, and many other landforms intruded into the path of the migrating Southern Athapaskans. Employing bow-and-arrow technology and the collective hunting techniques that had served their caribou-hunting ancestors so well in the past, the proto-Apacheans now sought to employ them in their pursuit of bison, whose populations were expanding across the northern and central plains region. By about 700 to 900 A.D., Southern Athapaskan groups had pushed as far south as Montana and Wyoming, meeting and then fighting, trading, and mixing with other nomadic peoples they encountered along the way.[18]

Besides bows, arrows, and collective hunting techniques (such as game drives and impounding), there is some evidence that the Southern Athapaskans introduced small side-notched projectile points and circular stone shelters to their new neighbors on the northern plains. Several scholars have associated the Avonlea Complex (200 to 750 A.D.) of southern Alberta and Saskatchewan, Montana, northern Wyoming, and the Dakotas with Southern Athapaskans who pursued a "free wandering way of life," shifting their base camps frequently in response to the movement of bison herds.[19] According to Thomas F. Kehoe, the Avonlea sites on the northern plains provide "the first indisputable evidence for large-scale communal bison hunting, which is essentially identical to circumboreal caribou/reindeer drives," and that Avonlea arrow points reflect "the movement of Athabascans skilled at caribou driving onto grasslands blossoming with bison."[20] The "cornerstone" of the Avonlea hunting complex, anthropologist J. Loring Haskell argues, was the pound (or game drive). A pound was a crude pen into which hunters drove large quantities of bison. At times, the pen lay at the base of a precipice. Hunters then lured or drove a bison herd into a chute of brush and logs and pressed them forward over the precipice into the pen, where other hunters quickly dispatched the wounded and stunned animals with spears and arrows.[21]

The proto-Apacheans could have selected any number of routes to take them south. Many scholars believe that they moved southeast along the flanks of the Rocky Mountains; others suggest that small groups of Southern Athapaskans simply drifted south through the Great Plains, keeping well east of the Rockies. Some scholars posit a western route, arguing that the Southern Athapaskans moved into east-central Idaho and southwestern Montana and then crossed over the Rockies onto the plains via the Wyoming Basin. Still others suggest an intermountain route down the Roan and Colorado plateaus, or through the Great Basin, where the Apacheans gained exposure to the mixed horticulturalist-hunting Fremont culture (500 to 1700 A.D.) of Wyoming, Colorado, and Utah. These bands then drifted back east and crossed the Continental Divide in Colorado or northern New Mexico. The remaining option for Southern Athapaskan immigrants would have been a highland path or mountain corridor along the Rockies. "The mountains from Colorado to New Mexico were an avenue by which the Apaches moved south," Richard Perry argues. "The mountain ranges from the Subarctic into the Southwest were the medium for Apache sustenance, and hence their travel route as well." George Hyde, meanwhile, has speculated that the proto-Apacheans probably engaged in a two-prong movement: one group moved down through the plains while another migrated south-ward through the interior plateau country lying west of the Rockies. The choice of route depended more on the availability of food, water, and the presence of other tribes than on the smoothness of terrain, although simply drifting down the Great Plains would have been the easiest of the various routes. While scholars do not see eye-to-eye about the exact travel itinerary that the early Apacheans selected, most would agree that the migrants began showing up on the central and southern plains at some point between 1000 and 1500 A.D.[22]

The Plains culture area is one of significant diversity and contrast in landforms, vegetation, wildlife, and people. The region's sudden changes in daily temperatures, extended droughts, cyclonic storms, and late-winter blizzards have exercised a profound influence on human existence and the

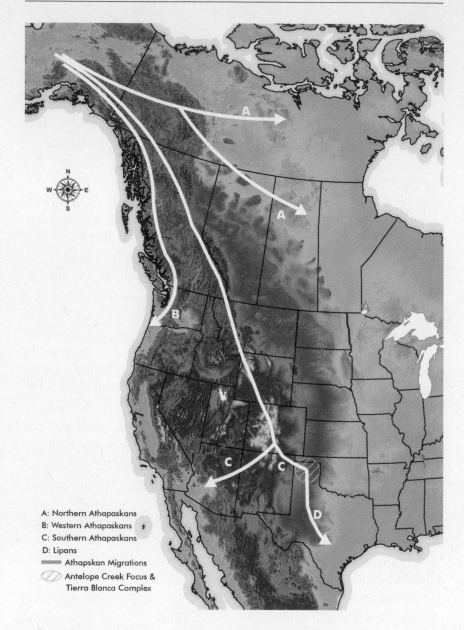

A: Northern Athapaskans
B: Western Athapaskans
C: Southern Athapaskans
D: Lipans
▬▬▬ Athapaskan Migrations
⬭ Antelope Creek Focus &
     Tierra Blanca Complex

Athapaskan migrations. *Map created by Matthew A. Crawford.*

evolution of Amerindian economies and cultures. The arrival of small groups of Apacheans on the western plains periphery would have coincided with a rather prolonged period of global climatic change (sometimes called the Medieval Optimum, the Medieval Warm Period, or the Medieval Climatic Anomaly) that occurred between 900 and 1300 A.D. On much of the Great Plains and in the American Southwest, rising temperatures and increased aridity brought drought conditions that persisted for decades at a time (e.g., from 1130–1180 A.D.), exerting considerable cultural and demographic changes that may have benefited the Apachean newcomers. Plains horticulturalists, for example, moved eastward to the edge of the plains in search of more reliable water sources, thus clearing away any opposition to incoming peoples.[23]

The so-called "Medieval Optimum," however, did not affect the Great Plains uniformly. On the southern plains, for example, summer precipitation levels in the Texas Panhandle and southwestern Oklahoma were sporadic, and may have actually increased at times, prompting inmigrations of animals and people from the drought-stricken north. In addition, the huge subsurface water reserves of the Ogallala aquifer would have partially offset climatic uncertainty on the southern plains, making the river valleys of the Texas Panhandle a more attractive site for settlement. Around 1350 A.D., there was another abrupt change in atmospheric circulation, ushering in the "Little Ice Age," which lasted into the mid-nineteenth century. The Little Ice Age introduced greater amounts of cool, moist air; lowered temperatures; and may have increased precipitation across the Great Plains, leading to a recovery of grasslands and bison herds. Peoples who had vacated the plains during the drought-bearing Medieval Optimum now returned home in droves to hunt bison, as did newcomers seeking a fresh start.[24]

The proto-Apacheans responded to these climatic changes in predictable ways. Most remained secure in the mountains, maintaining a lifestyle that would have been familiar to their ancestors. Although precipitation levels at different locations varied, the higher altitudes generally enjoyed greater precipitation, which would have ameliorated the effects of periodic drought. Some bands clung tenaciously (if not perilously) to their encampments on the western edge of the plains and foothills on the eastern slope of the Rocky Mountains. This latter group included tipi dwellers whose remains archeologists have excavated on the Chautauqua Plateau in southeastern Colorado. Tipi ring sites, some dating back to the early fourteenth century, appear to be the habitations of a foraging population, and some scholars point to the Apaches as the group most likely to have constructed them.[25] A few intrepid bands may have decided to try somewhere new, drawn south initially by news of increased precipitation and better bison-hunting opportunities.[26] By the fourteenth and fifteenth centuries, therefore, bands of Apachean peoples inhabited a broad expanse of territory stretching along the Rocky Mountains and western plains peripheries of southern Wyoming, Colorado, Kansas, Oklahoma, and northeastern New Mexico. The precise limits of their range to the north and east remain obscure, while to the southeast, the Texas Panhandle provides tantalizing hints of a fourteenth century Athapaskan presence in what Spaniards would later call the Llano Estacado or Staked Plains.

The 25,000-square-mile Texas Panhandle is a broad, flat plain that lies between the 100th and 103rd meridians and south of the 36°-30' line. Drained by the Canadian River and the upper tributaries of the Red River, the Panhandle is part of a broader region known as the Texas High Plains, which stretches across much of northern and western Texas to the Pecos River. Lying just south of the Panhandle is the Llano Estacado (or Staked Plains), an even flatter region that extends south from the Canadian River valley and west of the rugged Caprock, a rock-hard layer of soil that at one time underlay the Llano Estacado before wind erosion exposed its rough, craggy face. The climate of the Texas Panhandle and Llano Estacado is hot, dry, and windy, with little moisture and very low humidity. Hundreds of years ago, however, the Panhandle ecosystem supported a surprisingly wide variety of animals and migratory waterfowl. Playa lakes captured precious rainfall, while springs from the vast underground Ogallala aquifer meandered their way through most canyons. Edible plants and abundant grasses provided rich pasturage for herds of bison, elk, and pronghorn antelope, as well as for multitudes of rabbits, squirrels, and prairie dogs. Mule deer, bear, and turkeys, meanwhile, foraged in and around stands of live oaks that grew along the canyons and canyon bottoms.[27]

The Texas Panhandle also has a long history of human occupation. Waldo Wedel notes that rock shelters and campsite locations in the Texas Panhandle include complexes dating back to the first ten centuries of the Christian era. Between 200 A.D. and 900 A.D., the Lake Creek people maintained an economy based on foraging over a broad area along the Canadian and Red rivers. They engaged in trade relationships with Woodland peoples to the east, and with Southwestern desert dwellers to the west. From the thirteenth century through the mid-fifteenth century, the Antelope Creek people settled in numerous semipermanent villages and temporary hunting camps situated throughout the northern Texas and Oklahoma panhandles. Archeological evidence gives indications that the Antelope Creek inhabitants were skilled in working with bone, shell, pottery, and stone, and that they were involved in an expansive trade network both with the Pueblos to the west, and with Plains Caddoan speakers to the northeast. From the Puebloans, the Antelope Creek people secured luxury goods such as obsidian, turquoise, Olivella shell jewelry, pipes, and painted pottery. In exchange, the Antelope Creek traders provided elbow pipes, a wide variety of bone tools, and various perishable items such as bison hides and meat, Osage orange wood for constructing bows, salt, and tobacco. Prehistoric residents of the Texas Panhandle also traded flint from the Alibates flint quarries (located about thirty-five miles north of present day Amarillo). The Pueblos used the warm-reddish colored flint chips, flakes, and cores to devise an assortment of knives, scrapers, and hammer stones. Like their Plains Caddoan neighbors (or relatives), the Antelope Creek people farmed corn, beans, squash, and tobacco; hunted; and gathered wild plant foods. That the Antelope Creek people did not trade for Pueblo-grown corn or beans indicates that they were more or less self-sufficient—at least in food.[28]

There was a noticeable uptick in trade between Plains and Pueblo peoples during the fourteenth and fifteenth centuries. Anthropologists cite increased intermarriage and expanding social relationships between the two groups, climatic fluctuations that resulted in seasonal periods of famine, and/or the expansion of Pueblo populations as possible explanations for the expansion in commerce. Coinciding with these developments were significant changes taking place in the demographic makeup of the southern plains. Where there had once been semisedentary horticulturalists who did some hunting and gathering on the southern plains (i.e., the Antelope Creek people), by the mid-to-late fifteenth century, the region's inhabitants had become almost exclusively hunter-gatherers.[29]

Two factors merged over time to undermine the position of the Antelope Creek people of the Texas and Oklahoma panhandles. As noted earlier, drought conditions had persisted in many parts of the Great Plains during the Medieval Optimum, but wetter conditions during the Little Ice Age fed the expansion of grasslands and increased the number and range of bison. As herds drifted southward into Antelope Creek territory, immigrant peoples followed in their wake, challenging Antelope Creek hunters for choice hunting grounds and territory. Changes in Antelope Creek architecture of the fourteenth century confirm that such pressures were becoming acute. The size of buildings decline as time goes on, and the large contiguous rooms of their earlier history vanish altogether. Antelope Creek people also responded to the invasion by dispersing into smaller settlements, or by attempting to expand their trade relationship with the Pueblos. The presence of large bison herds feeding on the mixed grasses of the southern plains, however, acted as a magnet for incoming nomadic peoples in search of a steady, dependable food supply. Some of them were undoubtedly interested in gaining entry into (or perhaps taking over) the burgeoning trade network that linked Pueblos in New Mexico, Antelope Creek people in the Texas Panhandle, and semisedentary peoples residing on the central plains. At some point in the thirteenth or fourteenth century, the first Apachean immigrants appeared on the southern plains. Although constituting a small minority, these tough, resilient, and adaptive newcomers quickly gained a foothold in the vast treeless expanses of the northern Texas Panhandle. Before long, they managed to plug into the Pueblo-Plains exchange network, and over time, they usurped the important economic position once enjoyed by the Antelope Creek people. Trophy skulls, disarticulated skeletal remains, and burned dwellings unearthed at the Antelope Creek focus indicate that violence was prevalent in the region—perhaps in response to competition with the proto-Apaches over bison meat and hides, or for control of the Alibates flint quarry. By the mid-to-late fifteenth century, the Antelope Creek people had vanished—perhaps withdrawing to the northeast to join Caddoan relatives, to the west where they merged with their old Pueblo trading partners, or simply abandoning agriculture altogether and merging with the Apachean newcomers. As historian Gary Clayton Anderson has noted, some indigenous peoples adapted to the various challenges that they faced through the dual processes of ethnogenesis and cultural reinvention—altering themselves culturally "to forge unity with other groups, abandoning languages, social practices, and even economic processes to meet the needs of the new order."[30]

In the 1980s, West Texas anthropologist Jack T. Hughes identified a protohistoric component that he named the "Tierra Blanca complex" (ca. 1450 A.D.–1650 A.D.) located in present-day Deaf Smith County in the northern Texas Panhandle. According to Hughes, the Tierra Blanca complex represented semisedentary and seminomadic bison-hunting and possibly corn-growing people who were very involved in trade with the Pueblos. Hughes speculated that the Tierra Blanca peoples were likely Apachean, and quite possibly the group that had supplanted or assimilated the once-dominant Antelope Creek inhabitants. The Tierra Blanca Apacheans had been slowly infiltrating the Texas Panhandle from the central plains and southeastern Colorado since the early 1300s. By the mid-fifteenth century, they were apparently strong enough to displace the Antelope Creek peoples, taking over the latter's bison-hunting range and usurping their role in the trade network with the Pueblos. This displacement, however, did not take place without a fight. Archaeologists working at various Antelope Creek sites have uncovered "occasional evidence of hostilities as reflected in butchered human remains, the presence of non-indigenous trophy skulls, and healed arrow wounds on skeletal remains."[31]

Lithic remains from Tierra Blanca complex sites reflect an economy focused almost exclusively on hunting. Archeologists have unearthed small triangular, unnotched and notched projectile points, scrapers, knives, and drills. Although Jack Hughes postulated that the Tierra Blanca peoples might have supplemented their bison-based economy by growing corn, new scholarship suggests that they brought a highly specialized, nomadic, bison-oriented lifestyle to the Texas Panhandle. Confirmation of their hunting prowess is borne out by archeological evidence indicating a dramatic increase in bison remains at various southern-plains sites during the two centuries before European contact. Drawn perhaps by a sudden increase in southern-plains bison herds, climatic changes that rendered horticulture less productive or less predictable, or possibly by an increased Pueblo demand for bison hides and meat, the Tierra Blanca Apacheans opted for an economy that, at least in the short term, satisfied their base subsistence. But it was this near exclusive reliance on a bison-based economy that encouraged the Tierra Blanca people to look west to the Pueblos as a source for corn, beans, and other food items (besides pottery, blankets, jewelry, and other manufactured products) that could provide salvation for their families should the bison economy decline.[32]

While knowledge of the Pueblo-Plains trade network was probably one of the factors that contributed to the southward migration of Apacheans into the Texas Panhandle during the fourteenth and fifteenth centuries, the expansion of this trade during the ensuing three centuries ushered in an era of Apache dominance on the southern plains. Anderson's examination of the major exchange networks in Texas during the sixteenth and seventeenth centuries identifies the major "centers of production" or "core communities" of the southern-plains macroeconomy. These included the Pueblo towns along the upper Rio Grande, Caddoan communities in eastern Texas, and in the various Plains Caddoan towns located along the Red and Arkansas rivers. Over time, Anderson argues, the plains themselves became a center of production, as various native groups harvested bison meat and hides, raised horses and mules, and raided one another for captives—a particularly valuable commodity that commanded high prices at the various trade fairs held each year. During the sixteenth and seventeenth centuries, the major players in this rapidly changing and expanding market included the Jumanos, Caddoans, and Apaches. In the early eighteenth century, the Comanches—powerful new players—would force themselves into the mix, altering the economic and political status quo on the southern plains.[33]

In south Texas, Jumano farmers and traders congregated around La Junta de los Rios (the confluence of the Conchos and Rio Grande rivers), where they tended their irrigated fields of beans, squash, and corn. There were additional Jumano farming communities scattered along the middle Rio Grande as far west as El Paso, however, where they traded with numerous small bands of Coahuiltecans. At some point in their history, drought may have been so severe that Jumano groups conducting seasonal hunts on the southern plains decided to remain there, shifting their encampments in response to the migrating bison herds and living in hide tents. Over time, this tribal division became somewhat permanent, although the corn-growing "River Jumanos" and the bison-hunting "Cibola Jumanos" remained in contact with each other, often trading meat for corn. Both groups also traded with the Pueblos, and became intermediaries of sorts connecting the Pueblos with various indigenous groups in east Texas. After concluding their business in New Mexico, Jumano traders headed east to trade with Coahuiltecans, Karankawas, Atakapans, and Hasinais, at times riding as far north as the Red River to exchange goods with various Caddoan groups in northeast Texas.[34]

In north Texas, meanwhile, a second major trade network existed in the sixteenth century that connected Pecos, Taos, and Gran Quivira pueblos to Plains Wichita (or Plains Caddoan) villages situated along the Canadian River and forks of the Red River in present-day Oklahoma, and to Caddo villages located on the Red River farther east. Like the Jumanos to the south, the Plains Wichitas benefited enormously by controlling the flow of high-status manufactured goods that passed through their hands. By their close proximity to the bison herds, the Plains Wichitas traded hides and meat to the Pueblos to the west. Traders could then pack their bags and head east to their Caddoan relatives in east Texas to exchange meat, hides, and manufactured items they had recently acquired from the Pueblos. Like the Jumanos, the Plains Wichitas sought to expand their share of the southern-plains trade network to ensure their people a reliable supply of corn, beans, cotton blankets, and specialty items such as pottery and jewelry that they could use themselves or trade to neighbors residing in distant locales.[35]

The southern-plains trade network attracted the Southern Athapaskans "like ants to sugar," and ambitious Apache bands quickly thrust themselves into the center of it. Jumano, Plains Wichita, and Apache leaders understood that control of the bison trade offered them an important avenue for the accrual of power, status, and prestige, not to mention a secure hold over a vital component of their peoples' livelihoods. During the early 1500s, the Athapaskan newcomers eroded the Caddoans' share in the southern-plains economy, and by the end of the sixteenth century, the Apaches had the Pueblo trade on the southern plains well in hand. Thereafter, they looked covetously at the Jumanos' still substantial role in the trade network, which was showing signs of weakness and vulnerability. Drought, epidemic disease, and the gradual retreat of bison herds northward were natural disasters beyond the Jumanos' ability to respond. Spanish penetration of New Mexico in the seventeenth century, meanwhile, accelerated their loss of market share, as did growing threats

from the expansion-minded Apaches. The efforts of several Jumano leaders to obtain Spanish assistance against the Apaches provide evidence of
their growing desperation. In October 1683, for example, seven Jumano
chiefs visited Spanish officials at El Paso requesting missions for the
various indigenous peoples of south Texas. One of the Jumano leaders
even claimed to have had a Constantine-like revelation in which a cross
appeared in the sky during a battle with the Apaches. Unfortunately for
the hard-pressed Jumanos, the Spaniards were not impressed or convinced, and no missions were forthcoming. As the Jumanos' situation
continued to deteriorate during the early eighteenth century, their old
trading partners in east Texas watched with concern as their own access
to meat, hides, and trade goods fell under Apache influence and control,
contributing to the growing envy and hatred held by virtually all Texas
Indians for the powerful Athapaskan intruders.[36]

Circumstantial and anecdotal evidence suggests that the fourteenth-
and fifteenth-century bison-hunting Apacheans who settled in the
Texas Panhandle, traded with the Pueblos, and later dominated the
trans-Texas bison-hide trade included groups that were ancestral to
the Lipan Apaches. Proving such a proposition, however, is difficult. As
Albert H. Schroeder observed, "The historical relationships of the various Apacheans of the Southwest have been the subject of several anthropological papers, no two of which agree in their reconstructions."[37] The
following discussion, therefore, is an attempt to link the nomadic bison
hunters of the Tierra Blanca complex to the various Apachean peoples
that came to dominate the southern-plains trade economy, and whom
Spaniards first encountered in the sixteenth and seventeenth centuries.

Early in May 1541, Spanish conquistador Francisco Vasquez de
Coronado set out from Pecos Pueblo on an expedition in search of
Gran Quivira, the legendary Indian settlement on the northern frontier of New Spain. After a march of three or four days, Coronado's men
constructed a bridge over the Pecos River near present day Santa Rosa,
New Mexico. Ten days after crossing the Pecos, Coronado came upon
a vast plain covered with an immense herd of bison calves, cows, and
bulls. Some of his men noticed marks in the ground and suspected that
warriors dragging their lances had made them. Curious, the party followed the tracks to a ranchería of some fifty nomadic bison hunters,
who, Coronado reported, lived "like Arabs" in hide tents and employed

well-trained dogs to carry loads of bison meat, hides, and other items. It was the dogs dragging the tent poles, the Spaniards quickly discerned, that were responsible for the scratches in the ground. Coronado later referred to these nomads as the Querechos, a term derived perhaps from *Tágu-kerésh* (the Pueblo word for Apache), or *Keretsâ* (the Pueblo word for the Navaho tribe). He described the Querechos in glowing terms— as being gentle, faithful in their friendship, and skilled in the use of sign language. Coronado also praised their physical attributes, stating that the wandering natives had "better figures than the Pueblo Indians, are better warriors, and are more feared." Five to six days march from the Querecho encampment (perhaps near Palo Duro Canyon, or the canyons of the Brazos River east of present-day Lubbock, Texas) lived a second group of bison hunters who were enemies of the Querechos, painted their bodies and faces, and lived in "pueblos of *rancherías*." Coronado referred to these people as the *Teyas*.[38]

Nearly fifty years later, the Bonilla-Humaña expedition departed from Pecos Pueblo and headed east onto the plains. After several days travel, they encountered great herds of bison near the Canadian River and the deserted rancherías of nomadic hunters they called *Vaqueros*. When Jusephe Gutiérrez (a member of the Bonilla-Humaña expedition) briefed New Mexico governor Juan de Oñate in 1599 about what he had seen on the journey, Oñate dispatched Vicente de Zaldívar to the Canadian River country to locate the buffalo and to explore the region. In the autumn of 1600, Zaldívar visited several small bands of Vaqueros who had only recently returned from an expedition to the Pueblos to trade meat, skins, fat, tallow, and salt for cotton blankets, pottery, corn, and some green turquoise. The Vaqueros hunted bison on foot; they also constructed blinds near watering places, and then waited for the animals to come to drink so they could shoot them with bows and arrows. Dogs, carrying as much as one hundred pounds of supplies each, served as beasts of burden since the Indians had not yet acquired horses.[39]

Although the identity of the Teyas remains a matter of considerable debate, there is general agreement among scholars that Spanish reports of the Querechos and Vaqueros were actually referencing the very same group of people. They were nomadic bison hunters who resided on the grasslands of the northern Llano Estacado, between the Canadian River in the north and the tributaries of the Red River in the south. They had a close trade relationship with the Pueblos and participated in annual or seasonal trade fairs, at times (especially during the winter months) establishing encampments in the foothills just east of their Pueblo associates. These general characteristics match up fairly well with those of the earlier Tierra Blanca complex, leading to speculation that the Querechos/Vaqueros were descendents of the Athapaskan-speaking Tierra Blanca people. According to Albert Schroeder, by the end of the sixteenth century, the Vaqueros begun dispersing—some drifting west into New Mexico, others east into Oklahoma, and still others content to remain in the Texas Panhandle.[40]

Some of the Querecho/Vaquero groups that remained on or near the Texas Panhandle in the late sixteenth and seventeenth centuries were the proto-Lipan Apaches. In an effort to clarify and simplify their genealogy, I have divided the groups most often associated with the Lipans into three main categories:

1) The *Cancy* (*Canci, Gantsi, Kantsi, Cances*). Early Spanish maps of west Texas refer to the people residing there as the Cancy (Canci, Gantsi, Kantsi, Cances), which may derive from the Caddoan word *kantsi*, which means "deceiver" or "liar" and was the Caddoan name for the Lipan Apaches. The Cancy, moreover, had a principle village named Quiriches, which calls to mind Coronado's Querechos. Frenchman Bénard de La Harpe, who toured the Red River country in 1719, noted the presence of a "very populous village" of Cancy who possessed swords, lances, bows and arrows, and many fine horses, but also employed dogs to carry loads. The Cancy and the Caddoan tribes, La Harpe observed, were "so hostile toward each other that the victors eat the vanquished; they do not spare even the women nor the children." The Lipans, interestingly, were the only modern Apacheans known to have engaged in the ritual cannibalism of captives taken in war.[41]

2) *Chipaynes, Limitas, Trementinas*, and *Sejines*. In late August 1715, a force of Spanish soldiers and Indian allies under the direction of Don Juan Páez Hurtado set out from Santa Fe, New Mexico, in pursuit of Apache raiders who had been conducting forays in the surrounding area for corn and horses. Hurtado later reported that bands of Apaches known by various names including Chipaynes (Chilipaines, Cipaynes), Limitas, Trementinas, and Sejines—but known more generally as the Faraone (or Pharaoh), lived along the Canadian River in the north Texas

Panhandle. They were primarily bison hunters, but they may have grown a little corn, relying on trading with or raiding the Pueblos should the harvest fail. They lived for part of the year (presumably winter) in houses made of wood plastered with mud. When weather conditions improved, they roamed the plains in search of bison.[42]

Scholars have interpreted the Hurtado report in several—often conflicting—ways. Karl Schlesier segregates the Cipaynes as well as the Limitas and Trementinas as distinct Apachean peoples that merged with other groups to form a composite community of families and bands that the Spaniards knew as Lipan Apaches. The Faraones, however, he associates with the Perrillo Apaches and the Sierra Blanca Apaches, all forerunners of the Mescaleros. Albert Schroeder, on the other hand, argues that people knew the Limitas and/or Lementinas as Cipaynes, all of whom were Lipan—the name apparently a corruption of Cipanyes or Chilipaynes. Like Schlesier, he associates the Perrillos and Sierra Blancas with the Faraones.[43]

3) The *Escanjaques*, *Pelones* (or "hairless ones"), and the *Ypandes*. Historian George Hyde argues that the Escanjaques were most likely early Lipans, although other scholars lean toward an Escanjaque affiliation with the Pueblos or with the Wichitas.[44] The name "Pelones" first appears in the historical record in 1706, and by the 1740s, Spaniards listed them as one of the three main Apache divisions along with the Natagés and Jumanes (Jumanos). According to William Edward Dunn, the Spaniards often treated the Pelones as identical with another group called the Ypandes (Ipandes, Ipandis, Ypandis), people frequently associated with the Lipans. The Ypandes' close allies were the Natagés, and Spanish observers described them as outstanding equestrians and horse thieves. Interestingly, Frederick W. Hodge argues that the Spanish or Indian corruption of the Athapaskan appellation Ipa-n'de ("Ipa" being a personal name and "n'de" meaning "people") provides the basis for the name "Lipan." So closely did the Spaniards associate the Ypandes and Pelones that they often referred to them as "Ypandes alias Pelones." Dunn speculates that the Pelones were among the first Apacheans whom Comanches compelled to give up their lands on the Red River, and that they became known as Ypandes. Other people associate the "Pelones" with different Indian groups altogether. Gary Clayton Anderson, for example, argues that the Pelones were immigrants from Mexico, who

like the Jumanos merged with various Apachean bands and other fragment peoples to become Lipan Apaches.[45]

Given the conflicting historical evidence about Lipan Apache identity (what historian George H. Hyde termed "an amazing tangle"), it is little wonder scholars have reached different conclusions about the identity of the sixteenth- and seventeenth-century inhabitants of the southern plains. After 1700, Spanish documents often refer to Texas Indians in terms of individual bands—and the number of band names increases rapidly. Where once only large numbers of Querechos or Vaqueros were mentioned in reports, during the eighteenth century a lexicon of new names appear, so muddying the already murky association of names to people that we may never know with any certainty just who was who in seventeenth- and eighteenth-century Texas.[46] That being said, there are legitimate reasons for one to consider that a common thread connects several of these groups (Tierra Blanca, Querechos, Vaqueros, Cancy, Chipaynes, Limitas, Trementinas, Sejines, Escanjaques, Pelones, and Ypandis), and that over a considerable expanse of time, they (or their progeny) would coalesce—through ethnogenesis and cultural reinvention—to become Lipan Apaches. If that is indeed the case, their forefathers were among the first Southern Athapaskans to forsake their mountain sanctuaries and inhabit the plains regions extending from the Canadian River south into the Llano Estacado.

As the Southern Athapaskans migrated southward during the early years of the second millennium, groups became isolated from one another and began to specialize their economies—some hunting deer and elk in the mountains, some experimenting with agriculture, and others moving out onto the plains to pursue a nomadic bison-hunting economy. By the end of the sixteenth century, therefore, Apachean culture was becoming increasingly diverse as various groups responded and adapted to their geographic location, local resources, subsistence needs, and degree of interaction with sedentary peoples living on the margins of buffalo country. James and Dolores Gunnerson have noted that in the face of the growing diversity in material culture among Apacheans, there remained remarkable unity of nonmaterial culture that allowed various families or bands to merge with one another when necessary. This associational fluidity also helps explain the constant shifting of Apachean populations and the creation of new Apache identities.[47]

Over time, a broad division emerged within the *Apachería*. Western Apache groups (including the Navajos, Chiricahuas, Mescaleros, and Western Apaches) resided primarily in the mountains and timbered uplands of New Mexico and Arizona. They developed a semisedentary lifestyle with a mixed economy of hunting, gathering, and farming. The Eastern Apache groups (Lipans, Jicarillas, and Kiowa Apaches) adopted many facets of the Plains Indian culture complex and relied almost exclusively on hunting. The Lipans resided primarily on the plains of eastern New Mexico and west Texas, while the Jicarillas lived in northeastern New Mexico, where they adopted a mixed hunting-horticultural lifestyle. The Kiowa-Apaches, who may have split off from their brethren during the initial stages of the Southern Athapaskan dispersal at the end of the first millennium, roamed the central plains and Oklahoma Panhandle together with their Kiowa allies. Not surprisingly, subtle language variations also developed over time, with each of the seven major Apache divisions adopting its own distinct tongue. Athapaskan linguist expert Harry Hoijer divides Southern Athapaskan languages into two categories: (1) Kiowa Apachean, restricted to the Kiowa-Apaches, and (2) Southwestern Apachean, which includes all the rest. He further divides the second category into two groups, separating the Lipans and Jicarillas from the others. According to Hoijer, the Lipan dialect is most similar to Jicarilla, and their divergence occurred approximately 250–350 years ago (circa 1600–1700 A.D.). The Kiowa-Apachean language, furthermore, shares phonetic similarities with Lipans and Jicarillas that it does not share with the other Apachean dialects, suggesting to some linguists that the Kiowa-Apachean divergence from Lipan and Jicarilla may have occurred as recently as four hundred years ago (circa 1550 A.D.), contradicting theories of a much earlier separation.[48]

The sixteenth and seventeenth centuries were a "Golden Age" of sorts for the proto-Lipan Apaches of the Panhandle plains region. Life centered on the pursuit of bison, deer, pronghorn antelope, and the occasional bear that happened to wander within the range of Lipan hunters. While bison remained the staple food source, women contributed to their family's subsistence by gathering edible plants, fruits, and nuts, as well as important medicinal plants such as redbuds, purple coneflowers, and dandelions that grew at various places across the plains environment. Annual trade fairs at Pecos or Taos pueblos provided Lipan families with opportunities to acquire corn, beans, turquoise, cotton blankets, and ceramics. As has been noted, by the end of the sixteenth century, the Apaches had cornered the bison-hide trade across the southern plains, and were expanding their dominance southward into the Jumanos' trade network. By the first decades of the seventeenth century, proto-Lipans were meeting regularly with Spanish and Pueblo traders at Pecos and Taos, bringing home iron goods such as axes and knives, fabrics, worked leather, copper pots, mirrors, buttons, and other trinkets that must have astonished their families and heightened further their interest in expanding their trade relationships. As the proto-Lipans broadened their reach into central and south-central Texas during the seventeenth century, they absorbed remnant bands of Jumanos and Coahuiltecans as well as other Apachean groups, and by the end of the seventeenth century possessed a population of around five thousand people.[49]

Two tribes residing on the northern periphery of Texas in the seventeenth century that would play an ominous role in Lipan Apache history were the tribes of the Wichita Confederacy and the Comanches. In the mid-sixteenth century, the Wichitas consisted of two main groups. The first included the Tawakonis, Taovayas, and Guichitas, who resided east-northeast of the Great Bend of the Arkansas River in Kansas; the second group was the Iscanis, who roamed the region along the Canadian River and forks of the Red River in present-day Oklahoma. It may have been members of this latter group that the Spaniards named "Teyas" and against whom Tierra Blanca Apaches competed for control of the bison trade. An affiliated tribe, the Kichais, lived farther down the Arkansas near the mouth of the Verdigris and Neosho rivers. By the end of the seventeenth century and in the early eighteenth century, the tribes of the Wichita Confederacy were migrating slowly southward into Oklahoma and Texas. Among the factors responsible for their exodus was a desire to gain greater access to French traders based along the Red River and to escape attacks from the powerful Osage tribe to the northeast, and from Comanches and Apaches residing to the west and northwest.[50]

Coinciding with the Wichita movement into Texas was that of the Shoshonean-speaking Utes and Comanches from areas north of the headwaters of the Arkansas River. By 1700, the Comanches had entered the Great Plains from passes in the Front Range and appeared in eastern Colorado and western Kansas. Within a couple of decades, they overran

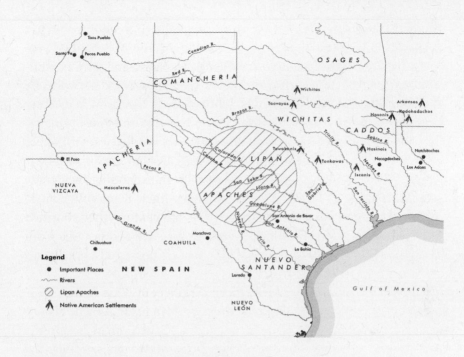

Texas Indians in the mid-eighteenth century.
Map created by Matthew A. Crawford.

Apacheans residing on the Dismal River, sending them south to join
their brethren in Texas, Oklahoma, and New Mexico. Desirous of gaining a foothold in the southern-plains macroeconomy, and eager to position themselves closer to trade outlets, slave raiding opportunities, and
bison herds, Comanches visited the Pueblos in 1705. During the ensuing decades, Comanche strength steadily increased, and by the close
of the eighteenth century, the Comanches had transformed themselves
from a "scrounging, poor, militarily weak rabble" into a "mounted, well-
equipped, and powerful people."[51]

The arrival of the Wichitas and Comanches, as we shall see in the
next chapter, would force the ancestral Lipan Apaches to vacate the
Texas Panhandle, continuing a tradition of southward expansion that
had started over one thousand years earlier when bands of Athapaskan
speakers from Alaska and northwestern Canada initiated their great dispersal. Known to early Spanish visitors to the plains as Querechos and

Vaqueros, the relationship between these nomadic bison hunters and the Spaniards in the decades immediately following contact was relatively cordial.[52] During the seventeenth century, the Apaches expanded their dominance southward, eventually usurping the Jumanos' trade network and becoming the bane of their Indian neighbors, and of the Spaniards as well. Even so, the arrival of the Comanches and the reappearance of the Plains Wichitas in Texas during the late seventeenth and early eighteenth centuries spelled the end of Apache hegemony on the southern plains. As the Lipans and other plains Apachean bands retreated southward into central Texas, they would face new challenges coming north from Mexico, providing tantalizing commercial opportunities, but also forcing them to make difficult choices about how best to maintain their lifestyle and their freedom.

CHAPTER TWO

The Lipan Apaches in Spanish Texas, 1700–1749

IN THE EARLY DAYS after the emergence of all living things from the under-world, the large and dangerous animals challenged the smaller, kindlier ones to a moccasin game (or game of hidden ball). The stakes were high. A victory for Big Owl, Bear, Mountain Lion, Water Snake, Eagle, and the other dangerous animals would have meant death and perpetual darkness in the world for Deer, Skunk, Gopher, and all the little birds and other harmless animals. Fickle Coyote could not decide which group to support, so when one side appeared to be winning, he went over to that team. When its fortunes declined, he quickly abandoned his teammates and joined the other. By their shouts and threats, the protagonists of unending night attempted to frighten and demoralize their opponents, but the small animals persisted, and with a little trickery from Gopher (who burrowed beneath the ground to see which moccasin held the ball), they finally saw the sun rise on their triumph. Since that time, man has had to war relent-lessly against the superior forces that seek to intimidate and overawe him, but if men are brave and persistent like the small and harmless animals of the emergence, they too will be victorious over their enemies.[1]

❨

DURING THE EIGHTEENTH and nineteenth centuries, the Lipan Apaches faced numerous protagonists who sought to frighten and demoralize them, and the story of the small animals' victory over seemingly insurmountable odds inspired them to persevere. Adaptive, brave, and resilient, the Lipans waged a relentless campaign for survival, seeking alliances with, and/or protection from, both Indian and non-Indian peoples. Their climactic struggle began in the early eighteenth century when, for a variety of reasons, they embarked on a slow exodus from the Panhandle region of Texas. During the 1720s and 1730s, they endeavored to establish themselves in the hill country north of San Antonio, where they sought anew to halt what to them was the advance of perpetual darkness.

Throughout the century and a half following their Querecho/ Vaquero forebears' encounter with Francisco Coronado and various other Spanish explorers, the scattered Southern Athapaskan bands that would later coalesce to become Lipan Apaches continued their nomadic, bison-oriented lifestyle on the plains, traveling west periodically to conduct trade with the Pueblos and with Spaniards in New Mexico. By the end of the sixteenth century, the proto-Lipans and their Jicarilla cousins were no longer in contact with the Western Apaches and the Navajos, and in the ensuing century, the Lipans and Jicarillas too would part ways as linguistic and cultural distinctions developed between them.[2] The Jicarillas remained at the northeastern edge of the Apachean territory in New Mexico, advancing cautiously into the Texas Panhandle to hunt bison, but never abandoning completely their mountain-based sanctuaries. Bands of proto-Lipans, as noted earlier, had ventured onto the southern plains at some point in the fourteenth century, gradually displacing the inhabitants of the Antelope Creek focus. For the next hundred years (ca. 1500–1600 A.D.), the Southern Athapaskan hunters who made up the Tierra Blanca complex ranged over a broad area in pursuit of game, wild plants, and new trade opportunities—simultaneously guarding their territory against those who hoped to commandeer their place in the exchange network linking the Pueblos with the plains.

At some point during the late seventeenth and early eighteenth centuries, the proto-Lipan Apaches began leaving the Texas Panhandle, continuing a tradition of southward movement that stretched back over a millennium. By the early 1700s, a new migratory cycle had developed where nomadic Apache bands that would later become known as the Lipans, Natagés, Mescaleros, Llaneros, Faraones, and so forth, spent their summers near agricultural villages along the Pecos and upper Rio Grande rivers, where they traded with the Spaniards and Pueblos. In the autumn, they moved back east to hunt bison along the San Sabá, Llano, and Pedernales rivers. During the winter months, some bands ventured further north into the Colorado and Brazos river regions to continue their hunting activities, while others hunkered down on the foothills and plains just east of the Pueblos. As spring approached, the Apacheans drifted back south to plant crops and harvest a variety of wild plants, nuts, and berries.[3] But they did not conduct the exodus simply for tradition's sake; powerful, irresistible forces were at work in the Apache world that compelled them to move southward onto new lands that differed markedly in climate, terrain, and available resources. As is the case with most demographic migrations, a combination of "push" and "pull" factors accounted for the Lipans' decision to move.

One factor luring the Lipans and their Apachean relatives south was the Pueblo Revolt of 1680, which resulted in the expulsion of Spanish forces from New Mexico. While the Pueblos celebrated their new—albeit short-lived—independence, plains tribes that depended on the Spaniards for assorted manufactured items and horses probably experienced mixed feelings about the abrupt loss of a valued trade partner and the high-status trade goods that would become more difficult to acquire. The Lipans may have moved southward, consequently, in hopes of reestablishing this important commercial relationship and retaining their access to Spanish trade.[4]

A second factor influencing the Lipan migrations of the late seventeenth and early eighteenth centuries was the pressure of powerful Indian newcomers to the central and southern plains. The westward migrations of Kansas, Oto, Iowa, Ponca, and Omaha peoples to areas beyond the Missouri River encouraged a southward movement of the remaining Apachean groups that had settled on the south-central plains. The various Caddoan-speaking tribes of the Wichita confederacy, meanwhile, under pressure from the French-armed Osages, moved south from the Great Bend of the Arkansas River, where they sparred with various Apachean bands to secure captives, horses, and access to bison herds. Meanwhile, tribes such as the Shoshonean-speaking Comanches and

Utes moved eastward onto the Great Plains through passes in the Front Range. Drawn southward by the lure of slave-raiding and trade opportunities, and nudged in that direction by Cheyennes, Kiowas, and Pawnee warriors armed with French guns, the Comanches and Utes soon challenged both the Apaches and the Wichitas for access to hunting grounds and control of the lucrative bison-hide trade. Over time, the Comanches and Utes severed the Apaches' trade links in New Mexico, while to the east, Apache traders saw their access to French markets curtailed by the Osages and Wichitas. The collapse of the Apaches' trade networks weakened their resistance to repel the onslaught, and they began to scatter in different directions.[5] In 1706, Penxaye Apaches north of Raton Pass in south-central Colorado were retreating southward in the face of Comanche attacks, and the Jicarillas found themselves so pressed that they considered falling back to Navajo country west of the Rio Grande. According to George Hyde, the "purpose of the Utes and Comanches was always the same: to catch the Apaches off guard at their *rancherías*, to make a sudden assault, kill as many Apaches as they could, capture some women and children for the slave trade in New Mexico, and plunder the *rancherías* and destroy the huts and crops."[6] Historians often cite a climactic nine-day battle that allegedly occurred in 1723 between Comanche and Lipan warriors at "El Gran Cierra del Fierro" (Wichita River). According to fragmentary accounts, the Comanches caught the Lipans by surprise, killed several men, and carried off an untold number of women and children into captivity. The attack so weakened the Lipans that they could not retaliate, opting instead to retreat southeast to the region between the Colorado and Brazos rivers.[7]

Some scholars dismiss the above-mentioned climactic battle as fictitious. Karl H. Schlesier argues that the alleged Comanche-Lipan engagement could not have taken place as stated, because the Comanches already had their hands full raiding various Apache bands in eastern Colorado and countering attacks from still other Apaches residing in western Kansas. Morris Opler, on the other hand, challenges the validity of the nine-day battle, since our only knowledge of the event is a Spanish account written in the 1780s—nearly sixty years after the engagement allegedly occurred. Absent contemporary accounts of the episode, and given the fact that nine-day battles were "not too common in American Indian annals," Opler's reservations are certainly understandable. The

Lipans' relocation to south Texas, Opler counters, must be viewed as part of the general southward movement of Apachean peoples in the fifteenth, sixteenth, and seventeenth centuries.[8]

During the first decades of the eighteenth century, Lipan Apache bands spent a considerable part of each year dispersed widely across the Edwards Plateau region of south-central Texas. Lacking deep soils suitable for farming, the Edwards Plateau was nonetheless excellent grazing land, its short grasses and mesquite shrubbery providing ample forage for herds of bison, horses, and cattle.[9] The Apachean push into the Edwards Plateau reverberated strongly among peoples already occupying the region. Scattered bands of Coahuiltecans and Jumanos, for example, under pressure from Spaniards expanding northward from Mexico, now found themselves in an increasingly perilous position, facing a burgeoning Apache movement south. The Coahuiltecans responded to Apache expansion by migrating south and west, by entering Spanish missions for protection, and by merging with Jumano band remnants that were equally imperiled. Other small tribes such as the Cocoimes (Cocomas), Chisos (Chizos), and the warlike Tobosos, were overwhelmed and apparently absorbed by the Lipans and other Apache groups.[10]

The mid-seventeenth century had been a particularly difficult time for the indigenous peoples of south Texas. The introduction of epidemic diseases, along with recurring drought and starvation, decimated Indian populations, while the establishment of Spanish missions at El Paso, La Junta, and in northern Mexico absorbed thousands of refugees seeking food, shelter, and protection from enemies. South Texas Indian groups migrated to new areas, united with other groups, or adopted outsiders, continuing a tradition of "ethnogenesis" that, according to David LaVere, is applicable to virtually all Indian peoples of Texas who "made and remade themselves over and over again." Thus, by the early nineteenth century, the original native peoples of south-central Texas were either culturally or biologically extinct because of assimilation, disease, and attacks by other Indian groups. In their place stood the new "composite peoples," who would likewise have to contend with Comanches, Mexicans, Americans, and other powerful newcomers who sought hegemony over south Texas.[11]

At some point during the first quarter of the eighteenth century, several of the Apache groups whose ancestors had once dominated the southern plains emerged as Lipan Apaches—a distinct tribe comprising a broad assortment of both Athapaskan and non-Athapaskan peoples who had merged under a variety of circumstances in order to survive. The first reference to the Lipans may have come in 1715 from a Taos Indian named Don Geronimo, who reported to Spanish officials that there was a group of plains dwellers living to the east, whom the Taos called the "Chipaynes," but who referred to themselves as the Sejines. In the 1720s, the Spaniards employed the name "Ipande" (or Ypande, Yxandi, Hipandis, Lipanes, Hipanes, Lypanes), while anthropologists and linguists also attribute several variations of the Caddoan word "Canecy" to the Lipan Apaches. Maria Wade, who has studied early Native American history in the Texas Edwards Plateau, states that the name "Lipan" does not appear in Spanish records before December 1732, and that one must exercise caution in attributing early anti-Spanish activities to them. Anthropologist Karl Schlesier believes that the Apaches who raided in and around San Antonio in the 1720s were probably members of what he calls the "Pecos Division" of Apaches that included the Faraones and Natagés, all of whom were forerunners of the Mescaleros. William Edward Dunn, meanwhile, states that between 1718 and 1750, "the tribes chiefly known in Texas were the Lipan and the Natagés, especially the former." They went under various names, but in the early part of the period, the Spaniards made no distinction between the different Texas bands and included all of them under the generic name "Apaches."[12]

While the Apaches' migration southward pushed thousands of Coahuiltecan, Jumano, and other Indian peoples into the enthusiastic embrace of Franciscan missionaries, officials in Mexico City were growing increasingly apprehensive about the security of New Spain's northern frontier. Reports from the region indicated that the Apaches were increasingly dominant in south-central Texas, they were stealing horses, and that several Indian groups desired Spanish assistance or protection against the invaders.[13]

The Spaniards had good reason to worry about Lipan Apache expansion into south Texas. They were already familiar with other Southern Athapaskans who, by their incessant attacks and raids, had made Spanish colonization of New Mexico difficult and expensive. Policymakers in Mexico City must have engaged in some serious hand-wringing as they reflected back on the challenges they had faced in pacifying the region lying just south of the Rio Grande. As the Spanish mining and mission frontier expanded northward during the latter half of the sixteenth century, the seminomadic tribes of the Mexican central plateau had fought tenaciously to expel the intruders. Employing early conquest policies that had worked so well against the stratified and extended empire of the Aztecs, the Spaniards sought to likewise incorporate these widely dispersed seminomadic peoples into their vast tributary domain. But there was no Montezuma or unhappy Indian vassals to exploit in the north. Due to increasing and unrelenting Indian resistance, the Spaniards began stationing soldiers in strategic or economically significant places from which they could venture out to make campaigns, initiating the so-called *presidio* system. Persistent Indian raids, however, discouraged Spanish colonization of the northern frontier, disrupted silver mining and the development of the regional economy, and pinned down large numbers of soldiers in remote locations. The mission system adopted at the end of the sixteenth century, in many respects, was an effort on the part of Spanish authorities to encourage (or bribe) Indians to accept Spanish authority, Christianity, and a sedentary lifestyle (or "reduction"), which they viewed in the long run as a far cheaper and more humane method of solving their "Indian problem."[14]

Spanish anxieties about the security of the northern frontier and the valuable silver mines of northern Mexico gained renewed intensity in response to the activities of French explorer René Robert Cavalier, Sieur de La Salle, who in 1682 led a successful expedition to the mouth of the Mississippi River. The familiar story of his murder and the ultimate demise of the St. Louis colony need not be recounted here, except for its effects on Spanish policy. The Spaniards, having learned about LaSalle's activities, dispatched several expeditions to locate and destroy any French colony they might discover. To discourage further French trespassing, officials in Mexico City also began formulating plans to heighten the Spanish presence in east Texas, taking the first tentative steps into a region that would severely test Spain's imperial ambitions to pacify and develop its northern frontier.[15]

After much delay, a Spanish expedition headed by Captain Alonso de León arrived in east Texas in May 1690. At a site located on San Pedro Creek, the Spaniards founded the mission San Francisco de los Tejas in hopes of evangelizing members of the Hasinai Caddo (Tejas)

Confederacy—longtime enemies and economic rivals of the various Apache peoples residing in Texas. Within a year, the Franciscans
founded a second mission, Santísimo Nombre de María, on the Neches
River about five miles away. Neither mission was successful. The Hasinais
were apparently disinterested in hearing the Gospel, and were outraged
by the conduct of Spanish soldiers who routinely violated their women.
When de Leon failed to punish the attackers, Hasinai leaders demanded
that the Spaniards vacate the area immediately. Although the Hasinais
allowed the Franciscans to remain in Tejas country, sickness and death
at the missions were rampant, and supplying the distant outposts from
northern Mexico proved expensive and difficult. By the end of 1693, even
the priests had worn out their welcome, and the Hasinais demanded
that they leave too. As one Hasinai man observed at the time, the greatest enemies to the success of Spanish missions were the Spaniards
themselves. Spanish officials may have hoped that "time would heal all
wounds," since over two decades passed before they attempted a return
to Tejas country.[16]

Discouraged by the Hasinai debacle, but undeterred in their determination to push northward, the Spaniards planted three new missions along their northern frontier between 1699 and 1703. In June 1699,
the Franciscans established a mission for Coahuiltecan peoples on the
Sabine River, some twenty-five miles north of Lampazos, Nuevo León.
Named in honor of John the Baptist, the mission San Juan Bautista lasted
only a few months before being relocated further north to present-day
Guerrero, Coahuila. Situated just five miles from the Rio Grande, the
mission was strategically located near a series of crossings into Texas,
and would later serve as an important staging area and supply depot for
military campaigns and settlements north of the river. In March 1700,
the Franciscans added the nearby mission San Francisco Solano, and
two years after that, the mission San Bernardo.[17]

Spanish fears of French penetration into Texas received new urgency
when, in the summer of 1714, the French cavalier Louis Juchereau de
Saint-Denis appeared at San Juan Bautista in hopes of enticing the
Spaniards to open trade relations with French Louisiana. Their arrival
in July shocked officials there, who promptly arrested the Frenchmen
and sent them to Mexico City for interrogation. In August, Spanish
authorities in the capital, possessing indisputable proof in the person

of Saint-Denis that the French in Louisiana were casting a covetous eye west, counseled that swift action be taken to discourage their rivals from acting on such desires, and Viceroy Duque de Linares ordered that preparations for an *entrada* (or campaign) be made immediately. In April 1716, a party of twenty-five soldiers under the command of Alférez Domingo Ramón—along with forty men, women, and children; nine Franciscan priests; and three lay brothers—set out from San Juan Bautista to reestablish a Spanish presence in east Texas. Guided by Saint-Denis, the Spaniards arrived in east Texas by the end of July and accomplished the expedition's primary purpose—establishing six missions and a presidio among the Hasinais. From these new settlements, the Spaniards were close enough to the French trading posts on the Red River to keep an eye on Saint-Denis's people.[18]

Keen to prevent the type of disaster that had befallen the first Spanish missions in east Texas, viceregal officials in the capital made sure that women and children accompanied the soldiers to assuage Tejas fears of renewed Spanish assaults on their women. They also approved the establishment of a mission and presidio midway between the Red River and the Rio Grande, reducing nearly by half the four hundred miles of open country that lay between San Juan Bautista and the new east Texas missions. On May 1, 1718, Fr. Antonio de San Buenaventura Olivares laid the foundations of the mission San Antonio de Valero, while Captain Martín de Alarcón established the presidio San Antonio de Béxar, and the settlement of Villa de Béxar four days later.[19]

From their scattered encampments in the hills of the Balcones Escarpment and river valleys in the Edwards Plateau, the Lipan Apaches observed the Spaniards' movements closely and with growing concern. Having hunted, traded, and skirmished with Spaniards in Texas and New Mexico for nearly a century, the Lipans understood the significance that Spanish guns and horses held for the various Indian peoples of south Texas. Their very survival depended not only on acquiring trade items, but also on preventing their enemies from doing so. Of particular concern was the Spaniards' apparent disposition to trade with the Lipans' enemies—particularly the Hasinai Caddos. The Hasinais and Lipans had been warring on and off since the 1690s, preying on each other's horse herds and seizing women and children as captives. Following the Spaniards' initial establishment of missions in east Texas, the Tejas were quick to enlist the

military assistance of their new allies. In August 1692, for example, the
Spaniards joined the Hasinais in a campaign against the Apaches, traveling westward until they happened across an Apache encampment. Things
did not go well for the Tejas. Had it not been for Spanish firearms, Fray
Francisco Hidalgo reported, not one of the invaders would have returned
home alive. Joseph de Urrutia, who lived among the Hasinais for several
years, later boasted that he had led his Tejas captors on several successful
campaigns against the Apaches during the 1690s.[20]

Lipan concerns about the Spanish-Tejas relationship deepened in
April 1717 when a band of seventy warriors came across a Spanish supply
train en route to San Juan Bautista after having wintered with the Tejas.
Possessing clear numerical superiority, the Apaches attacked them and
made off with twenty-seven mules. Because they believed there were
Frenchmen traveling with the Spaniards, however, the Apaches did not
press the confrontation for fear of jeopardizing possible trade opportunities in Louisiana. Diego Ramón, who had served as an escort for the
supply train, boasted that if he had had fifty men, he would have pursued
his attackers, since the "friendly" Indians in east Texas, as well as several coastal tribes, were "offended at the Apaches" and had called on the
Spaniards to come to their defense. Should a Spanish-Apache war ensue,
Ramon predicted, "the result would be that the friendly Indians and their
enemies would be brought under the yoke of Spain and of the Gospel."[21]

Given the record of Spanish assistance to the hated Tejas, the Lipan
Apaches probably viewed the establishment of missions and a presidio
at San Antonio with considerable suspicion. Fending off attacks from
Comanches and Wichitas on their northern flank, and from Hasinai
Caddos and other tribes to the east, the Lipans now had to be wary of
Spanish soldiers to the south. While the Spanish threat had not yet risen
to the level posed by their numerous Indian adversaries, they were at best
the "friends of their enemies," and therefore subject to Lipan attacks. The
Spaniards' provocative new position on the outskirts of their territory
consequently heightened the Lipans' acute sense of insecurity, compelling them to launch a campaign of hit-and-run attacks to alert the Spanish
trespassers that their presence in south Texas was not welcome.

Nor did the relative isolation and vulnerability of the San Antonio
population go unnoticed among Lipan warriors eager to demonstrate
bravery and boldness by raiding Spanish horse herds. Supply trains

moving north and south between San Antonio and San Juan Bautista, loaded with food, clothing, and other supplies, also made tempting targets for men eager to acquire high-status trade goods and the recognition of their people. Attacks and raids served the additional purpose of satisfying Lipan desires for revenge. Since the Spaniards were openly aiding the Tejas, they too bore responsibility for the death or capture of Lipan men, women, and children. As Carlos Castañeda has pointed out, "When the Tejas were befriended and aided in their campaigns vs. the Apaches, the seeds for Apache hatred for the Spaniards were sown."[22]

Hostilities with the Tejas and the establishment of Spanish missions and a presidio in east Texas also had the effect of restricting the Lipans' access to trade with the French, who enjoyed a close, profitable, and unobstructed economic relationship with a wide array of Indian peoples. Motivated primarily by the desire for profits, the French exhibited little inclination to Christianize the Indians or force their assimilation. Instead, they strove to work within Indian cultures and to exchange manufactured goods with Caddo and Wichita hunters for deer and buffalo hides, horses, and Apache captives. Throughout the eighteenth century, historian Juliana Barr has noted, French posts in western Louisiana were the nuclei of the slave trade in Apache women and children brought by Caddos, Wichitas, and Comanches. The Caddos and Wichitas rapidly drew the French traders into kinship relations (some through marriage and others through ritual adoption), often referring to them as "brother" or "father." They expected their French "kinsmen" to reciprocate with gifts of guns and other merchandise, provide wise counsel when they had to deal with the Spaniards, and assist them in their wars against the Lipans to the west and the Osages to the northeast. The absence of Spanish kinship relations with the Texas tribes, consequently, permitted the French to outmaneuver the Spaniards in acquiring Indian allies. Moreover, while the indigenous peoples of east Texas proved eager to accept Spanish gifts and trade goods, they remained unyielding in their determination to protect their French kinsmen.[23]

For the hard-pressed Lipan Apaches, acquiring firearms via French or Indian intermediaries (such as the Hasinais and Bidais) was crucial to their survival, and the prospect of trying to defend themselves against better-armed adversaries weighed heavily on their minds. Prohibition of the sale of firearms to Indians remained one of the fundamentals of official Spanish trade policy during the first half of the eighteenth century, and while some traders certainly skirted the ban on occasion, the Lipans realized that they could not depend on the Spaniards for weapons. Consequently, the Apaches' need for guns and ammunition was acute. Complicating matters further was securing the requisite trade items. Their former dominance of the bison-hide trade increasingly overshadowed by the Comanches, the Lipans were less able than ever to obtain goods to trade with the Spaniards—or with anyone else, for that matter. Acquiring captives was no longer a reliable option either, since their enemy's greater strength cut off the source of supply for the slave trade. "As a result of their greatly increased needs, and their greatly decreased effective economic demand," Frank Secoy has noted, "the Apache trade relation with the Spaniards became increasingly unsatisfactory. Their only alternative was to seize the items they required by force."[24]

For a variety of reasons, therefore, Lipan-Spanish relations were somewhat volatile after the founding of San Antonio in the spring of 1718. Warriors attacked supply trains moving north from Coahuila, stealing horses and mules, and at times killing the drivers and escorts who tried to stop them. In 1720, newly appointed Texas and Coahuila governor Marqués de San Miguel de Aguayo and an army of five hundred men marched north from Monclova into Texas to reestablish Spain's presence in Texas and to restore the missions they had abandoned to the French a year earlier during the so-called "Chicken War." Interpreting this new Spanish encroachment into their territory as a direct threat, the Apaches reportedly stuck arrow shafts in the ground near the Béxar presidio. The arrow shafts had red pieces of cloth attached to them like small flags, which may have represented their own "declaration of war." But Aguayo would not permit the Apaches to draw him into a fight. To the contrary, he distributed presents to the Indian peoples that he encountered on his trip east, prominent chiefs receiving blue cloth coats and silver-handled batons. Aguayo also instructed his men to erect several crosses along the way, both "to exalt the cross in the midst of so much idolatry" and to serve as beacons of peace to the Apaches.[25]

The Spaniards had initially envisioned forging alliances with the Apaches in hopes that the latter would serve as a barrier against French expansion, and Aguayo's instructions stipulated that he pursue a conciliatory policy toward them. Policymakers reckoned that the Lipans would respond favorably to peace overtures in light of the looming threat that the Comanches posed to them from the north. Several factors, however, rendered a Spanish-Apache alliance untenable at this time. First, the Spaniards' continued courtship of traditional Apache enemies such as the Tejas (and later the Wichitas and Comanches) both confounded and infuriated the Lipans. The Lipans had been warring with the Tejas for decades, and the cycle of raid and reprisal was an enduring and essential element of their warrior complex. Since the Spaniards had demonstrated on several occasions that they were willing to side with the Tejas, one can hardly fault the Lipans for concluding that they were untrustworthy. In addition, the Lipans were suspicious about Spanish proscriptions on selling weapons to Indians, and may have interpreted the affront as a hostile act aimed at keeping them in a weakened position vis-à-vis their better-armed opponents. The various tribes of Texas needed guns and ammunition for hunting and protection against their traditional Indian enemies, yet Spanish authorities refused to sell or trade firearms to Indians who did not adhere to official policies. Native peoples in east Texas responded to such strong-arm tactics by turning to the French, while the Lipans, due to their more distant geographic location and the presence of numerous Indian enemies blocking their access to Louisiana, watched helplessly as the balance of power shifted to their Comanche, Wichita, and Tejas nemeses.[26]

During the early 1720s, warriors from the various Lipan bands residing in south-central Texas conducted frequent raids on the presidial horse herds of San Antonio Béxar. Raiding parties were usually small, as was the case when a group of five men managed to steal fifty horses in the spring of 1722. Trying to control a herd that size must have slowed them down, and a detail of eleven soldiers recovered the horses, returning to San Antonio with the heads of four of the offenders—a grisly deterrent to other would-be horse thieves. The death and decapitation of four warriors confounded and infuriated the families of the deceased, who were obligated to retaliate and seek vengeance for the deaths of their loved ones. They had expected the Spaniards to attempt to recover their stolen horses, but to execute four warriors was, from the Lipan perspective, an unnecessary and excessive escalation of violence.[27]

The Lipans associated the moon with cloud cover and rain, and the presence of a crescent moon indicated that a storm was near. It may

have been the occurrence of a crescent moon, therefore, that encouraged a small group of warriors to plan another raid on the troublesome
Spaniards. On a dark, stormy night in August 1723, an Apache raiding
party made a daring foray on the Béxar horse herd. Despite the fact that
the horses were under a ten-man guard and enclosed in a locked corral,
the Apaches managed to break in and run off eighty animals. Captain
Nicolás Flores y Valdéz, a career soldier who had risen through the ranks
due to his bravery and ability, gave immediate pursuit, but returned
empty-handed the next day. After regrouping, Flores led a force of thirty
soldiers and an equal number of mission Indians to follow the Apaches'
trail. Flores pressed his men hard, stopping only briefly to decide which
of five trails to follow after the Apaches split up to confuse their pursuers. On September 24, more than a month after leaving their presidio, they discovered an Apache ranchería of two hundred people near
present-day Brownwood, Texas. According to Spanish reports, a six-
hour battle ensued in which thirty-four Indians were killed and twenty
women and children taken captive. Flores's forces apparently routed the
Indians, who fled with their families down a ravine and across a river
(Pecan Bayou?) to escape. The Spaniards "recovered" about one hundred
and twenty horses, together with a large quantity of plunder consisting
of painted saddles, bridles, knives, spears, food, and clothing that Flores
presumed had been stolen. The Spaniards reportedly suffered only three
light casualties during the engagement (including the captain, who lost a
tooth). Fray Joseph González, a missionary in San Antonio who was not
present at the battle, condemned the Flores expedition for attacking an
innocent band of Indians "behind their backs" and killing and capturing victims as they were fleeing for their lives.[28]

González's criticism was not unexpected, considering the divergent
goals of missionaries and soldiers. The Franciscans' objective was the
spiritual salvation of the Indians, their adoption of a sedentary lifestyle,
and "civilized" behavior. The military, on the other hand, was interested
in pacifying frontier tribes and forcing their subjection to Spanish rule.
The Spaniards targeted women and children to capture as prisoners in
hopes of using them to force their husbands and fathers to make peace.
While policymakers believed these secular and religious goals to be
compatible, missionaries and soldiers on the frontier increasingly took
exception to each other's "meddling," particularly when Indian raids

continued into the 1730s and 1740s. Priest and soldier came to view one another as adversaries rather than allies, precipitating a ceaseless stream of letters to Mexico City in an effort to illuminate the other's outrages and failures.

The argument between soldiers and priests that erupted after the Flores expedition illustrates the ambiguity and diversity of views regarding the formulation and implementation of Spanish Indian policy in the New World. As David J. Weber has noted, there was no monolithic Indian policy that Spanish administrators observed, and local forces often shaped the various imperial policies in effect at a given time. In addition, there was no real guarantee that Spanish officials "on the ground" would obey decrees sent from distant capitols, and they devised numerous ways of reinterpreting policies that they found misguided or unworkable. That being the case, there were many different views on how best to treat with *los indios bárbaros* to bring peace to the frontier and to advance the Crown's interests. Some groups favored integrating native peoples into Spanish society via reduction on missions; other groups were uninterested in assimilating the Indians and instead held out trade and commerce as the proper vehicle for pacifying the frontier. Some frontier officials advocated treating with Indian peoples as quasi-sovereign nations—forging alliances and lists of mutual obligations and boundary lines that each party was bound to respect. Finally, there were the proponents of force, who counseled a policy of meeting violence with violence and terminating Indian depredations by killing or exiling Indian raiders. Spain's frontier officials, military officers, and clergy, Weber argues, represented just a few of the "several competing interest groups, each divided into reformers and defenders of the *status quo*, who shaped and reshaped Indian policy into the twilight years of the Spanish Empire."[29]

The policies Spaniards employed toward Indians depended as much on Indian responses as on Spanish initiatives, and Indians often took the initiative, forcing Spaniards to respond. The Spaniards' evolving Apache policy confirms this crucial point. An important reason why Flores had seized Apache captives was to gain useful intelligence and to use them to encourage their families and leaders to make peace. From a forty-year-old Apache woman, for example, Flores learned that her people raided around San Antonio so they could acquire horses to trade with the "other

Spaniards" to the north. By "other Spaniards," Flores took her to mean
the French, thus confirming Spanish concerns about foreign penetration
into Texas. If the Spaniards could somehow make allies of the Apaches, he
reasoned, they could use the Indians as a bulwark against the French and
other trespassers. With the Apache threat neutralized, moreover, Spain
could more easily develop trade networks between New Mexico and east
Texas, further consolidating its hold over the northern frontier. Seizing the
opportunity at hand, in early October 1723, Flores dispatched the woman
to her own people astride a horse loaded with gifts for her chiefs, to entice
them to discuss peace and gain the release of their family members. In late
December, a party of thirty Apaches arrived in San Antonio to resume
negotiations, and Fr. González welcomed them warmly, promising to
release their loved ones at once. Captain Flores, however, had different
ideas. Rumors were rampant that the Apaches were not at all interested
in peace, but only in securing the release of the captives. According to
a Coahuiltecan neophyte named Gerónimo (hardly an objective informant), the Apaches were angry about Flores's earlier campaign and were
planning an assault on the presidio as soon as the captives gained their
freedom. With these concerns in mind, Flores countermanded the padre's
pledge to the Apache delegation. Indignant at his colleague's refusal to
free the prisoners, Fr. Gonzáles charged that Flores never intended to
release them, because he wanted to employ the Apaches as servants in
San Antonio. Unmoved by the priest's criticisms, Flores flatly refused
to release the captives until all the chiefs had agreed to end hostilities.
Disappointed and angry, the Indians departed empty-handed, issuing
vague promises that they would return later to make peace. Fr. González
was equally upset, and in a letter to his superiors, complained that Flores
had exacerbated Apache relations through his unwarranted attack the
previous autumn, his mismanagement of the presidio, and his stubborn-
ness during the recent peace negotiations. If the viceroy saw fit to appoint
him to lead a contingent of seventy men to Apache country, González proposed, he would treat the Indians kindly, restore their wives and children,
and again secure peace. The padre's complaints were not without effect,
and in April 1724, Viceroy Marqués de Cuellar removed Flores from command. Although the embattled captain fought successfully for reinstatement, the rift between missionaries and soldiers at San Antonio expanded,
complicating further the Crown's objectives in Texas.[30]

The Lipans, meanwhile, had good reason to be frustrated and angry. The Spaniards had attacked one of their encampments, killed many warriors, and seized several captives. The imprisonment of their wives and children must have infuriated and humiliated the Lipans, whose notions of honor and masculinity (not to mention strong familial attachments) required men to risk their lives to secure the captives' release. When a group of Lipan leaders journeyed to San Antonio with the expectation of retrieving their family members, however, the Spaniards rebuffed them. The French, meanwhile, were trading guns to several Caddoan-speaking tribes residing along both sides of the Red River in northeast Texas, such as the Wichitas and the Hasinais, whom the Spaniards referred to collectively as *Norteños* or the "Nations of the North." The Norteños (the Taovayas and Kichais in particular) were in turn arming the Comanches, who by the early 1730s had taken over most of the river valleys of the southwestern plains as well as the bison-hide trade with New Mexico.[31] Such ominous developments, at first glance, should have forced the Lipans (however grudgingly) to consider making peace with the Spaniards. But such considerations were out of the question. The Lipans felt little but contempt for the Coahuiltecans and Jumanos who had accepted Spanish protection, trading their dignity and freedom in exchange for a life that offered warriors hard work and little in the way of status acquisition or respect. Spanish efforts to build alliances with east Texas tribes also grated on the Lipans—who desired trade, but not at the cost of limiting their freedom of action. The only path open to them, Lipan leaders concluded, was to raid Spanish settlements and missions to acquire the means to ransom their loved ones, to defend themselves against the Comanches, and to make life so difficult for the Spanish intruders that they would retreat south of the Rio Grande.[32]

Such a course was admittedly dangerous, given the Spaniards' superior firepower, and the Lipans could ill afford to take heavy casualties (as they had at Brownwood). Lipan warriors also understood, however, that they had to face their fears head-on if they expected honor and respect from their people. That did not mean they should act recklessly, but that they should employ strategies and tactics their ancestors had honed over centuries of conflict with their various Indian enemies. These included fighting only when the odds were in their favor and on terrain of their choosing; attacking isolated and vulnerable targets; and luring their enemies into ambush or other exposed positions. Cease-fires would hold only as long as they benefited the Lipans. If achieving short-term objectives necessitated a promise to make peace, the Lipans would honor it if the agreement advanced their interests. A Spanish withdrawal, the Lipans calculated, would give them temporary breathing room to face pressures from the north and east. In the meantime, if they could cultivate a trade relationship with the French, they could regroup and reclaim a position of security and strength.

While some Lipan leaders may have thought along the lines suggested above, there was no "macro-Lipan foreign policy," given the autonomous nature and widely dispersed locations of the twelve to fourteen Lipan bands that inhabited Texas. While leaders could and did consult with one another regarding important issues that affected their respective peoples, each band ultimately made its own choices regarding how best to deal with the Spaniards. Some band members apparently decided in the months following the failed peace conference in San Antonio that it was in their individual interests—and perhaps in their band's interests—to step up raiding activities, and the years 1724 and 1725 witnessed an increase in attacks and raids. On March 9, 1724, for example, six warriors attacked two Spanish soldiers en route from San Juan Bautista to San Antonio. They shot one of the Spaniards out of his saddle, but the other escaped. When Captain Flores arrived with a relief party the next morning, they found the badly mutilated body of the soldier. The Lipans had stripped the man of his clothing, shot him with arrows in the stomach and back, scalped him, and torn away the flesh from the calf of one leg. The search party found the soldier's hat, shoes, and shield a short distance from the road. Flores took up the attackers' trail, but when night closed in, he turned the relief party back north to San Antonio. Later that month, the Apaches helped themselves once again to the horse herd at presidio San Juan Bautista. Raiding parties did not spare the mission Indians from their fury, perhaps trying to drive them away as a prelude to a Spanish withdrawal. Texas governor Fernando Pérez de Almazán responded to the mounting aggression with a policy of conciliation, giving orders that if his men should encounter any Apaches, they were to bring the Apaches back to him unharmed, so that he could give them presents and dispatch them as messengers offering friendship and alliance to their chiefs. Such a policy, Thomas Schilz has noted, only encouraged the aggression of the Lipans, who probably interpreted such conciliatory overtures as a sign of weakness.[33]

For reasons that elude scholars, Lipan attacks in and around San Antonio declined in the years 1726–1730. Perhaps there had been changes in band leadership, or, as Maria Wade has speculated, they were busy fighting Indian enemies such as the Comanches or Wichitas, or east Texas tribes such as the Hasinais. While raids for horses did not end entirely, the Spaniards residing at San Antonio no doubt appreciated the relative quiet they enjoyed during those years. But the break proved short-lived and came with mixed blessings. It was during this lull in hostilities that Brigadier General Don Pedro de Rivera arrived in Texas to conduct an inspection of the frontier presidios and to check the management and efficacy of the troops. Once in possession of this information, he could make fact-based recommendations in hopes of reducing the expenditure of royal funds connected with their maintenance. His 1728 report calling for a general reduction in forces throughout Texas (from fifty-three soldiers to forty-three at Béxar) was met with howls of protest from local officials and even the Franciscans, who understood that once the Apaches became aware of the troop reductions around San Antonio, they would renew their hostilities. The Spaniards had good reason to fear the renewal of Apache attacks. According to one estimate, between 1718 and 1731, Spanish officials attributed 22 percent of all recorded deaths of their compatriots in Texas to the Apaches.[34]

Rivera's recommendations of 1728, despite considerable objections, became official policy a year later in *los Reglamentos de 1729*. The cuts to troop strength at Béxar were even deeper than expected—the final number of soldiers shrinking from forty-three to thirty-eight. "These Indians have learned by experience what the soldiers can do in the exercise of their duty," Rivera explained, and "they observe a certain restraint which minimizes the need for vigilance." Don Pedro argued vehemently against the current policy of sending large numbers of troops into the interior to assist missionaries in their efforts to force Indians into missions. Convinced that the intrusion of a large Spanish military force would only provoke hostilities, Rivera counseled that in the future, commanders send only two or three soldiers to accompany the padres.[35]

While the number of troops stationed at Béxar declined, the number of people requiring their protection increased following the removal in 1731 of three missions from east Texas to San Antonio. In addition, Spanish officials endorsed the establishment of the villa San Fernando de Béxar, and sixteen families from the Canary Islands received land grants to entice them to settle in the area. The reduction of the garrison, coupled with the expansion of settlement, enhanced San Antonio's vulnerability—and therefore its attractiveness—to Lipan warriors, who lost no time launching raids on outlying horse and cattle herds. The sudden increase in Spanish activity on what the Lipans considered Apache lands also fueled attacks, as did the proliferation of missions that served as refuges for their enemies. In January 1731, Lipans under the leadership of Cabellos Colorados attacked a wagon train near San Antonio, killing a woman and taking a boy captive. Lipan attacks continued in mid-September when raiders struck San Antonio in broad daylight, getting away with sixty horses. Don Juan Antonio Pérez de Almazán, captain of the presidio, sent a sergeant and five soldiers in pursuit. When the captain rode out with eighteen reinforcements a short while later, he found his advance party in a desperate struggle with about forty Indians. As Almazán and his men charged in to rescue their comrades, several hundred more mounted and armed Indians emerged from their hiding places. The ensuing battle lasted two hours, the outnumbered Spaniards finally dismounting at the foot of a tree to make a last stand. The Apaches, who had killed two soldiers and wounded thirteen more, were seemingly on the cusp of a complete victory when they suddenly broke off the attack and rode away with the stolen horses. Had the Indians pressed their advantage, Castañeda has speculated, they very well could have overrun San Antonio, since fourteen soldiers were away on duty near the Rio Grande, leaving only three or four men at the presidio.[36]

Captain Almazán, in a process that would come to characterize virtually all subsequent communications between the Texas frontier and policymakers in Mexico City, complained about the inadequacy of his forces and requested additional troops. Recruiting civilian volunteers was virtually impossible, he argued, because Rivera's recent regulations had barred Spaniards from exploiting (that is, enslaving) their Apache prisoners. Absent such incentives, raising a volunteer militia was unattainable. His superiors responded by authorizing a campaign of 150 soldiers and Indian allies from neighboring presidios, adding caustically that no more men were needed, but rather, *more efficient management* of them. In a move designed to side-step—without actually negating—the Crown's ban on the enslavement of Indian prisoners, viceregal officials ruled that to "prevent the Indian allies from killing such captives as might be taken . . . it would be best to send [the captives] to other provinces and bring them up in the Catholic faith." To lead the campaign, policymakers turned to newly appointed Texas governor and former presidio commander Don Juan Antonio de Bustillo y Ceballos.[37]

The Bustillo expedition departed from San Antonio on October 22, 1732—an impressive force consisting of nearly 160 Spaniards, 60 mission Indians, 140 pack loads of supplies, and 900 horses and mules. After a two-week march, the Spaniards reached the Little River, a tributary of the Brazos. Following the Little River northwest, the Spaniards crossed the Colorado River and entered the heart of Apache country. On December 8, an Indian scout reported that he had located the enemy on the banks of what Bustillo named "El Rio San Sabas de Nueces" in honor of Saint Sabbas, a fifth-century monk and hermit whose feast day happened to fall around that same time. Halting to convene a war council, Bustillo decided to move closer to the ranchería with about half his men. After an all-night march, the Spaniards halted to regroup, and after receiving absolution from the priests, advanced in two ranks to within eyesight of the enemy. Before them lay not one but four Apache encampments, with an estimated four hundred tipis and seven hundred warriors. The ensuing battle lasted five hours. The well-disciplined Indians, mounted and wearing leather breastplates, fought tenaciously, timing their attacks to coincide with the interval after the Spaniards had discharged their weapons. Perhaps fearing that the Spaniards would desecrate the bodies of fallen warriors, the Indians threw their dead into the San Sabá River. Among those killed was a chief who carried a silver-tipped cane, which a friendly mission Indian delivered to Bustillo. Fighting at close quarters against superior firepower, the Apaches slowly retreated, leaving behind an estimated two hundred dead kinsmen and thirty women and children captives. The Spaniards seized seven hundred horses and one hundred mule-loads of hides and other plunder. Remarkably, the attackers suffered only seven casualties and one death. Flush with the spoils of war, Bustillo's party marched back to San Antonio amidst persistent Apache sniping, arriving home a few days before Christmas on December 22, 1732.[38]

Far from curbing Apache attacks in south-central Texas, the Bustillo campaign ignited a decade-long period of retaliatory attacks, murders, kidnappings, and theft. Having pierced the Apache heartland, the Spaniards struck a nerve that must have resonated strongly among Lipans who had been feverishly fending off enemy attacks along their northern and eastern peripheries. The slaughter of two hundred warriors (albeit a probable Spanish exaggeration) must have been as shocking as it was demoralizing to the Lipans, prompting warriors to question what they had done—or not done—to offend the supernatural forces that controlled their lives. The loss of hunters and providers, meanwhile, would have brought considerable distress to extended families and to the structural integrity of the affected bands. Warriors who had not acquitted themselves with the requisite daring and bravery could expect their in-laws to chasten them for bringing disgrace to the family, while band members sought to identify sorcerers, witches, and other scapegoats for censorship or death. Children, perhaps scared and bewildered about the events swirling about them, would have turned to their grandparents for an explanation, the latter reciting folktales and myths from the distant past to bolster their failing courage.

The loss of the seven hundred horses and one hundred mule-loads of supplies would have been, in some respects, equally disastrous for the Lipans—particularly coming in the middle of winter. Replacing seven hundred animals involved numerous raids, probably stretching over months—and horse theft, as we have seen, inevitably brought retaliation. The historical record does not itemize the Apache goods seized as plunder, but it is reasonable to assume that the one hundred Spanish pack mules trudging south to San Antonio bore thousands of pounds of meat, corn, flour, beans, medicinal plants and roots, hides, clothing, gunpowder, cooking utensils, and more.[39] Given the fact that food acquisition—particularly in wartime—was an essential and often time-consuming activity among the Lipans (and most other Texas tribes for that matter), the loss of such an immense quantity of foodstuffs at the San Sabá battle would have driven some bands to the brink of starvation.

The Lipan bands that had lost so much at the San Sabá were astonished when in mid-January 1733, two of the women the Spaniards had taken captive the month before appeared with invitations from their Spanish enemies requesting that they come to San Antonio to discuss peace. If

Lipan woman and child on muleback (circa 1853).
Friedrich Richard Petri, Center for American History, UT-Austin, di_04091.

the chiefs were interested in the Spaniards' offer, the women added, they were to proceed south to San Antonio and light a large fire to signal their arrival. While the Lipans were eager to secure the release of their captives, they may have also suspected a trap. If any of them were familiar with the events of the previous decade where one Spanish leader had promised to release Apache captives while another refused, they would have been understandably skeptical. To learn more about their enemies' true intentions, therefore, the Lipans sent three warriors and one of the women back to San Antonio.

On January 31, 1733, Governor Bustillo received word that a smoke trail was rising in the distance, indicating that the Apaches had arrived to discuss peace. Two days later, he welcomed the four Indians to San Antonio and treated them as honored guests. During their brief stay, the visitors insisted that their leaders were indeed interested in peace, and on February 5, they departed for home, promising to return within two months. In an expression of goodwill, Bustillo permitted groups of Apaches to enter and leave San Antonio as they pleased, and small groups of warriors visited the presidio and villa San Fernando to conduct trade. On March 27, however, as two soldiers were escorting an Apache woman and three men safely out of the settlement, a band of twenty-four warriors surrounded the two Spaniards, killed them, and flayed the flesh from their bones—as one priest commented bitterly—to "satisfy their vengeful appetite." The atrocity caused panic in San Antonio. Priests struggled to restrain mission Indians from fleeing to safety, while soldiers petitioned to have their families moved out of harm's way to San Juan Bautista. In response to frantic appeals for assistance, officials in Mexico City appointed fifty-five-year-old Don Joseph Urrutia as captain of the Béxar presidio. A veteran of numerous skirmishes with Indians, Urrutia had lived among east Texas tribes for seven years after they took him captive in the early 1690s. Well-versed in matters relating to Indian affairs, Urrutia appeared to be a wise choice at the time. The viceroy also called in reinforcements from neighboring presidios, and Bustillo received authorization to levy additional troops from presidios outside his jurisdiction.[40]

Apache raiders, meanwhile, ravaged south Texas. Cabellos Colorados seized two Spaniards and hauled them back to his encampment, where he reportedly set them to performing tasks usually assigned to women, such as dressing skins. The range of Apache attacks also expanded, with reports of depredations coming in from the lower Rio Grande Valley and northern Coahuila. According to William Dunn, seven Apache chiefs went so far as to establish rancherías on the Rio Grande to simplify the organization of raids in the region. In 1736, assaults on San Antonio were particularly frequent, perhaps because of widespread desertion on the part of presidial soldiers, which left the settlement practically defenseless. In September, a party of Apaches ambushed a Spanish supply train under a ten-man guard en route to San Juan Bautista, leaving two soldiers wounded. A short time later, Cabellos Colorados struck again, making off with forty horses from the mission San Francisco de la Espada. Some Apache raiding parties targeted the mission Indians. Soldiers found two slain Indian women at mission San Juan Capistrano and two more at mission Concepcíon—unusually brutal slayings, and uncharacteristic of the Lipans, who usually preferred taking women and children as captives. Stress levels ran so high at San Antonio that a simple gunshot sent residents into a state of panic. Concerns about the rising numbers of false alarms prompted the governor to issue an order forbidding residents from discharging their weapons unless it was in direct response to Indian attack.[41]

The year 1737 brought no respite from the violence. A particularly heinous atrocity occurred near the mission San Francisco de la Espada when five Pacaos Indian women and two young boys ventured a couple of miles outside the mission to gather fruit. A band of Apaches seized them, killed the five women (three of whom were reportedly pregnant), and carried the two boys away into captivity. In September, Apaches struck the Béxar horse herd again. A guard of ten soldiers was pasturing the herd about thirty miles away from San Antonio at a secluded spot on the Rio del Cíbolo (Cibolo Creek), which up to that time had been free of attack. The Apaches wounded one of the guards before riding off with over one hundred horses. Captain Urrutia immediately dispatched a detachment of soldiers to recover the horses, but the weary men returned home three days later empty-handed. Now thoroughly exasperated, Urrutia increased the guard at Rio del Cíbolo from ten to eighteen men, urging them to be especially vigilant for Indian raiders. Nonetheless, a couple of months later, the Apaches again targeted the herd. According to Juan Galbán, a junior officer at Béxar, the Indians struck at night and stampeded the horses, scattering the animals in groups each going in a different direction, and carried off more than three hundred of them.[42]

Embarrassed at having lost over four hundred horses in the span of three months, Urrutia ordered his men to move the herd back near the presidio, and he detailed a guard of twenty men to protect them. On December 11, 1737, the soldiers set out at daybreak to count the horses and captured a warrior who was apparently reconnoitering for yet another raid. Under interrogation, the Apache confessed that Cabellos Colorados and fifteen others (half of whom were women) were encamped about twenty miles away. Although the presence of so many women indicated that Cabellos Colorados was almost certainly not preparing for a new raid, Urrutia assembled nearly thirty soldiers and sent them to capture the notorious Lipan horse thief. The Spaniards must have surprised Colorados, since they captured his entire party and marched them under close guard back to San Antonio. After a few days of imprisonment, Colorados requested that the Spaniards send one of the captives to inform his people of his arrest, promising that they would return stolen animals in exchange for his release. Texas governor Prudencio de Orobio y Basterra selected a Lipan woman for this errand, instructing her to tell her brethren that he would release the prisoners when they handed over the stolen horses, and she rode off promising that her people would return the horses in twenty days. Forty days passed, however, before she reported back to San Antonio. She claimed there were some Lipans waiting nearby, but they possessed only sixteen horses with which to ransom the prisoners. As Urrutia scanned the horizon, however, he saw a far greater number of horses, and he sent out a detail to see what was afoot. The spies later reported that there was a host of armed Indians in the vicinity, and that the horses were little more than a ploy to lure the Spaniards into an ambush. Perhaps with Almazán's earlier experience in mind, Urrutia refused to take the bait, and after five days passed, the war party rode off. At various times later that year, small groups of Apaches appeared at San Antonio in an effort to win the release of the prisoners—presumably the immediate family members of Cabellos Colorados or the other prisoners. When Apache attacks resumed a couple of months later, Basterra decided to send the Lipan prisoners, including Cabellos Colorados and his two-year-old daughter María Guadalupe, to confinement in Mexico City. In mid-February

1739, a mixed guard of soldiers and civilians escorted thirteen of the sixteen Lipans (including Cabellos Colorados and his daughter) from Béxar on the first leg of their long journey south. They traveled for over three months on foot before reaching Mexico City in late May. Two of the Apache prisoners died en route, and seven others perished in prison. None of the survivors would ever see Texas again.[43]

By the spring of 1738, the Lipan strategy to force the withdrawal of Spanish forces from south Texas through a persistent and bloody series of raids, ambushes, kidnappings, and killings was showing signs of success. According to Captain Urrutia, the people of San Antonio lived in a state of constant terror and were afraid to venture outside the settlement to work their land or to attend to their livestock. Some families, unable to cope with the unrelenting fear and anxiety, packed their belongings and moved away. Mission Indians also deserted in droves, fleeing southeast to the Texas Gulf Coast, or northeast to the Monte Grande (Western Crossed Timbers) region. The presidio of Béxar, Urrutia freely admitted, was entirely insufficient to address the Apache problem. His rather unimaginative solution was to make one or more vigorous campaigns against them, and in May 1738, Urrutia petitioned the viceroy both for permission to wage the campaigns and for reinforcements.[44]

Notably absent from Urrutia's request was a reasoned assessment of why a campaign was necessary at that time, and exactly how the campaign would lead to Lipan Apache pacification. The Flores campaign of 1723 and Bustillo expedition of 1732 had certainly not accomplished this objective, and in some respects only exacerbated tensions. To dispatch an adequate force to chase one party of Apaches (who might or might not be the ones responsible for raids in the first place) exposed the settlement and missions to the depredations of countless others, and ascertaining with any precision the identity of the raiders was virtually impossible.[45] While the record of Apache attacks was voluminous in 1738, so too had it been earlier in the decade. Urrutia may have been looking for a military success to bolster his chances of becoming governor. The sixty-year-old commander may also have been seeking a glorious finale to a long military career that was certainly in its twilight. That viceregal officials gave their consent absent an analysis of how the campaign furthered the Crown's long-term interests suggests administrative incompetence, laziness—and/or that when it came to Indian affairs, decision makers at the local level received considerable leeway in formulating policy. Lacking adequate numbers of troops, equipment, and imagination, Spanish frontier officials (and their accomplices in Mexico City) found themselves engaged in a struggle that increasingly resembled intertribal wars with their endless cycles of raid and retaliation. But by allowing the Lipans (and other Texas Indians) to dictate the terms of the struggle, the Spaniards forfeited any pretense of imperial power, instead adopting the characteristics and objectives of any other "tribe" looking to guard its territory and people from predation. Lacking a grand strategy or purpose, therefore, Spanish officials organized campaigns that resembled obligatory reprisals having more to do with relieving their citizens' growing sense of frustration and helplessness than accomplishing a viable, long-term military objective. And while their tactics and technology differed to some extent from their Indian adversaries', the Spaniards' short-term goals were basically the same as those motivating the Lipans: they desired vengeance against those who had been raiding their horse herds and killing their citizens; they sought to acquire plunder and enemy captives, and to allow individuals (as in the case of Urrutia) to gain status and prestige as a means of social mobility. The apparent degenerative nature of Spanish campaigns was not lost on the Franciscans, who had long suspected that frontier commanders were motivated primarily by the lure of taking captives and other economic considerations.

The details surrounding the Urrutia campaign of 1739 remain poorly documented. Like most Spanish military ventures of the period, bureaucratic obstructions and fumbling caused delays, and the initial April launch date came and went. Not until the winter of 1739 did Urrutia and his cohorts ride out of Béxar en route to the San Sabá River country. They surprised an Indian encampment on the north side of the San Sabá, and took many captives. Father Benito Fernández de Santa Ana, who had other ideas about how best to deal with the Apaches, expressed disgust with the campaign. In a letter to the viceroy, he complained that Urrutia had allowed the soldiers to commit "disorders" that left many of his men heavily in debt—suggesting that gambling had been a popular distraction in camp. As for the campaign accomplishing its objectives, Santa Ana stated that the soldiers' primary concern had been gaining possession of Indian horses, bison hides, and captives, rather than serving their king.[46]

The long campaign into Apache country convinced Joseph Urrutia that his heretofore distinguished forty-year military career was over. Shortly after his return to Béxar, he passed command of the presidio to his thirty-year-old son Toribio. The new commander inherited a situation similar to that which had plagued his father—renewed Apache attacks and violence coupled with a financially strapped bureaucracy in Mexico City, possessing little inspiration regarding how to pacify the frontier. During the latter part of 1742, Toribio Urrutia, stressing the need for the subjection of the Apaches, requested permission to launch a new series of campaigns against them. Like his father (who had died on July 16, 1741), Urrutia offered no compelling rationale as to how the campaigns would end Apache depredations. Instead, he appealed to his superiors' economic interests, dangling the possibility of securing information about the rich mineral deposits that allegedly lay unexploited in Apache country. After the usual delays and bureaucratic paralysis, the necessary permissions were granted, and in April 1745, Urrutia, with a force of about fifty Spaniards and several Indian allies, marched north once again. More than two hundred miles to the northwest of San Antonio, just beyond the Colorado River, Urrutia surprised an Apache ranchería of Lipans and Natagés. Since many warriors were absent, perhaps out hunting to secure food after the long winter, acquiring large numbers of captives was a simple task. Father Santa Ana, a frequent critic of the senior Urrutia, depicted the aims of this latest campaign in characteristically unflattering terms, suggesting once again that its primary purpose was to plunder and enslave the Apaches, and that evil consequences would be the result.[47]

And evil consequences there were. Vengeance-seeking Lipans and Natagés soon descended on San Antonio, killing nine people within three weeks' time. On the evening of June 30, 1745, residents of San Antonio received an additional scare when 350 Lipans and Natagés, including an undetermined number of women and children, attacked the presidio with the intention of setting it on fire. The presence of women and children among the attackers was highly uncharacteristic of the Lipans (who generally sent their families into hiding during campaigns), and their role in the episode was probably more as spectators than as participants. The Indians divided their forces, with two groups attacking the presidio while a third remained outside in ambush. The arrival of

Camp of the Lipan by Theodore Gentilz (1845).
Frenchman Jean Louis Theodore Gentilz came to Texas in 1843. The painting shows the activities of a Lipan band on the Medina River. Courtesy of the Witte Museum, San Antonio, Texas.

one hundred mission Indians from Valero turned the tide of the battle, however, and the attackers retreated. According to William Dunn, the Lipans and Natagés were not of one mind regarding the cessation of hostilities. The Spaniards held the Lipan chief's daughter captive, but after receiving assurances that she had received kind treatment and that the Spaniards desired peace, he called off the attack. The Natagé leader was infuriated with the change in plans, but absent his erstwhile allies, he had little choice but to retreat as well.[48]

The Lipan band (or bands) involved in the San Antonio raid of June 1745, perhaps fearing that their loved ones confined at San Antonio would suffer the fate of Cabellos Colorados and his followers, scaled back their incursions around the settlement in the months immediately following the attack. Other Lipans (and perhaps even those alluded to above) raided south of San Antonio along the Rio Grande, so much so that San Antonio residents feared that an Apache attack might come from the south. The Lipans faced new challenges and concerns in the mid-1740s that marked a watershed of sorts in their relationship with their Indian enemies to the north and with the Spanish to their south. A particularly ominous development was the formation in 1746 of a Comanche-Taovayas alliance. The French had sponsored the relationship in hopes of expanding their commercial activities, but the Spaniards unwittingly contributed to the merger when New Mexican officials prohibited all trade with the Comanches. Finding New Mexico closed to them, the Comanches reached out to the Taovayas with the understanding that the relationship would gain them access to the French trade. Various Norteño tribes soon became intermediaries in the Comanche-French exchange network, trading the Comanches' hides, horses, and captives to the French for weapons, gunpowder, and other coveted items. By the middle of the eighteenth century, the predominance of "Canneci" (Lipan Apache) women in the enslaved Indian population in Louisiana became so pronounced that French governor Louis Billouart de Kerlérec abandoned any thought of adding the Apaches to the list of Louisiana's native trade allies.[49]

Coinciding with—but separate from—the Comanche-Taovayas alliance was the construction of new Spanish missions on the eastern periphery of Lipan country. In early June 1745, seventeen Indians from Ranchería Grande, located along the middle Brazos River Valley, arrived at San Antonio and requested that the Spaniards erect missions for them. Since the early part of the eighteenth century, refugee Coahuiltecans, Ervipiames, Tobosos, and Tripas Blancas, as well as Jumanos, Yojuanes, Deadoses, Mayeyes, and Cocos, had gathered at Ranchería Grande for protection against both the Spanish and Apaches, and the encampment had evolved into an important trade site. The Ranchería Grande emissaries, who had received a visit the previous year from Father Mariano Francisco de Dolores y Viana, refused to relocate to San Antonio, but indicated that they would be willing to allow the Spaniards to construct missions in their own country, where they were somewhat safer from Lipan attacks. Thrilled at this unexpected opportunity, Father Dolores wrote to his superiors requesting authorization and assistance. Proponents of the missions maintained that they would form a barrier between hostile Lipan Apaches and the coast and discourage the Lipans from trading with the French. After much delay, in December 1747, Viceroy Revilla Gigedo authorized three new missions (Nuestra Señora de los Dolores del Río San Xavier, San Ildefonso, and Nuestra Señora de la Candelaria) along the San Xavier (San Gabriel) River.[50]

In the face of renewed pressures on their northern, eastern, and southern fronts, the Lipans' future appeared bleak. Indian enemies were working in concert to raid their horse herds and to seize their women and children as commodities to trade with the French. From the French, meanwhile, these same Indian enemies were relatively well equipped with guns, powder, and lead, thereby enjoying not only numerical superiority, but technological supremacy as well. In light of the Spaniards' ban on weapons sales to Indians, the Lipans faced the unpleasant quandary of depending on their enemies or unaligned coastal tribes (who were also wary of the Lipans) to gain access to the French trade. To the south, the Spanish had conducted several expeditions into their country and carried off hundreds of women and children into confinement at San Antonio and beyond. They continued to hold their loved ones, demanding that the Lipans return the hundreds of horses they had stolen from presidial herds—horses that the Lipans desperately needed both to trade for firearms and to replenish their own herds ravaged by the Wichitas and Comanches. The Spaniards had repeatedly shown a willingness to befriend the Tejas and other Nations of the North, and were now in the process of expanding their presence in Texas and attempting to sever the Lipans' access to the coast, where they might trade directly with the French. From the Lipan perspective, therefore, they had but one choice: to continue waging war on all fronts to defend their territory, their families, and their independence.

The priests and soldiers assigned to the new San Xavier missions reported that the Lipans launched a series of attacks as soon as they discovered what the Spaniards were doing. In 1747 they attacked four different times, the fiercest engagement coming in May when sixty warriors rode up to the mission. Although more than two hundred mission Indians, priests, and soldiers were present, the arrival of the Apaches sparked such terror that many simply fled, leaving the buildings and supplies to be ransacked by the attackers. As the Lipans rode off with their plunder, they bumped into twenty-two Coco mission Indians that had been out hunting buffalo, and in the unpleasant encounter that followed, the Lipans killed two of the latter group and flayed the flesh from their bodies. As a result, many of the Cocos and other Indian groups that had earlier requested missions deserted and fled into the wilderness. To remedy the missions' lack of security, the viceroy approved the creation of a presidio (San Xavier de Gigedo) on the San Gabriel River, and in March 1751 appointed Captain Felipe de Rábago y Terán as its commander. By virtually all accounts a ruthless and unscrupulous scoundrel, Rábago's decision to carry on an illicit affair with the wife of a Spanish settler led to his alienation from the missionaries he was supposed to protect. When the woman's husband and a priest were found murdered in May 1752, Spanish officials removed Rábago from command and placed him under house arrest in Coahuila. Rábago's replacement at San Xavier was his maternal uncle—Pedro de Rábago y Terán, the governor of Coahuila and captain of presidio Santa Rosa de Monclova. Recurring Apache attacks, however, combined with drought, epidemic disease, and internal strife, proved too much for the padres. In late summer 1755, they, along with Rábago and his men, acted on their own and moved all operations to the banks of the San Marcos River. In October, reports from the San Gabriel missions indicated that San Ildefonso was deserted, San Xavier had one friar ministering to seventy Ervipiames and Mayeyes, and the Cocos had abandoned mission Candelaria, promising to return after the Spaniards provided adequate protection.[51]

After enduring over a quarter century of Apache raids and depredations in south Texas, Spanish officials began considering an alternate pacification policy that differed significantly from the reactionary military expeditions of the recent past. Instead of unsheathing the sword of the Spanish empire, they would instead send out the cross. The idea of establishing missions in Lipan Apache country was certainly not a new one. Prior to 1743, there had been at least three definite proposals for missionary work among the Lipans—none of which authorities acted on. In March 1743, however, Fray Santa Ana wrote Viceroy Fuenclara urging that he approve active steps to convert and reduce the Apaches, and that one of these steps should include the establishment of missions in their own land. The probability of success was favorable, Santa Ana argued, because of the ongoing hostilities between the Lipans and Comanches. While the Lipans, he conceded, would be entering missions primarily to obtain Spanish protection against the Comanches, once they were reduced, they could serve as a bulwark against further Comanche advances and against the troublesome French in Louisiana. Having touched on the strategic benefits and the ease by which the Lipans could be enticed to accept mission life, Santa Ana appealed to the Crown's economic interests, arguing that missionizing the Lipans would open a region that was rich in gold, silver, iron, and other valuable minerals.[52]

While interested in establishing missions in Apache country, Viceroy Fuenclara was not prepared to endorse them. Captain Toribio Urrutia had also been busy writing letters, seeking permission to launch an entirely different sort of campaign into Apache country. Additional reports emanating from the frontier also dampened the appeal of missions. In August 1744, for example, Spanish bureaucrat Thomas Phelipe de Winthuysen issued his evaluation of the presidios and missions in Texas. His assessment of the Apaches differed considerably from that of the Franciscans. The Apaches, he wrote, "because of their warlike nature, not only refuse to give quarter to, or accept it from the Spaniards or from any other tribe of Indians, but also, under the pretext of coming to grant peace . . . concealing their deprived intentions, they are hostile and destructive as they can be either on their arrival or departure." The mission Indians, meanwhile, were "so pusillanimous that, as soon as they see the garrison of some *presidio* divided or reduced, they flee and return to the forest for fear of the Apaches."[53]

As Spanish officials in Mexico City mulled over establishing missions for the Apaches, Comanche attacks into Lipan country escalated. Father Santa Ana had long warned his compatriots that the bloodier and more severe a campaign against the Apaches might be, the more vindictively did they retaliate. Given the ongoing intertribal war, and concerns that the Spanish might bear the brunt of Apache reprisals, officials in San Antonio decreed that in all subsequent campaigns, soldiers should take care not to kill any Indian except in self-defense. When Apaches attacked mission Concepción and stole several cattle in March 1749, Captain Urrutia immediately set out in pursuit. Near the Guadalupe River, some fifty miles away from the presidio, the Spaniards encountered a ranchería of two or three bands of Lipans that had gathered to conduct a buffalo hunt (and therefore were unlikely to have been the cattle thieves). Since most of the men were away pursuing bison, the Spaniards quickly overran the encampment, and Urrutia marched back to San Antonio with thirty men, ninety women, and forty-seven children—a total of 167 captives. In possession of this considerable bargaining chip, Captain Urrutia and Father Santa Ana concluded that the moment had at last arrived to establish a permanent peace with the Apaches. Repeating a process that had never worked well before, however, they dispatched three of the captives as messengers to their leaders, instructing them that if they would live in peace and friendship, the Spaniards would release all Apache prisoners held at San Antonio.[54]

Seven tense months passed before the Apaches responded. In November, the messengers returned with news that four Apache chiefs, each with one hundred followers, were waiting near the Guadalupe River to make peace. After staying a few days in San Antonio, the messengers departed, and a week later columns of smoke signaled their arrival on the outskirts of town. Captain Urrutia, meanwhile, had a large building constructed on the plaza to receive the Apache delegates. In late November 1749, Urrutia, with all his troops, missionaries, and the citizens of San Antonio in attendance, greeted the Apaches and invited them to a feast of beef, corn, squash, and fruit. On November 28, Spaniard and Apache alike attended mass. Afterwards, they concluded peace negotiations and Urrutia released the Apache captives.[55] A detail of soldiers dug a large hole in the center of the plaza, and in this they placed a live horse, a hatchet, a lance, and six arrows. Urrutia, joining hands with the four chiefs, then danced around the hole three times, the Indians afterwards repeating the ritual with missionaries and citizens. At a prearranged signal, the dancing ceased and everyone rushed to the hole, scooping up dirt and burying the instruments of war. After additional handshakes and embraces, the Apaches took their leave, each side promising to treat the other as friends and brothers. The citizens of San Antonio, meanwhile, rejoiced that their thirty-year ordeal was over. Happiest of all were the missionaries, who saw in the peace both the culmination of their efforts, and a long-awaited opening for spreading the Gospel to the Lipan Apaches.[56]

For the Lipan bands that participated in the peace proceedings in 1749, the event had achieved a crucial goal—the release of their family members. Beyond that significant objective, one can only speculate what was running through their minds as they rode north to their homes.

From their perspective, the agreement was a narrow one—they had promised to cease raids on San Antonio—but this did not obligate them to end such activities in east Texas or New Mexico. The Spaniards had made no promises of assistance against the Comanches and Norteños, although the Lipans understood that they could expect protection should they decide to enter a mission. That distasteful option, however, was a last resort that could wait until their situation was truly desperate. Should that day come, they mused, their people would have to endure mission existence until they could regain their freedom and resume their traditional lifestyle. Just as the little creatures had defeated their powerful enemies shortly after the emergence, the Lipans would have to exercise patience, bravery, and intelligence. During the second half of the eighteenth century, they would need these characteristics in abundance.

CHAPTER THREE

Lipan Apache Missions in Spanish Texas, 1750–1770

⌇

COYOTE WAS VERY HUNGRY. As he prowled about looking for a meal, he came across a rather peculiar sight—a gray lizard perched atop a sotol stalk. He crept forward, opened his mouth, and was just about to devour the lizard when the reptile, in an anxious voice, ordered, "Hush, I've been put here to hold up this stalk. The stalk is holding up the sky. If I let go, the sky will fall." Coyote sat back and studied him. When the wind blew, the stalk began to sway. "See, it is swaying," Lizard yelled frantically. "I ask you to help me. Hold it!" Coyote rushed up then and began to hold onto the stalk. "It still sways," the frightened lizard hollered. "Our hands might slip and the sky would fall on us. I had better go get some help!" Growing increasingly worried, Coyote agreed, and Lizard scrambled down the sotol stalk and ran away to safety. A long while passed, and Coyote called and called for the lizard to return, but the little creature had vanished. Lizard had only wanted to get away from the hungry coyote, and had told a lie because he did not want Coyote to eat him.[1]

☾

DURING THE 1750s, the Lipans may have felt a little like the vulnerable gray lizard: in the face of very real dangers, they had to react quickly if they were to escape the predations of their numerous foes. Caught between Comanche, Norteño, and Spanish efforts to expand their reach deeper into Texas, the Lipan Apaches clung tenaciously to their sotol stalk, facing the unenviable prospect of matching wits with not one but three dangerous enemies. Reminiscent of the little gray lizard in the folktale, the Lipans would engage in a bit of trickery to elude their attackers. At variance with the folktale, however, failure would most certainly bring the sky crashing down on their world.

The much-heralded Spanish-Apache peace agreement of November 1749 gave fresh impetus to the movement for Apache missions, ushering in a new (albeit short-lived) era of good feelings between the two peoples. Much planning and organizing had to take place before the missions could move beyond the theoretical, however, and the devil—as usual—was in the details. From the Lipan perspective, accepting Spanish missions and presidios in their country was at best a necessary evil. From their encampments scattered across the hill country north of San Antonio, they watched with contempt as Indian neophytes from weaker nations labored in the fields, dug irrigation ditches, constructed buildings, and adopted (at least outwardly) various cultural manifestations of Spanish "civilization." But they also noticed (and periodically attacked) the frequent supply trains of food and supplies that made their way north from San Juan Bautista; the large herds of cattle, sheep, and horses (which they also attacked) around San Antonio; and the relative security that the neophytes enjoyed as a result of their association with the Spaniards. Consequently, the Lipans pursued a policy aimed at taking advantage of Spanish military protection and supplies, while simultaneously spurning—or at least postponing—their reduction to mission life and the abandonment of their culture. For the Apaches, as David LaVere has observed, missions provided refuge or sanctuary from Comanche and Norteño attack, and were temporary way stations where they could pick up food and supplies, rather than a place to settle permanently.[2]

Lipan concerns about Comanche attacks gained greater urgency in the early 1750s when several bands of Kotsoteka Comanches pushed south to the Balcones Escarpment. From the Comanches' perspective, the new Spanish–Lipan Apache alliance threatened not only their dominant position in the horse and bison economy, but also their access to trade with the Norteños and the French. Shortly after their arrival, therefore, the Comanches opened a ferocious new offensive against the Lipans. By 1755, the Lipans were in such dire straits that they invited Comanche delegates to peace talks along the banks of the Guadalupe River. Despite engaging in ceremonial gestures such as singing together and touching weapons in token of friendship, the peace quickly unraveled, and the deadly cycle of raids and counter-raids resumed. Unable to check the Comanche advance, the Lipans turned to their Spanish allies for support, promising in return to accept Christianity and a sedentary lifestyle. While some Franciscans suspected that the Indians had ulterior motives for their sudden interest in missions, they were willing to push ahead, nevertheless, in hopes that a heartfelt Lipan desire for reduction might yet take place once they realized the temporal and material benefits that came with "civilization."[3]

The Spaniards' apparent zeal for Apache missions, meanwhile, was equally complex and not altogether genuine. While the missionaries certainly possessed a sincere and passionate desire to spread the Gospel and Christian civilization to the various "indios bárbaros," Spanish civil and military officials possessed a series of ulterior motives that were as self-serving as those of the Apaches. The establishment of missions in Lipan country, officials hoped, would quiet Indian troubles along the lower Rio Grande frontier, safeguard the nascent Spanish settlements located north of that river, and allow for the extension northward of the imperial domain. A Spanish-Apache alliance would also stunt French penetration into Texas and serve as a buffer against Comanche and Norteño attacks. Rumors of rich silver and gold deposits in the San Sabá and Llano river country, meanwhile, had long enticed Spanish investors. Once Apache interference abated, Spaniards could finally explore and develop the region.[4]

While anxious to take advantage of the nascent Apache peace, priests stationed at San Antonio disagreed over where to construct the new missions. One faction sought to relocate the Béxar presidio to the Pedernales River as a prelude to building missions there, while another called for the construction of new missions on the Guadalupe River. In June 1750, new voices entered the debate when concerned local officials convened a *junta* in San Antonio to consider Apache missions. Not surprisingly, participants rejected calls for relocating the Béxar presidio to the Pedernales for fear that any troop redeployment would expose them to attacks from the Julimes, Natagés, and other hostile tribes. Contributing to the junta's security concerns were sporadic raids that the Spaniards attributed to the Apaches. In late July 1750, Texas governor Pedro del Barrio issued a curfew in response to the Apaches' "repeated robberies, killings, and insults," as well as their "well-known and proved fickleness and treachery."[5]

A year and a half later, yet another voice joined the debate over Apache missions. In February 1752, Fr. Alonzo Giraldo de Terreros became president of the Texas missions. A veteran missionary who had worked in east Texas, Fr. Terreros established the first formal mission for the Texas Apaches in 1754, locating it along the Rio Grande near presidio San Juan Bautista. Acting on the request of an Apache leader named Pastellano, Terreros chose a site and assigned missionaries; but Pastellano's people apparently changed their minds and deserted the mission on the first night. Undeterred, the zealous Franciscan established a second Apache mission (San Lorenzo) near San Fernando de Austria in northern Coahuila. The Apache neophytes, including Lipan leaders El Gordo, El de Godo, and Bigotes (Vigotes) appeared committed to reduction. They helped construct buildings, dug irrigation ditches, and by March 1755, Terreros reported fifty-two Apaches residing at the mission. But the new San Lorenzo mission effort was also short-lived. When Franciscan superiors called Fr. Terreros away temporarily from the mission, the promising start that he had made quickly unraveled, and on October 4, 1755, the unhappy Apache neophytes set fire to the mission and fled into the wilderness.[6] While some Spaniards attributed the failure of the two Rio Grande missions to the "natural inconstancy" of the Apaches, the fact that both were located so far to the south bolstered the padres' arguments that they should construct future missions in Apache country.

In April 1752, meanwhile, orders from Mexico City arrived at San Antonio authorizing an exploration of south-central Texas to determine the region's potential for missions. Over the course of the next four years, three separate expeditions explored the San Sabá River region to assess its potential as a mission site. The Juan Galván expedition of 1753, however, was sidetracked after an Apache told them about a hill of red ochre (hematite) located nearby, leading to the discovery of the Los Almagres mines. In the end, all three expeditions reported favorably, commending the region's good arable land, abundant water, and mineral wealth—and most importantly, the Apaches' interest in reduction. During the second expedition in late 1754 and early 1755, for instance, Spanish commander Pedro de Rábago y Terán came across an Apache ranchería containing more than one hundred people under the leadership of a man they called "Captain Pintas." Pintas received the Spaniards cordially, and no doubt hit the right chord by claiming that he knew of ten other Apache captains with large groups of people who also desired missions.[7]

At a council held in Mexico City on February 27, 1756, Spanish officials weighed the arguments for and against the construction of Apache missions in Texas. The establishment of a mission and presidio at San Sabá, they believed, would serve as "the sword's point" of a more aggressive policy aimed at crushing the threat posed by French-armed tribes such as the Comanches and Norteños. Such a "sword's point" could also act as a wedge to expand Spanish influence in the area. Armed with the three favorable reports, the enticing prospect of the Los Almagres mines, and their laundry list of benefits that reduction would bring both to the Apaches and to the Crown, the position of the priests reigned supreme. Adding still greater weight to the proposal was Captain Pedro de Rábago y Terán's unexpected (and unauthorized) abandonment the previous August of the San Xavier missions and presidio and removal to the San Marcos River. What were Spanish authorities to do with the soldiers, Indian neophytes, and missionaries? An expedient solution to this dilemma lay right in front of them. Solving several problems at once, the council recommended transferring the San Xavier garrison to the San Sabá River. Secondly, they suggested dispersing the remaining San Xavier neophytes throughout the existing San Antonio missions. Finally, the council called for the relocation of the San Xavier missionaries to the San Sabá to establish three new Apache missions under the direction of Fr. Mariano de los Dolores. On May 18, 1756, an optimistic Marques de Amarillas signed off on the proposal. The viceroy envisioned the future establishment of a pueblo at San Sabá surrounded by neat cultivated fields, increased interprovincial trade, and the development of a string of self-supporting communities in Lipan country. Thus, nearly thirty years after the Franciscans had requested them, Apache missions were at last to become a reality.[8]

Fr. Dolores, the newly appointed superintendent of the San Sabá mission effort, had little time to savor his good fortune. While the wheels of the Spanish bureaucracy churned slowly in Mexico City, his Franciscan brother and rival Fr. Alonso Terreros had secured a pledge of 150,000 pesos from his wealthy cousin, Don Pedro Romero de Terreros, to finance the San Sabá mission effort for three years. Don Pedro was the owner of rich mines at Pauca and Real del Norte and was founder of the National Pawn Shop in Mexico City. His offer, however, came with strings attached. In exchange for his financial backing, Don Pedro insisted that the viceroy place his Franciscan cousin in charge of the missions, rather than Fr. Dolores, and that he select a new team of friars to staff the mission in place of the San Xavier priests. Thrilled at this unexpected offer, Viceroy Amarillas accepted the new plan, glad to reduce royal expenditures. A second significant change to the San Sabá operation became necessary following the death of Captain Rábago in early 1756. In his place, the viceroy appointed Colonel Diego Ortiz de Parrilla, a veteran officer and Indian fighter who had served with distinction in Cuba, Puebla, Sinaloa, and Sonora. A man of action but also an egotist, Parrilla would soon clash with Fr. Terreros (who was no pushover himself) over the timing and details of the expedition to the San Sabá.[9]

As the Spaniards prepared for their ambitious new mission effort, life among the Lipans centered around more immediate concerns. Acquiring food for their families, gathering medicinal plants and herbs, constructing and repairing weapons and tools, training their children, and tending to their horse herds consumed their time; meanwhile, they had to keep a sharp eye out for Comanche and Norteño raiders. While the men hunted bison, deer, and wild pigs, Lipan women gathered wood, hauled water, and harvested sotol and yucca plants, mesquite pods, wild onions, gourds, and a variety of wild fruits. At night, the men would gather around a fire and boast about their hunting prowess and their fearlessness as warriors. As the men smoked and made plans for the next day's activities, teenagers stood in the shadows listening and learning from their elders. Taking a puff from a pipe or sotol-leaf cigarette was an activity reserved for the men, the Lipans teased, and boys could not smoke until they could run down a coyote. Invariably, the talk turned to the various romances that were the source of band gossip and intrigue. The poor soul without a mate, and with few prospects for acquiring one, would frequently be the object of good-natured kidding. The Lipans joked that smoke was drawn toward lonely people, and bachelors were quick to alter their position around the fire to avoid the smoke's indictment. For warriors who had lost wives and children to slave raiders, however, loneliness, anger, and a desire for vengeance were constant reminders of the precariousness of Lipan life in the mid-eighteenth century. From their point of view, the recent alliance with the Spaniards provided perhaps their last chance to acquire the horses and firepower needed either to rescue their loved ones, or to exact revenge on the peoples who had taken them.[10]

In the fall of 1756, Colonel Parrilla and Fr. Terreros began their movement north from Mexico City to San Antonio. On the way, they picked up nine Tlascalan Indian families from Saltillo to serve as instructors for the Apache neophytes. They encountered scattered bands of Apaches encamped in northern Coahuila who, after seeing the huge supply train, promised to head to San Sabá forthwith to enter the mission. The party arrived in San Antonio in early December and quickly sent out messengers to invite Apache leaders to discuss the San Sabá project. Several Lipans arrived shortly thereafter, apologizing for the absence of their Natagé, Mescalero, and Pelone relatives, explaining that they were simply too far away to make the meeting. When the missions were ready, the Lipans promised, the other groups would come to the San Sabá. As the Lipans prepared to leave, they asked for corn, sugar cane, tobacco, and other gifts—requests that were in keeping with Lipan notions of hospitality and reciprocity, but which irritated Colonel Parrilla and sowed the first seeds of doubt in his mind about the Apaches' sincerity. On the other hand, Fr. Terreros and his chief assistant Fr. Francisco de la Santísima Trinidad had no misgivings whatsoever, and were eager to head north to the San Sabá as soon as weather permitted. Impatient to get the missions planted, the priests chafed at Parrilla's apparent lack of urgency, accusing him of dragging his feet and causing unnecessary delays. Not until April 9, 1757, did Parrilla finally give the order to move out—a decision that Frs. Terreros and Trinidad had been awaiting for months.[11]

On April 18, 1757, the Spaniards arrived at the San Sabá River, but much to the missionaries' disappointment, there was not an Apache in sight. Disgusted, but perhaps not surprised, Parrilla suggested that they call the whole thing off, or at least delay construction of any buildings until they could learn more about the Apaches' disposition. Terreros would hear none of it. If the captain did not order that work begin immediately, the Franciscan warned, he and his fellow priests would march back to Mexico City and inform the viceroy about the captain's perfidy. Parrilla reluctantly gave in and ordered his men to begin building a presidio on the north side of the San Sabá River. The priests, meanwhile, supervised the construction of mission Santa Cruz de San Sabá a few miles to the east but on the south side of the river, a decision that made sense to missionaries who did not want soldiers butting into their business, but with dangerous implications from a strategic standpoint. After they had completed the construction of quarters for the priests, storerooms for supplies, a church, and stables, the soldiers erected a wooden stockade around the entire compound. The padres then laid out plots of land along the river, and with the help of the Tlascalans, dug irrigation ditches and planted crops. Colonel Parrilla, meanwhile, oversaw completion of presidio San Luis de Amarillas, named in honor of the viceroy. The only thing missing was the Apaches.[12]

When word reached San Antonio that there were no Indians congregating at San Sabá, a priest (Fr. Benito Varela) rode out to locate them. At San Marcos, Varela learned that the Tejas had attacked some Lipans on the Colorado River, thereby disrupting their plans to relocate to the new mission. When Chief El Chico (or Chiquito) visited San Antonio a short while later, officials there encouraged him to take his people to the San Sabá, and he gave assurances that he would do so. By the middle of June 1757, various Lipan and other Apache bands (numbering perhaps three thousand people) began congregating near the San Sabá mission. El Chico's people resided in thirty-two tents and numbered around three hundred, while Lipans under the leadership of Chief Casablanca (Casacablanca) possessed more than three hundred tents and 2,700 horses and mules. Terreros's jubilation quickly soured, however, after he learned that most of the assembled Indians were preparing to embark on their summer buffalo hunt, rather than to enter the mission. Chief Casablanca, bent on making a campaign against the Comanches and Tejas to avenge the recent attack on the Colorado (where he had lost a brother), was busy enlisting warriors to that end. As the Indians prepared to depart, they gave assurances that once they had completed their business up north, they would return to settle down at the mission. In a last-ditch effort, the padres pleaded with the Apaches to at least leave their women and children behind while they conducted their hunts, but the Indians declined. They needed their women to help skin and prepare the bison carcasses, and parents were reluctant to depart without their children. With that, they rode off, leaving behind several dejected missionaries and a presidial captain smug in the knowledge that his predictions had come true.[13]

Two weeks passed and the Apaches had not returned. A few days later, however, hopes rose momentarily when El Chico and his people appeared at the mission loaded down with bison meat. Much to the chagrin of the missionaries, the Apaches lingered only briefly before continuing south. Over the course of the next several weeks, this pattern continued as small bands of Apaches appeared at San Sabá to receive food and hospitality, only to pack up and ride south. By summer's end, three of Terreros's Franciscan brethren, having abandoned hope in the San Sabá endeavor, packed their bags and left as well. Some of the Spaniards sensed apprehension and fear in the eyes and demeanor of the Apaches, and they soon discovered the source: a large contingent of Comanche and Norteño warriors were reportedly moving south in their direction, angry at the recent Apache reprisal attacks and outraged with the Spaniards for befriending them. Some of the Apaches were apparently so scared that they fled south of the Rio Grande to escape their enemies' fury.[14]

Beginning in the 1750s, the Comanches and the various Nations of the North had opened a new offensive against their enemies to the north (the Osages and Kansas) and their principal foe to the south—the Lipan Apaches. By 1757, the largest Norteño group (whom the Spaniards called the Taovayas) had relocated to the Red River to escape the damages they had suffered at the hands of the Osages and to improve their commercial opportunities. In addition, the Taovayas and their Comanche allies continued their onslaught against the Lipans in an effort to drive them completely out of the Red River country. The Lipans stoked their fury by boasting widely of the splendor of their new mission and the power of their allies, insinuating that the Spaniards were their protectors and advocates. The Lipans were probably hoping to intimidate the Comanches and Norteños to get them to ease up on their attacks. Contrary to Lipan expectations (or perhaps just as the Lipans had anticipated), their bragging drew the jealous wrath of both groups on the San Sabá settlement. The retaliatory raids that El Chico and Casablanca had conducted in 1757, therefore, were engagements in a conflict that had begun fifty years earlier (when the Comanches first appeared in north Texas) and had intensified significantly in the short period following the Comanche-Taovayas peace agreement of 1747.[15]

Whether or not the Spaniards understood fully the gravity of their decision to befriend the Apaches remains unclear. As winter approached and no Comanche-Norteño attack materialized, the Spaniards began questioning if the alleged threat was nothing more than another Apache excuse to put off entering the mission. After all, the Apaches had never been at the mission—why then would the Comanches and Norteños blame the Spaniards for the Lipans' recent attacks? While the missionaries and soldiers operating the San Sabá mission and presidio attempted to reassure themselves that they had nothing to fear, the harsh winter of 1757–1758 struck with unexpected fury. Before the end of the year, a frigid combination of wind, ice, and snow left hundreds of dead horses, cattle, and sheep. In February 1758, Fr. Terreros and Colonel Parrilla sent a letter to Viceroy Amarillas requesting permission to come to Mexico City to discuss the San Sabá effort and evaluate their plans. Before the viceroy could reply, however, the future of the San Sabá mission was decided for them.[16]

In late February, Indian raiders stole fifty-nine horses from the presidial herd at San Sabá. Colonel Parrilla dispatched a detail of fifteen soldiers in pursuit, but the men returned empty-handed, reporting that the area was crawling with Indians. With that information in mind, Parrilla ordered a second detail of six men to ride south to warn an inbound supply train to proceed with caution. As the detail approached the Pedernales River, twenty-six warriors attacked the Spaniards and wounded four of the six soldiers. When the bloodied troopers returned to report the attack, Parrilla ordered a second detail to ride south to protect the supply train. In mid-March, after seeing smoke signals rising to the north and east, the colonel sent a runner to Fr. Terreros and the few remaining priests at mission Santa Cruz, urging them to come at once to the presidio for protection. Fr. Terreros refused to budge, however, unconvinced that an attack was imminent and preferring to stay at the mission to care for his people and property. Remaining with him were two priests, eight soldiers, four San Antonio mission Indians and their wives, some servants, and some of the soldiers' children—about thirty-five people in all. Occupying the

San Luis de Amarillas presidio, meanwhile, were approximately eighty soldiers and 237 women and children. On the afternoon of March 15, Colonel Parrilla rode to the mission in a final, but equally unsuccessful, attempt to convince Terreros to evacuate.[17]

There is no shortage of stories detailing the attack on the Santa Cruz de San Sabá mission that occurred in the early-morning hours of March 16, 1758.[18] A large force (estimated at more than 2,000) of mounted, well-armed Taovayas and Comanches—and according to some reports, a smaller number of Bidais, Tonkawas, and warriors from other east Texas tribes—gained entrance into the mission stockade and began pillaging the various buildings. Fr. Terreros and a Spanish soldier named Joseph Garcia were shot and killed almost immediately. The attackers took what supplies they could carry off, killed the livestock, and then set fire to the buildings. A portion of the Comanche-Norteño force then rode to the San Luis de Amarillas presidio and set fire to the grass around the fort to draw the garrison out into the open. The stunt failed to achieve its objective, however, and a standoff ensued for the next couple of days. On March 18, the Indians began moving off to the north, unwilling to expose themselves to the firepower of the hundred or so soldiers (twenty-two soldiers from the supply train had arrived during the night of March 16) holed up inside the presidio.[19]

Not until March 20 did Colonel Parrilla deem it safe enough to send a detachment to the mission to investigate the damage. What they witnessed on their arrival must have sickened and infuriated them. The mission had been burned and practically everything inside destroyed. At the front gate lay the bodies of Fr. Terreros and Joseph Garcia. Inside, they discovered the mutilated bodies of five soldiers. At first, the searchers could not find the remains of Fr. Santiesteban, and they speculated that the fire had consumed his body. A few days later, however, searchers discovered it, the head completely severed from the body. Final casualty reports differ, but place the total number of Spaniards killed at between eight and twelve, with four people wounded. The number of Indian attackers reported killed was seventeen.[20]

Attributing causation for a particular historical event is always a tricky business, especially when participants come from diverse cultural traditions and speak different languages, and, as in the case of the San Sabá episode, only one side recorded its version of what took place.

Constructed in 1757 near present-day Menard, Texas, the San Sabá presidio and nearby mission came under fierce attack by Taovayas and Comanches a year later.

Historian Robert Weddle writes, "The story of the Mission Santa Cruz de San Sabá is one of Apache perfidy, Spanish gullibility, and the disastrous consequences of both."[21] But one might just as accurately interpret the story as one of Comanche and Norteño insecurity, blind Spanish ambition, and Apache self-preservation. Given the fact that the Comanches and Norteños acquired a sizeable portion of their guns, powder, and bullets from the French, one could also add "French intrigue" or "French instigation" to the story line.[22]

As has been discussed in previous chapters, the Comanches and Norteños were economic rivals and bitter enemies of the Lipan Apaches. They would have viewed any Spanish-Apache détente—let alone alliance—with considerable jealousy and trepidation. They may have also speculated that the apparent Lipan-Spanish alliance was an Apache attempt to secure arms to "level the playing field." The timing of the San Sabá mission effort was also significant, coming immediately after the Tejas raid on the Apaches near the Colorado River and the southward movement of the Comanches and Taovayas. These latter groups may have suspected that the Apaches and Spaniards would in time launch joint retaliatory raids—a concern that gained greater force after Apache warriors, as they were prone to do on occasion, planted articles of clothing and shoes worn by the soldiers to cast suspicion on them. Spanish soldiers accompanied Apaches on bison hunts, a symbolic act of friendship that apparently took place more than once during the summer and fall of 1757, which heightened Comanche and Norteño insecurities further. In short, the Comanches and Norteños interpreted the Spaniards' construction of a presidio and mission at San Sabá for the Apaches as a hostile act . . . a virtual declaration of war.[23]

While there was certainly a degree of gullibility in the Spaniards' mistaken belief that the Apaches were keenly interested in reduction, one might just as easily make the case that blind ambition on the part of the Spaniards was the real instigator behind the San Sabá fiasco. Bent on extending their domain, curbing French penetration into Texas, and hitting the mother lode at the fabled Los Almagres mines, Spaniards apparently ignored important lessons they should already have known by heart. Possessing two centuries of experience dealing with various Indian nations in Texas, the Spaniards nonetheless assumed that they could befriend the enemy of an ally without turning the ally into an enemy. As Maria Wade has noted, "The assumption of the Spaniards [was] that they could be friends with everyone regardless of Native internal enmities, as well as the political arrogance [or ineptitude] of making new alliances without informing former allies, especially when the new alliances were made with bitter enemies." Such behavior, she concludes, "would not be tolerated in any political or military setting; why would it be countenanced by Native Americans?"[24]

And what about the Lipan Apache role in the San Sabá story? Virtually all historians have interpreted their behavior in a negative light—as fickle and indecisive, or as devious, self-serving, and treacherous. Another way to interpret their behavior is as a determined effort at self-preservation and to retain their independence and way of life. In the face of pressures from both north and south, the Lipans engaged in a strategy aimed at pitting their enemies against one another. "None of the Apache missions was successful," Wade asserts, "because for the Apache, missions were temporary and expedient solutions to a problem. The Apaches were not fickle; they were politicians. They played the game was that proposed to them to their best advantage." Even if they had been genuinely interested in entering the San Sabá mission, no responsible Lipan leader could have allowed his people to place their lives in the hands of Spanish soldiers who held them in contempt, distrusted them, and whose notion of a "fortress" consisted of a log stockade with a couple of gun platforms surrounding a few mud-and-straw huts. After reviewing these unimpressive preparations, the Lipans understandably concluded that the Spaniards were not serious about protecting them. They may have even suspected that the Spaniards were setting them up for their enemies to destroy.[25]

The destruction of the San Sabá mission proved to be a "pivot" in the history of Spanish Texas. The Spaniards had planned the mission and presidio as a "sword's point" from which to crush the threat posed by unfriendly tribes so that they could penetrate the southern plains and establish trade routes across Texas to New Mexico. The loss at San Sabá altered these ambitious plans, leading instead to the eventual withdrawal of Spanish forces from San Sabá and other far-flung Spanish settlements to form a defensive line paralleling the present international boundary with Mexico. Second, it marked the first time that the Spaniards encountered a large native force armed with muskets and skilled at using them—validating the reasoning behind establishing the presidio in the first place. Subsequent military campaigns would need to adapt to this new reality if the skeleton Spanish presence in Texas was to persist. The attack also brought Spain into open warfare against the Comanches and Nations of the North, a conflict that would persist off and on until the Spanish expulsion from its once vast American empire.[26] Finally, the disaster at San Sabá sent shockwaves through the capital city of New Spain, forcing Viceroy Amarillas to face its possible implications, the most ominous of which was the collapse of the entire frontier defense system, with its thin line of missions and presidios. Spanish policymakers, consequently, had to address two questions at once: (1) what to do about the Comanche and Norteño "insult," and (2) what to do with the San Sabá mission and the whole project of reducing the Apaches.[27]

The answer to the first question was predictable. Colonel Parrilla pressed for a chance to vindicate Spanish arms, while the Lipans declared that they would not settle at the mission until they were satisfied that their enemies had been subdued. There had to be a swift and strong response to the recent outrage, Viceroy Amarillas reasoned, or Spain faced losing what remained of its prestige among the various Indian peoples in Texas. The viceroy also determined, for the same "face-saving" reason, to retain the San Sabá mission at least for the time being. To retreat in the face of defeat was not an option—at least not an option for the viceroy. In early April 1758, several soldiers from the San Luis de Amarillas presidio petitioned Colonel Parrilla to consider relocating the garrison to a safer location, and the commander wrote the viceroy arguing for the removal of the mission and presidio to the Guadalupe and San Marcos rivers or to the Llano River to protect the Los Almagres mines. Viceroy Amarillas would hear none of this, however, and in July, he decreed that the mission and presidio should remain at San Sabá pending the organization of a war council to aid Parrilla in planning a campaign of retaliation.[28]

The Comanches and Norteños, meanwhile, maintained pressure along the San Sabá frontier for the remainder of 1758. In the spring, a huge party of Norteños surprised El Chico's band and nearly destroyed them while they were out hunting buffalo. In mid-December, Comanches surprised a party of thirty-four Apaches, killing all but thirteen of them. A short time later, a group of Norteño warriors armed with French muskets threatened presidio San Luis while Comanche horse thieves staged a raid on the presidial horse herd. Rumors of an impending Comanche-Norteño attack on San Sabá as well as on San Antonio fueled tensions further. It was within this context of heightened anxiety that the war council convened on January 3, 1759, in San Antonio. The first order of business was to secure reinforcements, and to this effect, the council requested that Governor Juan Manuel Muñoz of Nuevo León dispatch one hundred fully equipped militiamen to reinforce the garrisons at San Antonio and San Sabá. Governor Muñoz complied immediately with a call for the men and threatened a fifty-peso fine if they did not muster as ordered. His urgent appeals, however, met with opposition and stonewalling from settlers who were concerned about leaving their own homes unprotected while they were away fighting Indians in Texas.

Lipan Apaches in Spanish Texas.
Map created by Matthew A. Crawford.

The good citizens of Nuevo León, furthermore, were not eager to bear the expense of equipping and supplying the detachment.[29]

Meanwhile, the Comanches continued to wreak havoc on the northern frontier. In late March 1759, they conducted a devastating raid on San Sabá presidio, killing nineteen soldiers and stealing 750 horses and mules—far heavier losses than the initial assault a year earlier. Of particular concern to Spanish officials was the fact that the Comanches had only used firearms in the attack—no arrows—and had stripped the soldiers' mutilated bodies of clothing and equipment. Such audacity spurred the San Antonio war council to take action, and it quickly authorized the creation of a five-hundred-man force with provisions for a four-month campaign. Given the broad dispersal of Spanish regulars on the northern frontier, organizing an army of this size required assembling an ad hoc assortment of volunteer militiamen, Indian auxiliaries, and regular Spanish troops.[30] The militiamen (whom Leslie Byrd Simpson has described as "badly armed, untrained, indifferent, and resentful") accounted for nearly half of Parrilla's army. The Indian auxiliaries, which included 30 Tlazcalteco warriors, 93 mission Indians from Texas and Coahuila, and 134 Apaches, were excellent fighters but lacked training in Spanish tactics. Maintaining command and control over indigenous forces during a campaign invariably tested the patience of frontier commanders who misinterpreted the Indians' unfamiliarity with (or contempt for) Spanish tactics as further evidence of their barbarism. In spite of their attitude of superiority, Spanish officials acknowledged the need to seek aid from the "primitives" they sought to dominate, and recruited Indian fighters through a combination of gifts, privileges (e.g., military rank and titles of nobility), and intimidation. There were obvious limitations to recruiting by intimidation, however, since unwilling allies were prone to desertion in battle. The Parrilla expedition did not depart from San Antonio until mid-August, accompanied by two Franciscans, more than 1,500 horses, a pack train of several hundred mules laden with supplies, and a sizeable herd of cattle for food.[31]

Parrilla's force spent a week at the San Sabá presidio before setting out on September 7 on what would be a four-hundred-mile trek northeast to the Red River. On October 2, 1759, they encountered a Yojuane (a Tonkawan tribe) village on the East Fork of the Little Wichita River in present-day Clay County. Although the Spaniards could not have been certain if the Yojuanes had participated in the San Sabá battle, their hunger for revenge was intense, and in the attack that followed, the Spaniards killed 55 warriors and took 149 captives.[32] The prisoners claimed that they knew the location of a large Norteño encampment, and Parrilla selected a couple of them to serve as guides. With the Yojuanes leading the way, the Spaniards continued their march northeastward toward the Red River. On October 7, the Yojuane guides alerted the colonel that they were very close to the enemy. After traveling about fifteen miles farther, the Spaniards suddenly came under attack by a group of sixty or seventy warriors, followed closely by a second wave of attackers. Parrilla quickly formed his men in a line, charged the Indians, and killed three of the enemy before the warriors melted into the woods. The Spaniards gave pursuit, rushing into the trees before their quarry could alert reinforcements. When they emerged on the far

side of the woods, however, Parrilla's men were astonished to discover
a large fortification on the east bank of the Red River. The fortification
included several oval-shaped huts, a wooden stockade complete with
firing ports, all surrounded by an earthen rampart and a moat.[33] The
large coalition of Norteño and Comanche warriors inside, confident in
the impregnability of their position, laughed and taunted the Spaniards
to attack. As the Spaniards prepared frantically to formulate a strategy
to cross the river and engage the enemy, a swarm of mounted Taovaya
and Comanche warriors attempted to flank Parrilla's men on either side,
while those holed up inside the palisade opened fire. Parrilla ordered
several frontal charges, but the deep sand undercut the maneuverabil-
ity of his cavalry and the Spaniards were unable to gain entry into the
palisade. Lipan scouts searched for a suitable place to cross the river,
but the enemy guarded the only two passes they discovered. Spanish
cannon fire proved equally ineffective in turning the tide of battle, the
cannon balls bouncing harmlessly off the stockade's sturdy timber fortifications. Mounted warriors, each with a companion on foot to keep
loaded weapons ready, protected the fort's flanks while harrying those
of the Spaniards. One Taovaya chief, who carried a shield of white buckskin and wore a helmet of white buckskin plumed with red horsehair,
was especially valiant, and his death reportedly caused great anxiety on
the part of his people. The Spaniards and their Indian allies somehow
managed to hold their ground, but as night closed in after nearly four
hours of combat, Parrilla abandoned any hope of taking the fort and
ordered a retreat. At a hastily convened council that night, the beleaguered Spaniards took stock of their situation. The troops were completely discouraged: The dead, wounded, and missing totaled fifty-four
(nineteen dead, fifteen wounded, twenty missing). They had abandoned
two of their cannons to the enemy, and had lost a significant number of
horses and mules. Convincing themselves, nonetheless, that a "glorious
military exploit had already been attained" and Spanish honor restored,
Parrilla's officers convinced him to return forthwith to the San Sabá.[34]

    While historians have interpreted both the conduct and results of
the "Battle of the Wichita Fort" in different ways, most concur that the
conflict was harmful to Spanish aims in Texas, and of significance to
the evolution of Spanish relations with the Lipans. Foremost among
the results was the damage wrought to Spanish respect and prestige,

attributes already shaken after the San Sabá episode two years earlier. "Parrilla's impotence against the northern tribes," Weddle has asserted, "confirmed the conclusions drawn from the San Sabá massacre. The [Wichita Fort] battle bore out all the more lucidly that the Spaniards, in their northern advance, faced a new type of enemy with overwhelming capabilities." Although Weddle's new study of the Parrilla campaign, *After the Massacre*, questions his earlier assessment that the battle was an unmitigated disaster, the Battle of the Wichita Fort was a watershed event in the evolution of Spanish Indian policy in Texas.[35] The days of launching retaliatory raids into strange lands, using small numbers of regulars and untrained and ill-equipped militias, were over.[36] The enemy, who enjoyed the advantage of fighting on familiar terrain, was now well armed, and more skilled in the use of those arms than were the Spaniards. The Parrilla expedition also produced fissures among Spanish officials. One group sought to continue the current policy of subduing the Nations of the North by force of arms, while the other group, convinced that the Norteños were the more appropriate ally to begin with, argued that they should abandon the San Sabá mission and wage war instead against the Lipan Apaches.[37]

The Lipan Apaches also brought away valuable lessons from the Parrilla expedition. While the historical record is silent about their perceptions of the events that took place on the Red River, they celebrated the fact that they had engaged the enemy and returned home virtually unscathed.[38] According to some accounts, they also managed to capture a large number of enemy—and perhaps Spanish—horses. Soon after the singing, dancing, and storytelling had died down, the realization of their precarious situation set in—the dismal performance and desertions of the militiamen and the derisive taunts and laughter of the Comanches and Norteños echoing loudly in their minds. Initially hopeful that alliance with the Spaniards would prevent—or at least forestall—the southward advance of their Indian enemies, the Lipans realized that their new allies were not as valuable as they had hoped they would be. Had Parrilla's force made a better showing, the Lipans might have been more willing to overlook the San Sabá debacle and stick with the Spanish a while longer—certainly not as neophytes laboring away in missions, but as allies in checking Comanche expansion southward. Instead, the Apaches—like the Comanches and Norteños—pegged the

Spaniards as weaklings: unremarkable as warriors, but still potentially useful as a source of supplies, and perhaps as pawns in their longstanding intertribal war.[39]

Colonel Parrilla traveled to Mexico City in the summer of 1760 to defend his actions during the previous year's campaign and to receive instructions regarding the future of San Sabá mission and presidio. Much to his disappointment, the colonel learned that the viceroy had reassigned him to command the Santa Rosa presidio, a position the veteran soldier had neither sought nor desired. His replacement as commander of the presidio San Luis de Amarillas was Captain Felipe de Rábago y Terán (the nephew of Pedro Rábago y Terán), whom Spanish authorities had only recently released from an eight-year imprisonment after he received absolution of charges made against him during his scandal-ridden tenure at San Xavier. Rábago had been busy orchestrating a vicious whispering campaign about Colonel Parrilla, seeking to discredit him by portraying the commander's behavior at the recent battle at the Wichita Fort in a decidedly unfavorable light. Described as possessing a "domineering and overbearing nature" and being "vain and jealous of command," Rábago seemed an odd choice to oversee Spain's northernmost frontier post at such a critical juncture, and the Franciscans at San Sabá strongly protested the appointment.[40]

Upon arriving at the San Sabá presidio in late September 1760, Captain Rábago displayed unusual vigor and enthusiasm—a testament perhaps to his resurrected military career—by immediately getting to work improving the condition of the one hundred men under his command. He ordered tons of supplies, weapons, and ammunition, and did his best to restock the presidial horse herd. Rábago did not neglect the material structure of the presidio, replacing the old log stockade and deteriorating mud huts with sturdy limestone structures. A little more than a year after his arrival, he reported proudly that the new presidio (which he renamed the "Real Presidio de San Sabá") was a veritable castle (complete with moat), and the garrison was at full strength and well mounted. He also expended considerable energy and money courting the Lipans, plying them with gifts of tobacco, corn, sugar, bridles, and clothing.[41] Consenting to their requests for protection, Rábago permitted soldiers to continue accompanying the Apaches on bison hunts. By doing so, he believed, the Lipans might come to the realization that the maintenance of friendly relations with the Spanish would best serve their material well-being. Captain Rábago, as Tunnell and Newcomb have pointed out, had few alternatives. If the Lipans were to become his enemies, whether they joined forces with the Comanches and Norteños or not, the chances that the presidio could long survive were poor. The Spaniards needed support from some quarter, and the Lipans were the only ones available that could give it. By turning to the Lipans, however, Rábago ensured that the major obstacle blocking peace with the powerful northern tribes remained in place.[42]

The Lipans, in many respects, were in the same predicament as the Spanish. Unable to prevent Comanche and Norteño expansion southward, they too were in dire need of allies. While Spanish troop performance had been less than stellar in recent years, there were few alternatives to maintaining amicable relations with them. Should the Spaniards befriend the Comanches and Norteños, their own survival would be seriously imperiled. Allying with the Spanish, moreover, had the benefit of providing access to supplies and horses. In the months following the Parrilla expedition, Lipan band leaders continued to visit the San Sabá presidio to receive gifts and a good meal. The Spaniards, who remained susceptible to vague promises of Lipan interest in missions, kept the spigot of supplies and gifts open. Several chiefs, for instance, gave Captain Rábago their assurances that they and their people would take up mission life once they had secured meat after a "last" bison-hunting excursion. Yet none of these promises ever panned out. Given the decentralized nature of Lipan political and social organization, various bands adopted different survival strategies: some sought to stick close to the Spaniards for supplies and for protection, while others professed peace but kept their distance. Some warriors continued the old game of raiding the Norteños and Comanches and then fleeing back south for protection. A few Lipan leaders did not even bother feigning friendship, and continued attacking Spanish supply trains, ranches, and other vulnerable targets. Most Lipans would have seen nothing wrong or inconsistent with making peace with Spanish officials in Texas, for instance, and then launching a raid into neighboring Coahuila. For the time being, therefore, maintaining the status quo appeared to be the last best option afforded them.[43]

While overseeing the transformation of the old San Luis de Amarillas presidio into the new, castle-like Real Presidio de San Sabá, Felipe de

Rábago reconnoitered the territory west of San Sabá to locate additional sites for Spanish installations. A few Lipan band leaders, meanwhile, convinced Captain Rábago that they would soon be ready for missions. In the fall of 1761, Rábago met with the Lipan chief El Gran Cabezón and several other leaders who reiterated their intention of accepting reduction. Assisting the captain in these discussions was Fr. Diego Jiménez, president of the missions on the Rio Grande, who arrived at San Sabá in November. The Lipans insisted that the Spaniards meet four conditions before they would enter a mission. First, they refused to settle at the old San Sabá site. The vulnerability of the area to Comanche and Norteño attack was established fact, and the close proximity of priests' and soldiers' graves ran contrary to Lipan strictures about death. Instead, Gran Cabezón requested a new mission forty leagues south of San Sabá near El Río de San José (the upper Nueces), a rugged, isolated country that had not yet been penetrated by the northern tribes, but nowhere near where the viceroy had in mind when he dispatched Rábago to explore the region west of San Sabá. The Lipans also requested that a detachment of Spanish soldiers accompany them on an upcoming bison hunt so that they could enter the mission fully provisioned with food. Gran Cabezón's third stipulation was that Rábago help them secure the release of a Natagé relative's daughter whom Spanish authorities were holding captive in Nuevo León. The final condition, which Rábago prudently declined, was for an additional detachment of soldiers to accompany them on a campaign against the Comanches. The Spaniards' rejection of this request was probably not a surprise to the Lipans, and from Gran Cabezón's perspective, not a deal breaker. Eager to act while the Lipans appeared willing to accept a mission, yet mindful of the viceroy's certain displeasure regarding the location of new outposts, Rábago and Fr. Jiménez opted to proceed without first seeking official authorization. The Lipans, meanwhile, rode off to conduct their bison hunt.[44]

Gran Cabezón and his band returned from their *carneada* in late December 1761 and declared themselves ready to open a new chapter in their lives. In response, Rábago detailed thirty soldiers to accompany the Indians on their one-hundred-mile journey south to El Cañon, the name given to the perspective mission site on the Nueces River (near present-day Camp Wood in Real County). The captain and his entourage followed a few days later, and by mid-January 1762, the party was encamped near the spring at El Cañon. Fr. Jiménez and Fr. Joaquin de Baños arrived on January 16, bringing axes, iron bars, tools, and several yokes of oxen, along with a supply of corn, tobacco, candy, clothing, and hats for the Indian leaders. Accompanying the Franciscans were some Coahuiltecan neophytes from mission San Bernardo to help the Lipans construct irrigation works and clear fields for planting. On January 23, Rábago led a procession of officers, priests, and Indians to a flat knoll above the spring where they would soon commence building the mission. Fr. Jiménez blessed the site, said mass, and named the new mission San Lorenzo de la Santa Cruz (but more commonly called Mission del Cañon). Gran Cabezón uprooted some grass, drew water, and then poured the water over some stones he had picked up, symbolizing that his band of three hundred Lipans were taking possession of the site. Rábago then appointed him "captain" of Santa Cruz.[45]

Before Rábago returned to his post at San Sabá, Fr. Jiménez drew him aside and handed him a petition requesting that additional troops be assigned to the new mission. Like Fr. Baños, Jiménez was a veteran of the San Sabá mission. Uppermost in his mind was the need for an adequate number of soldiers—not only to protect against a repeat of the San Sabá massacre, but also to assure the Lipans that the Spaniards were committed to the project. Contrasting the Coahuiltecan missions of northern Mexico with the heretofore unsuccessful efforts with the Apaches, Jiménez argued that keeping the "proud" and "haughty" Lipans satisfied would be problematic. The latter people were nomadic bison hunters, possessed large herds of horses, and had acquired arms and munitions from the French. When compared to the impoverished Coahuiltecans who had entered missions in order to survive, the Lipans appeared to be very well-off. Jiménez was also worried about the unofficial status of the San Lorenzo mission and feared that without official sanction, the enterprise would face insurmountable supply and logistical problems. But Rábago was reluctant to report his actions to the viceroy. Establishing a new mission one hundred miles to the south of San Sabá rather than to the northwest of the river ran contrary to his orders. Such disobedience, coming so soon after his reinstatement to command, could very well bring a second—and this time permanent—end to his military career.[46]

In addition to Gran Cabezón's people, other Lipan bands—whose total number Fr. Jiménez estimated to be around 3,000 people—visited

San Lorenzo and expressed interest in having similar missions established for them. A band leader named "Captain Teja" reportedly desired a mission, as did another named "Captain Panocha." While Rábago was still on the Nueces, in fact, a messenger arrived reporting that a third Lipan leader, El Turnio, had recently visited the San Sabá presidio, requesting that the Spaniards establish a mission for his people. Keen to act before these opportunities slipped away, the captain and Fr. Jiménez hurried back north to meet with him. El Turnio, whose band numbered between four hundred and five hundred people, sought a new mission about ten miles below San Lorenzo (near present-day Montell, Texas). Although Rábago was reluctant to spare an additional detail to guard the proposed settlement (thereby further weakening the defenses of the San Sabá presidio), the opportunity apparently held such appeal that the captain again, without acquiring permission, agreed to the establishment of a second mission on the Nueces, and on February 6, 1762, Fr. Jiménez presided over the founding of mission Nuestra Señora de la Candelaria.[47]

During the ensuing months, several Lipan bands visited the new missions, both out of curiosity and in hopes of receiving gifts. Fr. Jiménez reported, for instance, that besides Gran Cabezón and El Turnio, Lipan leaders Teja, Boruca, Bordado (Zapato Bordado), and El Cojo stopped by from time to time. Lacking adequate supplies and military protection for the existing Lipan neophytes, the Spaniards could hardly insist that these bands remain at the missions. In a letter to the viceroy dated January 24, 1763, Fr. Jiménez stated bluntly that without financial assistance and a competent garrison of soldiers to defend the Apaches against their enemies, there was little hope for the two settlements and the estimated four hundred Lipans (primarily women and children) gathered near them. Fr. Jiménez had some grounds for optimism, however, since the Lipans had apparently lost their fear of settling in permanent villages lest the immobility make them sick. A few of the men had even offered to help with some of the fieldwork, and they had not left the missions without permission. When the Lipans went out to conduct hunts (or raids), they left their women and children in the care of the Franciscans. "These and other things," Fr. Jiménez remarked, "convince us of the good condition of these Indians for being settled."[48]

Despite the promising beginning, however, the fate of the new Apache missions at El Cañon soon became hostage to a series of developments that Captain Rábago and Fr. Jiménez never could have expected. In 1762, the government of King Charles III of Spain entered the Seven Years' War on the side of France. Three months prior to the formal cessation of hostilities in February 1763, France, in an effort to prevent all its American territories from falling into British hands, secretly transferred Louisiana to Spain. With a stroke of a pen, therefore, the burden of defending Texas against Franco-Indian alliances abated, as did the Crown's immediate interest and financial investment in the troublesome province.[49]

At the new El Cañon missions, meanwhile, the dreams of a Lipan holy man named "El Lumen" were causing considerable anxiety. In June 1762, men from Gran Cabezón's band departed from mission San Lorenzo to conduct a bison hunt. While they were gone, El Lumen had a dream that the missionaries had abandoned the missions, taking the wives, children, and horses of the hunters with them. He apparently shared his dream with the hunters, as several hurried home to see if it was true. On arrival at San Lorenzo, the relieved Lipans found that all was in order and returned north to finish their hunt. Nevertheless, El Lumen continued to be a disruptive presence. He speculated that the Spaniards had been cohabiting with his band's women, and that they were plotting deceitfully to kill the Lipans. He suggested that before other soldiers came to join those already at the mission, the Indians should rise up and kill them instead. On still another occasion, El Lumen scandalized the Franciscans with his demand that they give him an altar cloth to use as a breechcloth. So unsettling was El Lumen's presence that Fr. Jiménez wrote the viceroy, reporting that the eccentric Lipan's behavior had created an "uneasiness which almost caused everything to be lost."[50]

A third unwelcome development for the nascent Apache missions was the unrelenting attacks of the Comanches and Norteños. In March 1762, the Comanches destroyed a Lipan encampment in one of the canyons near mission San Lorenzo. Two months later, they attacked a second Apache settlement, killing forty persons, and a July raid resulted in the loss of fourteen more Lipans. Captain Rábago spent a fortune provisioning, clothing, and acquiring livestock and horses for his soldiers, but the Comanches and their allies intercepted and robbed about half of the supply trains. They also targeted the San Sabá garrison. In June, a party of Taovayas and other Norteños raided the presidio, killing two soldiers and seizing seventy horses. In the ensuing weeks, they struck a

Lipan ranchería on the Frío River, as well as one on the Guadalupe, and killed several Lipan bison hunters on the Colorado. In mid-August, a Norteño force under the leadership of Tejas chiefs Sanches, Canos, and Nason gathered on the San Antonio River to pursue the Lipans, and dropped by the Béxar presidio to meet with Texas governor Angel de Martos. Angry with the Spanish for protecting the Lipans, the Norteños demanded missions and presidios for themselves. Caught in a trap of their own making, Spanish officials responded with gifts and vague promises of more even-handed treatment in the future.[51]

Reports of Comanche-Lipan violence also plagued Spanish authorities serving in New Mexico. In the fall of 1763, Governor Tomás Vélez dispatched seven mission Indians from Pecos to deliver letters to San Sabá, and to locate a good route to reach the presidio San Luis. Following the Pecos River south and east from New Mexico for nearly a week, the party came across a large Lipan ranchería located about two hundred miles southeast of Pecos, near Coyote Springs in present day Loving County, Texas. The mission Indians remained with the Lipans for five days, and were about to continue on their errand when the encampment came under attack by a contingent of twenty-one Comanches and two women. The Lipans annihilated the vastly outnumbered Comanches, killing every one of the attackers save one woman. In the celebration that followed, the Comanche woman, writes Castañeda, was "properly roasted" and then "joyously devoured in a triumphant banquet." The mission Indians then proceeded on and visited a second Lipan encampment, and then a third situated near Paint Rock under the leadership of Chief Bigotes.[52]

An uptick in Lipan raiding activities by those living near El Cañon and those residing away from the missions constituted a fourth vexing problem for the Spaniards. Since the El Cañon missions were operating without viceregal recognition or royal grant, the only way for Captain Rábago to feed his wards was to permit them to go on buffalo hunts. The Indians took advantage of this freedom, however, to conduct raids into Coahuila, where they stole food, supplies, and livestock. The El Cañon bands also used the missions as a sanctuary to make raids on their Indian enemies. After each buffalo hunt, the old men and women returned to the missions while the young men proceeded on into the lands of the Comanches and Norteños to take revenge. After striking their enemies, they would flee southward to the hill country between the Frío and Nueces rivers. Employing an old tactic, the Lipans would leave hats, shoes, and other items of Spanish manufacture to convince their enemies that the Spaniards were co-perpetrators. At times, they would seize their enemies' arrows and clothing and commit similar raids on Spanish settlements to cast suspicion on the northern tribes.[53]

After enduring months of Lipan thefts and raids, even the patience of longtime Apache defender Fr. Mariano de los Dolores was wearing thin. On August 6, 1762, Dolores wrote Governor Martos, complaining, "The Indians of the Apache Nation are slaughtering, stealing and wreaking destruction with unprecedented disorder, disrespect, and insolence and their almost daily persistency is becoming insufferable." The Apaches were not only killing cattle, Dolores added, but also deliberately targeting cows rather than bulls to reduce procreation. The "natural evil propensities" of the Apaches were the source of these outrages, he maintained, warning that a war of extermination against them might become inevitable. Employing rather "un-Franciscan-like" language, Fr. Dolores concluded his rant by opining that the atrocities "should dissolve the pious rationalized sermons of love toward the Apaches that habitually destroy whatever is offered them under simulated peace promises."[54]

A final problem undermining the success of the El Cañon missions was a devastating smallpox epidemic that struck missions San Lorenzo and El Candelaria in 1763 or 1764. Of the forty-five children and twenty-nine adults that the missionaries hastily baptized during the outbreak, the majority died. A concerned Fr. Jiménez reported the emergence of a nativistic movement that many Lipans embraced in the aftermath of the disease. The Lipans were "seeing" an old man, who would appear and then vanish. He was a shape-shifter, and at times took the form of a woman. He advised the Indians to wage a continuous war with neighboring tribes and with the Spaniards. He also warned them not to accept baptism, as death would follow shortly after the ceremony. The old man appeared during battles, was killed, but then reappeared alive. Lipans understood this to mean that should they die in battle, they would live on after death, reuniting with other Lipans who had passed away before them.[55]

According to anthropologist Philleo Nash, "nativistic cults arise among deprived groups" and "may occur within the framework of either acceptance or rejection of values and skills associated with white culture." The occurrence of such a movement among the Lipans in the 1760s, therefore, is hardly surprising. In response to more than a century of both direct and indirect contact with Europeans, and the introduction of horses, firearms, alcohol, and a multitude of other trade goods, revolutionary changes shook the very foundations of Lipan culture. In the face of continued warfare and epidemic diseases, their numbers were in drastic decline, disrupting the social ties and affinal obligations that held bands together. Desperate to offset their powerful Indian enemies, some Lipans turned to the Spaniards in hopes of gaining protection and urgently needed supplies. But the Spanish alliance quickly proved its inadequacy. There were too few presidios, and the soldiers and officers that manned them were as ill equipped and unmotivated as they were disinterested (or incompetent). Befriending the Spaniards also came with a price tag: the abandonment of ancient traditions, independence, and way of life. As Tunnell and Newcomb have observed, the Lipans "found themselves in an intolerable situation for which there was no practical solution." The vision of the old man, however, with "his supernatural gifts, offered a way—a plan of action and a road to salvation. To what extent the Lipans embraced the creed is unknown, but that he appeared at all is symptomatic of their condition."[56]

As Fr. Jiménez had feared, Rábago's failure to obtain official approval and economic support for the El Cañon missions, combined with growing Lipan reluctance to live at the settlements, made their success increasingly unlikely. By 1765, the number of Lipan bands visiting the sites plummeted as they retreated south to the Rio Grande or west to the Pecos in an effort to escape Comanche and Norteño attacks. The year 1766 brought renewed unrest to the region. On January 21, four hundred Comanches and Norteños stormed into the Nueces valley and overran the Lipan encampment near mission San Lorenzo, killing six and taking twenty-five captives. The Norteños also rounded up a sizeable herd of livestock, and to add further insult, spent the night in the Apache camp. Unbeknownst to the sleeping Norteños, Captain Rábago had learned about the planned invasion, and had dispatched forty-one Spanish soldiers from San Sabá to ambush the invaders on their return home. On the evening of January 23, the Spaniards engaged the retreating Norteños as they neared the Llano River, employing their cannon with such deadly efficiency that losses among the northern tribes may have surpassed two hundred. According to two Lipan eyewitnesses, they could hear the Norteños weeping as they trudged northward to their homes.[57]

While pleased to see their Norteño attackers bloodied, the Lipans at El Cañon had little cause for optimism. Fed up with mission life and lack of protection, El Turnio's band deserted El Candelaria early that fall. In October 1766, an estimated three hundred Tejas warriors armed with muskets, lances, and hatchets besieged mission San Lorenzo. Fierce fighting ensued between the attackers and the thirty Spanish soldiers and handful of Lipan defenders inside. Unable to reach the mission walls due to Spanish cannon fire, the Tejas gave up and rode away, taking a herd of mares with them and leaving several Spaniards wounded. Undeterred, a second group of Indians (perhaps Comanches or Wichitas) made an attempt on the mission a month later. Again undermanned, the Spaniards disguised their numerical weakness by ordering the women into soldiers' overcoats and hats and placing them with guns along the wall. Perceiving that the Spaniards were actively defending the mission, the attackers retreated to a grove of oak trees a short distance away. A chief came galloping up and rode leisurely around the mission three times under a hail of Spanish bullets before riding back to his awaiting warriors. The combatants kept up a continuous, but in the end useless, discharge of musket fire, neither side causing the other any known damage.[58]

The Norteño and Comanche raids of 1766 along with the bloody Battle of the Llano River marked, in the words of Gary Clayton Anderson, a "watershed in the history of the southern plains." While convincing the Norteños to cease major campaigns against the Apaches, the raids further weakened Spain's already shaky resolve to maintain a viable presence north of San Antonio. During the winter of 1766, the San Sabá garrison came under repeated assault. In a desperate plea for help, Captain Rábago wrote that raiders had destroyed or stolen virtually all his supplies and livestock. Wichitas, Caddos, Tonkawas, and Comanches controlled the roads, set pasturelands on fire, and attacked anyone who ventured outside the presidio. By the summer of 1767, the Spaniards at San Sabá and at El Cañon were virtual prisoners within the walls of their respective outposts, the few remaining Lipans having long since abandoned the missions.[59]

The Lipans' decision to forgo mission life and their relationship with the Spanish also marked an important watershed in their history.

They had never been keen about missions in the first place, agreeing to "reduction" only as a temporary expedient rather than from any sincere desire to remake themselves in the image of Europeans. Of the five missions that the Spaniards established for the Lipans and affiliated bands between 1750 and 1762, they occupied none of them continuously for more than a few years. As has been noted previously, Comanche and Norteño attacks, inadequate supplies, and ineffective Spanish defenses compelled the Lipans to reconsider their decision to ally with the Spaniards. When combined with their tepid commitment to mission life, the resulting collapse of the "era of good feelings" that followed the Spanish-Lipan peace of November 1749 seems a foregone conclusion. But the Lipans must have realized that they could not go back to their plains-based economy and remain dependent on buffalo if the Spaniards could not protect them. Consequently, the Lipans faced a crisis in the 1760s as Comanches and Norteños denied them access to winter buffalo herds in the Colorado River valley. Without buffalo, they possessed little in the way of trade goods to secure corn, beans, and other critical supplies. With their economy in shambles, Lipan bands drifted south to the Rio Grande, where they turned increasingly to raiding and stealing.[60] The Spaniards, for their part, looked with dismay on the renewal of Lipan depredations, particularly when Spanish ranches, supply trains, missions, and presidios were on the receiving end. Having sacrificed their time, treasure, and lives in an effort to "uplift" the Lipans, the Spaniards fumed angrily at the ingratitude, treachery, and unreliability of their erstwhile allies. Such attitudes were especially significant during the summer of 1767, as Spanish officials contemplated a complete recalibration of their position in Texas, and of their relationship with the Indians of that province.

(

In an effort to find ways to curb royal expenditures, to economize in its operations on the northern frontier, and to formulate an effective Indian policy, King Charles III dispatched José de Gálvez, a Spanish-trained lawyer and administrator, and the Marqués de Rubí, a field marshal in the Spanish army, to conduct a thorough inspection of the vast area between California and east Texas. In the spring of 1766, Rubí inspected the presidios and military organization of the northern frontier from Sonora to

Texas. Accompanied by military engineer Nicolás de Lafora and cartographer Joseph de Urrutia, the Rubí team covered over seven thousand miles in the span of two years. In June 1767, the Spaniards arrived in Monclova, Coahuila, at which point they turned northward to begin an inspection of Texas. Near Santa Rosa presidio and the nearby town of San Fernando de Austria, the Rubí party reported the presence of Lipan Apaches who were trading with citizens of the town and presidio. In mid-July, the Spaniards reached the Rio Grande, where they observed Lipan rancherías with cultivated fields. Using a "Lipan canoe," the party crossed the river, where they encountered yet another Lipan ranchería containing wickiups. Heading northeast to the Nueces River, they visited the abandoned Candelaria Mission before moving on to San Lorenzo. At this latter mission, Rubí found two missionaries, but no Lipan neophytes. Thirty soldiers and an officer from the San Sabá presidio guarded the vacant establishment. The Rubí party then inspected the presidio San Luis de Amarillas on the San Sabá. From there, they headed back south to San Antonio, reaching the settlement on August 8.[61]

The reports of Gálvez and Rubí awakened policymakers in Madrid and Mexico City to the nature and magnitude of the Indian problem on New Spain's northern frontier. The region possessed wide topographic diversity and climatic variation, and an equally diverse scattering of culturally distinct Indian tribes that seemed indifferent or openly hostile to Spanish efforts to civilize them. Frontier governors and military commanders complained that the Crown's interest in pacifying Indians through missionization—rather than by military campaign—was hampering the accomplishment of their objectives. Even when presidial commanders received authorization to undertake a campaign, they found their efforts impeded by shortages of men, horses, and supplies, not to mention the slow-moving cogwheels of the Spanish bureaucracy. The frontier sorely needed significant administrative changes, they maintained, since Texas and other northern provinces were located such a great distance from Mexico City and were far removed from the viceroy's attention. Not surprisingly, frontier officials urged that policymakers place effective control of this large area in the hands of military men, with headquarters located closer to the scene of the problems so that they could take quick action as circumstances required.[62]

Rubí's recommendations, which provided the blueprint for the "New

Regulation of Presidios" (or *Reglamento of 1772*) issued in September 1772, held crucial significance for the Lipan Apaches. First, Rubí ventured the opinion that the concern of Spanish officials to maintain the northern provinces as a buffer against foreign encroachment was misplaced. The real threat, he argued, came from within—namely, the hostile tribes that inhabited the region, especially the Apaches. That being the case, Rubí recommended the establishment of a defensive cordon along a more "realistic" frontier consisting of fifteen presidios spaced one hundred miles apart, each staffed by fifty men and officers. In hopes of preventing Apache raids into Chihuahua and Coahuila, six presidios were to guard the region between El Paso and San Juan Bautista. Of particular concern was cutting off Lipan and Mescalero access to the Bolsón de Mapimí corridor that stretched from the Big Bend of Texas south into the heart of Mexico. Described as so dry and hot that "even the cactus pads appeared to be toasted," the Bolsón de Mapimí nonetheless came alive in the spring and summer as groups of warriors rode south to prey on the ranches and villages of northern Mexico. The frontier provinces, according to Rubí's recommendations, would no longer act as buffers against foreign encroachments, but against Indian penetrations into the interior of New Spain.[63]

The Rubí report also recommended an entirely new policy regarding the Apaches, and the Lipans in particular. A review of Nicholas Lafora's notes taken during the Rubí inspection helps explain why. In his vivid descriptions of Apache war-related atrocities, Lafora accused them of exhibiting "extreme cruelty" toward vanquished foes. The Apaches "tear off their living flesh and eat it. They shoot arrows into them and, in short, inflict every imaginable cruelty on them." Lafora also maintained that the Apaches "have cut open living pregnant women and after taking out the infants beat them together until both were dead. They are extremely indolent and plant little or nothing. Thus they are compelled to steal their food." The provinces of Texas and Coahuila had suffered at the hands of the Apaches, Lafora continued, and "although these provinces are friendly to the Lipanes, they receive from them a thousand injuries, which are gradually bringing their unhappy subjects to ruin."[64]

Having established the barbarity of the Apaches, Lafora offered several suggestions for Spanish policymakers, and a rather stinging indictment against military commanders residing on the frontier. Simply adding soldiers and presidios to the frontier region, Lafora argued, would not halt "the impunity with which the Apaches commit their depredations." Instead, better training, tactics, and experienced commanders were required, since the Spaniards allowed the enemy to come and leave at will, took too long to order an effective pursuit, and were ignorant in the handling of muskets. "The enemy," on the other hand, "are amazing in their conduct, vigilance, speed, order, and endurance when they are raiding and retreating with their prizes," Lafora continued, "but all their precautions cease the moment they think they are safe within the limits of their own territory." For this reason, he concluded, "The only method of terrorizing, subjecting, or even annihilating these Indians . . . is a continuous offensive in their own territory. By this means they would be exterminated in a short time, simply by depriving them of their one means of subsistence, which is robbery."[65]

Field Marshal Rubí concurred wholeheartedly with his subordinate's assessment of Apache character, describing them as a perfidious, vile, and untrustworthy "mob of savages." After talking with officers close to the scene, he concluded much the same as Lafora had that the Spaniards' principal course of action should be to make total war on the Apaches. Henceforth, Rubí counseled, the Spaniards should abandon all commitments to the Apaches and make efforts instead to forge an alliance with the Comanches and Norteños (or better still, foment intertribal warfare to weaken or destroy them all). Implementation of such a policy, Rubí believed, would lead to either the subjugation or extermination of the Lipan Apaches.[66]

As Spanish officials in Madrid and Mexico City digested the contents of the Rubí recommendations, scattered bands of Lipan Apaches maintained their precarious position in south Texas. The long cycle of raids, ambushes, and retaliatory attacks against their Comanche and Norteño enemies continued, as did their depredations on Spanish settlements and supply trains north and south of the Rio Grande. Numerically weakened because of the constant violence, epidemics, frequent dislocation, and the consequent difficulties in obtaining food, supplies, and medicines, the Lipans' future, at least to the outside observer, appeared bleak. Their abandonment of the upper Nueces missions, Weddle concluded, "appears to mark the end of the Lipan Apaches as a powerful and decisive factor in the affairs of Texas and northern Mexico. Their raids and thieving were troublesome in subsequent years, but no longer did they threaten the very existence of Spanish settlements and ranches."[67]

Such a dark prognosis, however, would have surprised the Lipans. A strongly resilient and adaptive people, the Lipans of the mid-to-late eighteenth century had grown up in an environment of conflict and adversity; in fact, they had known little else. For nearly two generations, moreover, they had fought an uphill battle against an alliance of powerful Indian enemies. The Spaniards, one must remember, were in the process of retreating to the Rio Grande to construct a new line of defense aimed at protecting against Apache attacks. They certainly did not view the Lipans as a spent force. Should Comanche and Norteño pressures become unbearable, the Lipans could always fall back to one of several sanctuaries. The lower Rio Grande border region, even after the installation of the new presidios, remained porous and exposed sizeable gaps in the Spanish defense cordon. The Lipans could easily cross the river and disappear into the mountains of northern Mexico. Southeast Texas, having been virtually abandoned because of the presidial realignment, might also provide refuge should the need arise, as could the Big Bend region in far west Texas. Forging alliances with similarly pressed tribes (such as the Mescaleros, Jumanos, Coahuiltecans, or some of the Gulf Coast peoples) were other options open to the Lipan Apaches, continuing a tradition of ethnogenesis and cultural reinvention that had been at work in Texas for generations.[68] A few Lipans may have even speculated that they could coax the gullible Spaniards into another alliance. In other words, the Lipans, while weakened, would not have necessarily considered their position hopeless. Like the little gray lizard of their oral tradition, the Lipans were not prepared to submit themselves to the mercy of their enemies or to adopt wholesale modifications to their culture and traditions. "Change that is deep and meaningful," psychologist Lourdes V. Lapuz reminds us, "hardly ever occurs without conflict. Its adoption tends to be uneven, erratic, tentative, and ambivalent for some time."[69] Bound by attitudes and traditions that dated back to the earliest times, the Lipans considered their lives and activities predestined by the supernatural forces at work in their world, and by the experiences and examples of their ancestors. As long as they followed those examples and adhered to their traditions, the future would work itself out.

CHAPTER FOUR

A War of Extermination

Lipan Apaches in Spanish Texas, 1770–1800

∽

THE LIPANS AND COMANCHES were bitter enemies who frequently raided each other's horse herds, seized women and children captives, and killed each other's men. During one such engagement, the Comanches succeeded in taking the life of a young Lipan warrior who recently had married. After the battle, his widow got out her special ceremonial buckskin dress and followed the Comanches as they retreated home, determined to exact revenge on the people who had killed her husband. The woman knew that a good wife must be the servant of her husband's people even after his death, and she could never marry again unless her in-laws gave their consent. She walked a long distance from the battlefield, and when she found the Comanche village located far to the north, she hid herself until the enemy was engaged in a scalp dance celebrating their recent victory. Once the dance had begun, she donned her beautiful beaded buckskin dress and, after waiting until it was late, quietly joined the festivities. She looked around until she found the chief who had killed and scalped her husband. The chief was drunk, and when the young woman walked up and invited him to dance, he readily agreed. As they danced, she noticed that her husband's scalp dangled beside the chief's knife attached to a belt around his waist. The chief attempted to put his arms around her, and the woman knew what the Comanche had on his mind. As he escorted her away from the encampment, she started to run, heading toward some tall weeds and brush where nobody could see or hear them. According to the story, the woman, lacking a knife, used her teeth to slash the chief's throat and then scalped him with his own knife, took his clothes, and stole away on his horse. The woman returned to her husband's people, crying and singing the Apache war song. When her in-laws came to the door, she had the Comanche's scalp on a stick and she had his clothes. The Lipans put on a big dance of their own, and her in-laws released the woman from her obligation to them, telling her, "You are free and can marry again because you are brave and you are true." And she was brave and the Lipans respected her.[1]

❨

THE STORY OF THE COURAGEOUS Lipan woman was a popular one that elders told and retold, stirring the imaginations of children who crawled under their bison robes dreaming that they too might one day earn the respect and admiration of their people. The story also reinforced Lipan social strictures and the obligations that married couples held toward their in-laws. Violence and warfare were an important—and all too frequent—component of Lipan life, often bringing heartache and hardship to the families of victims, but also offering avenues to prestige, status, revenge, and social mobility. This chapter examines the thirty-year period following Spain's unsuccessful efforts to "reduce" the Lipan Apaches, and the dramatic escalation of violence and warfare that accompanied the reorientation of Spanish Indian policy toward an alliance with the Comanches and Norteños, and a war of extermination against the Lipans.

As the Spaniards studied the recommendations of visitor-general José de Gálvez and the Marqués de Rubí, frontier officials reported the presence of Lipans across south Texas and northern Coahuila. In 1768, Fr. Gaspar de Solis remarked that the Lipans and other Apache groups occupied lands between the Rio Grande and the Nueces River, while the Rubí party had reported seeing Lipans in three locations: in the mountains of Coahuila

just southwest of the Big Bend of Texas, across the Rio Grande above present-day Eagle Pass, and on the Pecos River. Other Lipans were reportedly
living far to the west near the Natagé and Mescalero Apaches around El
Paso. Thomas Schilz writes that several small Lipan bands under the leadership of Cabellos Largos, Poca Ropa, El Chico, Flacco, and others, fearing Spanish attack in northern Coahuila, fled northeastward in the early
1770s to the Nueces, and perhaps as far north as the Leon River (about
one hundred miles southwest of present-day Fort Worth). Other scholars,
meanwhile, believe that Lipan bands drifted east toward the Gulf Coast
of Texas, where they fostered social and economic relationships with the
Bidais, Atakapas, and Akokisa (Orcoquisas) peoples through intermarriage and trade. These east Texas tribes carried on a clandestine trade
with British merchants from West Florida, exchanging hides and horses
for guns and other manufactured goods. Beyond acquiring firearms, the
Lipans may have gained a sense of security from their budding relationship with the east Texas Indians—something they had not experienced in
a very long time.[2]

On September 10, 1772, more than four years after the completion
of the Gálvez and Rubí inspections of the frontier, King Charles III of
Spain issued the "New Regulations for Presidios." Drawing partly on
one of Gálvez's ideas, the Regulations grouped the northern provinces
of Nueva Vizcaya, Sonora, Sinaloa, California, New Mexico, and Texas
into a new administrative unit called the *Provincias Internas* (Interior
Provinces) and placed frontier garrisons under the immediate supervi-
sion of a "commandant-inspector." Of even greater consequence was
the regulation's inclusion of Rubí's recommendations regarding the
realignment of frontier presidios. The Spaniards would thereafter curtail
sharply their presence in east Texas, and relocate the provincial capital
from Los Adaes to San Antonio. They were to abandon all existing missions and presidios in the province—save those at San Antonio and La
Bahía—and get to work establishing a new line of forts along the Rio
Grande. Finally, the regulations called for the adoption of an Indian
policy aimed at securing alliances with the Comanches and Norteños as
a prelude to an all-out war of extermination against the Lipan Apaches.
As David J. Weber has observed, Spain's policy with respect to the
Apaches was an exception to the Crown's standard policy (in place since
1573) that permitted short-term campaigns, but prohibited offensive

Lipan man with hair-pipe breastplate (1852).

Plains and Eastern Woodlands Indians wore "hair-pipes" made up of shells, bone, copper, or stone. Pendant in the middle is silver. Friedrich Richard Petri, Center for American History, UT-Austin, di_04093.

wars against unconquered Indians—testifying to the importance the Spaniards placed on addressing the "Apache problem."[3]

New Spain viceroy Antonio María de Bucareli had the task of putting the new regulations into effect. To that end, he appointed Don Hugo Oconór as the first commandant-inspector of the Provincias Internas. Well-respected as a tenacious and aggressive officer, Oconór (or "El Capitán Colorado," as the Indians reportedly called him) wasted little time carrying out his new duties. Traveling back and forth across the vast northern frontier, Oconór oversaw the closure, removal, and construction of presidios along the lines recommended in the Rubí report, and raised several companies of cavalry to serve on the northern frontier. He also kept an eye on the Apaches, waiting patiently until time and circumstances permitted an all-out campaign against them.[4]

Coinciding with Oconór's efforts on the northern frontier were those of a remarkable Frenchman named Athanase de Mézières. Following the French cession of Louisiana to Spain in 1763, De Mézières offered his services to the Spanish, and in 1769, Louisiana governor Alejandro O'Reilly appointed him lieutenant governor of the trading post at Natchitoches. De Mézières was well-known and influential among the various Native peoples of the Texas-Louisiana border and could converse in several Indian languages, and the Spaniards hoped to use his connections to foster closer ties with them. The various Wichita tribes, in particular, would be critical in any effort to influence—if not control—the Comanches. In the spring of 1770, Mézières concluded an agreement with the Caddos, promising the Indians annual presents and expanded commercial opportunities in exchange for their allegiance to Spain. Later that year, the Caddos assisted De Mézières in arranging a council with the Kichais, Tawakonis, Taovayas, and Yscanis. These tribes of the Wichita confederation, driven both by the desire to acquire Spanish trade goods and their fear of the powerful Osages, proved amenable to Spanish overtures for improved relations, and De Mézières succeeded in getting a treaty signed in the summer of 1771 at a second council that he hosted at Natchitoches.[5]

Seeking to build on these successes, De Mézières traversed northeast Texas the ensuing spring in an effort to visit Spain's new Indian allies and to acquire intelligence about the Comanches. In June 1772, the Frenchman brought several Norteño chiefs to San Antonio to meet Governor Juan

María Vicencio, Barón de Ripperdá and to ratify their recent peace agreement. At a formal ceremony, the chiefs performed a feather dance as a
sign of peace and wrapped the governor in buffalo skins.[6] Afterward, De
Mézières returned home to Natchitoches, where troubling reports awaited
him that four Apache chiefs and their bands were en route to the Bidais
and Hasinais to conduct trade and to establish alliances. The Hasinais, in
particular, appeared the most vulnerable to the Lipans' overtures. As the
Comanches increasingly came to dominate trade in Texas and with the
French, the Hasinais' position as middlemen in the Comanche-French
trade relationship had steadily eroded. Forming an alliance with the
Lipans, however, could provide the Hasinais with the horses and livestock
necessary to acquire firearms and reestablish their former trade connections with Louisiana—but adopting such a course would most certainly
displease both the Spanish and the Comanches. Fearing that a Hasinai-
Lipan alliance would destabilize Spain's delicate diplomatic arrangements
in east Texas, and sensing an opportunity to test the Hasinais' commitment to their Spanish ally, Don Athanase sent instructions to the Hasinai
chief Bigotes to ambush the Apaches by pretending to welcome them, and
then attacking as soon as their guard was down. Employing such treachery was a common staple in Indian warfare, and a compliant Bigotes
busied himself setting the trap. Most of the Lipans, however, stopped to
hunt along the way, and only seven delegates showed up at Bigotes's village. The Hasinai leader received them as guests, and in the pre-arranged
attack that followed, Tejas warriors seized three of the Lipans and publicly
beheaded them. The Apaches did not forget the Hasinais' treachery, and
according to one writer, their cries for vengeance "surged across the land
like a storm wind stirring dust devils." The turbulence lasted for nearly
a year—buffeting the Hasinais and neighboring tribes with rumors that
the Apaches were planning a mass invasion in retaliation for the deaths
of their brethren.[7]

   For Spaniards residing in Texas, the Comanches and the Lipans
headed the list of troublesome Indians who required pacification; yet
the Regulations of 1772 adopted separate policies for each group. Unlike
most Spanish frontier commanders, Lt. Colonel Oconór possessed the
ability and willingness to differentiate between bands of hostile and
friendly Indians of the same tribal identity. In 1773 and 1774, for example, he made peace with several Lipan bands in Texas. Significant among

these were Lipans under the leadership of Cabellos Largos and Poca Ropa. Lipan bands residing in Coahuila, on the other hand, who stood accused of raiding back and forth across the Rio Grande, were subject to military pacification. Reflecting on Spanish-Apache relations a few years later, Oconór recommended that the Apaches be accorded "the best treatment and friendship, tolerating in them some mistakes or slight excesses and trying to induce them by good example and persuasion to admit missionaries and that they submit to the King's rule." If the Lipans refused to make restitution for stolen horses or other misdeeds, however, only then should the Spaniards wage a campaign against them. Once authorities determined that a campaign was necessary, they should take care to inflict "the least harm possible so as not to offend the spirit of the entire nation." Not all Lipan bands, in other words, should bear Spanish punishment for the actions of a few rebellious warriors.[8]

In an ongoing effort to bolster the new chain of frontier fortifications against Indian attacks, Oconór organized cavalry units (or "flying companies") of seasoned veterans, new recruits, and Indian scouts. Unlike fixed presidial companies, flying companies were always on the move, crisscrossing the frontier in constant search or pursuit of the enemy. By increasing the number of Spanish patrols, relocating the presidios, reforming the military supply system, and leading several short campaigns, Oconór hoped at least to reduce the number of hit-and-run attacks that were the bane of Spanish Texas. By the fall of 1774, he had progressed sufficiently with the reorganization of frontier defenses to mount a more substantial offensive against the Apaches. According to historian Frank Lockwood, the Irishman aimed "to strike the Indians' hip and thigh, front and rear, in camp and on the move. Buffeted from this direction and that, whether they stood or retreated, they would be found, repulsed, and beaten."[9]

To accomplish this ambitious and rather brutal goal, Oconór began formulating plans early in 1775 that called for putting nine large forces, totaling 2,228 men, into the field. Although the actual number that participated was far less (perhaps 1,500 men), Oconór succeeded in assembling one of the largest armies ever gathered to fight the Apaches. Drawing troops from Coahuila, Nueva Vizcaya, New Mexico, and Sonora, the Spaniards hoped to converge on the Apaches from all directions, "squeezing them together in a lump that could be either exterminated or driven northward out of the reach of the settlements of northern Mexico."[10] The campaign, which began in September 1775, lasted nearly four months; but of the nine separate Spanish forces that Oconór had initially proposed, only three materialized. On September 29, 1775, Coahuila governor Jacobo Ugarte and 184 men reached the presidio Monclova Viejo on the San Rodrigo River. A couple of days later, they crossed the Rio Grande at a point just above Piedras Negras and proceeded northward. On the evening of October 2, three Indians appeared at the Spaniards' encampment, anxious to find out against whom the Spaniards were marching. It was Cabellos Largos, one of the Lipan bandleaders who had made peace with Oconór a year earlier, accompanied by two warriors. Ugarte assured Cabellos Largos that his band was not the target, and the three Lipans spent the night in the camp. As word spread across the Rio Grande frontier that the Spaniards were planning a great campaign, Lipan captains Poca Ropa, Boca Tuerta, El Cielo, El Flacco, Panocha, Rivera, Javielillo, Paxarito, and Manteca Mucho also met with Ugarte and received similar assurances about their safety. As the Spaniards continued their march northward, they passed several Lipan rancherías, many of them empty, since the women and children had been hustled away to safety until the Spaniards' intentions could be determined. A few days later, Ugarte dispatched a detail to the San Sabá under the command of seventy-six-year-old Don Vicente Rodriguez, who reported later that he had encountered a handful of Lipan hunters encamped among some pecan trees. Pursuant to orders, Ugarte's force then turned west toward the Pecos.[11]

Although Governor Ugarte's scouts found considerable evidence that Apaches inhabited the Stockton Plateau region, they did not encounter any hostile groups until they reached the Rio San Pedro (Devil's River), located just east of the Pecos. On December 22, a Spanish scouting patrol stumbled upon a large Lipan force on the Devil's River, and lost three men before reinforcements arrived. In a skirmish with about fifty Lipan warriors a day later, Ugarte's army killed or wounded six Apaches.[12] Thus, after having spent several weeks in the field in search of Lipans and Mescaleros, Oconór's great pincer movement had managed to entrap precious few Indians.[13]

Despite the many weeks of arduous travel and hardship, the Oconór campaign of 1775 (and a subsequent campaign in the fall of 1776) failed to stop Apache raids into Mexico.[14] In a letter to Viceroy Bucareli dated

November 7, 1776, Governor Ugarte reported that Indian attacks into Coahuila continued, that the raiders had seized numerous horses and mules, and that near the village of San Fernando attackers had left two residents dead before riding off with some captured children. On November 1, a fourteen-year-old boy named Juan Domingo Ochoa appeared in Santa Rosa after having escaped from a Lipan Apache encampment. The boy recounted how a large party of Lipans had captured him while he was out herding some goats near his village. After capturing young Juan Domingo, the Lipans seized several horses and three additional children, but later abandoned two of them (probably infants) to starve and die. When the raiding party arrived back at their encampment, the Lipans beat the boy and cut off his left ear. The encampment's composition was of particular interest to Spanish officials. According to Juan Domingo, there were many families residing there—some of whom had arrived only recently after fleeing from the Comanches. There was also an adult Spaniard residing with the Lipans, an escaped convict named "Andres," and a mulatto man who had his entire upper lip cut off. The mulatto served as a scout for the Lipans, and he had taken a Lipan wife. He urged both Juan Domingo and Andres not to run away, and described his life among the Lipans as free and easy-going—at least compared to his lowly status and hardscrabble life among the Spaniards. Juan Domingo managed to escape his captors, however, and volunteered to guide a Spanish rescue effort to the Lipan encampment.[15]

By this time, however, Oconór's service on the northern frontier had ended. Reflecting on his considerable efforts, the commandant-inspector admitted that even with the reforms he had carried out, "attacks, robberies, deaths, and other hostilities will never be lacking on the frontiers" since it was simply impossible to prevent Indians from passing through the line of defense. Broken in health (and perhaps in spirit), Oconór requested a transfer to a less arduous assignment, and was awarded with the governorship of Guatemala. "Thus marked the end of an era," Bernard Bobb has observed, "and the beginning of a new concept" with respect to New Spain's northern frontier.[16]

The "new concept" took effect in May 1776 when Spain's Council of the Indies, concerned about the security of the northern provinces, placed the Provincias Internas under the command of a military governor known as the *comandante-general*. According to Donald Worcester, the Spaniards created the new "Commandancy General of the Interior Provinces" to cope with the Apaches—something they had done for no other tribe of Indians. To administer this new area (the Californias, Sonora, Sinaloa, Nueva Vizcaya, New Mexico, Coahuila, and Texas), King Charles III appointed Teodoro de Croix, a thirty-year army veteran, as both governor of Texas and comandante-general. Arriving in Mexico City in December 1776, Croix immersed himself in a thorough examination of written reports and documents relating to the vast region that he was to oversee. In December 1777, he convened a war council at the Monclova presidio to discuss Indian policy and obtain answers to several important questions:

1) How long had the Apaches been known on the frontier and when did they begin waging war against the Spaniards?

2) What military successes had the Spanish achieved against the Apaches—particularly in the previous five years?

3) How many warriors did the various Apache tribes possess? What was the relationship between them?

4) What types of arms did they possess? Where did they live? Where did they get their food? How and where did they wage war against us?

5) Who were the Apaches' enemies?

6) Of what good are peace pacts with the Lipans? What conveniences or inconveniences would result by maintaining the peace or declaring war on them?

7) What did the Council think about the Nations of the North?

8) What benefits could the Spaniards secure by waging war against the Nations of North and allying with the Lipans? What benefits could they secure by waging war against the Lipans and allying with the Nations of the North?

9) Were there currently sufficient Spanish troops to conduct a campaign against the Lipans and other Apaches and/ or the Nations of the North? If not, how many more men were needed?

10) If an alliance were concluded with the Lipans or the Nations of the North, which would be the one most suitable to guarantee the good faith of the alliance?

11) If Spain commenced war against the Lipans or the
Nations of the North, when and where should the
campaign be directed?[17]

The recommendations offered at Teodoro de Croix's war council
parroted most of the policies set in motion five years earlier with the
Regulations of 1772. The Monclova junta determined that the Lipans were
the primary enemy on the northeastern frontier, that peace necessitated
that the Spaniards target them in their campaigns, and that military
officials cultivate an alliance with the Norteños and Comanches—even
though the Comanches continued to misbehave. Since the Comanches
and Norteños were already allies, Croix reasoned, he had little choice
but to continue efforts to enlist the Comanches' support, lest he alienate
the Nations of the North. There were also practical considerations—the
Comanches and Norteños were numerically and militarily stronger then
the Lipans, and Croix did not want to "bite off more than he could chew."
Croix also mulled over how his people should respond to Apaches who
sued for peace and requested Spanish protection. Well aware of past difficulties with the Lipans, Croix devised a policy that was as impractical as it
was unrealistic—a veritable recipe for failure. In effect, Croix called for the
creation of *establecimientos de paz* ("establishments of peace"). Spanish
authorities thereafter would require Apaches who sought peace to gather
their families near a designated presidio, build houses to live in, and settle
down in pueblos as peaceful vassals of the king. The Apaches needed permission to leave their settlement, and had to promise to obey the orders
of the presidial captain. Under Croix's plan, the Spaniards also obligated
the Apaches to accept priests to instruct them, and expected Indian children to live as faithful Catholics. Finally, the policy required that the
Apaches take up farming for their subsistence, although the Spaniards
agreed to issue rations for the first year. Croix cautioned his subordinates
to extend the terms only to families who voluntarily presented themselves
at the presidios and appeared eager to accept reduction. Not surprisingly,
Croix's "peace terms" only inspired more Apache depredations, harden-
ing the commandant-general's resolve to crush them through an alliance
with the Comanches and Norteños.[18]

In February 1778, meanwhile, De Mézières arrived at San Antonio
to review Croix's plans, and to discuss how best to proceed with the
Norteños and Comanches. Although he had long believed the various

Nations of the North would make excellent buffers to Osage and English penetration of Spanish Texas and Louisiana, De Mézières saw no reason why the Spaniards could not first employ the Norteños to wipe out their hated Apache nemesis to the south. With the appropriate timing (in September, after the Indians had completed their harvest) and with adequate supplies, the Norteños would quickly "earn their keep," he argued, both in their loyalty to the Spanish, and in Apache lives. As for the Comanches, De Mézières offered the protection of the "Great Captains" of Louisiana and the Provincias Internas if they would agree to cease their hostilities and return stolen horses.[19]

Spain's Indian problem grew even more perplexing in the summer of 1779. An inexperienced Colonel Domingo Cabello had become the new Texas governor the previous fall, while the indispensable De Mézières lay recuperating in Natchitoches from injuries sustained after a freak horse-riding accident. Worse still was word from Spain, notifying Croix that the king had rejected plans to conduct a general war against the Apaches. Spain's alliance with the French and pending entry into the war against Great Britain ruled out any new expenditures of men and resources to the Provincias Internas. Furthermore, the Crown rejected, on humanitarian grounds, the forcible subjugation or extermination of Indians, urging instead a policy of peaceful persuasion and kind example as the preferred means of pacification. Thereafter, commanders were to treat hostiles that surrendered to Spanish authorities with gentleness, humanity, charity, and good faith. In place of forcible reduction, the Royal Order of February 20, 1779, instructed commanders to ply the Indians with supplies and gifts—including firearms. The guns should be defective, however, with weakened barrels and stocks that would make them easily damaged and in continual need of repair. This would lead both to further Indian dependence upon the Spaniards for necessary repairs and gunpowder, and to hasten the decline of their skills in making and using aboriginal weapons.[20]

To say that Croix disapproved of the Royal Order of February 20, 1779, is an understatement. Experience, the commandant-general believed, dictated that peace with the Apaches would be fleeting, since self-preservation motivated them rather than "true sentiments of humanity." The Lipans, he complained further, "came to the *presidios*, overbearing and proud, with hands bloody from victims . . . whom they had sacrificed in their fury, [demanding] food, presents, and gifts. They not only murdered in the interior of the province, but even at the doors of *presidios*, and threatening a general invasion, attacked the *presidio* Aguaverde." In short, Croix concluded bitterly, "the Lipan Apache are not worthy of the sovereign piety his royal Catholic spirit dispenses them in the royal order of February 20, 1779."[21]

During his first year in Texas, Domingo Cabello must have wondered what wrongs he had committed in his life to account for his "promotion" to the governorship of Texas. An experienced army officer with combat experience in Europe, Cuba, and Central America, the fifty-three-year-old Cabello considered his new position in Texas to be the "absolute nadir of a promising career," and he tried every means possible to gain a better post.[22] Upon his arrival in Texas in late October, 1778, he found his orders a mess of contradictions. On the one hand, his superiors expected him to avoid any rupture with the Lipans until they authorized a general campaign against all Texas Apaches. At the same time, Commandant-General Croix expected him to cut off the Lipans' access to British trade goods by isolating them from the Tejas and Bidais. But how could he keep the Lipans happy without upsetting Spain's Norteño allies? Keeping a lid on this pressure cooker required skilled diplomacy and long experience dealing with Texas Indians, which Cabello sorely lacked. Croix had hoped that Athanase de Mézières would help fill the void, but the Frenchman's poor health and Cabello's distrust of his advice negated that possibility. While de Mézières had counseled a pro–Comanche and Norteño policy, the new governor instead adopted a conciliatory attitude toward the Lipans.[23]

On March 6, 1779, a delegation of eighty Apaches—both Lipans and Natagés—met with Cabello at San Antonio. A Lipan chief named El Joyoso reported that a large Norteño and Tonkawa war party had attacked them, killing or capturing more than three hundred people and seizing many horses. The Apaches yearned for revenge and requested Spanish assistance as well as powder and shot. Alarmed at the news, Cabello nonetheless refused their request. The Norteños and Tonkawas were friends of the Spanish, he explained, and had done nothing to him. After distributing a box of cigars and two *piloncillos* (sweet cone cakes), he ended the meeting, pleased that he had managed to defuse the situation. But the self-congratulations proved premature. Ten days later, El

Joyoso's people rode back into Béxar, boasting proudly that they had attacked the Tonkawas on the banks of the Colorado River, had killed four people, and had taken a woman and three children captive. Four fresh scalps hung conspicuously from their belts. Cabello offered the chief eight horses for the captives' release, perhaps thinking about how he could gain the Tonkawas' gratitude by repatriating their relatives. El Joyoso refused the offer, however, but did release one of the children to Luis Menchaca, a Spanish merchant in San Antonio who was on good terms with the Lipans.[24]

Cabello had little time to reflect on the fate of the Tonkawas. Disturbing rumors swept through Béxar in April that Spanish authorities in Coahuila were meeting with Mescalero Apache emissaries to plan a joint campaign against certain Lipan bands that resided in northern Coahuila. Cabello was stunned—not at the duplicitous behavior of his Spanish brethren in Coahuila, but at the realization that the campaign would undoubtedly send a stream of angry and vindictive Lipan refugees north into Texas, and he lacked adequate resources to resist them. Dashing off a letter to Croix, Cabello warned that while some Béxar residents would welcome the news of a campaign, many would be "very anxious about the harm which will befall their friends the Apaches-Lipanes, for in spite of the injuries and damages suffered at the hands of these Indians, so much affection is held for them" that he feared San Antonio residents would alert the Lipans in advance. Besides, he queried, had not the war councils of 1778 agreed that no such campaign should take place until reinforcements had arrived and the Norteño alliance was solidified?[25]

Unbeknownst to Cabello, his Spanish brethren in Coahuila and Nueva Vizcaya had in fact been scheming for some time to incite the Mescaleros and Lipans to make war against each other. Some Lipan bands had collaborated with the Spaniards in the latter's campaigns against the Mescaleros, but were shocked when Coahuila governor Juan de Ugalde joined with the Mescaleros to wage war against *them*. In a decisive late spring battle, the Spaniards inflicted heavy casualties on the Lipans, seized several hundred horses, and destroyed a number of rancherías. A month later, however, Ugalde led a force of over 150 soldiers and Lipan allies into the Bolsón de Mapimí against the Mescaleros. During a campaign that lasted over a month, Ugalde's men located and dispersed two enemy encampments, killed seven warriors, took nine prisoners, and freed a Spanish captive. A buoyant Croix crowed that with Mescalero-Lipan discord sown, "there are solid hopes that it may be increased to the point of igniting hatred between these two flocks of the Apache. And if this is completely achieved, it will mean a most happy period for these provinces."[26]

On the afternoon of August 3, 1779, a beleaguered Chief Joyoso and several other Lipans appeared at the door of his friend Luis Menchaca at the Béxar presidio. The chief recounted the disaster that had befallen his people in Coahuila at the hands of the Spaniards and Mescaleros before finally getting to the point of his visit: were the Spaniards of San Antonio against them also? Menchaca assured Joyoso that this was not the case, and led the chief to Governor Cabello for additional assurances. In a lengthy conference with the governor, Joyoso requested permission for his people to settle near the presidio for protection. Cabello gave his consent, but warned that if they caused the least bit of harm, he would declare war on them and they would not be entitled to any redress. El Joyoso agreed readily to this condition, and as a token of goodwill, promised to look into the disappearance of some mules that had vanished from the presidio a couple of days earlier. With a box of cigars and piloncillos in hand, a relieved El Joyoso departed to rejoin his people, who were encamped on the Arroyo del León, just north of the Rio Grande.[27]

Three months later, Lipan chiefs Roque, El Joyoso, Josef Chiquito, and Manteca Mucho showed up once again at the presidio, professing that they were "extremely resentful" about the Tonkawas, but had held off from attacking them as a courtesy to Governor Cabello. The Lipans were equally angry at the treachery of the Mescaleros and Gileños— their Athapaskan cousins. Relatives or not, the Lipans were gearing up to inflict some well-deserved vengeance on those two disloyal groups. They asked Cabello if they could count on his support in such an undertaking, just as the Spaniards had assisted the Mescaleros in their attacks on the Lipans in Coahuila the previous spring. The governor responded that he would consider providing assistance on two conditions: First, the Lipans had to travel to Chihuahua to obtain the blessing of Commandant-General Croix. Second, the Lipans had to name a single leader or "supreme chief" with whom the Spaniards could negotiate, and who would accept responsibility for the actions of all his people.

Having to deal with such an excess of leaders, Cabello argued, was a waste of time and "annoying [him] greatly."[28]

Cabello's two conditions left the Lipan leaders astounded. They replied that they did not dare travel to Chihuahua for fear of encountering enemies "at whose hands those making the trip might perish." According to Cabello's read of the situation, the Lipans were "not displeased" about the second condition since they had ridden away "very contented" to discuss the idea of a selecting a "supreme chief." The next day, the four Lipan leaders returned and reported that their people had agreed to accept a "supreme chief" of Cabello's choosing. This time the governor was astounded. He protested that he could not possibly choose their chief, and that they should make the selection. Furthermore, they could not make such an important decision alone, but required the consent of all the Lipans. The chiefs apparently accepted the clarification (or were probably still confused about what precisely Cabello had in mind to begin with) and were preparing to depart when two Lipan warriors rushed in with news that Comanches had attacked a Lipan encampment near the San Sabá River and had made off with four hundred horses and an unknown number of captives. Outraged, the chiefs informed Cabello that they were leaving at once to gather their people, but they would return later to take up the discussion of a "supreme chief."[29]

By 1780, a rough division was developing among the Lipans that split the various bands into two large groupings reflecting their position with respect to the Rio Grande. The bands that composed what the Spaniards termed the "Upper Lipans" (*Lipanes de Arriba*) resided in Coahuila, the Bolsón de Mapimí region of Chihuahua, and in that part of Texas west of the Pecos River. The bands of the "Lower Lipans" (*Lipanes de Abajo*) lived toward the Gulf Coast in southeast Texas and northeastern Mexico (in present-day Nuevo León and Tamaulipas) and may have possessed upwards of 2,500 people living in villages scattered along the Nueces River Valley.[30] In response to their sociocultural traditions, as well as the pressures brought to bear by their numerous enemies, it would have been common for Lipan bands from either Upper or Lower groups to wander well outside their "areas of occupation." If one were traveling through Texas in 1780, for example, it would not have been unusual to find Lipans hunting bison near the San Sabá River, visiting with Spanish officials at San Antonio, or conducting trade at various Indian villages in east Texas. One wonders how Governor Cabello could have reasonably expected such a dispersed population to select a "supreme chief" to represent their varied interests. Residing nearby, and occasionally accompanying their Lipan relatives on hunts or raids, were related Apache groups bearing names such as Faraones, Mescaleros, Natagés, Llaneros, and Lipiyanes whose precise composition and identity remain obscure.[31] As has been seen, these Apachean peoples (the Lipans and Mescaleros in particular) did not necessarily view one another as natural allies, and in fact aided the Spaniards in campaigns against each other. When circumstances arose that either enhanced or threatened their prospects for survival, the interests of family, band, and tribe (in that order) trumped any affinity they may have felt for their Athapaskan-speaking relatives.

The Lipans have a saying that what you hit with the back of your hand will cripple and die. The Comanche raids on the Lipan Apaches in 1779 and their great victory at the San Sabá in late October was, in many respects, a terrible backhanded slap. Badly crippled and discouraged, the Lipans retreated south toward the Rio Grande. Governor Cabello described the Lipans as so "terrified and demoralized" that they "dare not leave the land bounded by the *presidios* of Béxar and Rio Grande, this *presidio* of Espiritu Santo, and the disemboguement of the Rio Grande into the sea." Afraid to venture out to hunt on the bison plains they had once dominated, these "Lower Lipans" poached cattle belonging to missions or individual ranchers, or from the vast wild herds claimed by the Crown. Other Lipans lingered near the coast, hunting deer. Upon learning in early January 1780 that the Spaniards had conducted a successful campaign against their Comanche adversaries, the Lipans celebrated and asked if they might trade with the Spaniards for some of the Comanche spoils. Cabello responded to their request with insults, taunting them to go out and take the spoils themselves, "fighting them as the Spaniards do." The governor then piled on further abuse, telling them "several things concerning their cowardice to which they had nothing to say in reply."[32]

Meanwhile, a new crisis struck south Texas when a smallpox epidemic swept through the province. Weakened himself by fever, Cabello reported that at San Antonio "one does not hear or see anything day or night except the tolling of bells and the sight of burials." Lacking medicine or doctors, Spanish settlers and mission Indians succumbed to the disease in alarming numbers. The epidemic also devastated the Lipans. In desperation, parents strung together bracelets and necklaces of gourd seeds for their children to ward off the sickness. Within weeks, however, they were gathering sage to burn at their loved ones' funerals. According to Cabello, a "huge body" of Lipans encamped about twenty-five miles from the presidio were falling victim to an outbreak of both smallpox and diphtheria. Fleeing in desperation to the missions, the Lipans were "being decimated to a degree inexpressible."[33] Despite the heavy toll in human suffering, Cabello confessed to Croix that he hoped that "not a single Lipan Apache lives through it, for these Indians are pernicious—despite their apparent peacefulness and friendliness."[34] Making matters worse for the Lipans, their encampment came under attack by nearly two hundred angry Laredo residents who mistakenly blamed them for some recent Comanche horse raids. The weakened and bewildered Lipans suffered three people killed and the loss of more than fifty horses and mules.[35]

In Coahuila, meanwhile, events were unfolding that would bear important fruit for the beleaguered Lipans in Texas. In 1781, Coahuila governor Juan de Ugalde launched the first of three campaigns against Mescalero and Natagé encampments located in the Bolsón de Mapimí and in scattered mountain sanctuaries in the Big Bend region of far west Texas. Leading a force of nearly six hundred soldiers and numerous Lipan auxiliaries, Ugalde remained in the field for a year, traveling over five thousand miles and engaging the enemy on twelve different occasions. Although costly in Spanish and Apache lives, not to mention pesos and horses, Ugalde's offensive demonstrated Spanish resolve and forced the surrender of three prominent chiefs and over 130 warriors. To ensure that they would not stir up any new trouble, Commandant-General Croix had them deported to the interior. In response to this loss, the Mescaleros and Natagés approached the Lipans at some point in late 1781 or early 1782 to reconcile their two-year-old quarrel. Weakened and desperate for allies following the smallpox epidemic and the constant battering they had endured at the hands of Comanches and Norteños, the Lipans readily agreed.[36]

The Lipans' rapprochement with their western relatives was a welcome, if unexpected, opportunity. They likewise explored opportunities to make alliances with some of the east Texas tribes. Lipan leaders Josef Chiquito,

El Joyoso, and Manteca Mucho had attended a conference in 1779 with representatives of the Hasinais, Tonkawas, Eyesh, Mayeyes, and Cocos to discuss the possibility of joining forces to protect themselves against the Comanches and Spaniards. In November and December 1782, an even larger gathering convened on the Guadalupe River. Andres Courbière, a contemporary of Athanase de Mézières whom Cabello had sent to spy on the proceedings, estimated that more than four thousand Indians were present at the assembly. Included in this number were Lipan leaders Josef Chiquito, Poca Ropa, and Flacco; Mescalero chiefs El Quemado and Volante; and representatives from the Mayeyes, Karankawas, Cocos, Bidais, and Caddos. Anticipating the acquisition of arms and ammunition from the east Texas tribes, the Lipans brought along an immense herd of three thousand horses to trade. The easterners proved unwilling, however, to part with more than a few hundred guns, citing a growing scarcity of firearms because Spain and England were at war, which led to reduced supplies in Louisiana. The disappointed Lipans had additional cause for concern when the notorious Tonkawa leader, El Mocho, proposed forming a grand confederacy (with himself serving as head chief) that could field perhaps 1,500 Lipan, Mescalero, Natagé, and Tonkawa warriors. With such a force, the Tonkawa leader boasted, they could drive the Spaniards clear out of Texas.[37] The Apaches remained cautious about his scheme, however, and they departed from the Guadalupe with their disappointingly small arsenal of new firearms, and still immense herd of horses.

A month later, Lipans under the leadership of Agar (Aga?) and Zapato Sas rode into San Antonio to meet with Governor Cabello. They were returning from having gone in pursuit of four Comanches who had stolen seventy-four horses from them about thirty miles from the presidio. They had chased the horse thieves northward for seventy-five miles before overtaking them at the Pedernales River, recovering their herd and killing three of the four Comanches. They brought along the lone survivor (and the smoked flesh of his dead companions), whom they turned over to Cabello for interrogation. The prisoner confessed that his people were indeed responsible for the recent string of raids and murders committed in the area, and that the Comanches were gathering near the San Sabá to prepare for another raid on the Béxar horse herd. Rattled by this disclosure, Cabello returned the prisoner to his Lipan captors, who led him away to what was assuredly a painful and gruesome death.[38]

Alerted to the possibility of renewed Comanche attacks, Cabello sent out patrols to reconnoiter all likely approaches to the presidio, and on May 26, scouts returned to Béxar with news that the Comanches had established a large ranchería across the Guadalupe River at Arroyo Blanco, and that they had discovered a fresh trail leading toward La Bahía. The governor quickly ordered two squads of soldiers, mission Indians, and settlers to ride out to Arroyo Blanco and engage the enemy. About a dozen Lipan warriors joined them, much to the dismay of Cabello, who preferred not to incite Comanche anger further by giving the appearance that the Lipans and Spaniards were working together. The Spanish-led force of over 140 men drove the Comanches north to the Pedernales and Colorado River country, but the Comanches avoided engaging their pursuers. For the next few months, smaller details of Spanish soldiers continued a dogged but ultimately vain pursuit of scattered parties of Comanches who abandoned their encampments moments before the soldiers arrived. A frustrated Governor Cabello could only shake his head in disgust as his weary men returned to Béxar empty-handed, likening his position as governor to a helpless victim entrapped in "pure bee glue."[39]

Cabello's "pure bee glue" grew stickier yet in the spring of 1784. Lipans encamped on the Medina River were stealing horses, while officials at La Bahía complained that Lipan raiding parties were slaughtering large numbers of cattle from neighboring ranches. In May, a one-hundred-man-strong Taovaya-Wichita war party rode toward La Bahía to avenge the deaths of four of their people at the hands of the Lipans. But the Norteños also helped themselves to Spanish herds and "devoured all the cattle that came within their reach." Exacerbating matters further was the arrival of a large party of Lipans en route to a bison hunt. Encountering five Taovayas, the Lipans killed four and took one captive. Under interrogation, the prisoner confessed that Governor Cabello had written the "chiefs of the Interior telling them to come and make war on the Lipanes." Outraged at the news, a Lipan chief rode to La Bahía to complain to the captain there, while his men set out in pursuit of the other Norteños. A couple of weeks later, Chief Casaca and other Lipan leaders paid a visit at San Antonio to register their own complaints about the Spaniards' deceit. Cabello was somehow able to talk himself out of what could have been a very serious situation. "Since I am all year long made to endure these and even greater impertinences," the self-pitying Cabello noted, "I likewise know how to placate them, so they went away quite content and satisfied."[40]

Under pressure from newly appointed viceroy Bernardo de Gálvez for a breakthrough regarding Texas's Indian problems, and keenly aware that no permanent solution could be found until the Comanches had been either pacified or neutralized and the Lipans either neutralized or exterminated, Governor Cabello initiated a new diplomatic offensive. In 1784, he dispatched peace emissaries to the Norteños to reconnect with them and kindle their alliance, which had deteriorated badly since the death of Athanase de Mézières in November 1779. He also reached out to the leaders of eastern Comanche (Kotsoteka or Cuchanec) groups that roamed throughout central and northeastern Texas. These efforts coincided with those of New Mexico governor Juan Bautista de Anza, who had been laboring since the early 1780s to secure peace with the powerful western Comanche (Yamparika, Jupe, and Kotsoteka) bands that resided in the eastern half of his province. By the summer of 1785, the Spaniards in Texas had managed to reestablish a relationship with the Norteños, and with Taovaya assistance, held a meeting with twelve Comanche chiefs in late August. Following several rounds of negotiations, the Comanches indicated that they were ready at last to make peace. In late September 1785, Cabello's emissaries returned to San Antonio accompanied by three eastern Comanche chiefs, and after another series of lengthy negotiations, they signed a formal treaty of peace in October. Governor Anza, likewise, concluded a peace agreement with Ecueracapa (aka Camisa de Hierro, Comisa de Yerro, Cota de Mala) and the western Comanches five months later.[41]

The Spanish-Comanche treaty of 1785 held ominous implications for the Lipan Apaches. One provision stated that the Comanches would be the friends and enemies of all the nations that were Spain's friends and enemies, but that they would not make war without first seeking Spain's permission. The Comanches pledged further that "they would be the declared enemies of all the Apaches and Lipanes and attempt as much as previously to make war on the latter in such a way that they may be totally exterminated." Cabello promised to notify the Norteños to "unite with them and come to assist them" in such an endeavor. The agreement permitted the Comanches and Norteños to keep "all they could take" from the Lipans, with the exception of horses carrying Spanish brands. The treaty also called on the Comanches to acquire permission from the Texas governor before entering Coahuila to attack the Lipans and Mescaleros, and if they received the "go-ahead," they promised to send someone to Béxar to advise the governor of the results. The last provision dealt with the distribution of annual gifts to the Comanches, which included horses, guns, and ammunition. When combined with goods furnished by Spanish traders, Cabello intoned, the Comanches would "realize the usefulness that will result from their remaining as our friends."[42]

At around the same time that the Comanche leaders were preparing to leave, Cabello received word that Lipans encamped forty miles from the presidio had learned of the new Spanish-Comanche alliance and were scheming to intercept the Comanches on their return trip home. Over 150 warriors were apparently en route to stage an ambush. Cabello decided quickly to augment his planned escort of twenty men with twenty more from La Bahía, and detailed additional militiamen to guard the presidial horse herd. On the morning of October 18, the reinforcements from La Bahía arrived, and Cabello held a final conference with the Comanches to reaffirm all that they had agreed to do. He outfitted the three chiefs in the uniforms of Spanish captains and presented each with a baton and gorget (a plate-mail cover for the neck and shoulders). The next day, the Comanches departed from San Antonio surrounded by a Spanish escort in battle formation marching smartly to the beat of the company's drummer. In light of the sizeable Spanish escort, the Lipans decided against their planned ambush. Nonetheless, a few Lipans did shadow the Comanches after they left San Antonio, shouting insults and threats at their stolid-faced adversaries. "The Spanish governor must be sick in the head for having made peace with them," the Lipans heckled, "since the Comanches had caused the Spaniards so much harm." Growing tired of their game, the Lipans withdrew to the Nueces River, carrying away six calves from a nearby ranch.[43]

Over the course of the next couple of months (December 1785–January 1786), Governor Cabello had the opportunity to further hone his skills as a host when small groups of Comanches stopped by Béxar to visit. Cabello lavished attention on his new friends, both to honor them and to encourage an all-out effort to exterminate the Lipans. Their success, he promised, would "motivate me to love them very much, give them gifts, and send them traders to supply them with all that they needed." At an important meeting in mid-January, the governor was able to arrange a parlay between the Comanches and some visiting Taovayas, Wichitas, and Tawakonis. He made a speech about the importance of unity and, not surprisingly, of the immediate need to make war on the Lipans. The assembled leaders nodded their heads solemnly in agreement, promising to "make every effort to finish them off" by taking the fight to the Lipans' hunting grounds and rancherías.[44]

The Nations of the North made good on their bloody pledge in the spring, when a war party of about 200 Norteños and 150 Tonkawas launched an early morning attack upon a large Lipan encampment on the Colorado River. Lipan women, children, and old people fled for safety, while their outnumbered warriors fought to hold back the attackers. In a battle that raged until late afternoon, the Lipans suffered more than thirty men killed, including their two chiefs—Cuernitos and Panocha. The Norteños and Tonkawas captured two women, six hundred horses, and countless supplies. As news of the catastrophe spread to other Lower Lipan groups, the survivors and their relatives led a retreat to the Nueces River to mourn their losses. Compounding their grief was the realization that their "great comrades" (the Tonkawas) had allied with the Nations of the North.[45]

Unable to obtain peace or trade, and under attack from virtually all the major tribes in Texas, the Lipan Apaches were truly in desperate straits. Scrambling to regroup, some bands turned to the strongest surviving Lipan leader, Zapato Sas, who apparently assumed stewardship of Chief Cuernitos's and Panocha's peoples following their fatal encounter with the Norteños and Tonkawas on the Colorado River. In early June 1786, two Spaniards visited their encampment, and Zapato Sas informed them he wished to speak with Governor Cabello. During their meeting later that month, Zapato Sas (whose demeanor Cabello described as "audacious and arrogant") requested peace terms similar to those enjoyed by the Comanches. Claiming to be the "chief with the greatest reputation among the Lipanes," he proposed that if Cabello would recognize him as "Great Chief" and provide his people with traders, the Lipans would relocate wherever the governor requested them to go. Zapato Sas also promised to rein in warriors who preyed on Spanish-owned cattle and horse herds, to return stolen animals, and to punish offenders severely.[46]

Aware that the Lipans were boxed into a corner, and convinced that their submissiveness was born more out of shock and fear than from a sincere desire for peace, Cabello rejected the chief's proposal, citing four reasons for his decision. First, he could not appoint Zapato Sas head chief, because the entire Lipan nation had not participated in the decision. Second, all other Lipan leaders needed to give up their titles of "chief" and testify that they supported Zapato Sas before the Spaniards would accept him. Third, the Lipans had to demonstrate their sincerity by making restitution for any branded horses they possessed, and finally, only the commandant-general could authorize peace with the Lipans. Cabello then delivered additional bad news: the Lipans were to clear out of south Texas and relocate above the headwaters of the Frío River—in the heart of Comanche country—to await the commandant-general's decision. Angry and confused by Cabello's unwillingness to make peace, Zapato Sas retorted that the governor was "hard-headed," but that he would nonetheless comply with his request. Well aware that Cabello was sending his people into the jaws of their enemies, the Lipan chief departed from San Antonio on June 20, with a few paltry gifts, after promising to prepare his people to move north.[47]

Shortly after the Lipans' departure, Miguel Peres, a Yojuane man who served as Cabello's emissary to the Tonkawas, informed the governor that the Norteños and Tonkawas were preparing to wage a new campaign against the Lipans. He was aware of Cabello's recent meeting with Zapato Sas, and claimed to know the whereabouts of the proposed Lipan encampment at the headwaters of the Frío River. The location was, according to Peres, "quite convenient for making a great strike against them." If Cabello ordered the Tonkawas to set out immediately for the towns of the Tawakonis, Iscanis, and Flechazos, Peres continued, the combined force could head forthwith to the Lipan encampment "in order to discharge [their] responsibility." Cabello found Peres's ideas "quite attractive," and he gave permission to alert the Tonkawas. Before departing, Peres mentioned that a group of 150 Lipan men, women, and children were encamped near the Bidais, and that the Tonkawas were planning to strike this encampment first before meeting up with the Norteños for their deadly business on the Frío River. The governor vetoed this idea, however, and instructed Peres to concentrate on Zapato Sas's encampment first, as there were more Lipans concentrated at that location. Once they had finished off that troublesome group, Cabello impassively observed, it might be possible to bring about the extermination of the second group, encamped near the Bidais.[48]

Jacobo de Ugarte, commandant-general of the Western Provinces, approved whole-heartedly of Cabello's initiatives regarding the Lipans.[49] The setback that the Norteños and Tonkawas had caused the Lipans the previous spring on the Colorado River, and the "humility" that the Lipans were demonstrating in Texas afterward were, according to Ugarte, "appropriate to their perfidious and cowardly character." He ordered Cabello to continue pressuring the Lipans, "not ceasing to have the friendly Indians move against them," while at the same time ensuring that no one could supply them with guns and ammunition. He also applauded Cabello's prudent decision not to accept Zapato Sas as "Great Chief" until there was sufficient proof of his good behavior, or the Lipans had been defeated and a just peace imposed on them.[50]

Viceroy Bernardo de Gálvez also advocated an especially bellicose policy regarding the Lipans. In his *Instructions for the Governing of the Interior Provinces of New Spain,* Gálvez expressed himself "very much in favor of the special ruination of the Apaches" and insisted that "war must be waged without intermission in all of the provinces and at all times against the Apaches *who have declared it.* They must be sought out in their rancherías, because it is the only method of punishing them, and the only one by which we may be able to achieve pacification of the territories." Secondly, he urged his subordinates to use trade as a weapon by cultivating Apache dependence on alcohol and on Spanish-manufactured guns and ammunition. Finally, Gálvez urged a continuation of fostering intertribal warfare as a means of weakening all the native peoples residing on the northern frontier. "The ancient and irreconcilable hatred between the Nations of the North and the Lipan Apaches must be promoted with much skill and discretion," Don Bernardo instructed, "but without *our* taking an open part in the aggravations." Intra-Apache factions should be similarly exploited, and a wedge be driven between the Lipans and Mescaleros. The future happiness of the Provincias Internas, Gálvez concluded, required the "voluntary or forced submission of the Apaches, or in their total extermination."[51]

Although serving in his final months as governor of Texas, Domingo Cabello must have had mixed feelings about Gálvez's *Instructions.* Taking the fight to the Apaches had long been a priority, and with the

Comanches and Norteños committed to the same end, the time seemed right to punish the Lipans like never before—whether they had started the fight or not. Cabello approved of Gálvez's instructions about using friendly Indians to carry out the destruction of the Lipans, and about sowing intra-Apache rivalries—so long as the Mescaleros did not drive additional Lipan bands north into Texas. Trading alcohol and firearms to the Lipans, on the other hand, seemed downright silly, and Cabello was no doubt relieved that he would be far away at his new assignment in Cuba when the Crown started supplying those volatile commodities to the Lipan Apaches. Even more troubling was Gálvez's suggestion that the Apaches be allowed to make peace, providing they locate their people at designated "peace establishments" (*establecimientos de paz*) located near presidios. As long as the Apaches behaved themselves, the Spanish government would provide them with food and provisions.[52] Don Hugo Oconór had expressed reservations about Croix's policy that permitted peace-seeking Apaches to encamp near presidios, skeptical that the Lipans would ever submit to a sedentary existence. In what must have been one of his final letters to the commandant-general, Cabello confessed that (to him at least) "the Indian [was] an incomprehensible being." The Comanches did not fulfill their promises, and if the Spaniards waited for them to do so, "it would be with extreme slowness and without the complete extermination of these perfidious Lipanes." The main body of Lipans under the guidance of Zapato Sas, meanwhile, had decided not to relocate to the Frío River after all, and instead encamped on the Atascosa River near San Antonio. For their subsistence, Zapato Sas sent out raiding parties to harvest wild cattle that ranged nearby. Cabello considered ordering a party of visiting Comanches to "inflict a few hard blows" on some small Lipan rancherías located nearby, but he resisted the temptation, fearing that one of the chiefs might be injured or killed in the process.[53]

While Cabello would not get the satisfaction of witnessing the destruction of the Lipans through force of arms, the arrival in San Antonio of Zapato Sas and fifteen warriors on September 19 provided the governor with an opportunity to find out what his enemies were up to, and where he could find them in the future. Zapato Sas, meanwhile, wanted to know what the Spaniards had decided about his peace proposal of the previous summer, and if they were prepared to recognize him as "Supreme Chief" of the Lipans. Cabello replied that since the Lipans had not fulfilled their promises, he could neither grant peace nor accept Zapato Sas as their leader. Using Cabello's own reasoning against him, the wily Zapato Sas argued that the reason why Lipan raids persisted was that the governor refused to name him chief. The discussion at an impasse, the exasperated governor told Zapato Sas that the matter would have to await future settlement. The Lipans then made a surprise announcement that they were heading to the San Sabá region to conduct a bison hunt. Cabello could scarcely contain his glee, happy to get them as far away from San Antonio as he could. As they prepared to leave, the governor dispensed cigars and piloncillos to the members of Zapato Sas's retinue. Cabello added additional presents for the Lipan chief, including a loincloth and two knives to help dress the bison hides. Cabello assured Zapato Sas that he held "great affection for him" and that he was "very much his friend." Zapato Sas was evidently "extremely happy and grateful," since he promised Cabello "to remain as long as possible in the location where he was going to conduct the hunt." Distance, apparently, does make the heart grow fonder.[54]

The arrival of Captain Rafael Martínez Pacheco in San Antonio on November 30, 1786, officially ended Domingo Cabello's tenure as governor.[55] As luck would have it, the new governor had barely unpacked his first box before a new crisis gripped the capital. In mid-December, Lipans rode in to report that a large party of Taovayas and Wichitas was on the way to steal horses and to avenge the deaths of two Taovaya horse thieves whom Spanish soldiers had gunned down a couple of months earlier. Pacheco sounded the alarm and deployed troops to ward off the attack. By experience distrustful of the Norteños, Pacheco lavished praise and gifts upon his Lipan guests, going so far as to dip into supplies earmarked by treaty for the Comanches and Nations of the North. The Lipans even convinced the new governor that they were sincerely desirous of peace, promising to congregate at the San Antonio missions and to adopt a sedentary lifestyle. By playing upon the naïve hopes of Governor Pacheco, the Lipans won a badly needed respite and obtained desperately needed provisions for a relocation to San Antonio that never occurred.[56]

Sitting in his office in Chihuahua, Commandant-General Jacobo Ugarte fumed over the recent actions of his new governor in Texas. In the span of less than a month, Martínez Pacheco had endangered a key component of Spanish Indian policy—cultivating a close alliance with the Comanches and Norteños as a prelude to the annihilation of the Lipan Apaches. Ugarte scolded Pacheco, lambasting him for his ill-considered settlement with the Lipans. If the Norteños, moved by their anger over Spain's apparent rapprochement with the Lipans, decided to break their armistice, the responsibility would lie squarely with the governor. "You must realize," Ugarte reiterated, "that the settlement of the Lipanes in your missions will undoubtedly bring upon us the displeasure and distrust of our friends, the Comanches and the other Indians of the North, whose peace is *most important* to every province." That being the case, the commandant-general ordered Pacheco to redirect the Lipans to Coahuila, where he would allow them to settle in peace—out of the sight of the Comanches and Norteños.[57]

Commandant-General Ugarte was not the only one fuming about Pacheco's acceptance of the Lipans' olive branch. The friars laboring at the San Antonio missions were equally displeased. The addition of an untold number of Lipans, Father José Raphael Oliva wrote the governor, would severely deplete the missions' already meager supply of food. If the Spaniards allowed the Lipans admittance, furthermore, the existing mission Indians would be disconsolate. In light of the Franciscans' previous efforts to reduce the Lipans, Fr. Oliva nursed understandable misgivings about the sincerity of Lipan declarations that they were ready to accept mission life. "They hate the missions," he charged, "and neither wish to distribute themselves among them nor to live with anyone else. . . . And thus they will be everywhere, with their violent and inconstant will."[58]

Although he was a career soldier and thereby accustomed to receiving and executing orders, Raphael Pacheco was no pushover, and he defended his conduct vigorously. Employing the lessons learned over the course of his thirty years dealing with both the Spanish bureaucracy and the Apaches, and insisting that he was merely following the dictates of Viceroy Bernardo de Gálvez, the king, and God Almighty, Pacheco refuted the objections of both Ugarte and Fr. Oliva. He had given the Lipans the option of relocating to La Bahía, to the presidio Rio Grande, or to one of the five missions at San Antonio. Due to the availability of supplies at the latter facilities, the Lipans had selected San Antonio. In fact, Pacheco reported, seven Lipan chiefs had gathered their people near El Atascoso to await the move. The "first fruits of the harvest of the

Lipan-Apaches" was already in evidence, Pacheco argued unconvinc-
ingly, citing that an elderly and sick Lipan woman had requested baptism and to be buried like a Spaniard.[59]

Unimpressed with Pacheco's explanations (and perhaps irritated with the condescending tone of his subordinate's letter), Ugarte
reminded the governor that since the latter's position was "temporary
and short-termed," he should abandon the project of relocating the
Lipans to San Antonio. Ugarte also claimed to have received intelligence
that provided a troubling explanation for the seven Lipan chiefs' delay
in riding to San Antonio. According to Ugarte's sources, authorities had
sent a Spanish escort with eight-and-a-half loads of supplies to provision
the Lipans during their relocation. The Indians had received the escort,
however, "with weapons in hand," taunting the soldiers that they would
come to San Antonio only after they had been defeated in battle.[60] The
incident confirmed Ugarte's opinion that the Lipans possessed a "perfidious and ungrateful character," and provided solid justification for
pursuing the extermination policy originally intended for them. Even
so, the Spaniards would still permit the Lipans to settle in Coahuila,
but would not supply the Indians with meat and corn as Pacheco had
promised them. Instead, they would receive food and supplies through
barter or exchange only—in other words, the Lipans needed to have
currency or trade goods, or to provide some useful service such as helping the Spaniards control the Mescaleros. Ugarte ended his letter with
additional admonitions that Pacheco consult with him before striking
out on any new ventures.[61]

In June 1787, Lipan scouts accompanied Spanish troops on a campaign against Mescaleros in the Big Bend. Commander Juan de Ugalde
had received reports that a large group of Lipyianes (Lipiyanes, Llaneros)
under the command of an important chief named Pica-gande (or
Picax-Ande Ins-tinsle, Picax-ende-Ynstixle) were warring against the
Comanches. Determined to meet the Lipyiane captain, Ugalde led his
force north toward the Colorado River. On June 26, three Lipyiane messengers rode into the Spaniards' camp to inform Ugalde that Picax likewise sought a meeting, and a few weeks later, the two men met on the
lower Pecos. Deeply impressed by the fifty-year-old Lipyiane leader's
appearance and attitude, Ugalde held several lengthy conferences with
him, and they entered into a preliminary agreement for an alliance. How

Ugalde could reconcile such an accord with the Spaniards' existing relationship with the Comanches is a mystery. Promising to meet again later in the year at Santa Rosa to solemnize the alliance, Ugalde turned back south to resume his campaign against the Mescaleros.[62]

While some Lipans were serving with Ugalde in the Big Bend, others were traversing back and forth across south Texas, in a state of flux now that the Spaniards had suspended their relocation to San Antonio. In April and again in August 1787, they had suffered strong attacks at the hands of the Comanches and Norteños, and the Spaniards' refusal to assist them put the Lipans in a decidedly hostile frame of mind.[63] Unable to convince Texas officials of their peaceful intentions, some Lipans again looked west to New Mexico for sanctuary. A Lipan chief called "Strong Arm Lipan," accompanied by three women and two men, rode into Santa Fe in November 1787 requesting peace from the new governor, Fernando de la Concha. After receiving assurances that Concha would consider their request after consulting with his superiors, the Lipans set out for a second meeting with the Jicarillas. Writing to Concha a couple of months later, Commandant-General Ugarte instructed him to preserve the peace only with the Comanches, Utes, Navajos, and Jicarillas. He was to extend neither peace nor trade to the Gileños, Pharaones, Natagés, Lipyianes, or to the Lipans. Instead, the governor was to wage a continuous war against Apaches who were not at peace. Spain's Indian allies should likewise wage war against them. Thus, Ugarte surmised, the Apaches would be in a crossfire between New Mexico and the frontiers of Chihuahua and Sonora, and between Spanish arms and those of their allied tribes.[64]

On March 6, 1788, nearly nine months after their initial meeting on the Pecos, Juan de Ugalde and the Lipyiane chief Picax-Ande Ins-Tinsle formalized a peace agreement in Santa Rosa. Noted for his soldierly bearing, character, and truthfulness, Picax greeted Governor Ugalde with the following memorable remark: "There are only three great chieftains, the Great One above, you, and I. The first one is looking down on us and listening to what we say so that we shall see who is lacking in truth."[65] The Lipyianes desired an alliance against the Comanches, but this was, of course, out of the question. What the Apache leader received instead was a promise that so long as his people remained at peace with the Spaniards, the Spaniards would leave them to deal with the Comanches and other Indian enemies by themselves. If they broke the peace, however, the Spaniards would join in a war of extermination against them. On a more positive note, Ugalde agreed to halt arms sales to Comanches in the provinces under his control, and he recognized Picax-Ande Ins-Tinsle as *Capitán Grande* of the entire Apache nation. As an additional honor, the viceroy issued a decree changing the name Picax-Ande to "Manuel Picax-ande Yns-tinsle de Ugalde."[66]

Having completed the new alliance with the Lipyiane Apaches, Ugalde departed from Santa Rosa for an inspection tour of Texas. In April, he visited with Lipan leaders at a large ranchería located on the banks of the Atascosa River about thirty miles south of San Antonio. There were approximately five hundred Lipans gathered in the area, which, according to Maria Wade, accounted for about half the total number of Lipans left in Texas. Another hundred Lipans were away with Zapato Sas, who had moved his people southward following the Norteño attack on the Frío River. The Lipans did their best to dissuade Ugalde from continuing his government's unfavorable policies toward them, holding a feast in his honor and reminding him of the long—if not always perfect—relationship between the Lipans and Spaniards. It was the Comanches, they argued, who were responsible for the violence and unrest in Texas. If Ugalde would reconsider his position, the Lipans would gladly fight alongside the Spaniards, as they had done so many times in the past.[67]

While Ugalde would later profess his great love for the Lipans, and at times demonstrated a sincere admiration and respect for individual leaders, he was a friend whom the Lipans needed to keep at arm's length. "Flouting law and custom, Ugalde dealt so treacherously with the Lipans and Mescaleros," one historian has observed, that no Indian or Spaniard "dared trust him in anything."[68] After receiving word in August that Comanches had killed Picax-Ande Ins-Tinsle, the short-lived Spanish–Lipyiane Apache alliance ended. A year later, Ugalde led campaigns alongside his Comanche allies against the Mescaleros and Lipiyanes near Piedras Negras, and against Lipans and Mescaleros near the old San Sabá presidio. On Christmas Eve 1789, Ugalde augmented his force with over fifty volunteers and eleven soldiers from Béxar. Roughly two weeks later, on January 9, 1790, Ugalde together with a large contingent of Norteño, Tonkawa, and Comanche warriors surprised a big encampment of Lipans and Mescaleros on Soledad Creek (a tributary of the

Medina River) near present-day Freer, Texas. In a battle that raged for several hours, the Spaniards killed an estimated forty to sixty Apaches, including two chiefs; took several women and children captive; and seized upwards of eight hundred horses and mules. This crushing defeat at the battle of Soledad Creek, Donald Chipman has written, "broke the back of Apache resistance in Texas."[69]

A change in leadership in 1790 brought another brief respite from the extermination policy that the Spaniards had pursued for over a decade. The new viceroy, Conde de Revilla Gigedo, disagreed with his predecessor's policies, and instructed Commandant-General Ugarte to commence peace negotiations with the Apaches. In the spring of 1790, consequently, Lipan leaders Agá, Canoso, and Cabezón traveled separately to San Antonio to make peace overtures, and in August, Agá lobbied on behalf of several bands interested in improving relations with the Spaniards. For the next two years, the relationship between Lipan bands and Spaniards fluctuated as individual band leaders voiced their earnest desires for peace, while others opted to continue raiding and horse stealing. Upper Lipans, in general, favored some form of peace settlement with the Spaniards, perhaps due to their closer proximity to the Comanches. The Lower Lipans, on the other hand, opposed any plan that restricted their freedom of movement and ability to conduct raids south of the Rio Grande border. The Spaniards appeared equally uncommitted to normalizing relations, pledging to protect the Lipans from attack and to provide them with trade opportunities when they were incapable and/ or unwilling to make good on either promise. In February 1791, a Lipan captain named José Antonio met with Commandant-General Pedro de Nava (Ugarte's replacement) at San Fernando de Austria to discuss peace terms for Upper Lipan bands encamped between the Sierra de Sacramento and Sierra Blanca mountains. Once they had accomplished this, the Spaniards reasoned, the Upper Lipans could help coax their brethren to the southeast to make peace as well. In the settlement that followed, the Lipans consented to move their rancherías south of the Atascosa River, to keep their distance from presidios, to refrain from stealing livestock, and to halt their illicit trade with the coastal tribes. In return, the Spaniards promised the Lipans trade opportunities and permission to enter the towns to barter buffalo skins with the residents. The Spaniards also pledged to do what they could to keep the Norteños at bay. Because of the peace accord, F. Todd Smith writes, most of the Upper Lipans relocated their settlements south of the Atascosa River.[70]

The peace held only so long as the Spaniards were able and willing to enforce its provisions, which was sporadically at best. The Lipans proved equally willing to ignore treaty stipulations regarding their behavior. Chief Canoso, for example, not only refused to relocate his people south of the Atascosa River, but also continued trading with Akokisas for firearms and ammunition. In May 1791, Lipan chief José Limbreña and six others paid a visit to Commandant-General Nava in Santa Rosa. An argument apparently broke out between them, and the heated exchange turned violent when one of the Lipans drew his knife and stabbed Nava twice in the shoulder. In the melee that followed, Spanish soldiers stormed in and killed all seven Lipans. Sporadic raids and retaliatory strikes occurred throughout the remainder of the year, prompting Zapato Sas to lead an attack in February 1792 on the Spanish settlement of Reynosa. Spanish detachments sent out from presidio Rio Grande pursued the Lipans back across the river into Texas, killing the Lipan chief and fifteen of his warriors.[71]

But the violence did not end there. In hopes of protecting his province from Lipan attacks, Don Manuel de Escandón, the governor of Nuevo Santander, concluded a separate treaty with certain Lipan bands and gave orders allowing them to encamp outside Laredo to conduct trade, provided they remained north of the Rio Grande. Before the year was out, however, Lipan raids so terrorized settlements along that river that authorities called in additional troops from presidio Rio Grande. In southeast Texas, meanwhile, bands of Lower Lipans reportedly committed depredations near La Bahía and the new mission of Nuestra Señora del Refugio on Matagorda Bay. In the latter part of 1792, for example, Lipan warriors attacked the Karankawa neophytes, burned their huts, and even killed their dogs. The raiders pillaged the settlement, stealing the horses—and just to be ornery, absconded with a yoke and plow with which the padres had hoped to sow crops in the spring.[72]

Such behavior only strengthened the long-standing prejudices that many frontier officials nursed regarding the Lipans. Colonel Ramon Castro, Nava's assistant in the Eastern Provinces, opposed the ongoing peace negotiations with the "Lipanes." In a letter to Viceroy Gigedo in April 1792, Castro expressed his skepticism of achieving a lasting peace with people whom he characterized as deceitful, arrogant, malicious, and inherently perfidious. He warned that Lipan interest in peace negotiations was little more than a ploy to acquire intelligence about the Spaniards so that they could "attack our presidios and settlements when we are most confident in their friendship" and "perform their bloody feats and cruel damages." Since the Lipans would never willingly acquiesce to Spanish rule and remain peaceful (that would take "a miracle of God"), Castro concluded that there was no other way to deal with them but by extermination.[73]

Viceroy Gigedo, being either a realist or a humanitarian, rejected his subordinate's pleas to resurrect the old extermination policy; but not until the spring of 1793 did the Lipan bands in Texas come to peace terms with the Spaniards. In August 1792, Gigedo authorized frontier officials to make a specific peace overture to those Upper and Lower Lipans who likewise sought an end to hostilities. In many respects, the viceroy's plan mirrored the Marques de Croix's "establecimientos de paz" of a decade earlier. At a council held at Presidio del Norte in late September or early October, Spanish officials met with several Lipan leaders and presented a twelve-point draft for their consideration:

1) That all hostilities between the Lipans and the Spaniards should cease in the provinces of Nueva Vizcaya, Nuevo Mexico, Coahuila, Texas, Nuevo Reyno de Leon, and the Colonia del Nuevo Santander.

2) That both Lipans and Spaniards would release captives.

3) That the Lipans present their livestock to Spanish officials so they could be branded and thereafter identified as Lipan property.

4) That the Lipans permit Spanish soldiers to conduct periodic inspections of their livestock and give up unmarked animals.

5) That the Lipans give up to Spanish authorities for appropriate punishment all horse thieves and other individuals who violated the peace agreement.

6) That the Lipans willingly assist Spanish troops in pursuit of enemies—even if they were pursuing Lipans who had broken the peace.

7) That the Lipan captain of each settlement mark his peoples' territorial boundaries and clearly state which lands they would use for hunting and harvesting wild fruits. (According to Pedro de Nava—the commandant-general of the Eastern Provinces, the Spaniards should settle the Lipans in places where there were no mountains close by. That way, it would be easier for the Spaniards to punish them or to exterminate them should they break the peace. Settling the Lipans away from mountain refuges carried the additional benefit of enabling the Norteños and Comanches to strike them should they wander too far from their respective settlements.)

8) That the Lipans would not prey on *mesteño* (wild) cattle.

9) Should the Lipans wish to relocate their settlement, they would need to get written permission from the local presidial commander before doing so.

10) Each Lipan family that settled on presidial lands or up to four leagues (fourteen miles) away would receive two measures of corn or wheat, four small cigars, one piloncillo of sugar, half a handful of salt, and a portion of meat each week. (The Lipan captain's share would be slightly larger, as would that of families with children. Minors, incidentally, would not receive cigars!)

11) If the Lipans selected two main captains to lead them (one for the Upper Lipans and one for the Lower Lipans), the Spaniards would consider them as chiefs and allow them a degree of self-rule.

12) The Spaniards would permit Lipans, provided they remained peaceful, to enter borderland towns to conduct trade, so long as they left their weapons with the guards.[74]

In the spring of 1793, Lipan leaders Canoso, Chiquito, and Moreno met with Governor Manuel Muñoz in San Antonio and agreed to the Spaniards' peace terms. The three chiefs also consented to renounce their illicit trade with the coastal tribes, provided the Spaniards rein in the Norteños. For the next decade or so, the Lipans hunted bison west of San Antonio and then traveled to Béxar to sell the hides and to enjoy the hospitality of their Spanish customers. The Comanches and Norteños continued to be a menace, however—so much so that all three Lipan leaders moved their bands south of the Rio Grande in the late 1790s. Chiquito emerged as the principal spokesperson for these groups, who continued their hunting, gathering, and at times raiding activities along the Rio Grande frontier. Writing in 1796, Antonio Cordero reported that the Lipans were "acting in good faith" toward the Spaniards, and had "separated themselves from our enemies, not so much by reason of affection as out of respect for our weapons."[75] Three years later, Pedro de Nava also commented on the Lipans' peaceful disposition, and expressed the hope that the Comanches too might be enticed (or coerced) into accepting Spanish hegemony. For the time being, however, Nava advised his superiors to adopt a policy of salutary neglect in regards to the Comanches, pretending not to see minor violations of their 1785 peace accord and to leave matters of compliance to the chiefs.[76]

As the dawn of a new century approached, the Lipan Apaches, though battered and weakened after having endured two decades of Spanish, Comanche, and Norteño attempts to annihilate them, remained unconquered. As late as 1787, their presence around San Antonio remained so menacing that even the Comanches balked at visiting the Béxar presidio, preferring instead for the Spaniards to establish a trading post at the old San Sabá fortress.[77] That the Spaniards had singled them out for destruction gives added weight to their reputation as a fierce and indomitable people. As had been the case earlier in the eighteenth century, Spain's Indian policies always made exceptions when it came to the Lipan Apaches. While busy attempting to civilize and Hispanicize the indigenous peoples of east Texas during the first half of the century, the Spaniards carried out numerous campaigns against the Lipans. When at mid-century they sought to pacify Texas Indians by force of arms, they experimented with missions for the Lipans in south-central Texas. When in the latter decades of the century they sought to win the allegiance of Texas tribes through treaties, trade, and gifts, Spanish authorities endeavored to employ a "divide-and-conquer" strategy against the Lipans, urging the Comanches and Norteños to destroy them, while simultaneously working to seal off the Lipans' access to trade with the east Texas tribes. It should come as no surprise, therefore, that the Lipan Apaches probably felt a little like the "Ishmael of the Plains."[78] The next half century would bring new challenges and opportunities as the Spanish empire collapsed and a new Mexican Republic emerged. Such developments set the stage for the birth, shortly thereafter, of an independent Texas. In order to stay a step ahead of these developments, the Lipan Apaches would need to summon the courage and daring of people like the brave Lipan widow who slew the Comanche chief to avenge her husband's death and her people's honor.

CHAPTER FIVE

The Lipan Apaches, Mexico, and Texas, 1800–1845

∽

WHEN A TURKEY HEN was going out with her brood, she walked ahead and her chicks followed along behind in single file. A female coyote came along and asked, "How do you make those children follow you in line so nicely?" "Oh, I put a string through their necks and lead them in line that way," the turkey hen explained. Then Coyote started back home, thinking "I'll do the same thing." She thought it was very good that those children followed their mother. When she arrived home, she started to do what Turkey Hen had instructed. She put holes through the necks of her children, ran a string through them, and began to lead the pups in line. After a few steps, one dropped, then another. "Oh, you are getting sleepy already," the mother scolded. In a few minutes, she was dragging all of them, for they were all dead.[1]

☾

THE AIM OF THIS CHAPTER is to examine Lipan responses to rapidly changing political, economic, and social circumstances during a tumultuous period in Texas history. Throughout the first half of the nineteenth century, the Lipan Apaches were witnesses to, and at times active participants in, a series of intense struggles over control of their homeland. These included the Mexican Revolution and the final collapse of the Spanish empire, the emergence and demise of the short-lived Mexican empire, the creation of the Mexican Republic, the Texas Revolution and the birth of the sovereign nation of Texas, and at the end of 1845, the transformation of Texas from a sovereign nation to a new state in the United States. While Spaniards, Mexicans, Texans, and Americans sparred with one another to advance their national aims and objectives, they kept a close eye on the various Indian peoples of Texas whose allegiance was critical in determining the contest's outcome. The Lipans struggled to discern the correct path to follow and which side to support, concerned more with their immediate needs than with the long-term consequences of their actions. In some respects, the Lipan Apaches found themselves in a position similar to that of the mother coyote—under pressure to modify their behavior and traditions, to vacate their lands, and to accommodate the powerful, new, and (at times) attractive forces at work in their world. The Lipans looked to their elders for guidance, and the latter cautioned their people against straying too far from established traditions and conduct lest they become like the pitiable mother coyote, who by her disregard for customary behavior destroyed the very existence of her children.

During the first decade of the nineteenth century, Texas remained a sparsely settled territory, heavily dependent on the Spanish military for its protection and economic viability, and continually exposed to Indian depredations.[2] With the United States's acquisition of the Louisiana Territory in 1803, however, Texas resumed its historic position as an important buffer area, protecting the interior provinces of New Spain against foreign interlopers. Desperate to shore up its beleaguered northern frontier to offset Indian attacks and discourage commercial penetration from American merchants and traders, Spanish officials reinforced San Antonio with troops from northern Mexico and authorized the establishment of new settlements on the Trinity, Brazos, Colorado, San Marcos, and Guadalupe rivers.[3] Although these efforts succeeded in temporarily increasing Texas's Hispanic population (San Antonio's population was estimated at over three thousand by 1810), events were taking shape far to the south in Guanajuato that would render these labors useless as Spain faced a new challenge from within the heart of its empire.

The tenuous Spanish-Lipan peace agreements negotiated in the early

1790s, meanwhile, frayed, but did not break. Writing in 1799, Lieutenant José Maria Cortes commented that pacifying and civilizing the Apaches remained "the most important goal facing us in the Interior Provinces of New Spain" and required a "sane, deliberate, and thought-out system" of governance. But the existing Spanish policy of settling nomadic bands near presidios (at the so-called establecimientos de paz or "establishments of peace"), where they could be watched and pacified with supplies and gifts, was expensive, and settlers grumbled about having to pay extra taxes to feed and provision their longtime adversaries. Mission Indians were equally resentful. In addition to constructing buildings, irrigation systems, and toiling in the fields, they were subject to floggings and being worked in chains for leaving their villages without permission. It is little wonder then that these "friendly" Indians bristled at the Spanish double standard that provided "barbaric" Apaches with rations and the freedom to come and go as they pleased.[4]

Persistent intertribal warfare also tested the limits of Spanish-Indian relations. The Comanche-Spanish peace agreement of 1785 had always been difficult to enforce among the Kotsoteka Comanches of Texas, and Comanche-Lipan violence threatened to undo the years of diplomatic efforts invested by Spanish frontier officials. In 1801, a series of mishaps nearly ended the tenuous peace. In autumn of that year, unidentified Spaniards killed two Comanches who were en route to San Antonio, one of whom was the son of Chief Blanco, a prominent Western (Yamparica) Comanche leader. A short while later, Spaniards stood accused of killing three more Comanches near Mission San José. A much more grievous incident occurred in early 1802 when a party of Lipans attacked a Kotsoteka Comanche encampment near the Rio Grande and killed twenty-five followers of Chief Yzazat. Rumors swirled that Spanish troops from Coahuila had assisted the Lipans in the slaughter. After sending a delegation to San Antonio to register his complaints with Governor Juan Bautista Elguezabal, Yzazat dispatched a 225-man war party to pursue and exact vengeance on the Lipans. The presence of such a large contingent of enraged warriors in south Texas (and a coincident increase in horse thefts) sparked a panic among settlers, who in turn implored the governor for protection.[5]

A third episode of Lipan-Spanish violence directed against Comanches occurred in the winter of 1803. According to Chihuahua governor Fernando

Chacón, a group of soldiers from Laredo together with some Lipans had attacked a group of eastern Comanches near Chope. Corporal José Maria Nabayra, one of the participants, then sold the Lipans the ears, hair, and parts of the skin of three dead Comanches. In his report to Viceroy José de Iturrigaray, Chacón lamented that the corporal's poor judgment would only encourage Comanche unrest. "Nothing will incite them to renewed violence such as Texas is beginning to experience except seeing themselves offended without cause or motive, or helping their bitter enemies the Lipans. Nothing should be done to alienate either group."[6]

The escalating tensions between Spanish and Comanche forces in Texas coincided with the United States acquisition of the Louisiana Territory from France in May 1803. Fearing that the purchase was a pretext for an American invasion of Texas, Spanish frontier officials mobilized their available forces to repel the expected attack. In an effort to dispel intertribal enmities and gain desperately needed allies in the upcoming conflict with the United States, Governor Antonio Cordero met with Comanche and Lipan leaders, and in September 1806, they agreed to settle their differences and make peace. The following spring, Governor Cordero sponsored a formal peace council that included Lipan chiefs Canoso and Morrongo, a Comanche chief named Cordero, and the Tawakoni leader Daguariscara. Agreeing that their old feuds were not in the best interests of their respective peoples, the assembled leaders accepted the principle of tribal boundaries in order to prevent misunderstandings and possible bloodshed.

Surprisingly, the peace endured for the next two years, but Spain's feeble hold on its northern provinces witnessed new challenges that would strain its resources to the breaking point.[7]

Like a wind on smoldering embers, Spain's Indian problems gained renewed intensity following Fr. Hidalgo's September 16, 1810, "Grito de Dolores." As Spanish troops rushed south to quash the rebellion, warriors from across south Texas seized on opportunities to plunder ranches, missions, and unwary travelers along the Rio Grande frontier. So desperate was Texas governor Manuel Salcedo for military reinforcements that he entertained the idea of recruiting Lipan warriors to serve as auxiliaries.[8] Making matters worse, between 1811 and 1813, Texas was the scene of two additional episodes of rebellion against Spanish rule. Already displeased with sporadic pay and lack of equipment, men serving in locally recruited militia units in south Texas balked at leaving their families exposed to Indian attacks while they were off fighting Hidalgo's rebels in the interior. In the latter part of January 1811, Juan Bautista de las Casas, a retired militia officer and Hidalgo supporter, marshaled this growing discontent, leading a mutiny of the Béxar garrison and establishing a short-lived revolutionary government. A year-and-a-half later, José Bernardo Gutiérrez de Lara, a Hidalgo supporter from Nuevo Santander, and Augustus William Magee, an American artillery officer and West Point graduate, embarked from Louisiana on a campaign to separate Texas from Mexico. Magee, Gutiérrez, and their small force of sixty men (the so-called "Republican Army of the North") crossed the Sabine River in August and captured poorly defended Nacogdoches. Before moving on to La Bahía, they enlisted the support of Peter Samuel Davenport, a wealthy merchant and trader who had important commercial ties to several Texas Indian tribes. Davenport not only furnished the rebels with arms and ammunition, but also assisted in raising a group of volunteers from east of the Trinity River. Along with fellow filibuster Samuel Kemper, Davenport reached out to the Lipans and Tonkawas, promising trade goods in exchange for their military assistance.[9]

Initially, few Indians responded to calls from either Republicans or Royalists for support, but their caution apparently dissipated following the Republican capture of La Bahía in November. Among the three hundred or so Texas Indians who joined the invaders were Tonkawas, Lipan Apaches, and a few Tawakonis.[10] A significant Lipan leader who enlisted was Cuelgas de Castro, who would later represent his people in treaty negotiations with Mexico and the United States and serve as a scout for the military.[11] After enduring a four-month siege by nearly 1,000 Spanish forces under the command of Governor Manuel Salcedo, the rebels marched west toward the capital. On March 29, 1813, on a prairie near the confluence of Rosillo and Salado creeks nine miles southeast of San Antonio, Gutiérrez's men engaged Spanish forces under the command of Governor Salcedo and Nuevo León governor Simón de Herrera. In a brief but bloody fight, the rebels inflicted heavy casualties and captured an enormous supply of firearms, cannons, and horses. Gutiérrez permitted the Lipans and other Indian auxiliaries to count coup and keep captured weapons, and he distributed presents worth $130 for their involvement. The Battle of Rosillo resulted in the unconditional surrender of Spanish forces and the capture of San Antonio on April 1. Five days later, the victors established a republic of Texas with Gutiérrez as president, but the new nation proved short-lived. On August 18, 1813, General Joaquín de Arredondo, leading a 1,800-man Spanish army, clashed with Republican forces about twenty miles south of San Antonio at the decisive Battle of Medina. The Republican army had swelled to about 1,400 men by this time, including Tejanos, American adventurers, and perhaps as many as one hundred Lipan, Tonkawa, Tawakoni, and Taovaya auxiliaries. They were no match, however, for Arredondo's well-organized and disciplined regulars. After a furious four-hour battle involving infantry, cavalry, and artillery, the Republican army broke ranks and ran. General Arredondo later reported that the Indian allies had proved of little value to the Republicans and were among the first to flee the battlefield. In hindsight, their flight proved prescient considering that Arredondo's men caught and executed the retreating rebels, allowing fewer than one hundred to escape alive.[12]

General Arredondo remained at San Antonio for several months after the Medina battle to oversee the restoration of royal control. He dispatched hundreds of troops to Nacogdoches to clear remaining rebels from east Texas, and retributions against those deemed disloyal to the Crown were severe. Arredondo was also interested in subjugating hostile Indians—particularly those who had assisted the rebel cause. In October 1813, he sent Colonel Cayetano Quintero to Nacogdoches to punish the Lipans. Quintero's force attacked a Lipan ranchería of more than three hundred lodges, routed them, and seized most of their supplies and possessions.[13]

Yet Spain's tenuous hold on Texas continued to deteriorate in the aftermath of General Arredondo's victory at Medina. As authorities diverted money and troops away from frontier defenses to combat unrest in the interior of New Spain, the establecimientos de paz collapsed, and troop morale at presidios plummeted. Settlers fled south to escape the growing lawlessness, while inadequate provisions and pay reductions drove soldiers to conduct illegal trade with the Indians. To compound problems further, five interim governors served at San Antonio between 1813 and 1817. Not until May 1817 did a permanent replacement, Colonel Antonio María Martínez, take office. Just weeks after his arrival in Texas, Governor Martínez—the last governor in Spanish Texas—wrote his superiors in

Mexico City in a desperate plea for assistance. His troops were sick and deserting, he reported, and some were at the point of mutiny because of their families' sufferings. The plight of Spanish officials, soldiers, and settlers grew even more precarious after a Lipan Apache group led by El Cojo made a short-term truce with the Comanches. In exchange for bison-hunting privileges in Comanche country, the Lipans opened south Texas to Comanche raiders, at times serving as guides since they knew the terrain, the location of villages, and the position of Spanish troops. In October 1817, Martinez reported that Comanches, Lipans, and Tonkawas were conducting increasingly frequent raids near San Antonio. "They know we are powerless," the governor complained, "and are not afraid to carry their hostilities within the town itself." The following year, a joint Lipan-Comanche raiding party sacked the town of Refugio near the Gulf Coast, killing several settlers, slaughtering livestock, and stealing several thousand horses and mules.[14]

An additional complication for both Spaniards and the indigenous peoples of Texas was the arrival of increasing numbers of "immigrant tribes" from the southeastern United States—peoples that had either been pushed south by hostile northern tribes, or forced west by the expanding American frontier. In its ongoing efforts to both populate and protect its own northern frontier, the Spanish government had extended invitations to various tribes to settle in northeastern Texas. During the first decade of the nineteenth century, for instance, Texas governor Antonio Cordero had encouraged Kickapoos, Shawnees, Delawares, Choctaws, Chickasaws, Coushattas, and Cherokees to reside in Texas, and by 1820, there were approximately 2,000 "immigrant Indians" residing in the province.[15] Over the course of the next decade, the number swelled to nearly 10,000. Some of these immigrant groups, such as the Alabamas and the Coushattas, took advantage of the power vacuum in east Texas and established themselves as intermediaries in the trade between Texas tribes and Louisiana smugglers. Other enterprising Indian groups acquired manufactured goods from American suppliers and took them to La Bahía and San Antonio, where they exchanged them for horses and mules. Among the many customers eager to acquire these illicit goods were Spanish settlers and even presidial soldiers desperate to obtain provisions for their families. Not surprisingly, the demand for horses, mules, and cattle skyrocketed, as did the number of Indian attacks.

Well aware of the Spaniards' dire predicament, Lipans staged a raid on the remnants of the San Antonio horse herd on the morning of May 11, 1819, killing five soldiers and wounding another. A Spanish punitive campaign dispatched from San Antonio the following February failed to engage their adversaries, however, since most of the 228-man force lacked horses. By the summer of 1820, Lipan and Comanche raids and killings had become so onerous that Spanish officials managed to piece together a force of two hundred soldiers from northern Mexico, and another fifty militiamen from La Bahía, to strike back at their assailants. The Spaniards marched to the Guadalupe River, where they discovered a Lipan ranchería, and in an early morning attack, killed eight Apaches and forced the rest to withdraw, leaving behind crucial supplies of dried bison meat, ammunition, and over 250 horses.[16]

The hard-pressed Spaniards in Texas received another bit of welcome news that summer when a settler staggered up to the presidio Rio Grande after having escaped a month-long captivity among the Lipans. He reported that during his time encamped near the headwaters of the Colorado River, the Tawakonis had staged a daybreak raid on his Lipan captors. The Lipans sent out eighty-five warriors to engage the Tawakonis, while a rear guard hastily gathered up the women and children and retreated to a safer location. A short while later, the man recollected, the Lipans sent back seven men to reconnoiter the battleground and discern the fight's outcome. They returned in haste bearing terrible news: there had been a horrific fight, and nearly all their warriors were "dead on the ground." Amidst the wailing, disorder, and confusion that ensued, the settler managed to escape. He reported that the Lipans were holding at least forty other prisoners, and that other Apache encampments also possessed numerous captives, primarily children whom, he claimed, the Indians treated kindly.[17]

If indeed the great Tawakoni slaughter of the Lipans actually occurred,[18] the result would have been utterly devastating to a people whose total population numbered perhaps 800 to 1,000 people at the time, about 5 percent of the total estimated Texas Indian population of 20,000.[19]

Unable either to bury their dead or to destroy the deceased's property at the place where their deaths occurred, some Lipans shuddered at the prospect of their loved one's ghost persecuting them for their failure to do so. At night in particular, a sense of foreboding swept across the survivors' encampments, and the hoot of an owl or a raven's caw—which the Lipans associated with death—would have sent youngsters scrambling for cover.[20] The presence of so many captives, particularly children, indicates that the Lipans were seeking to replenish their numbers, although some bands may have been more interested in ransoming their captives than in keeping them. The Comanches, too, were enduring a demographic crisis following a smallpox epidemic in the winter of 1816 that may have claimed as many as 4,000 lives. To make up for the losses, the Comanches kidnapped hundreds of Tejano women and children, as well as women and children from other Indian tribes. Such actions, though born partially from demographic distress, confirmed the negative perceptions that most Spaniards held of Comanches and Lipans. At the end of 1819, Juan Antonio Padilla, secretary to the commandant-general of the eastern Provincias Internas, charged that the Lipans "unite all the vices of the Comanches with those peculiar to themselves—the quality of being very astute and daring in their hostile expeditions." Such qualities were well-known to the residents of San Antonio Béxar, who in November 1820 petitioned their leaders to dispatch a force of experienced frontier troops to follow the Comanches and Lipans until they were "exterminated or forced to an inviolable and lasting peace."[21] Such requests lacked the urgency of other pressing issues, however, as Spanish officials in Mexico City and throughout Spanish America fought to maintain their grip on a rapidly eroding empire. On August 24, 1821, Viceroy Juan de O'Donoju met with the rebel leader Augustín de Iturbide and signed the Treaty of Córdoba, signaling an end to Spain's long tenure in America and gaining Mexico its independence.

The Lipan Apaches had contributed significantly to the decline of Spanish power and control of its northern frontier. In a conflict that stretched back to Spain's first tenuous steps into central Texas in the early 1700s, the Lipans had waged a long, asymmetrical war against Spanish troops, missionaries, and settlers. Protecting an empire is expensive, and New Spain spent a fortune financing the construction of presidios and outfitting campaigns to combat Lipan raiders. Frontier officials, meanwhile, tapped the royal treasury repeatedly to provide gifts and supplies to appease Lipan chieftains, or to purchase the support of Indian allies to help them in their campaigns against the Lipans. Spanish missions,

ranches, and military fortifications lost countless horses and cattle to
Lipan rustlers, while additional expenditures went to ransom captives
held in far-off rancherías. The Lipans could also claim at least partial
responsibility for New Spain's failure to lure settlers to its northern frontier. Without settlers, there could be no towns, ranches, farms, busi-
nesses, or other signs of European-style civilization. Efforts to establish
civil settlements near presidios also came to naught, as settlers quickly
realized that their protectors were no match for well-armed, mounted
Indians who could attack without warning—and then seemingly vanish
without a trace. Thus, Spain's optimistic vision of transforming Texas
into a region of prosperous farms and ranches, and of integrating its
Spanish and Indian subjects into a burgeoning interregional trade network evaporated as the northern frontier fell prey to a host of indigenous
peoples that refused to participate in the type of transformation envisioned in distant capitals.

After signing the Treaty of Córdoba, Augustín de Iturbide traveled to
Mexico City, where on May 19, 1822, he proclaimed himself Augustín I,
emperor of Mexico. Although his reign was short-lived (lasting just over
a year), it was not without significance in regards to the Lipan Apaches.
In fact, even before Iturbide's accession to power, Mexican officials—like
their Spanish predecessors—were scrambling to piece together a coherent
strategy to deal with persistent, deep-rooted problems on the northern
frontier. The Mexican revolutionaries' Plan de Iguala, adopted in February
1821, included a provision that all inhabitants of Mexico, regardless of
race, were citizens and entitled to legal protection and equality. Emperor
Augustín later confirmed this citizenship clause, as did the state constitution of Coahuila-Texas, which broadly defined citizenship as including "all men born in the state and domiciled in any part of the territory
thereof." Nevertheless, an individual's ethnicity often determined his or
her rights as a citizen. The Spanish-Mexican population, for example,
excluded conquered Indians from voting and holding office. An inspector
from Mexico sent to the northern frontier in 1834 characterized "barbarian" nomads such as the Lipans and Comanches as part of the "extended
Mexican family," who might qualify for citizenship, but only if they
pledged allegiance to the government, adopted Catholicism, and joined
settled communities. But how were authorities in Mexico City to incorporate the various indigenous peoples into the social and political fabric

of the Mexican nation—particularly those who resided in remote areas who heretofore had resisted Hispanicization? Since no answer was forthcoming to address this dilemma, state and federal authorities continued to deal with Indians as the Spaniards had done before them, signing peace treaties with various tribes as though they were sovereign nations rather than fellow citizens. The Plan de Iguala (and the subsequent Mexican Constitution of 1824) was equally ambivalent about the critical issue of Indian land title. Indians, in the viewpoint of Mexican officials, did not possess property rights, although both the national and state governments possessed the authority to grant lands to them. The rights to lands not specifically granted, however, remained with the national government.[22]

In the weeks following independence, Mexican authorities dispatched emissaries to contact the various Texas tribes in order to alert them that a new government was in power. In November 1821, don Gaspar López, the commandant-general of the Eastern Provinces, issued a proclamation promising Texas Indians equal rights, the privileges of citizenship, a liberal system of government, and protection. The new Mexican government, the proclamation pledged, would forgive all transgressions committed in the past. In exchange, the tribes had to agree to lay down their arms, cease further raiding, restore captives, and send their leaders to Mexico City to formalize the peace. Earlier that summer, General López had sent word to José Francisco Ruíz and Vizente Tarín, former revolutionaries known to have close ties to the Lipans and the Comanches, requesting that they serve as peace commissioners to those tribes. In July, Lipan chiefs Cuelgas de Castro and Volcna Poca Ropa (Yolcha Pocarropa) visited with Mexican officials at San Fernando de Austria in northern Coahuila, and a month later, López signed a peace treaty with several Lipan leaders at Monclova. The following spring, Cuelgas de Castro and Volcna Poca Ropa, along with a seven-soldier escort, set out for Mexico City to formalize the peace. The Lipans had promised the Comanches that they would wait for them so they could go to Mexico City together and negotiate from a position of strength, but the Comanches arrived late, and the impatient Lipans set out by themselves. The party arrived in the capital in the latter part of May, soon after Iturbide's coronation as emperor. The Lipan delegation remained housed in the Colegio Apostólico de San Fernando monastery for over two months, perhaps awaiting the formation of the new regime's bureaucratic structures. On August 17, 1822, Castro and Poca Ropa signed a treaty promising to obey the laws of the Mexican empire, to state the definite limits of their territories, to release all the Tejano captives in their possession, and to provide warriors for campaigns against hostile tribes. Mexican officials, on the other hand, promised to provide the Lipans with protection against their enemies, to grant them lands along with rights to water and pasturage, to make annual gifts of gunpowder and corn, to release Lipan prisoners, and to permit Lipan bands to catch and sell wild horses.[23]

The Mexican government's diplomatic overtures to improve its relations with the Lipans and other Texas tribes complemented ongoing efforts to populate its northern frontier and regulate the burgeoning illegal trade network that was operating unchecked in various parts of the region. In the months following Mexican independence, Anglo-Americans trickled west across the still undetermined Texas-Louisiana border, and by 1823, there may have been upwards of 3,000 illegal immigrants in the province. Over the course of the next decade and a half, another 25,000 Anglo-Americans arrived. In 1821, Stephen F. Austin, acting on a Spanish land grant made to his father, Moses Austin, settled over 150 families between the Colorado and Brazos rivers.[24]

The arrival of ever-growing numbers of Americans in Texas and New Mexico ushered in a bonanza of new and expanded commercial opportunities for Indians and their Mexican and American trading partners. As early as mid-November 1821, New Mexico was trading with American merchants based in Missouri, leading to the creation of the Santa Fe Trail, the most important trading route between the United States and northern Mexico. In 1822, American and Mexican traders exchanged an estimated $15,000 worth of goods, and that amount doubled every two years—$30,000 in 1824, $60,000 in 1826, and a staggering $500,000 by 1843. Not surprisingly, this lucrative trade network lured prominent Mexican families to join in the exchange of Indian commodities—such as bison and deer hides, meat, horses, cattle, and captives—for guns, powder, bullets, alcohol, cloth, and assorted manufactured goods. Freed from the constraints imposed by the Spaniards' reluctance (and inability) to provide them with adequate supplies and firearms, Texas Indians turned northward and eastward to their new American neighbors, who offered them higher quality guns than the colonial-era antiques and Napoleonic

War surplus ordinance typically available to Mexican soldiers. Within a decade of Mexico's independence, notes Andres Resendez, a "web of local and regional economic interests increasingly tied Texas and New Mexico to the economy of the United States, thus affecting the livelihood and ultimately the loyalty of key social groups within the Hispanic, Anglo-American, and Native American communities."[25]

The scattered bands of Lipan Apaches who periodically hunted and traded in east Texas enjoyed a comparatively good relationship with the newly arrived Texans of the Austin colony. The Lipans had been active participants in the illicit trade network with Americans in Louisiana, and some had been supportive of the Magee-Gutiérrez Expedition of 1812–1813. In 1807, Dr. John Sibley, the U.S. Indian agent in the Orleans territory, had described the Lipans as "shrewd, remarkably honest" and "warmly attached to the Americans." The Lipans mingled peacefully with the Austin colony on the lower Brazos River, pleased to have found an indiscriminating trade partner with whom to conduct business and perhaps obtain assistance against the Comanches, who had intensified their captive-taking excursions in order to meet the demands of the burgeoning regional market.[26] One can find evidence of the promising relationship in a "passport" that Austin issued to Lipan captain Juan Novale, stating that Texans should consider the Lipans the "friends and brothers of the American settlers in this province." Some Lipan bands also established cordial relations with Tonkawas, and set up encampments near each other for mutual protection. On occasion, Texan militiamen aided the Lipans and Tonkawas in scrapes with Tawakonis and Kichais, while Lipans and Tonkawas reciprocated by helping the Texans ward off attacks from Comanches, Tawakonis, and Wacos. But the Texans were not always close enough (or sufficiently committed) to render assistance. In February 1827, for instance, Waco warriors joined with a large party of Comanches and overwhelmed an encampment of Lipans and Tonkawas located on the San Marcos River, killing several men and making off with hundreds of horses.[27]

In 1827, Mexican president Guadalupe Victoria appointed thirty-eight-year-old General Manuel de Mier y Terán to lead a scientific and boundary expedition into Texas.[28] Terán left Mexico City on November 10, 1827, and crossed the Rio Grande into Laredo in early February, 1828. Accompanying him on the mission were Rafael Chovell (a mineralogist),

Jean Louis Berlandier (a French-born and Swiss-educated botanist, zoologist, and artist), and José María Sánchez y Tapía (a cartographer and artist). The team spent over two weeks in Laredo, and although not particularly impressed with the town, commented favorably on the area's natural bounty—the herds of deer and wild horses in particular—which helps explain the presence of Lipan Apache bands in the area. Among them was that of Chief Cuelgas de Castro, who along with other Lipan leaders had traveled to Mexico City in 1822 to make peace. Three years later, Castro had received a lieutenant colonel's commission in the Mexican army for his assistance against the Comanches. He apparently spoke good Spanish, and during a short visit to Laredo, he promised the Mexicans that he would punish warriors who violated the five-year-old peace accord. Although the commissioners were impressed with the Lipans' physical appearance (Berlandier described the Lipans as "erect, lithe, well-proportioned, graceful in their movements," and wearing clean and well-made clothing), they remained critical of Lipan character and behavior. Sánchez believed them to be both "cruel" and "deceitful," and parroted the age-old maxim that peace was possible only after they had been totally exterminated. General Mier y Terán concurred, and suggested that the Mexican government dispatch two thousand troops to "set upon the Lipanes, Comanches, Tahuacanos, Huecos, etc. for a period of six months," and then do to them what the Americans had done with their troublesome Indians: subjugate them and send them beyond their borders. Berlandier, meanwhile, depicted the Lipans as thieves and beggars, whose visits to the garrisons were a "distinct annoyance because of their unending demands for gifts."[29]

After departing from Laredo, the Terán commission headed east, reaching the Nueces River on February 23. The men marveled at the region's plentiful resources—and commented favorably on the numerous flocks of wild turkeys and herds of deer, cattle, and horses. A week later, they rode into San Antonio. According to Sánchez, the city's 1,425 residents were hard-pressed to make ends meet. They could do no farming, because of the constant threat of Indian attack, and the garrison of Mexican troops assigned to protect them was of little use. Lacking adequate supplies and thoroughly demoralized at having to go long stretches without pay, the soldiers' chief means of subsistence was hunting wild game. Just a few years earlier, a large band of Comanches had ridden into the city, barged into houses, and helped themselves to whatever they could carry away. The commander of the Bexár garrison, José Francisco Ruíz, had served as the Mexican government's liaison with the Lipans and Comanches five years earlier, and the Terán party relied on him for information about the status of various Texas Indian tribes. According to Ruíz, the Lipans were excellent equestrians, adept at handling weapons, and "the most cruel of all the barbaric nations." They were at war with the Comanches, Tawakonis, Wacos, and Tawehash (Taovayas), and at times entered the settlements to barter and steal. They wandered about hunting bison in south Texas, and at other times entered east Texas and the Bay area with their Tonkawa allies. When time and circumstance permitted, they planted corn, watermelons, and squash along the Llano, Guadalupe, and other rivers. The Lipans were still redeemable, Ruíz maintained, and their "vagrant ways could be vastly improved" if the government granted them land to cultivate, farm implements, and protection against their enemies. If the Mexicans did not do something to help them, he warned, the Lipans would be forced to ally with the Comanches.[30]

After spending six weeks in the capitol, Terán and his men rode eastward toward Nacogdoches, battling sweltering heat, hazardous river crossings, fever, and mosquitoes. Arriving at the important commercial center in early June, they observed the entry of various bands of Hasinai Tejas, Cherokees, Kickapoos, Delawares, Alabamas, Kichais, and others to conduct trade. They also viewed with alarm the growing number of American settlers in east Texas, and the absence of any government precautions to check their advance. In his subsequent report, Terán recommended that officials in the capital take stronger measures to arrest American expansion into Texas. To that effect, he suggested strengthening the existing garrisons at San Antonio, Goliad, and Nacogdoches, and establishing new ones in east Texas. The government needed to redirect trade with Texas, meanwhile, away from the United States and toward Mexico. The subsequent Law of April 6, 1830, incorporated many of Terán's suggestions and rescinded all *empresario* contracts not yet completed.[31]

Although the Spaniards only partially and haphazardly implemented the Law of April 6, 1830, the new rules contributed mightily to the nascent revolutionary fervor that would culminate in the Texas Revolution five years later. Mexican authorities proved incapable of halting the influx of American settlers, redirecting trade southward, and were only partially successful at enhancing their military occupation of the northern frontier. Adopting a "velvet glove" rather than an "iron fist" approach to addressing the Indian problem, Mexican frontier officials hoped to pacify hostile tribes through persuasion, commerce, gift-giving, and enlisting Indian allies as auxiliaries and militiamen, rather than by military force alone. Like their Spanish predecessors, however, Mexican authorities lacked the necessary resources and efficient institutional structures to carry out an effective and coherent Indian policy. Endorsing the maxim that a "bad peace was preferable to a good war," they responded both timidly and inconsistently to renewed Indian depredations in Chihuahua, Coahuila, and in Texas during the early 1830s. From the perspective of apprehensive Texas settlers, therefore, the arrival of Mexican troops after 1830 illuminated two important—albeit paradoxical—truths that would prove salient during the ensuing five years: first, Mexico's show of strength was aimed at restricting their expansion, commerce, and liberty; second, the Mexican military was weak and incapable of protecting them against incessant Indian attacks.[32]

Details about the activities of the Lipan Apaches during the period immediately preceding the Texas Revolution are sparse. Lipan raiders were reportedly active in eastern Chihuahua and Coahuila, and together with the Tonkawas, jointly plundered settlements between the Brazos and Colorado rivers. According to historian Ralph A. Smith, Apache warriors used one of six major trails to conduct their raids into Mexico.[33] Along the way, they "slew woodcutters in forests, shot down shepherds, and cut field workers to pieces. They left travelers bristling with arrows on the roads, and settlers slumped in the doorways of their straw and stick huts, and washer women dying along the stream banks." Desperate government officials along the northern Mexican frontier responded to such behavior by hiring scalp hunters, such as the notorious "scalp lord" Santiago Kirker, to track down and kill as many Apaches as they could find.[34] North of the Rio Grande, meanwhile, a large force of Lipans engaged a party of Texans led by Jim and Rezin Bowie while the latter were en route to the old San Sabá mission. The Bowie brothers, drawn by tales nearly a century old, were apparently searching for the legendary silver mine of Los Almagres. In a vicious fight in November 1832 that lasted the better part of twelve hours, warriors under a Lipan chief named "Tres Manos" drove the invaders back south after setting fire to the grove of live oaks sheltering the Texans. Some Lipans continued serving as auxiliaries of the Mexican army. In February 1832, as many as fifty Lipan and Tonkawa scouts and trackers rode alongside Mexican troops and militiamen in an ambitious campaign to drive the Comanches out of south Texas altogether. Led by Captain Manuel Rudecindo Barragán of presidio Rio Grande, the Barragán Campaign netted meager results in several small skirmishes with the Comanches.[35]

The Lipans believe comets are an indicator or omen of serious trouble or misfortune, so when Haley's Comet flashed across the Texas sky in the closing months of 1835, Lipan elders worriedly discussed what it could mean for their people.[36] They did not have to wait long before the anticipated trouble occurred, and their homeland became embroiled in a revolution that would have profound implications for all the Indian peoples of Texas.

Befitting people who possessed no centralized leadership or hierarchy, the Lipan Apaches responded to the Texas Revolution of 1835–1836 in different ways. Bands residing along the Nueces River (Lower Lipans) nurtured important trade relationships with the Austin colony and other settlements and were sympathetic to the rebel cause, although there is little evidence that they provided significant military assistance.[37] Some bands adopted a neutral stance because they were happy with the status quo, or they were reluctant to join the "wrong" side and jeopardize the relative autonomy that they had enjoyed since the collapse of Spanish rule in the late eighteenth century. According to anthropologist Andrée F. Sjoberg, the Texas Revolution broadened the division between the Upper and Lower Lipans. The Upper Lipans, Sjoberg claims, supported the Mexican cause, while the Lower Lipans heeded the example of Chief Flacco (a close friend of Sam Houston) and supported the Texan drive for independence. The oral tradition of one Lipan band indicates that the Mexican army prevented them from approaching or participating to help the Alamo defenders, so they instead watched the destruction of the old mission and the annihilation of its outmanned defenders. In the midst of the revolution's turmoil, some Lipan warriors, inspired by the lure of plunder rather than support for a Texas republic, seized the opportunity to conduct raids along the Rio Grande. Mexican general Vicente Filisola reported in 1836 that as his brigade passed along the Arroyo Aura en route to San Antonio, they found encamped there "hordes of Lipanes numbering more than five hundred, including men, women, and children." At the time, they were at peace, noted Filisola, but they "did not hesitate to steal some mules and horses from the brigades as they went by."[38]

Sam Houston's victory over *Generalisimo* Antonio Lopez de Santa Ana at the Battle of San Jacinto in April 1836 marked the beginning of the independent Republic of Texas. A month earlier, Texas revolutionary leaders had established an ad interim government and ratified a constitution that, among other things, excluded Indians from citizenship. The issue of Indian land ownership, meanwhile, paralleled earlier Spanish precedents. The Texans regarded Indians as tenants-at-will, and did not recognize tribal land ownership—except in cases where the central government had awarded a land grant. Earlier Mexican land grants to the Shawnees and Cherokees, however, did not receive recognition from the Republic of Texas. The fledgling Texas government, consequently, walked a tightrope of sorts in its initial dealings with its Indian peoples, seeking their friendship or neutrality while at the same time withholding any promises of recognizing their claims to land. Under the first Sam Houston administration (October 1836 to December 1838) Texas adopted an Indian policy that focused on "pacification and protection." Pacification, Houston maintained, required that the government give gifts, establish well-regulated commercial relationships, and negotiate treaties of friendship. By supplying the tribes with necessary trade items and maintaining even-handed justice with them, Houston remarked in his inaugural address, "natural reason will teach them the utility of our friendship." Although a protégé of Andrew Jackson and a veteran Indian fighter, Houston believed that launching retaliatory campaigns into hostile territory usually inflamed tribal animosities rather than assuaging attacks, and making war was to be a last resort. Protection, meanwhile, required the creation of militias and erection of forts. In December 1836, Houston signed a bill authorizing the creation of a battalion of 280 mounted riflemen to guard the frontier (increased shortly thereafter to 600 men), the construction of forts and trading houses, entering into treaty negotiations with Indian tribes, and the appointment of agents to reside among them.[39]

Convinced of the need to maintain flexibility in his dealings with native peoples, Sam Houston argued that some tribes deserved the support of the government, while others merited punishment. Immigrant tribes such as the Cherokees, Shawnees, Biloxis, Kickapoos, Coushattas and Choctaws were potential allies, he argued, while Comanches, Wichitas, and Caddos were treacherous and untrustworthy. The Lipan Apaches, meanwhile, held a somewhat ambiguous designation. In an unusual government report presented on October 12, 1837, the Committee on Indian Affairs recommended that the Tonkawas, Karankawas, and Lipans residing below the Nueces River be considered "as part of the Mexican nation and no longer considered as a different people from that nation."[40] Consequently, they had few if any legitimate claims to land. Congress apparently opted not to adopt the recommendation (or if legislators did adopt it, they promptly ignored its provisions), since a month later, on November 22, 1837, the Republic of Texas concluded a treaty of peace with the Tonkawas. Shortly thereafter, James Power, a former empresario and signer of the Texas Declaration of Independence, met with Lipan chief Cuelgas de Castro at Live Oak Point (near Aransas City) and negotiated a "treaty of peace and perpetual friendship between the Republic of Texas and the Lipan Tribe of Indians." In addition to peace and friendship, Texas promised the Lipans protection (so long as they remained peaceable and refrained from disturbing settlers) and trade opportunities. Chief Castro received $250 worth of gifts for his people, and in return, he promised to restore stolen livestock. The Lipans also promised to deliver lawbreakers to the proper authorities for punishment, and were to report violations committed by Texas citizens to the president so that he could ensure that Texas administered justice on the Lipans' behalf. On January 8, 1838, Chief Castro placed his mark on the Treaty of Live Oak Point, an agreement that most Lipans would adhere to faithfully until the U.S. annexation of Texas in December 1845.[41]

A significant fringe benefit for Lipan leaders maintaining peaceful relations with the Republic of Texas was the right to visit the capital city and enjoy the hospitality of government officials. Such demonstrations of generosity toward visitors, and the recognition that each party in an alliance held reciprocal obligations, were important traditions in virtually all Indian cultures, and Texas officials soon learned that the Lipans intended to perpetuate these traditions. In early March 1838, Chief Castro and ten of his captains rode into Houston to visit their new friends. The Texans did not disappoint them. Vice President Mirabeau B. Lamar, who nursed long-standing animosities toward Native Americans, nonetheless greeted the Lipan delegation warmly, referring to Chief Castro as "General," and "the enlightened chief of a powerful nation." After gently reminding his Indian guests of their duties and responsibilities (i.e., abstaining from all hostilities and violence), Lamar and other Texas officials showered the Lipans with gifts—including blankets, bead purses, bolts of cloth, jewelry, rifles, and snuff boxes—and serving them several sumptuous meals followed by cigars, whiskey, and brandy. The Texans also presented Castro with two cloth cloaks, nine blue frock coats, and three pairs of cashmere and satin pants. The chief had an opportunity to show off one of his new outfits at a ball held in his honor. According to one participant, Castro complimented the ladies, the recently deceased Erastus "Deaf" Smith, and General (George) Washington very handsomely, and bragged that he would "go any place Deaf Smith would go alone." Some Lipans reportedly responded with gusto to a speech that berated the Mexican government with shouts of "Muerte a los Mejicanos!" Texas secretary of state Robert A. Irion described Cuelgas de Castro as a "sagacious, shrewd and intelligent Indian" who was familiar with Mexican politics and apparently nursed a hatred of the Mexican people. From Castro, Irion also learned that the Lipans were warring against the Comanches, and would not conclude peace with them until the Comanches had come to terms with the Texans.[42]

Mirabeau B. Lamar's election as president in November 1838, with David G. Burnet as vice-president, signaled a significant departure from Houston's efforts at pacification and protection. Lamar was a native of Georgia and had joined that state's efforts to expel the Creeks in the 1820s. Like Andrew Jackson, who had recently completed his second term as president of the United States, Lamar rejected the notion of tribal sovereignty and insisted that the Indians remain subject to state laws. In his first message to the Congress of the Republic of Texas, Lamar made his position concerning Indians perfectly clear. He considered Houston's pacification policy a failure, and advocated instead a policy of retaliation and the prosecution of a war of extermination or expulsion against hostile tribes. To that effect, he called for the establishment of a line of military posts along the frontier to protect settlers, and the organization of a regular, permanent, and efficient armed force. Government officials could then call on that force to remove tribes that (in their opinion) possessed no rightful claim to reside in Texas. Native Americans who had signed treaties of peace and could establish a claim could remain—subject to their compliance with Texas laws. Like Houston, Lamar understood the necessity of regulating trade with the Indians, and he requested that agents be appointed to live among the Indians to conduct a "vigilant espionage," cultivate friendly relations, and prevent "all causes of interruption and collision between the Indians and our people." For those tribes that refused cooperation, Lamar warned that Texas would wage campaigns "without mitigation or compassion, until they had been made to feel that flight from our borders, without the hope of return, is preferable to the scourges of war."[43]

Lamar did not have to wait long to implement his policy of retaliation. In December 1838, the Texas Congress sent him a bill calling for the creation of a regiment of 840 men to protect the northern and western frontier. While the president assembled these instruments of coercion, a long-brewing crisis erupted in May 1839, when Cherokees under the leadership of Chief Duwali, angry over the government's refusal to recognize their territorial claims, threatened to go to war over the construction of a fort on the Saline River.[44] President Lamar responded to the crisis by dispatching a three-man delegation to persuade the Cherokees and all other immigrant tribes to remove from Texas peacefully. Should that effort fail, he issued orders that military officials remove them by force. When the commissioners reported on July 15 that discussions with the Cherokees had broken down, the army began its march. In sporadic fighting that lasted two days, the soldiers battled several hundred Cherokees, Shawnees, Kickapoos, and Delaware warriors armed with guns and with bows and arrows. Despite possessing superior numbers, the Indians retreated, leaving more than one hundred dead, including the principal Cherokee chief—the Bowl. Their territory devastated and their farms and cabins burned to the ground, the Cherokees fled north into Indian Territory, while a few escaped south to Mexico. According to David LaVere, by 1840, only a few isolated families of Choctaws, Chickasaws, Shawnees, Kickapoos, and Delawares remained in east or central Texas, since most immigrant Indians, at least as unified nations, had vacated the country.[45]

The Lipan Apaches, having made peace with the Republic of Texas in January 1838, enjoyed relatively good relations with the Lamar administration, and sided with the Texans in several of their military campaigns against tribes intent on preserving their land and way of life. Indian agent Joseph Baker, writing in January 1839, reported that the Lipans had not "committed a single act of hostility since the treaty was made," and that they were encamped east of the Guadalupe River hunting buffalo and laying up provisions. Baker opined that Lipans and Tonkawas were eager to go on expeditions against the Comanches whenever a small force of whites would accompany them. Verne Ray asserts that the Lipans' close friendship with Sam Houston played an important role in their decision to help the Texans, as did the opportunities that campaigns offered to take booty and weaken various tribal foes such as the Comanches. Having spent decades fighting the Spaniards, Comanches, and Norteños, the Lipans may have also determined that allying with the Texans was simply the best mode of protecting their interests, and ensuring that they preserved their access to firearms, powder, ammunition, and other crucial supplies.[46]

For a variety of reasons, therefore, the Lipans served as scouts and auxiliaries for Texas frontier troops. In late December 1839, for example, General Edward Burleson employed Lipan and Tonkawa scouts in a successful campaign against Cherokee holdouts at the Battle of Pecan Bayou. The Texans dispersed the Cherokee encampment, seized over twenty captives, and killed Chief Bowl's son John and another chief known as the Egg.[47] The Lipans also served in several expeditions against the Comanches. Angry that their May 1838 treaty did not delineate a clear boundary line between their lands and those claimed by Texas, the Comanches continued to harass the settlements, stealing livestock, taking captives, and killing settlers. General Burleson responded to such hostilities that fall by calling out the militia to conduct raids on the Comanches.[48] In the winter of 1839, Colonel John H. Moore led three companies of volunteers and a contingent of Lipans under Chief Castro on a campaign of chastisement against Comanches under the leadership of Chief Maguara (Muk-wah-ruh). In early January, Lipan hunters discovered a Comanche winter encampment about fifty miles northwest of present-day Austin. Too few in number to attack the Comanches, the Lipans reported what they had seen to Texas authorities. Certain that the Comanches would soon attack white settlements, the men of Bastrop and La Grange organized a campaign to attack the Comanches before they moved elsewhere. John H. Moore, a Texas Revolutionary

War veteran and founder of La Grange, assumed command of the expedition. The Moore expedition set out on January 26, and after enduring a miserable three-day winter storm, continued their march toward the Colorado River. On February 11, Lipan scouts led the Texans to Maguara's large encampment between the Colorado and Concho rivers, and Moore called for an early-morning attack the next day.[49] The Texans tasked eight of Castro's warriors with stampeding the Comanches' horse herd, while the remaining Lipans accompanied Moore's men on an assault of the encampment. In the melee that followed, the Texans killed between thirty to forty Comanches and wounded fifty to sixty more before Indian reinforcements compelled Moore to retreat.[50] According to participant Noah Smithwick, one wounded Comanche warrior lay on his back shooting arrows straight up so they would come down on the Texans. A young warrior named Flacco—the son of Chief Flacco—killed the Comanche with a lance and captured his shield. As the Comanches regrouped, however, the Texans quickly found themselves on the defensive, and half the attackers lost their mounts and had to walk home. Castro, meanwhile, rode away with over ninety horses and mules, perhaps assuaging his disappointment at not achieving total success over his hated enemies. He and his men later received payment of $1,140 from the Texas government for services rendered in the Moore campaign.[51]

Approximately a year following Moore's winter campaign, three eastern Comanches rode into Houston with a message for Texas government officials. Driven by Cheyenne and Arapaho attacks along the northern boundary of their territory, with losses suffered in several smallpox epidemics and the numerous military campaigns waged against them, the Comanches had decided to make peace. As a demonstration of their good faith, they promised to return all stolen property and liberate their captives. Remaining suspicious of Comanche sincerity, Texas officials nonetheless scheduled a conference in San Antonio to formalize the peace. On March 19, 1840, a party of over sixty Comanches arrived at San Antonio, led by the prominent chief Muguara. Accompanying them were several Mexican children and one sixteen-year-old white girl named Matilda Lockhart, who claimed that her captors had abused her, and that the Comanches were still holding other captives. When the Texas commissioners demanded the release of all the captives, Muguara responded that the particular Comanche bands holding them were

A lithograph, after a drawing by Arthur Schott, of a mounted Lipan warrior. *Dated between 1854–1857. UTSA's Institute of Texan Cultures, no. 070–0142. Courtesy of U.S. Dept. of the Interior Boundary Survey Report / 1857–1859.*

beyond his authority. Disappointed, but having prepared for such a contingency, Texas officials ordered awaiting troops to seize the Comanche delegates and hold them hostage pending the release of the remaining captives. During the ensuing "Council House Fight," the troops killed over thirty Comanche warriors and five women and children. The Texans also seized twenty-seven prisoners, the Indians' horses, and a large quantity of bison robes before permitting one of the female hostages to ride back to her people to arrange a prisoner exchange.[52]

The Council House Fight outraged the Comanches, who considered ambassadors immune from acts of war. Led by Chief Potsanaquahip (Buffalo Hump), the Comanches retaliated by attacking deep into Texas during the summer of 1840. Daniel W. Smith, the U.S. consul at Matamoros, reported in May that Comanche raiders operating north of the Rio Grande had taken several captives, along with some horses and mules. In early August, hundreds of Comanche warriors attacked southward along the Guadalupe River valley, focusing their wrath on the towns of Victoria and Linnville. In what became the largest of all southern Comanche raids, the Comanches seized hundreds of horses and thousands of dollars' worth of supplies, and took a number of captives. After a week of such activities, and with their vengeance spent, the Comanches rode back north, leaving over twenty people dead.[53]

Following closely on the heels of the retreating Comanches was a hastily assembled army of Texas volunteers. On August 11 and 12, 1840, they engaged the Indians near Plum Creek, inflicting over eighty enemy casualties and forcing the Comanches to move north toward the Colorado River. Texas authorities organized a second campaign in October under the leadership of John H. Moore. The second Moore expedition consisted of approximately one hundred Texas volunteers and many of the same Lipans who had participated in the winter campaign of 1839 (e.g., Castro and Flacco the Younger). After a long pursuit up the Colorado River, Lipan scouts located the Comanches' encampment at the river's Red Fork—about three hundred miles northwest of Austin. In a brief battle that took place on October 24, 1840, Moore's men routed the Comanches, killing 140 and capturing 34. According to Gary Clayton Anderson, the actual number of fatalities may have been twice that high, since many Comanches perished in the cold waters of the Colorado as they attempted to swim to safety. The Rangers burned everything in the camp, including tipis and food. They recovered as many as five hundred horses, pelts, and some of the remaining plunder from the Linnville raid, which they divided among themselves. The Texans' remarkable success at the so-called "Battle of the Comanche Village" (Moore's force took only two casualties) apparently stimulated a series of new campaigns directed against the Comanches later that spring, as Ranger companies rode out in pursuit of glory and plunder.[54]

The Lipans also aided Texas in its efforts to stave off sporadic incursions emanating from Mexico, which still refused to recognize the independence of its former province. Throughout much of 1841, a force of fifty Lipan warriors led by young Flacco served as a "Corps of Observation" for Texans, reporting on the movement of Mexican troops within the disputed border area.[55] In February 1842, General Rafael Vasquez led a Mexican army of several hundred mounted troops across the Rio Grande above Laredo, and by the first week in March, the Mexican force had entered San Antonio. Meanwhile, a second column of Mexican soldiers took control of the towns of Goliad and Refugio. When a party of Lipans rode into the latter city on the evening of March 6, the Mexicans attacked them, killed four warriors (including the nephew of Chief Castro), and seized the Lipans' horses and weapons. Three days later, a large contingent of Lipan, Mescalero, and Karankawa warriors retaliated by attacking a Mexican encampment below the Nueces River. The war party left fifteen Mexican casualties and seized several horses and cattle.[56]

John Coffee Hays, the legendary Texas Ranger, frequently employed Lipans as auxiliaries in campaigns against Comanche and Mexican raiders, and developed a close relationship with young Flacco. In a display of gratitude for his friendship and assistance, Texas government officials presented Flacco with a colonel's uniform, complete with a plumed hat and sword. A contemporary described him as "brave and unswerving in his fidelity to the whites, his many services had likewise won him friendship of all who knew him." A tragic incident in the fall of 1842, however, deprived the Texans of this important ally and led to a significant development among the Lipan Apaches. In October 1842, in retaliation for the Mexican army's persistent raids on Texas, President Houston (who had been reelected to office a year earlier) ordered General Alexander Somervell to organize an army to invade Mexico. A few Lipans volunteered for scouting duty, and Flacco was one of them. The Somervell expedition departed from San Antonio in November, and within a month had recaptured Laredo from the Mexicans. At this point, however, Somervell's army of volunteers, perhaps weary after spending weeks in the field, or disappointed at the meager plunder, began to pack their gear and ride home. Flacco and a Lipan associate also took their leave at this time, apparently content with the fifty horses they had stolen from ranches around Laredo. As they approached the Medina River, Flacco's companion became ill, and the two stopped to rest until his condition improved. That night, two Texans attacked and murdered the Lipans and stole their horses. Law-enforcement officials discovered the identity of the murderers several days later when they apprehended the cutthroats in Seguin, still in possession of Flacco's horses and blankets.[57]

Texas officials were both stunned and horrified when they discovered the bodies of the Lipan scouts, for such treacherous treatment of the son of an important tribal chief was no trivial affair. How would Chief Flacco's people respond? Fearing that the incident could spark a renewal of Lipan warfare, the Houston administration concocted a story that Mexican bandits had ambushed and murdered the two men.[58] Noah Smithwick, who delivered the tragic news to Chief Flacco, later recounted that the old chief sobbed upon receiving the report, gave away all his son's possessions, and began a lengthy fast.[59] In March 1843, Flacco wrote to President Houston requesting additional details about his son's death—an odd petition, considering the customary Lipan practice of never referring to the deceased. Since he shared his son's name, however, he also asked that the president refer to him as "Señor Yawney," since he no longer desired to hear the name "Flacco." Houston responded with a moving eulogy, extolling young Flacco's many virtues and promising that the Texans would not forget him. Just as "Flacco was a friend to his white brothers," Houston wrote, so too should his fellow Lipans "walk in the white path." Ending his tribute with a pledge to "hold my red brothers by the hand," Houston sent the letter along with several plugs of tobacco for the chief and some shawls for his wife. Flacco never got over his son's death, and suspected that Houston was not telling him the entire truth about what had happened on the Medina River—which helps explain his previously mentioned break with tradition. The incident soured his band's relationship with the Texans, so much so that he moved his people south into Mexico in 1843. This left Chief Castro's people as the largest remaining

Lipan group in Texas. His death in late 1842 or early 1843 removed another important moderating influence, although his son Juan Castro pledged to continue following his father's path of peace. Thomas Schilz writes that some of Castro's band took up residence with Tonkawas under the leadership of a chief named Placido, while others joined a smaller band of Lipans residing further west, led by Sandia.[60]

Even as the Lipan dispersal was taking place, the Houston administration was reaching out to Texas Indians in a continued effort to bring peace to the frontier and to undo Mirabeau Lamar's expensive, and ineffective, policy of extermination. The president dispatched licensed traders to contact disaffected tribes, and labored to rein in the aggressive Ranger units that, he believed, were responsible for exacerbating tensions. Peace commissioners contacted the various tribes, and in late March 1843, a council took place a few miles west of the Torrey Brothers' trading post—a series of log houses overlooking Tehuacana Creek (Tawakoni Creek, Tah-wah-karro Creek) southeast of present-day Waco. Houston's old friend and newly appointed commissioner of Indian affairs George W. Terrell headed the Texas delegation. Others in attendance included Pierce M. Butler—the former governor of South Carolina and U.S. Indian agent in the Indian Territory—and representatives from the Delawares, Caddos, Wacos, Shawnees, Ionies, Anadarkos, Tawakonis, Wichitas, and Kichais. On March 31, the conferees signed an agreement promising to cease hostilities and to attend a Grand Council to negotiate a permanent treaty of peace and friendship between the Republic of Texas and all the Indians residing within or near its borders.[61]

Houston's Indian policy again emphasized the necessity of establishing a well-regulated system of trade with the Indians. To accomplish this objective, he proposed establishing a line of demarcation running from the Red River southwest to the Rio Grande, separating the Indians from the settlements. Next, he called on Congress to fund the establishment of trading houses along the line to promote commerce and friendly intercourse. In January 1843, Congress passed legislation that specified the locations of the trading houses and centralized the administration of Indian affairs in an Indian Bureau attached to the War Department. President Houston also received authorization to appoint four Indian agents and a superintendent of Indian Affairs to oversee their conduct.[62]

While the Houston administration labored to formulate and lay the necessary groundwork for its Indian policy, it worked simultaneously to earn the trust and cooperation of Texas tribes. In late September 1843, Texas commissioners met again with delegates from the Delawares, Caddos, Wacos, and others at a council that took place at Bird's Fort, located on the Trinity River about twenty miles west of Dallas.[63] The few Waco, Caddo, and Wichita leaders who showed up made the habitual promises of peace and friendship, agreed to accept government-appointed agents to serve as their official liaisons, and also agreed to purchase goods only from licensed traders. The agents and traders were to see to it that the Indians purchased no alcohol or firearms, although the government promised to lift the ban on guns and ammunition once the tribes had demonstrated their compliance with the treaty's other provisions. Articles 11 and 15 called for the strict observance of the demarcation line, and chiefs and captains were charged with the task of ensuring that their people did not cross it "for any purpose whatsoever without authority and a passport from an agent." These two articles did not make it into the final treaty document, however, since it was useless to conduct a debate about the line without the Comanches present. The Indian signatories accepted responsibility for the conduct of their warriors and promised to "compel them to keep the peace and walk in the path made straight between the white and red brothers."[64]

The Texas Senate ratified the Treaty of Bird's Fort on January 31, 1844, and President Houston signed the accord a few days later. The vote provided a degree of legitimacy to Houston's peace policy, although the president had failed to reveal the Comanches' boycott. Over the course of the next several months, commissioners endeavored to entice the Comanches and Kiowas to place their marks on a similar agreement. Later that fall, Indian delegations converged at Tehuacana Creek, and by the end of September an estimated one thousand participants had gathered there. Sam Houston addressed the colorful assembly, mixing remorse for his predecessor's aggressive policies with appeals for peace in the future. A few months earlier, Robert Neighbors had visited a band of Lipans encamped along Boregas Creek south of San Antonio, and they had promised to attend. The Lipan delegation, which included Ramon Castro and Captain Chico, arrived late, but the two men signed the treaty document on October 9. Other signatories included delegates from most of the tribes present at the Bird's Fort council, with the notable additions of Comanche leaders Potsanaquahip (Buffalo Hump), Mopechucope (Old Owl), and Chomopardua. Secretary of war George W. Hill and attorney general George W. Terrell (the former Indian commissioner) also participated in the deliberations, further magnifying the council's significance. When the Texans submitted their ideas about a boundary line to separate the Texas tribes from the settlements, the Comanches insisted that the Texans push the line eastward—so much so that even Austin fell on the Comanche side of the line. As a result, the October 9 Treaty of Tehuacana Creek also omitted from the final draft those articles dealing with the boundary line. Participants agreed to hold a general council each year to discuss various issues, iron out any misunderstandings, and distribute presents from the government.[65]

From the perspective of Thomas G. Western, the superintendent of Indian Affairs, the Treaty of Tehuacana Creek signaled a bright new beginning for the peoples of Texas, since the Indians were "finding it advantageous to cultivate the peace and friendship of the Republic."[66] From the perspective of the Lipan Apaches, however, the "advantages" they had acquired by signing peace agreements and assisting Texans in campaigns against hostile tribes seemed fleeting at best. In fact, one can argue that the Lipans' overall condition (population, security, and self-sufficiency) deteriorated during the era of the Texas Republic. Possessing an estimated population of around eight hundred to one thousand people in 1836, Lipan numbers in Texas fell rapidly in the ensuing decade. Intertribal warfare and Flacco's migration to Mexico explain only part of the decline. In the late summer of 1843, epidemic disease broke out among the Lipans and Tonkawas, killing thirteen people in a single two-day period in October. According to one estimate, the sickness affected men more than women, and nearly 20 percent of the Lipan and Tonkawa warriors died. By 1849, therefore, the Lipan population in Texas had dipped to just five hundred.[67]

Lipan security and self-sufficiency also eroded in the late 1830s and 1840s. Treaties signed with the Texans ignored Lipan territorial claims, limited their freedom of movement, and called for the strict regulation of their commerce. Access to firearms and ammunition—critical to the Lipans' hunting economy, self-defense, and raiding activities—was now subject to the oversight of Texas authorities. Meanwhile, settlers who had once welcomed Lipan assistance against invasions from hostile tribes and from Mexico began a steady clamor for Lipan removal. As early as November 1838, the citizens of Bastrop (located about thirty miles southeast of Austin) raised a company of militia to evict Tonkawas and Lipans encamped on the Colorado River. Although the Indians had not committed any depredations, Bastrop residents were, in the words of one leading citizen, "generally . . . not satisfied to have them in too close proximity."[68] Comanche and Tawakoni depredations on Lipan encampments, meanwhile, continued unabated during the period, spurred on by the presence of Lipan scouts leading Texas militiamen on campaigns directed against them.

Additional—albeit tenuous—indications of distress among the Texas Lipans in the 1840s were their broad dispersion into subunits (or band fragments) and their constant motion—activities generally associated with difficulties finding food (particularly during winter months) or flight from enemies. Such responses to adversity were in keeping with earlier traditions, however, and may not have indicated an especially acute period of crisis. That being said, the Texans' perceptions of Lipan weakness and vulnerability help explain a special provision not included in the treaty document signed at the Tehuacana Creek council—that the Lipans and Tonkawas were to be segregated from other Texas tribes and permitted to reside east of the demarcation line. The explanation lawmakers gave for this special consideration appears to have been to prevent hostile tribes from attacking them.[69] A review of frontier correspondence for the years 1844 and 1845 suggests that the Lipans remaining in Texas were strewn widely across the southern portion of the republic, and that they were constantly on the move. In March 1844, for example, some Lipans were encamped near Goliad, while the majority seem to have been residing along the Rio Grande.[70] Three months later, residents reported Lipans near Corpus Christi, and on the Atascosa River fifty miles south of San Antonio.[71] At year's end, Indian agent Cambridge Green wrote that Tonkawas and Lipans were engaged in criminal activity near Bastrop,[72] while in February 1845, Texas officials reported Lipans residing on the Bosque River near Waco, and along Cibolo Creek near the crossing of the La Bahía Road.[73] While some of these accounts may have been cases of mistaken identity, when taken as a whole, they show that bands of Lipans were encamped along a southwesterly line on the

outer fringe of the advancing Anglo-American settlements.[74] They maintained a nomadic existence, depended on hunting and raiding for their
livelihood, and responded to threats (e.g., food scarcity or enemies) by
dispersing into multiple subunits based on extended families.[75] When
placed within the context of the mid-1840s and their segregation from
other Texas tribes, however, the Lipans' broad dispersal and frequent
relocation could have been an indicator of abnormal distress that would
grow even more acute in the final year of the Texas Republic.

This new source of distress was the alarming decision by Texas
authorities to remove the Lipans from their protective sanctuary near
the settlements and to place them instead on Comanche lands—in effect
placing a lamb in the lion's den. What caused the Texans to reconsider
segregation of the Lipans and Tonkawas from other Texas tribes merits
consideration. One explanation was the desire of settlers to have them
evicted. The citizens of Bastrop, as noted earlier, were particularly keen
on having the Indians removed from their midst, and in February
1845, Superintendent Western instructed Robert Neighbors to forbid
the Lipans and Tonkawas from entering the settlements without a pass
and to relocate the Tonkawas further west "as fast as practicable." That
summer, Lipans stood accused of stealing horses near Victoria, of killing an eighteen-year-old youth named James H. Kenney near Corpus
Christi, and of slaughtering cattle in Béxar County. According to one
local report, the Lipans "waylaid all western roads and murdered numerous travelers, and sometimes entered the settlements to plunder and
massacre families."[76]

Besides the recurring petitions from settlers for Lipan and Tonkawa
removal, the Comanches demanded that the Lipans relocate their
encampments away from the settlements. At one of the periodic councils held at Tehuacana Creek in the fall of 1845, the Comanche chief
Mopechucope had made it clear that "the great cause of difficulty between
his people and the whites was the Lipan tribe of Indians." Envious and
resentful that their historic foes were allowed to reside in south Texas
and conduct trade at San Antonio and with Mexican communities
south of the Rio Grande, Mopechucope insisted that the Lipans "must
be altogether removed from the white settlements." Texas commissioner
Colonel Leonard G. Williams concurred, promising to consult with
Superintendent Western to have the Lipans expelled. In late September

1845, at the conclusion of a conference that included Lipan leaders Ramón Castro, Chiquito, and Chico, commissioners advised President Anson Jones that the Lipans and Tonkawas had given their consent to the move. Within a matter of weeks, secretary of war William G. Cooke reported that the Lipans had indeed moved from the San Antonio River to the San Gabriel River, located about 150 miles to the north.[77] For the time being, the Lipans would reside under the watchful eyes of the Comanches.

For a people who placed strong emphasis on steady adherence to established traditions and the examples of culture heroes from the distant past, the first half of the nineteenth century must have seemed particularly chaotic to the Lipan Apaches. Although an incredibly adaptive and resilient people, their tenuous status as subjects of a distant Spanish king, as citizens in a Mexican Empire and a Mexican Republic, and as tenants-at-will in the Republic of Texas probably turned some of them inward. For the elders, at least, embracing their identity as "Lipan Apaches" was the only enduring foundation in a rapidly changing world. Since each of the nations that claimed to rule over them was weak, overburdened, and simply incapable of imposing their will, little progress (or effort for that matter) was made to integrate the Lipans into the social, political, and economic institutions these societies were endeavoring to create. Consequently, the Lipans' precarious existence remained similar to what it had been over a century earlier when the Spaniards first ventured north of the Rio Grande. So long as weak and numerically deficient challengers were all they had to fend against, the Lipans' tenure in Texas seemed relatively secure. But the United States' annexation of Texas in December 1845, and its acquisition of lands stretching to the Pacific Ocean in 1848, brought new and heretofore unknown pressures on the Lipans. When coupled with the northerly advance of Mexico's population and the emergence of additional Indian enemies at home, the Lipans' greatest challenges, as events will show, still lay ahead of them.

CHAPTER SIX

The Lipan Apaches
and the United States, 1845–1905

One moonlit evening, two Lipans raided a Kickapoo horse herd and captured over a dozen fine horses. When the Kickapoos realized what had happened, they sent a large war party in pursuit, and after tracking the Lipans for a few days, caught up with them at their encampment. A bloody fight ensued, and both groups lost important leaders. The daughter of one of the slain Kickapoo chiefs was heartbroken, and her crying became so unbearable to her people that they organized a second war party to seek revenge on the Lipans. The Kickapoos set out and discovered the Lipan ranchería by a stream under some pecan trees, and they quietly prepared for an attack. Initially oblivious to the danger lurking nearby, several Lipan men were playing hoop and pole while spectators reclined in the shade. One of them noticed the advancing Kickapoos, however, and sounded the alarm. In a flash, the Kickapoos swarmed through the encampment killing men, women, and children. A young Lipan warrior of fine appearance and with hair down to his hips fought bravely, but the Kickapoos silenced him with a hail of arrows. Another

Lipan warrior miraculously survived the encounter despite being the recipient of numerous wounds—a Kickapoo warrior had pierced him with a lance, clubbed him over the head, and then scalped him.

Years later, the Lipan survivors of the encounter met with some old Kickapoos, and each group recounted their heroic deeds. One of the Lipan participants, however, scolded the Kickapoos for their dishonorable conduct. "What I did was what men do," the old Lipan lectured, "but the way you people snuck up on our encampment and killed children who could do no harm—that is not the way men fight. If you wanted to fight, you should have shown yourselves and given us a chance. We are men too. You killed my children in a poor way. I say that is not what men do."[1]

❨

THE KICKAPOOS, along with the Seminoles and their Black Seminole allies, were new enemies that the Lipan Apaches encountered in the latter half of the nineteenth century. They joined an ever-growing list of groups that sought to banish or exterminate the Lipans from the Rio Grande frontier. This chapter explores the increasingly desperate efforts by small and widely scattered bands of Lipans to survive in the face of starvation, disease, and constant pressure from Mexican authorities, Texas Rangers, American soldiers, and a host of Native peoples that sought to destroy them. By the turn of the twentieth century, the condition of the Lipans paralleled the warrior described in the folktale above: they were battered, bloodied, and severely weakened—but miraculously still standing.

As the sovereign republic of Texas dissolved after its December 1845 annexation by the United States, the remaining three hundred or so Lipan Apaches residing in Texas were shuffling back and forth between encampments located south of San Antonio and north of Austin on the San Gabriel River. Geologist Ferdinand Roemer, for example, witnessed a Lipan encampment of forty people moving along the banks of the Guadalupe River near the town of New Braunsfels en route to San Antonio with bison and deer robes to trade. In response to pressure from angry Comanche leaders who resented the decision of Texas authorities to permit Lipans to reside near the settlements, and from settlers who were uncomfortable about having the Lipans as neighbors, government officials had relocated them to the San Gabriel River country. Just two months later, however, Indian agent Robert S. Neighbors noted that small bands of Lipan and Tonkawa holdouts were still encamped between the San Marcos and San Antonio rivers, that they had scattered in pursuit of game, and that once the weather warmed up, the Lipans intended to plant crops near their old encampment along Cibolo Creek. While pleased to hear that the Lipans were taking an interest in farming, Neighbors urged them to move north to the upper Guadalupe River region.[2]

Meanwhile, the Lipans residing south of the Rio Grande, who numbered around two hundred people, were under mounting pressure from Mexican authorities who had been waging war against several Apache groups. So desperate had the security situation become on the northern Mexican frontier that officials in Sonora and Chihuahua enlisted the assistance of paid killers and scalp hunters in an effort to rid their provinces of Apaches. At the end of 1845, Mexican authorities shuddered amidst rumors that a large contingent of Lipan Apaches was holding a war council in the Sierra del Carmen Mountains in northern Coahuila. The Lipans were allegedly planning a trip to southern New Mexico to convince the Mescaleros to join them in raiding expeditions they were planning in Chihuahua.[3]

Shortly after Texas's annexation, the James K. Polk administration dispatched commissioners Pierce M. Butler and M. G. Lewis to establish contact with tribes in the state, and to arrange for a conference to explain the new relationship between Texas Indians and the U.S. government.[4] The relationship was particularly confusing in light of the peculiar land situation that existed in the Lone Star state. As part of its annexation agreement, federal authorities had permitted Texas to retain control over all its public lands so that Texans could sell them and repay the state's hefty pre-annexation debts. As a result, there were no "Indian lands" or reservations set aside in Texas unless state officials opted to create them. That being the case, certain federal trade and intercourse acts that applied to other states with Indian reservations did not apply to Texas, although Texans still expected the federal government to bear the entire expense and shoulder the responsibility for managing the relationship between Indians and whites. Consequently, there existed in Texas a "peculiar situation" where "the laws of Texas were operative, while the United States was helpless, yet possessing nominal control over the Indians."[5]

Butler and Lewis spent much of January and February 1846 spreading the word that they were organizing a council at Comanche Peak, a 1,200-foot-high limestone bluff located in Hood County that was a popular Comanche meeting place. By the middle of February, bands of Wacos, Caddos, Tonkawas, Wichitas, and Tawakonis had converged to air complaints about how the Texans had violated past treaties, and to discuss their concerns about declining bison herds, the expansion of white settlements, and the boundary line that was supposed to prevent the reoccurrence of bloodshed between them. A delegation of Lipans arrived from south Texas on February 19, armed with lances and bows and arrows, and with their bodies painted red for the occasion. A few days after the Lipans' dramatic arrival, Butler and Lewis convened an evening conference with Lipan, Tonkawa, Cherokee, and Creek representatives who gathered around the council fire to hear Seminole leader Wild Cat's (Caocoochee) testimony about the benefits of peace and the desirability of living in Indian Territory. A couple of weeks later, Buffalo Hump (Potsanaquahip), the eloquent fifty-year-old Comanche chief, arrived with a group of 150 men, women, and children. Unwilling to make any agreement without conferring with other Comanche leaders, Buffalo Hump secured a brief postponement of the council pending discussion with his Comanche brethren. In the meantime, the assembled tribes enjoyed the hospitality of the commissioners and the various social activities that accompanied such gatherings. While the men exchanged stories and got acquainted, boys spent their time wrestling and conducting foot races, while the women prepared meals, attended to the children, and busied themselves getting ready for the evening's festivities. Elijah Hicks, a Cherokee attendee at the Comanche Peak conference, recalled that a Lipan couple took the opportunity to get married. The bride was dressed in a fringed buckskin jacket and fringed bootees ornamented with sleigh bells. Although Lipan weddings were ordinarily low-key events without elaborate ceremony, the presence of so many other Indian peoples with different traditions and expectations may have altered the couple's plans. According to Hicks, the bride and the groom locked arms, covered themselves with a rug, and marched around while friends followed along, beating drums, until they had completed a circuit around the encampment. There being no objection from any quarter, they were man and wife.[6]

As the council at Comanche Peak wound down in mid-March, additional Lipans arrived. On what must have been one of the final meetings, Commissioner Butler sat down with Comanche, Creek, and Cherokee delegates as well as "three Lippan Captains from Mexico." According to Hicks, Butler informed them about the purpose of his mission and assured them of his good feeling for them. He promised to give the Lipans "small presents and meat," but said that other matters would have to await the council that he and Commissioner Lewis were planning later that spring with the Comanches. The Lipans replied that they had been "oppressed" in Mexico and could not live there, and had subsequently moved their people back to the north side of the Rio Grande. Their chief (possibly Flacco), when informed of the Comanche Peak meeting, had sent them to see the commissioners and assure them of the Lipans' friendship.[7]

The council fires at the Comanche Peak conference were still smoldering when commissioners Butler and Lewis began preparing for the upcoming conference at Council Springs, located near the Brazos River in Robertson County. They maintained high hopes of securing permanent peace along the Texas frontier, and had promised tribal leaders a generous share of presents to ensure their attendance. When the Comanches failed to show up, the commissioners dispatched Delaware and Lipan emissaries to find them and inform their leaders that the commissioners insisted on their participation. After a few anxious days, the Comanches replied that deputations from three bands would take part. A second near-crisis occurred in late April when Indian agent Robert S. Neighbors arrived with news that Texas Rangers had attacked a group of Lipans on the Colorado River and had killed or wounded several people, including women and children. The news, Elijah Hicks recalled, set off "the most heart rending national mourning by the Lipan women encamped here, loud with their shrieks which lost their sound in the distant heaven."[8]

On May 13, 1846, the Council Springs proceedings got off to a rousing start with a huge feast hosted by the commissioners—consisting of coffee, corn bread, and over two hundred pounds of boiled beef that the cooks piled on a tent cloth and spread on the ground. The various tribal delegations, decked out in a fantastic array of colors, feathers, and beads, seated themselves around this culinary extravaganza and devoured it forthwith. After two days of speechmaking and discussion, leaders representing the Comanches, Caddos, Wacos, Tonkawas, Wichitas, and Tawakonis signed a treaty placing themselves under the protection of the United States government, and acknowledged that it alone had the right to regulate their trade.[9] The signatories also agreed to deliver up captives and to restore stolen horses. Indians guilty of murder or robbery were to be given up to federal authorities to stand trial, while U.S. citizens guilty of similar crimes committed against Indians were to be punished in accordance with state law. The treaty authorized the U.S. president to establish trading houses, agencies, and posts near popular Indian hunting grounds and encampments, both to protect the tribes and to ensure implementation of the treaty stipulations. Finally, each side pledged to maintain the peace in perpetuity, and the federal government agreed to disburse $10,000 worth of goods to the tribes at a council it would host the next fall.[10]

While the various Texas tribes were preoccupied at Council Springs, the long-simmering boundary dispute between the United States and the Republic of Mexico had precipitated a war. Texas officials feared that the war would encourage tribes to increase their raiding activities, and some Comanche and Kiowa bands apparently could not resist the temptation to attack the growing number of supply caravans traversing their territory along the Santa Fe Trail. In October, Texas pro tem governor Albert C. Horton penned an anxious letter to President Polk warning that the Indians were growing resentful that the government had not delivered the presents promised them at Council Springs. An additional concern was the presence of traders selling firearms and alcohol to Native Americans, as well as land speculators eyeballing Indian property. The governor confessed that he was powerless to stop such activities, and recommended that the federal government appoint agents to enforce treaty provisions. Despite such problems, the only cases of direct military contact between the Lipans and the U.S. army during the Mexican War occurred in mid-May 1847, when forces under the command of Colonel Alexander W. Doniphan engaged a band of between fifty and sixty Lipan warriors in northern Chihuahua. The Lipans had conducted a raid a couple of days earlier, and Doniphan's men positioned themselves near the only watering hole in the area (called *el Pozo* or "the well") to conduct an ambush. In the ensuing battle, the troops killed fifteen warriors, rescued thirteen Mexican captives (women and children), and recaptured a considerable quantity of plundered property. Frederick A. Wislizenus, who arrived shortly after the battle, witnessed a group of Mexicans lassoing the bodies of the dead Lipans and dragging them together into a heap. Some of the warriors possessed fine blankets and bows and arrows, and a few carried leather shields. The fallen leader wore a headdress of feathers and horns. Wislizenus looked on as Americans and Mexicans stripped the Lipans of "curiosities," and consequently saw no "impropriety" in taking something for himself—the skull of the Lipan captain, which he sent to a craniologist in Philadelphia for examination. In the ensuing months, there were additional encounters between Lipans and Texas Ranger units, which were under nominal federal control. In the summer of 1847, Lipans stood accused of attacking Captain G. K. Lewis and his escort, who were en route to Monterrey. Although badly wounded, Lewis managed to reach Laredo to sound the alarm. A contingent of Texas Rangers rode to the Lipan camp, and when the Indians began to string their bows, the Rangers opened fire on them. Several Lipans suffered wounds in the encounter, but they and the remainder of the band managed to flee westward, joining the upper Lipans on the Pecos. Lastly, in January 1848, a Ranger force led by Captain James B. Gillett—who allegedly sported a revolver holster fashioned from an Apache scalp—attacked and killed seven Lipans who he believed had stolen some horses.[11]

The return of peace did not translate into improved conditions for the Lipan Apaches in Texas. Two tragedies occurred in the months following the conclusion of the Mexican War that devastated the affected Lipan bands and ushered in an era of renewed conflict that lasted for the duration of the nineteenth century. The first tragedy occurred after surveyors and settlers began pushing into the upper Guadalupe and Medina River country northwest of San Antonio—the region where Agent Neighbors had relocated the Lipans just two years earlier. The Lipans responded by staging raids on the settlers' livestock herds, and in one such retaliatory mission, they absconded with some animals owned by a Texas Ranger named William "Big Foot" Wallace. In the spring of 1848, Wallace assembled a posse of about thirty Rangers, set off in pursuit of the Lipans, and located their encampment on the headwaters of the Frío River. After surrounding the Lipan ranchería, the heavily armed

Texans attacked on horseback, and within a half hour had killed over a dozen people. Wallace's men then began sizing up the plunder, which consisted of kegs of gunpowder, sacks of lead, blankets, robes, and some 170 horses. Wallace later reflected, "The Lipans never recovered from the fatal blow we gave them on this occasion. From having been, up to this time, a formidable tribe, able to send six or eight hundred warriors into the field, they rapidly dwindled away until now they scarcely number a hundred souls, men, women, and children, all told."[12]

While land speculators, settlers, and Texas Rangers were responsible for the first disaster that befell the Lipans in 1848, the second calamity came at the hands of the Comanches and the U.S. army. A Comanche war captain named Carnebonahit had been on his way to Mexico with a raiding party when a company of U.S. soldiers attacked him and dispersed his men. His Mexican raiding plans having gone awry, Carnebonahit followed the soldiers and, catching them off guard, managed to steal seven of their horses. Aware that the soldiers would undoubtedly pursue him, the Comanche rode northward with the horses until he came to the camp of the Lipan chief Chiquito. Chief Chiquito, whose name meant "Little One," was actually a tall, thin man who, according to one contemporary, had the appearance of one possessing "more than ordinary powers of endurance." The old chief eyed the branded horses with concern, and rebuked Carnebonahit for leading the stolen animals to his encampment and focusing the suspicion of American authorities on his people. "I don't care," Carnebonahit responded indifferently as he prepared to ride off. "You and your people have piloted the Americans to the Comanche camps." Chiquito had precious little time to prepare for what followed in the Comanche's wake. No sooner had Carnebonahit galloped off when Captain William G. Crump and a company of soldiers, having tracked the stolen horses to Chiquito's encampment, attacked the Lipans and killed over twenty of them. Chiquito later explained to Robert Neighbors that he had seen the soldiers coming and had tried to explain, but the Americans were too mad to listen. They attacked his encampment, killed several innocent people, and seized two hundred horses. As a result, Chiquito severed contact with U.S. officials and fled into Mexico with the remainder of his band.[13]

The line of settlements, ranches, and military installations in Texas expanded westward during the late 1840s and early 1850s, increasing the pressure on already declining bison herds and further depressing the Indians' available food supplies. As the bison herds retreated, ranchers, farmers, and land speculators moved quickly to fill the void. Since the state retained control over its public lands, Texas officials arranged for the quick survey and sale of immense tracts of territory in the western part of the state, leaving some tribes wondering if there would be any land left for them. Meanwhile, the introduction of new virulent strains of smallpox and other epidemic diseases continued to wreak havoc among the state's Indian residents. In the face of these new but familiar pressures, members of some tribes retaliated. Lena Clara Koch writes that in the year 1849 alone, Indian raids in Texas accounted for the loss of over 6,600 head of livestock valued at over $100,000. In addition, the Indians killed nearly two hundred people and took twenty-five people captive. The new line of forts erected by federal authorities to safeguard the frontier remained undermanned, however, and only a handful of Indian agents received appointments. Because of these shortcomings, state officials found it necessary on several occasions to organize militias to bolster security and to provide the stability Texas needed to continue its rapid economic development. As petitions flowed into Congress from state officials seeking compensation for these military-related expenditures, authorities in Washington, DC, countered with demands that Texas set aside territory for Indian reservations within which the federal government could exercise jurisdiction and maintain the peace. These discussions culminated in 1855 with the establishment (albeit short-lived) of two reservations on the Brazos River: the Brazos Agency for the Caddos, Wacos, Tawakonis, Tonkawas, Keechies et al., and the Comanche Reserve for various Southern Comanche groups.[14]

Unbeknownst to the Lipans, government officials had intended to settle them and their Mescalero kinsmen on the Brazos Reserve, but then changed their minds and began a long and ultimately fruitless discussion about establishing a third reservation west of the Pecos for the Apaches. As was their custom, each Lipan band responded to perceived threats or opportunities with the short-term, parochial interests of their own group uppermost in their minds. That being the case, there was no monolithic Lipan response to the pressures facing them in the early 1850s. The bands of the elderly chiefs Chiquito (who had evidently returned from his self-imposed exile to Mexico) and Chapota (Chipoti,

Chipota) encamped peacefully on the Concho River. They spoke of other Lipans residing further west on the Pecos River attempting to grow corn. New Lipan agent John H. Rollins estimated that there were no more than 250 Indians in Chiquito and Chapota's encampment, with few children and a disproportionate number of old people. Not surprisingly, the Lipans desired peace with the Americans, although the two old chiefs also expressed interest in participating in a new war against the Comanches. According to Rollins, the "Lipan[s] want a war because they hate the Comanches—they hope to get employment—[and] are anxious to show they are friends of the whites and thus be allowed to visit the settlements, especially San Antonio."[15]

Other Lipan groups held a more ambivalent attitude toward the Comanches, and apparently cooperated with them periodically to stage joint raids on either side of the border. In the decade following the end of the Mexican War, for example, the state of Nuevo León suffered over eight hundred Indian raids resulting in nearly one thousand casualties and millions of pesos worth of lost property. In 1850 alone, Nuevo León lost twenty-one men killed, twenty wounded, four children captured, and a thousand head of livestock stolen. Consequently, in September of that year, military officials in northern Mexico adopted a new policy regarding Indian raiders. Instead of seeking to make peace with the Indians, commanders were instead to wage a "vigorous war" against the Comanches, Lipans, and other tribes that roamed the northern frontier. These groups, Mexican authorities declared, shifted around "without forming settlements" or "cultivating the ground like other tribes," and "devoted themselves entirely to hunting and warfare of an atrocious character." Part of the Mexican government's new "get tough" policy was permitting Kickapoos, Seminoles, and other displaced tribes from the United States to settle along its northern frontier to act as a buffer against Lipan and Comanche attacks.[16]

During the first week in December 1850, representatives of several of the tribes that had attended the Council Springs conference four years earlier gathered at Spring Creek, a tributary of the San Sabá River, to reaffirm their commitments to peace and to one another. Buffalo Hump again headed the Comanche delegation, but his attitude had soured in recent years as the once formidable *Comanchería* steadily dwindled in size and power. Representing the Lipans were Chiquito, Chapota,

Yekehtasna, and Kehrauch, who may have remembered better days when their people had dominated the San Sabá River valley. Other tribes in attendance included the Caddos, Quapaws, Tawakonis, and Wacos. Special agent John H. Rollins and Captain Hamilton W. Merrill of Fort Martin Scott, meanwhile, represented the interests of the United States government. On December 10, the assembled dignitaries placed their marks on an agreement (the so-called Fort Martin Scott Treaty) that was similar in virtually every respect to the Council Springs agreement, with one notable exception. The Indians agreed (in article 15) not to go below the line of military posts that existed on the east side of the Colorado River, or below the Llano River without written permission from an Indian agent or military officer. U.S. officials, incidentally, never submitted the treaty to the Senate for ratification, since they regarded it merely as reaffirmation of the 1846 Council Spring treaty.[17]

The Fort Martin Scott Treaty accomplished virtually nothing, since sporadic attacks and hit-and-run raids continued into 1851. Raiding parties comprised of less than a dozen men reportedly walked into the settlements, took what they wanted, and then rode out on stolen horses. Texas governor Peter Hansborough Bell responded with a flurry of letters to military officials and Indian agents, demanding that they do something to curb what was in his view a broad-based Indian rebellion. Mexican authorities, meanwhile, were incredulous that "so small a number of savages could cause so much woe and escape punishment." Citing article 11 of the 1848 Treaty of Guadalupe Hidalgo (which required the U.S. government to "forcibly restrain" Indians from attacking into Mexico, and to punish those that did with the same energy and determination as if the incursions had occurred on U.S. soil), Mexican authorities demanded that their American counterparts fulfill their solemn obligations. The Texas press fanned the flames with incendiary accounts of thefts, assaults, and murders. No place in Texas seemed safe from Indian attack.[18]

In the face of mounting pressure from Governor Bell, the Mexicans, and the press, General George M. Brooke authorized a campaign to punish the Indians for their alleged violations of the peace. In late May 1851, Lieutenant Colonel William J. Hardee led a force of two hundred dragoons into the San Sabá country—not far from where federal officials had reaffirmed peace with the Indians just five months earlier. On May 28, Hardee's guides discovered the location of two encampments—one belonging to a group of Lipan Apaches, and the other occupied by southern Comanches. Exercising unusual restraint, since both camps possessed a large number of women, children, and old men, Hardee ordered his men to search the sites for captives, stolen horses, and other contraband. The Lipans turned over seventeen Mexican captives, while an investigation of the Comanche camp produced nothing. Later that fall, Indian agent John A. Rollins organized another meeting with Comanche, Lipan, and Mescalero leaders on the San Sabá River in an effort to convince them to halt their raiding and to adopt farming and a "civilized life." In remarks that could not have provided much solace to the Indian delegates, Rollins informed them that since the buffalo, deer, bear, and mustang were gone, they needed to go to work or face extinction. If they would make the transition to a sedentary lifestyle, Rollins exhorted them, they would enjoy "good homes and plenty of corn, cattle, horses, sheep, hogs, and other comforts like the White man of America." He warned them to cease crossing the Rio Grande to make raids into Mexico, but instead to "go to work and live like honest men and warriors."[19]

The responses of the Lipan delegates (Chiquito, Quaco, Colonel Lamos, and Manuel Hernandes) to Rollins's condescending remarks and unrealistic suggestions provide important insights into their state of mind in the early 1850s. Chiquito expressed interest in raising corn and becoming self-sufficient, but he placed particular stress on his peoples' need for a stable home where they would be protected from "further persecution"—homes that they could call their own and not be driven from as they had been in the past. Quaco also sought security and stability, stating that he had many children, was "tired of moving about," and desired a home to keep his family together and to maintain his herds of cattle and horses. Colonel Lamos similarly confessed to being sick of having his family "roving about like wild animals," while Hernandes stated his desire to be settled some place, with his family near him, where he could raise corn. At the conclusion of the conference, delegates signed yet another treaty acknowledging their obligations and promising to cease further raids into Mexico. Government officials also required the Lipans, in the future, to deliver up captives without expectation of ransoms or rewards—an exception being the return of runaway slaves, which brought a fifty-dollar bounty. On October 28, special agent John Rollins signed the agreement along with eight Comanche representatives, four Mescaleros, and nine Lipans, including Chiquito, Coyote, Quaco, Chapota, Manuel, Colonel Lamos, Captain John Castro, Captain John Flacco, and Manuel Hernandes.[20]

The Lipans' interest in corn and a secure homeland increased in the months following the San Sabá treaty-signing as military officials reported poverty and destitution among bands residing across south Texas. In July 1852, veteran soldier and Indian fighter George T. Howard, the superintendent of all Indian agents in Texas, wrote to Commissioner of Indian Affairs Luke Lea that Chief Chiquito had visited him near San Antonio, and that his people were starving to death. Desperate for relief, Chiquito requested permission for his people to hunt wild horses to feed their families, but Howard had to turn him away due to opposition from military officials and the local citizenry, who feared that their property might likely end up roasting over a Lipan campfire. Later that month, hungry Lipans near Fredericksburg stood accused of stealing food, killing livestock, and extorting food and supplies, and settlers soon demanded that the military remove them. "There is no exaggerating the starving condition of these Indians," wrote Indian agent Horace Capron, "and with every disposition on their part to be friendly, they are forced into predatory excursions to sustain life." Capron urged Lipans under the leadership of Chiquito, Chapota, and Cartre to move closer to the recently established Fort Mason (located in northern Gillespie County) to avoid further trouble with the settlers. When the post commander issued them strict orders not to go near the settlements without a pass, the Lipans' critical trade relationship with the settlers ended, and within weeks, they were again begging for food and supplies.[21]

In the fall of 1852, a rumor spread that a Lipan raiding party had wandered well below the Llano River boundary line and attacked a ranch located forty miles south of San Antonio. The raiders wounded several people and carried off dozens of horses, all the while announcing their identity as Lipans belonging to a band under the leadership of Manuel. Although Manuel's people were scrounging for food at Fort Mason (nearly two hundred miles away) at the time of the raid, military officials organized a campaign to teach the Lipans a lesson. In January, Lieutenant Colonel Philip St. George Cooke, the commander of Fort Mason's 2nd Dragoon Regiment, devised an elaborate plan to trap the

Indians, employing troops from nearby Forts McKavett, Chadbourne, and Terrett to block their avenues of escape. On January 12, Cooke overtook the Lipans while they were encamped near the head of the Guadalupe River. The Indians acted as though they were interested in a parlay, but at the last minute scattered, with several managing to escape. Cooke had his bugler sound the charge, and in the ensuing chaos, his men killed three Lipans, captured eighteen women and children, and seized 150 horses. The soldiers then set about burning the Indians' winter supplies, tipi poles, and other belongings, and seized as war trophies the presents that their Indian agent had only recently distributed to them. When the military learned of its terrible blunder and attempted to return the captured livestock, remedying the damage became impossible since many band members were either dead or wounded, and the survivors hopelessly scattered.[22]

As F. Todd Smith has detailed, during the 1830s and 1840s, settlers from the United States poured across Texas's porous borders, and by 1850, the non-Indian population had swelled to nearly 150,000 people. A sizeable number of immigrants—perhaps as many as 25,000—pushed into central Texas, vastly outnumbering the remnant bands of Lipans, Tonkawas, and Comanches residing on the periphery of the new settlements, and ending the Indians' dominance over the region.[23] Facing starvation, frequent and involuntary relocations, declining trade opportunities, and sporadic but deadly clashes with soldiers, the Lipan Apaches of the 1850s were in the most desperate position in their history—they were, in essence, teetering on the brink of extinction. That being said, the scattered, fragmentary Lipan bands that resided along the Rio Grande frontier during the second half of the nineteenth century maintained a disproportionately strong presence in south Texas. Between the years 1849 and 1881, for instance, the United States army participated in 219 "actions and skirmishes" against hostile Indians in Texas; the Lipans (who could field a total of perhaps fifty to one hundred warriors) accounted for nearly thirty of them—about 13 percent of the total, and second only to the far more numerous Comanches.[24]

The official number of "actions and skirmishes" military officials recorded as having taken place between Lipans and soldiers does not, of course, reflect the total number of raids, kidnappings, and murders that were attributed (appropriately or not) to the Lipans residing south of the

Rio Grande. The years 1854 and 1856 were particularly violent, owing perhaps to the Lipans' recognition of their precarious existence, or to the army's paranoia and mounting pressures to halt frontier violence. In the spring of 1854, the Lipans were again (like the Cooke campaign on the Guadalupe River) the victims of false identity. When Comanche and Wichita warriors raided ranches near Laredo in late March, a wagon master apparently recognized some of the attackers as Lipans. Without any additional investigation, Brevet Major General Persifor F. Smith ordered out five detachments of mounted riflemen to scour the countryside in search of the Lipans. In April, three men attacked and murdered a man named Forrester and his three young daughters at their home north of San Antonio. The Lipans were again accused, and a manhunt for the perpetrators was conducted. At Fort Inge, meanwhile, Lipan agent George T. Howard had Chief Chiquito and a number of his men incarcerated in the guardhouse pending an investigation. A few weeks later, marauders identified as Lipans swooped down on a wagon train near Fort Ewell (between San Antonio and Laredo), killing five men and making off with several mules and other plunder. Although most of the Lipans had been at, or near, Fort Inge at the time of the attacks and possessed reliable alibis, many Texans were convinced that they were the guilty party and merited having the military drive them from their lands and homes.[25]

The brutal Forrester family slaying, as it turned out, had been the work of some Wichitas, and the Lipans, in the words of one scholar, "must have burned with fires of unjust persecution."[26] General Persifor F. Smith stoked the fires still further with orders that military officials allow no Indians within twenty miles of Fort Clark (present-day Bracketville, Texas). According to W. W. Newcomb, the unfriendly order severed the last ties between the Lipans and the U.S. government, and by the winter of 1854–55, "virtually all the Lipans had crossed the Rio Grande" into Mexico. Those that remained in Texas were in awful shape. When Frederick Law Olmstead traveled through Texas in 1854–1855 as part of his larger tour of the South, he visited Fort Inge. Located three miles north of the fort was a hastily created Indian encampment, where Olmstead witnessed the desperate living conditions of about one hundred Lipans, Mescaleros, and Tonkawas.[27] According to Olmstead, the Indians exhibited "the most miserable squalor, foul obscenity, and disgusting brutishness," and he confessed being unable to find "one man of dignity" among those assembled there. Time had not been good to the Apaches, Olmstead observed, since "at least half the Lipans have been exterminated by powder and ball, in the open war of the last years."[28]

Employing a time-honored strategy, those Lipans who had escaped the "powder and ball" of the various regular army, volunteer militias, and Texas Ranger units that pursued them, fled across the Rio Grande border into Mexico for sanctuary. When conditions changed—either on the Mexican side or on the American side of the river—some bands might slip back across and return to familiar sites in south-central Texas that held special meaning for them. This cross-border fluidity continued for the remainder of the nineteenth century. In 1852, for example, authorities in Nuevo León organized a large campaign of about two thousand cavalrymen who scoured the northern and western reaches of the province in search of Comanche, Kiowa, and Apache raiding parties. Such activities sent the Lipans northward into south Texas for safety. During the summer and fall of 1854, however, small bands of Lipans slipped back into Mexico to escape the growing number of campaigns the Texans were waging against them, and to gain a respite from southern Comanche groups with whom they were again feuding.[29] Sharing the northern Mexican frontier with the Lipans were additional refugee tribes from the United States. As mentioned previously, during the 1840s and 1850s, small groups of Kickapoos, Seminoles, and even a few Shawnees, Cherokees, Pottawattamies, and Delawares had received permission from the Mexican government to live there in exchange for periodic military assistance, and to act as a buffer against Apache and Comanche raiders from the north. Both Mexican and U.S. authorities initially assumed that the Lipans made common cause with these immigrant groups, joining them in their raiding forays against their mutual enemies in Texas. If such a relationship did develop, it apparently did not last long, since the Seminoles soon complained that the Lipans were attacking them while they were out hunting or working in their fields.[30]

The Seminoles were not the only ones growing irritated with the Lipans. Fearing that their frequent cross-border raids would invite retaliatory invasions by Americans, Santiago Vidaurri, the powerful leader of northeastern Mexico during the late 1850s and early 1860s, moved quickly to rein in the Lipans. In March 1856, Vidaurri dispatched troops into northern Coahuila with instructions to carry out a war of extermination against the Lipans. After locating the Indians' encampment near the villages of Monclova and Múzquiz, the Mexicans attacked, and in the first onslaught captured more than one hundred Lipans, including thirty warriors whom the Mexican soldiers immediately executed. Under tight guard, soldiers marched the remaining Lipan captives south to Monterrey. According to one of the Mexican participants, some of the Lipan women commenced killing their infants rather than see them deprived of their liberty. This "unnatural action" so outraged the troops that their commanding officer (Captain Miguel Patiño) permitted the killing of more than forty more Lipans of both sexes. Meanwhile, a Mexican force of over 160 men, including forty Seminoles and twelve Black Seminoles, scoured the country seeking "to hunt down the [Lipan] fugitives like wild beasts." Those Lipans lucky enough to survive the campaign fled northward to the Pecos River country.[31]

As groups of Lipans escaped north out of Mexico in the late 1850s, their brothers in Texas—who may have numbered around 250—looked south to Mexico for sanctuary. Disinterested in living on a reservation in either Texas or in Indian Territory, and driven in desperation to secure their subsistence by raiding, the Lipans in Texas became the target of several military campaigns. In July 1857, Lieutenant John Bell Hood engaged a party of Comanche and Lipan warriors at the Battle of the Devil's River in southwestern Sutton County, killing nineteen Indians and wounding four others. Less than a year later, Lipans encamped on the Nueces River suffered a defeat by another army patrol that left several men dead and the Lipans' horse herd severely depleted. Meanwhile, a band of Lipans following Ramon Castro (son of Chief Cuelgas de Castro) were encamped along Verde Creek in Bandera County when in October 1858 they came under attack by the U.S. military—who apparently destroyed their upcoming winter food supplies, since many died of starvation later that year. For the Texas Lipans, therefore, the Big Bend region of far west Texas, or the mountains and deserts of northern Mexico appeared as oases amidst the bloodshed and suffering at home.[32]

The constant threat of Indian attack, and the failure of federal authorities to provide adequate security, was one of the primary reasons that Texas officials gave when explaining their decision to secede from the United States in 1861. As the pivotal presidential campaign of 1860 was getting under way, Texas officials busily adopted resolutions demanding compensation for the financial losses its citizens had accrued from the "shocking enormity of Indian massacres, robberies, and thefts" that had gone on since the state entered the union. In a letter dated March 24, 1860, Governor Sam Houston called attention to the "bleeding and suffering" citizens of Texas who were victims of "thefts, murders, and rapine." He also offered "proofs" showing that the Lipans and other tribes residing in Mexico "committed their depredations on our frontier inhabitants, and pass beyond the Rio Grande with their booty with impunity because our troops and citizens are not at liberty to pursue and chastise them on Mexican soil."[33]

During the Civil War years, the escalating demands on Texas troops stretched them thin. Many units received deployments outside the state, while others stood guard against potential federal advances coming from the east or along the Gulf Coast. Not surprisingly, Lipans, Mescaleros, Kickapoos, and other groups seized the opportunity to acquire cattle, horses, and occasionally captives from ranches and settlements in south Texas. In the fall of 1864, for example, a small party of Lipans raided the home of a German sheep raiser named Schwander near Camp Wood in Real County. The Lipans killed Schwander's wife and ransacked the house before making off with the couple's six-year-old son Albert. After spending several grueling nights of travel with little to eat or drink, the Lipans crossed the Rio Grande and sold the boy to a Mexican trader, who later ransomed the child back to his father. Heart-wrenching incidents such as this prompted Texans to resume their flood of petitions and pleas for government assistance once the Civil War had ended.[34]

The Civil War, which exercised such a profound influence on virtually all American peoples, left Lipan casualties as well. The Lipans who had been living outside Fort Inge during the early 1850s, for example, watched with dismay when their Tonkawa friends under the leadership of Chief Plácido agreed in 1854 to remove his people north to the newly created Brazos River reservation. A small number of Lipans—probably not more than twenty—accompanied the Tonkawas to the Brazos. After state officials abandoned the Texas reservations in 1859, they removed the Tonkawas and tag-along Lipans to a reservation near Fort Cobb in Indian Territory. Their new neighbors included Comanches, Kiowas, and other tribes that had a long history of hostility to them, and perhaps feared their reputation as cannibals. In addition to resenting the presence of the hated Tonkawas (they probably were not thrilled at the prospect of having Lipans as neighbors either), several pro-Union tribes resented the Tonkawas' willingness to serve as scouts for the Confederacy. Consequently, in late October 1862, in what was later described as "one of the bloodiest incidents ever witnessed on the Western frontier," pro-Union Indians (identified variously as Shawnees, Delawares, Osages, Comanches et al.) attacked Plácido's village on the Washita River and killed over 130 people (including Plácido), and several of the Lipans.[35] The survivors, led by Plácido's son Charlie, fled for safety to Fort Arbuckle, and after the war returned to Texas, where they settled near Fort Griffin.[36]

Texas officials struggled with demobilization, economic restructuring, and complying with the various Reconstruction policies emanating from Washington, DC. Providing substantial numbers of soldiers to patrol the frontier against small bands of marauding Indians, consequently, was not at the top of anyone's priority list. John H. Evans, a soldier who served along the Rio Grande border during the late 1860s, reported that the "portion of the frontier [between Eagle Pass and Laredo] was constantly overrun by bands of Lipanes and Kickapoos" who "pillaged and murdered indiscriminately" before stripping the area of its cattle and horses. The Kickapoos were particularly outraged over the January 8, 1865, Confederate attack on a group of peaceful Kickapoo emigrants en route from Kansas to Mexico. The so-called Battle of Dove Creek, notes Arrell Morgan Gibson, ushered in a twenty-year Kickapoo offensive against Texas that resulted in dozens of deaths and the loss of millions of dollars in stolen property. The Lipans, as we have seen, were also nursing several grudges against the Texans, and in March 1867, a group of warriors struck German immigrant communities in Kendall and Medina counties. While passing through the small village of Quihi, Texas (located in Medina County), a group of Lipans forced an old German settler named Gerdes to disrobe, and then proceeded to jab him with their lances, inflicting over fifty wounds before finally putting him out of his misery. Medina County judge H. J. Richards complained that Lipans and Kickapoos residing along the Rio Grande held several Texas children as captives, and he urged authorities to prohibit them from residing so close to border.[37]

Judge Richards was one of many people who believed that the solution to Texas's border troubles lay in forcing the "tribal fragments"
believed responsible to relocate deeper into the interior of Mexico, or
to reunite with their brethren in the Indian Territory. In January 1867, a
prominent Quaker citizen from Uvalde County named Reading Wood
Black requested permission from Governor James W. Throckmorton
to approach some of the Indian groups residing just south of the Rio
Grande in an effort to convince them to return to the United States.[38]
The governor approved Black's request, but the Quaker diplomat's rather
undiplomatic and outspoken Unionist sympathies led to his murder in
October 1867. Six months later, the state's Committee on Indian Affairs
appointed Stephen S. Brown, a merchant with considerable experience
working on the Rio Grande frontier, to assume Black's mission. The following summer, Brown met with several Kickapoo chiefs and warriors
at the courthouse in Múzquiz, Coahuila. He later described the Indians
as destitute and dependent on the Mexicans for their survival, but the
assembled chiefs gave no clear reply to Brown's offers to remove them
to the United States—due perhaps to their deep distrust of American
authority, or because they feared how their Mexican hosts might react
if they attempted to leave. A few of the Kickapoo participants suggested
that Brown arrange for a delegation of chiefs from their former homes
and reservations to come down and help arrange their removal.[39]

During the early 1850s, Kickapoo and Seminole immigrants had
encamped in northern Coahuila near the villages of Zaragosa, La Navaja,
and Guerrero. In 1852, however, the Mexican government approved land
grants for them forty miles to the south at El Nacimiento (located at
the head of the Sabinas River). According to Brown's estimates, there
were between 80 and 120 Lipans in Mexico in 1868, about the same
number of Pottawatomies, and around 800 Kickapoos. The Seminoles
were gone by then, having completed a return to Indian Territory that
began in 1857 following the death of their leader Wild Cat. Around 150
Black Seminoles remained behind, most of them residing in southwestern Coahuila. The Kickapoos settled near the village of Múzquiz,
although some groups still encamped at El Nacimiento and a few at
Allende. Brown reported that the Kickapoos attempted to plant crops,
but the dry climate required that they haul water to irrigate their fields.
Consequently, they could only produce enough food to feed perhaps a

quarter of their population. Although a few Kickapoos gained employment as servants or laborers, raiding became the Kickapoos' primary
(and from their perspective, most respectable) source of subsistence.[40]

The Lipans, meanwhile, were in no better shape, and along with
their Mescalero brethren, "hung like a cloud of destruction" upon the
Rio Grande frontier. Unlike the Kickapoos, who made continued efforts
to grow crops, the Lipans remained reluctant to depend on agriculture
for their subsistence, and the hot, dry climate of northern Mexico would
have discouraged them further. Consequently, the Lipans pursued an
economy based almost exclusively on raiding, stealing, and trading. As
General E. O. C. Ord testified in December 1877, the Lipans "never cultivate the soil, but subsist by plunder." Upon their return from a successful raiding foray, they exchanged stolen goods with the various
Mexican towns with whom they had trade relationships. At times, the
Lipans preyed on villages that were allied with other tribes (such as the
Kickapoos), and their long tradition of stealing horses from Indian enemies persisted in Mexico.[41]

The village of Zaragosa was the principal safe haven for the Lipans,
and villagers benefited from the raiding activities of Lipan warriors who
preyed on ranches and settlements north of the Rio Grande. Lipan raiders brought horses, mules, and cattle south to Zaragosa, for example,
and exchanged them for food, firearms, ammunition, and alcohol—
at rates that greatly benefited the Mexicans. The Lipans also provided
Zaragosa residents with protection against raids from other tribes in the
area—such as Kickapoos.[42] The Kickapoos, meanwhile, had a similar
arrangement with the village of Múzquiz, eking out a living as best they
could. After a devastating Kickapoo attack on Zaragosa in May, when
the Lipans lost twenty-six people along with some captives and horses,
the Zaragosa city council wrote their Múzquiz counterpart requesting that they return the stolen horses and Lipan captives. Lipan leaders Gicore, Soli, and Costilietos, meanwhile, considered relocating their
people to Fort Griffin (established in 1867 and located on the Clear Fork
of the Brazos River in Shackelford County), where around 150 Tonkawa
refugees from Oklahoma, and a handful of Lipans, had gathered at the
conclusion of the Civil War. According to Brevet Major General Edward
R. S. Canby, the commander of the 5th Military District, the Tonkawas
were anxious to merge with the Lipans, since their united strength

would give them perhaps one hundred warriors—a force that Canby hoped to organize as scouts and auxiliaries due to their "knowledge of the haunts and habits of the hostile Indians" of Texas.[43]

Commissioner Brown, meanwhile, did his best to bring about the removal of the tribes residing in northern Mexico, and his reports helped convince Congress to appropriate $50,000 to cover the removal costs of the Kickapoos alone. But Brown remained pessimistic about getting much help from his Mexican counterparts. The Indians provided them, after all, with a ready-made army of four to five hundred warrior-soldiers with an "implacable hatred" of Texas. Their raids and thievery brought thousands of dollars into the local economy; they provided protection against other wild Indians (such as the Comanches); and they could be used as leverage to extract concessions from Texas and U.S. authorities. Brown speculated that the Mexicans would eventually seek to scatter Indian families across its northern frontier and to incorporate the young men into the military. He believed that the Indians would resist these efforts, however, until desperation, starvation, and vassalage forced them to accept what Brown termed "tribal suicide."[44]

The Lipans tell a story of an incident that occurred around 1869 that provides insights into their lives in northern Mexico, and which commenced a slow, sporadic migration of Lipans out of Coahuila to New Mexico that continued into the early twentieth century. The incident took place near the Lipan-friendly town of Zaragosa. Some Lipans had settled down to live in town while others remained encamped in the hills, where they carried on a predatory existence, poaching cattle and robbing outlying settlements. One day these "Lipans in the hills" killed several family members of a wealthy Mexican rancher as the latter were traveling to their ranch to escape an epidemic that had recently broken out in town. The rancher was furious and used his influence to get the government to wage a military campaign against the Lipans. Before this could take place, however, a friendly Mexican named Diłtso warned the Lipans that they were in grave danger and needed to leave Zaragosa quickly. He told them to head north to the Rio Bonito (site of Fort Stanton in south-central New Mexico), where they would be safe. The Lipans prepared to leave, but had trouble securing provisions and ammunition, as the authorities had warned local merchants not to sell them any supplies. Some Lipans chose to remain in Zaragosa, therefore, while others opted to hide out deeper in the mountains. Several families heeded Diłtso's advice, however, and headed north. After eluding the Mexican army, they crossed the Rio Grande at Piedras Negras. The Lipans then headed west, making their way through the Guadalupe Mountains into New Mexico in search of sanctuary among the Mescaleros.[45]

Some of the Lipans who sought to escape did not remain north of the Rio Grande for very long. Morris Opler writes that three companies of Mexican militia under the command of Colonel Ildofonse Fuentes and Captain Antonio Guerra captured several Lipan refugees who were encamped near the mouth of the Pecos River. Colonel Fuentes then marched the prisoners back to Mexico. Not all those who found sanctuary with the Mescaleros stayed put either. Once Mexican tempers had cooled and authorities had abandoned the search for them, small parties of Lipans cautiously made their way back to Zaragosa. In the United States, meanwhile, the policy of removing Indians from sanctuaries in northern Mexico gathered steam among a broad range of interest groups. Texas cattle ranchers, for instance, were understandably enthusiastic about the prospect of an Indian-free frontier. "The cattle interest is one of the most important in Texas," wrote General Joseph J. Reynolds in the summer of 1869, "and is now second only to the cotton interest in this state." After consulting with the two largest cattle dealers in Texas, Reynolds threw his support behind the removal policy. In a second effort to effect the removal, American officials sent Kickapoo agent John D. Miles to Múzquiz in hopes of convincing the Mexican Kickapoos to consider relocating to Indian Territory. After several days of fruitless discussions, however, Miles returned home to Kansas empty-handed.[46]

In the spring of 1873, federal authorities tried a third time to negotiate the removal of Indians residing south of the Rio Grande border. On April 30, newly appointed "special commissioners" Henry M. Atkinson and Thomas G. Williams arrived at Fort Duncan on the first leg of a mission to visit the Kickapoos, Lipans, Pottawatomies, and other groups living in northern Coahuila. On May 15, the two men traveled to Saltillo, where they met with Governor Victoriano Cepeda. After securing his promise of cooperation, Atkinson and Williams departed for Monterrey to obtain a similar pledge from Governor José Eleuterio González. With these important agreements in hand, the two men departed for Múzquiz on May 22 to hold their first meeting with the Kickapoos. Before they had gotten seventy-five miles out of Monterrey, however, a courier rode up with alarming news—a large American force had marched across the Rio Grande and attacked Indian encampments near Remolino, killing several people and taking others prisoner.[47]

Little did commissioners Atkinson and Williams know that while they were traveling south to Texas in April 1873, top military officials were huddled together at Fort Clark plotting their own solution to the border problem. On April 11, Secretary of War William W. Belknap and Lieutenant General Philip H. Sheridan met with Colonel Ranald Slidell Mackenzie, an experienced Indian fighter who had recently arrived in south Texas with several companies of the Fourth Cavalry Regiment. Although no written minutes of their meeting exist, most scholars believe that Belknap and Sheridan ordered Mackenzie to put a stop to the border raids, but left the timing and details to the colonel. Over the course of the next month, Mackenzie prepared for his secret mission, gathering intelligence about the various Indian encampments in northern Coahuila and training his troops for the task ahead. By mid-May, civilian scouts had discovered the exact whereabouts of Kickapoo, Lipan, and Mescalero encampments near the village of Remolino, located on the southern fork of the San Rodrigo River about forty miles from the border. Mackenzie's force of 360 men set out toward the Rio Grande on May 17 and crossed the river later that evening. Riding all night, the force drew up to the outskirts of Remolino on the morning of the eighteenth, and once in position, charged the grass lodges that constituted the Kickapoo village. As the terrified Kickapoos fled for their lives, the soldiers set fire to the settlement; "the fierce crackling of the flames," First Lieutenant Robert G. Carter later recalled, "mingled strangely with the carbines, rifles, cheers, and yells." In a matter of minutes, the "battle" was over, and the troopers rode on to the other villages. The occupants of the Lipan encampment, which was located less than a mile away, had taken flight at the first sound of shots, and the soldiers moved unopposed among their deserted dwellings and set them afire. In minutes, the soldiers destroyed all three villages (around 180 lodges). Mackenzie later reported nineteen Indians killed and forty women and children taken prisoner. Costilietos, an elderly Lipan chief, and his daughter Teresita were among those captured, although most of the Lipans managed to escape before the army could corner them. Mackenzie lost one

Photo of Lipan Chief Costilietos and his daughter Teresita taken at Fort Clark shortly after the McKenzie's Remolino raid in 1873. *Courtesy of the Daughters of the Republic of Texas Library, San Antonio, Texas.*

man killed and two wounded. Shortly after noon, the Americans and their prisoners started for home. Fearing a possible ambush, Mackenzie drove his command straight through the scalding heat of the afternoon and evening before reaching the Rio Grande at dawn on May 19.[48]

As one can imagine, the news of "Mackenzie's Raid" had an unsettling effect on Commissioners Atkinson and Williams, and for several days afterward their "lives hung by a thread." Under a military escort for their own protection, the two men proceeded on to Múzquiz, arriving on May 28. The next day, they sent word to the Indians inviting them to a council, while simultaneously obtaining Mackenzie's promise that there would be no follow-up attacks until after the commissioners had completed their assignment. Reminiscent of the problems facing earlier efforts to promote Indian removal, Mexican officials placed a series of roadblocks in the path of the commissioners. They warned the Indians that the commissioners sought to poison them or to gather them in one place so that the soldiers could kill them, and they advised the warriors to murder the commissioners or hold them hostage to exchange for the women and children carried off by Mackenzie. Múzquiz merchants and municipal officials, meanwhile, collected funds to bribe the chiefs and headmen. Despite all the difficulties, Atkinson and Williams managed to meet Kickapoo and Pottawatomie leaders in a council held on June 1, 1873, and attempted to explain how it was that at the very time they were in Mexico to treat with them, the American army was attacking, killing, and capturing their kinsmen at Remolino. To this oft-repeated question, the commissioners could only say that the army had been following the trail of the Lipans, that it led to the Kickapoo encampment, and that the Kickapoos had received a blow intended more particularly for the Apaches. Although the Mackenzie raid had caused the commissioners some tense moments, they later admitted that its results contributed to their ultimate success by exhibiting the power of the United States, and by demonstrating clearly that Mexico could no longer shelter the Indians after their raids into Texas.[49]

By 1875, the three hundred or so remaining Lipan Apaches strewn across the Rio Grande frontier resided beside—or with—other fragment groups in an effort to bolster their numerical strength and odds of survival. Perhaps 150 Lipans occupied the region around Zaragosa, west to Remolino in northern Coahuila. Their feud with the Kickapoos was apparently over (or at least on hold), since they were encamped next to one another just prior to the Mackenzie raid. Another group of Lipans, perhaps one hundred or so, lived with their Mescalero kinsmen at the newly created Mescalero Reservation in the Sacramento Mountains of south-central New Mexico. These northern Coahuila–New Mexico Lipans traveled back and forth across the Rio Grande border as the situation warranted, always looking for a new place of refuge yet unknown to their enemies. On occasion, they drifted as far east as San Antonio, but never in large numbers. A third group of Lipans (numbering around twenty-five) had attached themselves to the Tonkawas and were encamped outside Fort Griffin, where they received periodic employment as scouts and trackers. In 1875, the War Department forbade any further issues of rations to Lipan and Tonkawa families, and post commander Colonel George P. Buell reported them in "deplorable condition, reduced to either depredating or starvation." A final small group of Lipans remained with Tonkawa or Kiowa Apache friends at Fort Sill in Indian Territory. They were survivors of the terrible massacre that had so decimated Chief Plácido's people in October 1862.[50]

Although Lipans from Fort Griffin served as scouts and trackers for Colonel Mackenzie during the Red River War in 1874, in the minds of most Texans, they remained a far greater liability than they were an asset. In 1875, Texas officials adopted yet another resolution to Congress requesting reimbursement for monies the state had spent to defend its territory. Employing characteristic hyperbole, the petitioners claimed that a "reign of terror" existed along the Rio Grande frontier that had prevented citizens from attending to their vocations, depreciated the value of property, stunted population growth, and directed millions of dollars' worth of property into the "haunts of [Mexico's] savage allies." To put it bluntly, the Texans maintained, they were waging a "contest between civilization and savagery" in south Texas, and the lives of countless settlers and frontiersmen hung in the balance.[51]

Aggressive efforts on the part of military officials to address the concerns of Texans residing along the Rio Grande frontier did little to mute the hue and cry that Indian depredations were making their lives unbearable. Steven M. Kerr, who has examined records of Indian attacks along the Rio Grande and Trans-Pecos frontiers in the late 1870s and early 1880s, argues that reports of Indian depredations were widely exaggerated during the period. According to Kerr, the Texans' clamor for federal assistance was often motivated as much by a desire to protect their pocketbooks as it was to protect innocent lives.[52] This is not to say, of course, that no depredations occurred, and military officials were quick to point out the real threat from the tribal fragments living just south of the Rio Grande.[53] American officials were convinced, furthermore, that Mexican authorities were negligent (if not duplicitous) in their efforts to "restrain" warriors from making cross-border incursions. General E. O. C. Ord testified that Indian raiders took "orders"

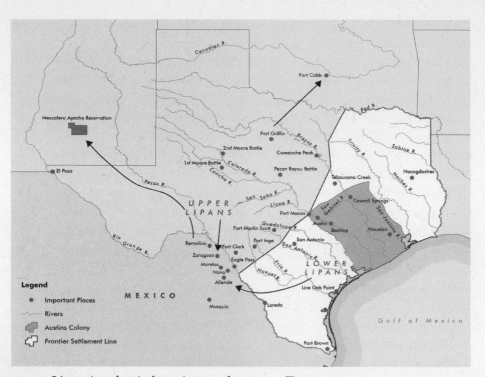

Lipan Apaches in late nineteenth-century Texas.
Map created by Matthew A. Crawford.

for specific items that their Mexican customers desired, and then stole into Texas to fill them. He also alleged that the illicit trade in towns like Zaragosa was so vigorous that some local officials, instead of reporting it to higher authorities, began to tax the contraband as a revenue generator. There were even reports of Mexican officials giving Indians "passports" so that they could move quickly and easily across the border without paying import duties.[54]

The cycle of raids, robberies, murders, and retaliatory strikes continued during 1877. Indian raiders attacked ranches as far north as San Antonio, while military authorities in the United States admitted that they had pressed as far as two hundred miles into Mexico in pursuit of hostiles. On June 29, Lieutenant John L. Bullis struck the trail of Indians heading toward the Rio Grande with a herd of stolen livestock.

He followed them across the river and continued the pursuit for three days. On the third day, Bullis and his men caught the Lipans while they were resting, and attacked at once. In an engagement that lasted an hour, Bullis's force wounded several warriors and recovered twenty-three stolen horses.[55] The Lipans suffered an even greater setback a few weeks later, when thirty Mexican Kickapoos launched a daybreak attack on a Lipan encampment located just west of Zaragosa. The Kickapoos, perhaps angry that the Lipans' raiding activities targeted them and also invited American retaliatory raids into northern Coahuila, killed seventeen men, captured several women, and seized 125 horses. As the townspeople of Múzquiz came out to greet them, the elated Kickapoos paraded the seventeen scalps through the streets to celebrate their triumph. Zaragosa residents, meanwhile, reported seeing two Lipan men and several women in town who were in mourning and had slashed their arms and legs, indicating some recent disaster. If the Kickapoos killed as many warriors as reported, one American military official commented, "it nearly wipes out the Lipans."[56]

The various military campaigns waged against the Lipan Apaches on both sides of the border, coupled with the devastating Kickapoo assault of July 1877, drove some Lipans to seek refuge elsewhere.[57] In mid-September 1877, an informant of Lieutenant Bullis living in Arizona reported that ten or twelve families of Lipans had arrived at the San Carlos Reservation a month earlier. A few of them joined the legendary Mimbreño (Warm Springs) Apache leader Victorio on his raiding campaigns into Mexico, New Mexico, and Texas. Other Mexican Lipans drifted north onto the Mescalero Reservation, where they joined relatives who had relocated there a decade earlier—although pending instructions from the Bureau of Indian Affairs, they were at first treated as prisoners.[58] Sensitive to ongoing American charges that Mexico was harboring Apache raiders, Mexican authorities authorized General Jeronimo Treviño to clear out Indian sanctuaries in northern Coahuila. In October 1878, Treviño led an army of five thousand troops to locate and destroy Lipan, Mescalero, and Kickapoo encampments—an impressive campaign that probably did more to improve Mexican-American relations than it did in halting the cross-border raiding problem. On April 14, 1881, a small party of seven Lipans committed the "last important Indian raid on Texas soil" when they attacked and killed a fourteen-year-old boy named Allen Reiss (Allen

Lease) and Mrs. John McLauren while they were out working near the
McLaurens' home on the Frío River. Two weeks later, Lieutenant Bullis
and thirty Black Seminole scouts received orders to pursue the killers.
The Lipans had made rawhide "shoes" to cover their horses' tracks, but
the sharp-eyed scouts were still able to pick up their trail. Bullis and his
men followed the Indians across the Rio Grande and trailed them to their
hideout in the Sierra del Burro Mountains. On May 2, they attacked the
Lipan encampment, killing four warriors and capturing a woman and
child along with twenty-one horses. During the ensuing year, twelve expeditions set out from various Texas military posts in search of their elusive
enemies. They covered 3,662 miles, but without finding the slightest trace
of Indian raiders.[59]

After 1881, there were no serious attempts on the part of the Lipans to
remain in Texas or to regain a foothold there, and their identity as a distinct people began to fade from the historical record. Fort Griffin closed
its doors in May 1881, and its single remaining army unit, Company A,
Twenty-Second Infantry, marched southward to Fort Clark. The Tonkawas
and Lipans residing outside the old fort were destitute, and when drought
conditions wiped out their meager crops, they began to starve to death.
In October 1884, government officials placed the remaining seventy-eight
Tonkawas and nineteen Lipans on a train and shipped them to Indian
Territory. They settled at the Iowa Agency for a couple of months, before
authorities relocated them one final time to the Oakland Agency (or Fort
Oakland), located in the north-central part of what would become the
state of Oklahoma. At the turn of the century, a few Lipans were also
reported living with the Kiowa Apaches.[60]

Far to the south, meanwhile, the remaining Lipans lived near
Zaragosa or with the Mescaleros in New Mexico. Magoosh, a Mexican-
born Lipan leader—whom some Lipans refer to as their "last chief"—
led his followers back and forth between southern New Mexico and
Zaragosa. In 1887, Magoosh's band was encamped among the Mescaleros
at the latter's reservation in the Sacramento Mountains when trouble
broke out between the two groups. According to oral accounts recorded
by anthropologist Eve Ball, a Mescalero chief named "San Juan" lay
dying, and his medicine man attributed the source of his illness to two
Lipans who had recently been feuding with the old chief. A few hot-
tempered Mescaleros armed themselves—as did the Lipans—but the

reservation agent was able to intervene and restore peace before they had shed any blood.[61] At Zaragosa, meanwhile, a few Lipan families followed a warrior named Venego. Fearful that Mexican authorities sought to impress their men into military service, and on the verge of starvation, they sent a young man named Antone Apache to New Mexico (circa late 1890s) to locate Chief Magoosh's people, and to inquire if they might be allowed to join them. Antone Apache's mission was successful, and the elderly (and apparently balding) Magoosh spoke with Mescalero Indian agent James A. Carroll about the possibility of removing the remaining Lipans to New Mexico. Carroll in turn requested the assistance of Father Luciano Migeon, the parish priest at Tularosa, New Mexico, who was fluent in Spanish. After some preliminary investigating, Fr. Migeon learned that in October 1903, the Mexican army had transferred a group of Lipans from Coahuila to northwestern Chihuahua. The priest then wrote Chihuahua governor Luis Terrazas seeking permission for the Lipans to relocate to the Mescalero Reservation; Terrazas was happy to oblige. In 1905, Fr. Migeon traveled to Chihuahua City to escort the Lipans to Mescalero. Upon his arrival, he found thirty-seven pitiful Lipan prisoners sitting in a corral on the outskirts of town. They were filthy, had no shelter to shield them from the sun, and wore little in the way of clothing. Their guards fed them ears of corn, thrown to them as if they were animals, which they consumed raw because there was no wood to make a fire. The next day, Fr. Migeon loaded them into the caboose of a train for their final trip home. Ten-year-old Philemon Venego, the son of the Lipan captain Venego, remembered the trip well, particularly when they detrained at Mescalero and there were Apaches at the train station to greet them. "How glad our people were to see each other," Philemon Venego later recollected. "Men embraced with tears streaming down their faces."[62]

❨

Thus, after two hundred years residing in south Texas, the Lipan Apaches no longer possessed a discernible presence in what was once their homeland. During the eighteenth and nineteenth centuries, the Lipans' fierce independence and indomitable spirit played a significant role in the history of south-central Texas and the lower Rio Grande valley. Their incessant raiding helped end Spain's determined efforts at expanding its empire beyond San Antonio, and during the 1820s, the Lipans enjoyed the relative autonomy that came with the departure of Spanish troops and Mexican independence. Some Lipan groups—for both economic and political reasons—cultivated good relations with the growing number of American settlers pouring into east Texas, and enlisted their help in campaigns against their traditional Indian enemies. Following Texas's annexation by the United States and the rush of land-hungry immigrants intent on fulfilling their manifest destiny, the demographic balance shifted away from the Lipans and other Texas Indians, leaving them increasingly marginalized. Beginning in the 1850s, therefore, several bands embraced a cross-border raiding strategy that led to the militarization of the Rio Grande frontier, and soured Mexican-American relations for the remainder of the nineteenth century.

To what extent the Lipans controlled their own destiny or were "victims" of forces beyond their control is a difficult calculation. On the one hand, their ancestors' decision to leave the mountains and reside on the open plains made them vulnerable to attack, and planted the seeds of their ultimate demise. The proto-Lipans' decision to adopt a nomadic bison-hunting economy and then to "corner" the bison trade on the southern plains, furthermore, made them the most hated group in Texas during the seventeenth and eighteenth centuries. Tied closely to their role in the bison trade was the Lipans' historic unwillingness to place much reliance on agriculture. Possessing many enemies, the Lipans had little choice but to keep moving—but relying on large-game animals for subsistence was a risky business. Enhancing their vulnerability further still was the Lipans' inability to forge lasting alliances with anyone—either Indian or non-Indian. Their enemies, on the other hand, proved adept at doing so—working closely with the Spaniards and French and in various intertribal alliances, such as those existing between the Comanches and Wichitas and between various east Texas tribes. Although some Lipan refugees joined with similarly destitute Tonkawa refugees during the first half of the nineteenth century, the Lipans were unique in their overall unwillingness to depend on others—even their Apachean relatives in New Mexico—until it was too late. By the time that the Lipans and Mescaleros began cooperating in the mid-nineteenth century, the demographic strength of both peoples had been shattered.

Of course, several forces over which they exercised no control also undermined Lipan tribal viability. Periodic epidemic diseases such as smallpox decimated Lipan band strength, forcing affected groups to combine or to fracture irreparably. The Lipans' inability to procure firearms at the same rate as their Indian enemies also placed them at a distinct disadvantage, forcing warriors to acquire by theft what they could not acquire by trade. The expanding market in Indian captives—primarily women and children—also worked to the detriment of the Lipans, as they became the favored targets of Spanish, Comanche, and Wichita slave raids. The Lipans' own involvement in this exchange of human commodities only heightened the desire of their enemies to do unto the Lipans before the Lipans did unto them. The steady increase of American settlers in Texas that began in the 1820s expanded mightily in ensuing decades, leading to a vast demographic advantage on the part of non-Indians. This development brought about a profound shift in power away from Texas's indigenous peoples—what historian F. Todd Smith has described as a movement "from dominance to disappearance." Finally, the Lipans remained a convenient target—even a pawn of sorts—for American and Mexican military officials seeking to demonstrate their country's commitment to solving the "border problem." In the aftermath of an especially bloody campaign that resulted in the death or capture of over one hundred Lipans, Mexican governor Santiago Vidaurri challenged military officials in Texas to match what his troops had accomplished in northern Coahuila. He boasted that the Mexicans' "chastisement" of the Lipans had surpassed his hopes, "the whole tribe having been made prisoners, most of the warriors killed, and the small remnant so dispersed that their insignificant number cannot inspire any fears for the future."[63]

☾

Career army officer and Indian fighter Richard I. Dodge related an incident that occurred in the early 1850s in which a Lipan Apache at Fort Martin Scott (near Fredericksburg) traded five beautifully dressed wildcat skins for a book of matches. After seating himself near a large stone, the Lipan struck one match after the other, curiously watching the flame of each, until all within the box were gone.[64] The forlorn image of the solitary Lipan observing the small tongue of fire as it made its way down the thin piece of wood may have carried deep symbolism for him.

The Lipans deemed wind and lightning as essential to the animation of all living creatures. Life began when wind and lightning entered the body, and ended when the lightning burned out and the wind abated. Thus, the Lipans referred to death by the phrase "he burned down"—not unlike the matches being observed by the Lipan trader. At the turn of the twentieth century, the flame that had once given life and strength to the Lipan Apaches of Texas was nearly exhausted . . . yet a faint flicker remained that in the early twenty-first century offered the possibility of rebirth and renewal, continuing a tradition of Lipan resiliency and adaptability that characterized their ancestors who once marched around the earth in search of a home.

EPILOGUE

☽

THE HISTORICAL RECORD of the Lipan Apaches ends rather abruptly
in the early twentieth century after the relocation of the Chihuahua
prisoners to the Mescalero Reservation. Like virtually all other native
peoples, the closing years of the nineteenth century marked a demographic nadir for the Lipans, and in the early twentieth century, various observers estimated that their population stood at fewer than forty
people.[1] While this figure seems somewhat low (particularly given the
arrival in New Mexico of between twenty and forty Lipans in 1905), a
smallpox epidemic that struck Mescalero settlements along Tularosa,
Nogal, Three Rivers, and Elk-Silver creeks between 1900 and 1910 killed
several adults and nearly half the children residing there.[2] Further exacerbating the Lipans' demographic collapse was a reported gender imbal-
ance that existed on the Mescalero Reservation in the early twentieth
century. According to Philemon Venego, one of the Lipans who relocated to Mescalero in 1905, there were very few Lipan females residing at the Mescalero Reservation, and most young men, consequently,
took Mescalero brides.[3] Given the Mescaleros' matrilocal-residence and
matrilineal-kinship reckoning system, parents of such unions would
have raised their children as Mescaleros.

As time passed, the Lipans living alongside larger tribes in New
Mexico and Oklahoma gradually assimilated, blurring cultural

distinctions and language traits that had once distinguished them from each other. During the Great Depression, Commissioner of Indian Affairs John Collier advanced a New Deal for Indians that led to the "reorganization" of several tribes. In March 1936, the Mescaleros approved a new tribal constitution that made longtime Lipan and Chiricahua Apache residents of their reservation full members of the Mescalero Apache tribe. Two years later, the Tonkawas in Oklahoma included a similar measure in their new constitution.[4]

By the beginning of World War Two, therefore, the Lipan Apaches had seemingly vanished—joining the Jumanos, Karankawas, Coahuiltecans, and other indigenous peoples that had once dominated the southern reaches of Texas. Government officials in Washington, DC, also appear to have lost track of the Lipans. As Frank D. Reeve noted in his 1946 article "The Apache Indians in Texas," about thirty-five Lipans were living on New Mexico and Oklahoma reservations in 1940, but they had "lost their official identity in the records of the Office of Indian Affairs."[5]

As the United States demobilized after the war, the federal government moved to terminate its guardianship responsibilities over Indian peoples, and to integrate Native Americans into the social and economic fabric of the country. As a prelude to such efforts, Congress sought to settle any outstanding claims that tribes had initiated against the federal government, and in 1946, created the Indian Claims Commission (ICC) to adjudicate long-standing Indian grievances. In February 1948, the entire Apache Nation filed a petition before the ICC for lands they had lost in Arizona, New Mexico, and Texas. A year and a half later, the Apaches amended the petition, declaring instead their desire to file separate claims for each distinct Apache group. That being the case, the Mescaleros and Lipans filed a new petition in 1959 seeking compensation for tribal lands they had lost in Texas during the nineteenth century. The ICC dismissed the petition, however, claiming that the Apaches had no aboriginal title to the land since the Republic of Texas had never acknowledged the existence of aboriginal land rights prior to its annexation by the United States in 1845 (see chapter five). The Mescaleros and Lipans appealed the decision, and in 1967 the Court of Claims in *Lipan Apache Tribe v. United States* (180 Court of Claims 487) reversed the ICC's decision, ruling that the Apaches could recover damages if they could show that the federal government had broken treaty promises that resulted in the loss of their lands. In February

1976, the ICC held new hearings on the Lipan and Mescalero claims, and on February 19, ruled that the Mescaleros could recover five million dollars for themselves, and an additional five million dollars on behalf of the Lipan Apaches residing on the Mescalero Reservation. Named among the Lipan Apache plaintiffs in the suit, incidentally, was Philemon Venego, who as a young boy in 1905 boarded the train in Chihuahua to join Chief Magoosh's people at the Mescalero Reservation.[6]

But the Lipan story does not end with the successful court case. On May 8, 1999, the newly incorporated Lipan Apache Band of Texas, Inc. (LABT), a federal, nonprofit organization headed by Daniel Castro Romero Jr., submitted a letter to officials in the Bureau of Indian Affairs giving notification that the LABT sought federal recognition as a viable and sovereign tribe and/or nation.[7] According to its bylaws, the LABT's mission is to serve "the cultural, social, educational, spiritual, linguistic, economic, health, and traditional needs" of its members, while preserving and sharing Lipan Apache culture, heritage, and traditional knowledge with the citizens of Texas.[8] But who is Daniel Castro Romero Jr., and to what Lipan Band of Texas was he referring? In order to answer these two pertinent questions, a quick rewind of Lipan history is required. The thirty-seven-year-old Romero traces his ancestry to the important Lipan Apache (or *Llanero* Apache) leader Cuelgas de Castro, one of the men who traveled to Mexico City in the early 1820s to sign a treaty with the newly established Mexican Empire.[9] Chief Cuelgas de Castro (or simply Castro) was also a contemporary of Texas presidents Sam Houston and Mirabeau B. Lamar, and knew each man personally. On occasion, Castro assisted military officials in their campaigns against the Comanches. According to Castro family oral tradition, after Chief Castro's death in the early 1840s, his son John (Juan) Castro moved his people to Laredo, and later south into Mexico, where they established a ranchería at Remolino alongside the Kickapoos. There they witnessed first-hand El Día de los Gritos (or The Day of the Screams) when Colonel Ranald S. McKenzie's Fourth Cavalry destroyed Kickapoo, Lipan, and Mescalero encampments situated along the San Rodrigo River.[10] John Castro, along with a son (Calixtro Castro) and a daughter (Juanita Castro), survived the assault, and somehow managed to escape capture and make their way to safety.[11]

The Lipan Apache Band of Texas, consequently, seeks to identify and enroll as members the descendents of those Lipans who survived the Remolino attack, as well as other Lipans who had fled into Mexico during the latter half of the nineteenth century, or who relocated to New Mexico in the late nineteenth and early twentieth centuries. As of December 2005, the organization had identified over 1,400 prospective members (300 in central Texas, 300 in south Texas, 150 in northern Texas, 480 in California, and 185 in New Mexico) and was encouraging them to submit tribal enrollment forms so that the LABT could verify their claims to Lipan ancestry.[12]

Besides enlisting new members, Daniel Castro Romero Jr. has sought to bolster his organization's petition for federal recognition by securing several municipal and state resolutions attesting to the Lipan Apaches' historic presence in Texas, and to the various contributions of the Lipans' "living descendents." In September 1999, the city of Selma, Texas, issued an "Official Proclamation" attesting to the fact that Selma residents and Lipan Apache Indians had "lived together in peace for over 140 years." Two and half years later, the Texas State Senate passed a resolution that recognized the Castro family's Lipan heritage going back six generations, and the many contributions the various generations had made to the state's history. Romero was also the driving force behind the introduction of legislation geared at protecting unmarked burial grounds and associated human remains in Texas, as well as artifacts recovered from Native American burial sites. In April 2006, he oversaw the restoration of ancient human remains at the Buckeye Knoll site in Victoria County. Of even greater significance, however, was the introduction in May 2005, of Senate Concurrent Resolution 34, which again called for recognition of Lipan Apache contributions to the state of Texas and to the nation. The resolution also contained a provision whereby the 79th Legislature would urge the U.S. Congress to recognize the Lipan Apache Band of Texas as a federally acknowledged Indian tribe.[13]

In western Louisiana, meanwhile, members of the Apache-Choctaw community of Ebarb (incorporated by the state of Louisiana in July 1977) trace at least part of their heritage to the Lipan Apaches. During much of the eighteenth century, Comanches, Wichitas, and Caddos raided Lipan encampments in central and south Texas and seized hundreds of captives (primarily women and children), whom they carried off to Louisiana to exchange for European manufactured goods. The numerous Spanish campaigns into Apache country also resulted in the capture of Lipan men, women, and children, whom they employed as servants in the households of the well-to-do. Lipan Apache slaves were present at Los Adaes (the capital of Spanish Texas from 1729 to 1773), and Lipan women married (or cohabited with) Spanish soldiers at the post, as well as with French soldiers and traders stationed at nearby Natchitoches. The descendents of those Spanish, French, and Lipan Apache unions later mixed with Choctaw emigrants from the Southeast who began passing through the Sabine River region in the 1780s. From the late eighteenth century to the present, the Choctaw-Apache of Ebarb (Sabine Parish) isolated themselves into what anthropologist Dayna Bowker Lee has termed "an endogamous cultural enclave" that the state of Louisiana and other Native American groups recognize as ethnically Indian. Like the Lipan Apache Band of Texas, the Choctaw-Apache Tribe of Ebarb is working toward acquiring federal recognition from the Bureau of Indian Affairs. According to Chief Tommy W. Bolton, tribal officials have deemed 3,276 persons eligible for membership with the tribe—nearly half of whom live within the ancestral boundaries, while the remainder are scattered across the United States. In September 2000, the Choctaw-Apache tribal council declared that they shared a "common heritage, culture, and kinship" with the Lipan Apache Band of Texas, and promised to assist them in acquiring federal recognition.[14]

The Lipan Apaches' quest for federal recognition hit a snag in the summer of 2007 in the form of an intra-Lipan feud. On July 27, Romero's Lipan Apache Band of Texas, Inc. received a summons to appear before the Bexar County District Court to answer a petition filed on behalf of Bernard Barcena Jr., a former vice-chairman of the organization. Drawing, perhaps, on the Lipan Apaches' historic affinity for decentralization, and the prerogative of any band member to set off on his/her own, Barcena sought to establish a new nonprofit (501c) organization entitled the "Lipan Apache Tribe of Texas, Inc.," which would also seek federal recognition and compete with Romero's Lipan Apache Band of Texas, Inc. for members. The court approved Barcena's request (as apparently did Romero) and authorized both Lipan entities to enlist members, but with the stipulation that individuals could hold membership in only one of the two Lipan organizations.[15] The reasons for the schism remain unclear, and the long-term impact on the Lipans' pursuit for federal recognition remains to be determined.

NOTES

((

PREFACE

1. Report of Texas governor Prudenzio de Orobio Basterra, 1738, Bexar Archives Translations, microfilm copy (hereafter cited BAT), series 1, reel 2, vol. 11, April 9, 1739–August 26, 1739, Hunter Room, University of Texas at Brownsville (hereafter cited UTB); William Dunn, "Apache Relations in Texas, 1718–1750," *Texas State Historical Association Quarterly* 14 (1911), 236–38.

2. Ibid.

3. Thomas Schilz, *Lipan Apaches in Texas* (El Paso: Texas Western Press, 1987).

4. John Upton Terrell, *The Plains Apache* (New York: Thomas Y. Crowell Company, 1975), 15.

5. Frederick W. Hodge, ed., *Handbook of American Indians North of Mexico*, pt. 1 (New York: Greenwood Press Publishers, 1907), 768–69; James Mooney, "Tribal Names and Divisions of the Jicarilla, Lipan, and Mescalero Apaches, 1897," manuscript 3785, Smithsonian Institution National Anthropological Archives, Washington, DC.

6. Albert H. Schroeder, *A Study of the Apache Indians* (New York: Garland Publishing, 1974), 495–96, 502.

7. Daniel Castro Romero Jr., Edinburg, TX. Email to author, December 10, 2005.

INTRODUCTION

1. "Killer-of-Enemies Creates the Deer," in Morris E. Opler, *The Myths and Legends of the Lipan Apache Indians*, Memoirs of the American Folk-Lore Society (New York: J. J. Augustin Publisher, 1940), 36:29–30.

2. Ibid., 29, 137.

3. Andrée F. Sjoberg, "Lipan Apache Culture in Historical Perspective," *Southwestern Journal of Anthropology* 9 (1953): 85–86; T. S. Dennis, *Life of F. E. Buckelew: The Indian Captive* (Bandera, TX: Hunter's Printing House, 1925), 91; Jean Louis Berlandier, *The Indians of Texas in 1830*, ed. and intro. John C. Ewers (Washington, DC: Smithsonian Institution Press, 1969), 128; Elizabeth A. H. John, "Views from a Desk in Chihuahua: Manuel Merino's Reports on Apaches and Neighboring Nations, ca. 1804," *Southwestern Historical Quarterly* 95 (1991): 149; Edward W. Gifford, *Culture Element Distributions: Apache-Pueblo*, Anthropological Records, ed. A. L. Kroeber, R. H. Lowie, and R. L. Olson, vol. 4 (Berkeley: University of California Press, 1940), 36–37; Carlos E. Castañeda, *Our Catholic Heritage in Texas, 1519–1936* (Austin: Von Boeckmann-Jones Co., 1936), 3:14; Ferdinand Roemer, *Texas*, trans. Oswald Mueller (San Antonio: Standard Printing Co., 1935), 106; William Bollaert, "Observations of the Indian Tribes in Texas," *Journal of the Ethnological Society of London* 2 (1850): 277; Frederick Law Olmstead, *A Journey through Texas: Or a Saddle Trip on the Southwestern Frontier* (Austin: University of Texas Press, 1978), 293; reprint of 1857 edition (page citations are the reprint edition).

4. Sjoberg, "Lipan Apache Culture," 86–87; Gifford, *Culture Element Distributions*, 36–37; José María Sánchez, "A Trip to Texas in 1828," trans. Carlos E. Castañeda, *Southwestern Historical Quarterly* 29 (April 1926): 251; Bollaert, "Observations of the Indian Tribes in Texas," 277; John C. Ewers, "Women's Roles in Plains Indian Warfare," in *Skeletal Biology in the Great Plains*, ed. Douglas W. Owsley and Richard L. Jantz (Washington, DC: Smithsonian Institution Press, 1994), 326; Stella La Paz, Antonio Apache, Perry Bigmouth Interviews, Morris Edward Opler Papers, Collection 14–25–3238, subseries D, box 44, Division of Rare and Manuscript Collections, Cornell University Library, Cornell, New York (hereafter cited as Lipan Interviews, *Opler Papers*).

5. Sjoberg, "Lipan Apache Culture," 85–86; Gifford, *Culture Element Distributions*, 36–37; Harry Hoijer, "The History and Customs of the Lipan, As Told by Augustina Zuazua," *Linguistics* 161 (1975): 27; Lipan Interviews, *Opler Papers*; Don Antonio Cordero, "Cordero's Description of the Apache, 1796," ed. Daniel S. Matson and Albert H. Schroeder, *New Mexico Historical Review* 32 (October 1957): 340; William W. Newcomb, *German Artist on the Texas Frontier: Friedrich Richard Petri* (Austin: University of Texas Press, 1978), 134.

6. Paul H. Carlson, *The Plains Indians* (College Station: Texas A&M University Press, 1998), 36–39; Waldo R. Wedel, "Some Aspects of Human Ecology on the Central Plains," *American Anthropologist* 55 (October 1953): 505; Frank G. Roe, *The Indian and the Horse* (Norman: University of Oklahoma Press, 1955), 22; Jeffrey D. Carlisle, "Spanish Relations with the Apache Nations East of the Rio Grande," Ph.D. diss., University of North Texas, 2001, 24.

7. Sjoberg, "Lipan Apache Culture in Historical Perspective," 80–81; William W. Newcomb, *The Indians of Texas: Prehistory to Present* (Austin: University of Texas Press, 1961), 91–92; Dan Flores, "Bison Ecology and Bison Diplomacy: The Southern Plains from 1800 to 1850," *Journal of American History* 78 (September 1991): 485; Opler, *Myths and Legends of the Lipan Apache Indians*, 124.

8. Gifford, *Culture Element Distributions*, 5–7, 9, 84, 89; Jose Cortes, *Views from the Apache Frontier: Report on the Northern Provinces of New Spain, 1799*, ed. Elizabeth A. H. John (Norman: University of Oklahoma Press, 1989), 68; James L. Haley, *Apaches: A History and Culture Portrait* (Garden City, NY: Doubleday & Company, 1981), 84–87; S. E. Banta, *Buckelew: The Indian Captive or The Life Story of F. M. Buckelew While a Captive among the Lipan Indians in the Western Wilds of Frontier Texas* (Mason, TX: The Mason Herald, 1911; reprint, New York: Garland Publishing, 1977), 76–77 (page citations are from the reprint edition).

9. Gifford, *Culture Element Distributions*, 5–7, 84–87; Hoijer, "The History and Customs of the Lipan," 30–38.

10. Morris E. Opler, "An Application of the Theory of Themes in Culture," *Journal of the Washington Academy of Sciences* 36 (May 15, 1946): 143; Opler, "A Summary of Jicarilla Apache Culture," *American Anthropologist* 38 (April–June 1936), 207–8; John, "Views from a Desk in Chihuahua," 153–54.

11. Gifford, *Culture Element Distributions*, 9–10; Banta, *Buckelew: The Indian Captive*, 71–72; Terrell, *The Plains Apache*, 34; Sandra L. Myres, "The Lipan Apaches," in Dorman Winfrey et al., *The Indian Tribes of Texas* (Waco: Texian Press, 1971), 131; Johns, "Views from a Desk in Chihuahua," 153–54; Carlisle, "Spanish Relations with the Apache Nations," 25–26; Morris E. Opler, "Problems in Apachean Cultural History, with Special Reference to the Lipan Apache," *Anthropological Quarterly* 48 (July 1975): 188–89; Donald E. Worcester, "The Spread of Spanish Horses in the Southwest," *New Mexico Historical Review* 19 (1944): 226; Sjoberg, "Lipan Apache Culture in Historical Perspective," 83; Juan Antonio Padilla, "Texas in 1820," trans. Mattie Austin Hatcher, *Southwestern Historical Quarterly* 23 (July 1919): 56.

12. Banta, *Buckelew: The Indian Captive*, 71.

13. Lipan Interviews, *Opler Papers*.

14. Opler, "Problems in Apachean Cultural History," 188; Frank R. Secoy, *Changing Military Patterns of the Great Plains Indians*, intro. John C. Ewers (Lincoln: University of Nebraska Press, 1992; reprint of 1953 edition), 30–32.

15. Sjoberg, "Lipan Apache Culture in Historical Perspective," 82–83; Terrell, *The Plains Apache*, 34; Newcomb, *The Indians of Texas*, 113–15; Berlandier, *The Indians of Texas in 1830*, 132–33; Cortes, *Views from the Apache Frontier*, 60; Dennis, *Life of F. M. Buckelew: The Indian Captive*, 93.

16. Sjoberg, "Lipan Apache Culture in Historical Perspective," 82–83; Gifford, *Culture Element Distribution*, 11–13; Hoijer, "The History and Customs of the Lipan," 31; Opler, *Myths and Legends of the Lipan Apaches*, 186; Banta, *Buckelew: The Indian Captive*, 72–73; Newcomb, *The Indians of Texas*, 115–16; James H. Gunnerson, "Plains Apache Archeology: A Review," *Plains Anthropologist* 13 (August 1968): 174; John D. Speth, "Some Unexplored Aspects of Mutualistic Plains-Pueblo Food Exchange," in *Farmers, Hunters, and Colonists: Interaction between the Southwest and the Southern Plains*, ed. Katherine A. Spielmann (Tucson: University of Arizona Press, 1991), 32.

17. Gifford, *Culture Element Distribution*, 13–15; Hoijer, "The History and Customs of the Lipan," 30–38; Lipan Interviews, *Opler Papers*.

18. Lipan Interviews, *Opler Papers*.

19. Sjoberg, "Lipan Apache Culture in Historical Perspective," 87–88; Gifford, *Culture Element Distributions*, 21–24; Hoijer, "The History and Customs of the Lipan," 27–28; Morris E. Opler, "The Apachean Culture Pattern and Its Origins," in *Handbook of North American Indians*, vol. 10, *The Southwest*, ed. Alfonso Ortiz (Washington, DC: Smithsonian Institution Press, 1983), 370–71; Opler, "Problems in Apachean Cultural History," 188; Newcomb, *The Indians of Texas*, 116–17; Dennis, *Life of F. M. Buckelew: The Indian Captive*, 105–6.

20. Gifford, *Culture Element Distributions*, 58–59; Lipan Interviews, *Opler Papers*; Sjoberg, "Lipan Apache Culture in Historical Perspective," 90; Merle Shover, "Apache Fiddles," *Indians at Work* 4 (1937): 46–47; Banta, *Buckelew: The Indian Captive*, 82.

21. Gifford, *Culture Element Distributions*, 52–57; Hoijer, "The History and Customs of the Lipan," 31; Sjoberg, "Lipan Apache Culture in Historical Perspective," 97; Haley, *Apaches: A History and Culture Portrait*, 162–63; Opler, *Myths and Legends of the Lipan Apache Indians*, 87, 203; Padilla, "Texas in 1820," 56–62; Virginia Wayland, "Apache Playing Cards," *Expedition* 4 (Spring 1962): 34–39; J. L. McConnel, *Western Characters or Types of Border Life in the Western States* (New York: Redfield, 1853), 57–58.

22. John, "Views from a Desk in Chihuahua," 156–57.

23. Morris E. Opler, "Lipan Apache Navigation," *The Masterkey* 49, no. 2 (1975): 70–72; Thomas Roy Hester, "Aboriginal Watercraft on the Lower Rio Grande of Texas," *The Masterkey* 46 (1972): 108–9; Gifford, *Culture Element Distributions*, 24–25; Hoijer, "The History and Customs of the Lipan," 34; Roemer, *Texas*, 106.

24. W. W. Newcomb, "A Re-Examination of the Causes of Plains Warfare," *American Anthropologist* 52 (July–September 1950), 317–30.

25. Sjoberg, "Lipan Apache Culture," 89–90; Gifford, *Culture Element Distributions*, 32–33; Berlandier, *The Indians of Texas in 1830*, 130; Hermann Lehmann, *Nine Years among the Indians, 1870–1879*, ed. J. Marvin Hunter (Albuquerque: University of New Mexico Press, 2001; a reprint of 1927 edition by Von Boeckmann-Jones Company), 26; W. W. Newcomb states that the Lipans did not paint their shields. See Newcomb, *A German Artist on the Texas Frontier*, 130.

26. Secoy, *Changing Military Patterns of the Great Plains Indians*, 26; Dunn, "Apache Relations in Texas, 1718–1750," 226–27.

27. Cordero, "Cordero's Description of the Apache, 1796," 345–46; Gifford, *Culture Element Distributions*, 71–72; John, "Views from a Desk in Chihuahua," 158–60.

28. Alfred B. Thomas, *Teodoro de Croix and the Northern Frontier of New Spain, 1776–1783* (Norman: University of Oklahoma Press, 1941), 90, 98.

29. Christon I. Archer, "The Deportation of Barbarian Indians from the Internal Provinces of New Spain, 1789–1810," *The Americas* 29 (January 1973): 376; Azar Gat, "The Pattern of Fighting in Simple, Small-Scale, Prestate Societies," *Journal of Anthropological Research* 55 (1999): 563–83.

30. Opler, "The Apachean Culture Pattern and Its Origins," 373; L. Bryce Boyer, "Stone as a Symbol in Apache Mythology," *American Imago* 22 (Spring–Summer 1965): 20–21.

31. Among the Lipans, Killer-of-Enemies possesses the attributes of both Southern Athapaskan culture heroes Killer-of-Enemies and Child-of-the-Water (or Wise One). Killer-of-Enemies is usually associated with the sun (fire), and the Child-of-the-Water with water, thunder, and the moon. See Opler, *Myths and Legends of the Lipan Apache Indians*, 16, 22.

32. Some Lipan groups associated Changing Woman as the wife—rather than the mother—of Killer-of-Enemies. Lipan Interviews, *Opler Papers*.

33. Opler, "The Theory of Themes in Culture," 138.

34. "The Woman Saved by Prairie Dogs," in Opler, *Myths and Legends of the Lipan Apache Indians*, 72–74, 75, 106; Opler, "The Theory of Themes in Culture," 138–39; Opler, "A Note on the Cultural Affiliations of Northern Mexican Nomads," *American Anthropologist* 38 (April–June 1936): 704.

35. Opler, "The Theory of Themes," 139.

36. Morris Opler, "Cause and Effect in Apachean Agriculture, Division of Labor, Residence Patterns, and Girls' Puberty Rites," *American Anthropologist* 74 (October 1972): 1144; Opler, "The Theory of Themes, 139–40.

37. John G. Bourke, "Notes upon the Religion of the Apache Indians," *Folklore* 2 (December 1891): 419.

38. Opler, "The Theory of Themes," 140–41; Opler, "The Apachean Culture Pattern and Its Origins," 373.

39. Opler, "The Theory of Themes," 141–42.

40. Ibid., 142–43.

41. Ibid., 157.

42. Ibid., 157–58; Lipan Interviews, *Opler Papers.*

43. Opler, "The Theory of Themes," 157–58.

44. Ibid.

45. John J. Honigmann, "Parallels in the Development of Shamanism among the Northern and Southern Athapaskans," *American Anthropologist* 51 (July–September 1949): 513; Morris Opler, "Remuneration to Supernaturals and Man in Apache Ceremonialism," *Ethnology* 7 (October 1968): 375–76; Sjoberg, "Lipan Apache Culture," 92–93; Newcomb, *The Indians of Texas,* 129–30; James W. Cornett, *How the Indians Used Desert Plants* (Palm Springs, CA: Nature Trails Press, 2002), 51, 59; Lipan Interviews, *Opler Papers.*

46. Weston LaBarre, "Twenty Years of Peyote Studies," *Current Anthropology* 1 (January 1960): 45–47; J. S. Slotkin, "Peyotism, 1521–1891," *American Anthropologist* 57 (April 1955): 204; Stacy B. Schaefer, "The Peyote Religion and Mescalero Apache: An Ethnohistorical View from West Texas," *Journal of Big Bend Studies* 12 (2000): 52–53; Edward F. Anderson, *Peyote: The Divine Cactus,* 2nd ed. (Tucson: University of Arizona Press, 1996), 3, 20–21, 83–84, 120–27, 174–78, 185–86; Omer C. Stewart, *Peyote Religion: A History* (Norman: University of Oklahoma Press, 1987), 3–4; Omer C. Stewart, "Origin of the Peyote Religion in the United States," *Plains Anthropologist* 19 (1974): 212–13; Kay Parker Schweinfurth, *Prayer on Top of the Earth: The Spiritual Universe of the Plains Apache* (Boulder: University of Colorado Press, 2002), 170.

47. Opler, *Myths and Legends of the Lipan Apache Indians,* 56–58. See Schweinfurth's *Prayer on Top of the Earth,* 170–73, for an alternative story about Lipan peyote use.

48. Morris E. Opler, "An Outline of Chiricahua Apache Social Organization," in *Social Anthropology of North American Tribes: Essays in Social Organization, Law, and Religion,* ed. Fred Eggan (Chicago: University of Chicago Press, 1937), 177–80; Harry W. Basehart, "Mescalero Apache

Band Organization and Leadership," in *Apachean Culture History and Ethnology*, ed. Keith H. Basso and Morris E. Opler (Tucson: University of Arizona Press, 1971), 37–41; Telephone interview with Victor Crayhon, BIA compliance officer of the Lipan Apache Tribe of Texas, September 2007; Opler, "The Apachean Culture Pattern and Its Origins," 369; Grenville Goodwin, "The Characteristics and Function of Clan in a Southern Athapascan Culture," *American Anthropologist* 39 (July–September 1937): 394; Gary C. Anderson, *The Indian Southwest, 1580–1830: Ethnogenesis and Reinvention* (Norman: University of Oklahoma Press, 2005), 126; Newcomb, *The Indians of Texas*, 124; Morris E. Opler, "The Lipan and Mescalero Apache in Texas," in *Apache Indians X* (New York: Garland Publishing, 1974), 218–19.

49. Terrell, *The Plains Apache*, 40; Berlandier, *The Indians of Texas*, 38–39; Basehart, "Mescalero Band Organization and Leadership," 43–46; Sjoberg, "Lipan Apache Culture," 93–94; Opler, "The Apachean Culture Pattern and Its Origins," 369.

50. Newcomb, *The Indians of Texas*, 121; Opler, "The Theory of Themes in Culture," 155–56; M. Jean Tweedie, "Notes on the History and Adaptation of the Apache Tribe," *American Anthropologist* 70 (December 1968): 1140; Morris E. Opler, "The Kinship Systems of the Southern Athapaskan-speaking Tribes," *American Anthropologist* 38 (October–December 1936): 622, 625; Opler, "The Apachean Culture Pattern and Its Origins," 370.

51. Cordero, "Cordero's Description of the Apache," 342; Bollaert, "Indian Tribes in Texas," 277; Terrell, *The Plains Apache*, 36–37; Newcomb, *The Indians of Texas*, 121; Opler, *Myths and Legends of the Lipan Apache Indians*, see note p. 42; J. M. Morphis, *History of Texas* (New York: United States Publishing Company, 1875), 433; Opler, "Apache Data Concerning the Relation of Kinship Terminology to Social Classification," *American Anthropologist* 39 (April–June 1937): 204; Gifford, *Culture Element Distributions*, 66.

52. Tweedie, "Notes on the History and Adaptation of the Apache Tribe," 1140; Opler, "The Apachean Culture Pattern and Its Origins," 370; Anderson, *The Indian Southwest*, 135.

53. Opler, "Remuneration to Supernaturals and Man in Apachean Ceremonialism," 376.

54. Morris E. Opler, *An Apache Life-Way: The Economic, Social, and Religious Institutions of the Chiricahua Apaches* (Chicago: University of Chicago Press, 1941), 82–87; Opler, "Cause and Effect in Apachean Agriculture, Division of Labor, Residence Patterns, and Girls' Puberty Rites," 1144; Anne Dhu Shapiro and Ines Talamantez, "The Mescalero Apache Girls' Puberty Ceremony: The Role of Music in Structuring Ritual Time," *Yearbook for Traditional Music* 18 (1986): 80–81; Opler, "The Theory of Themes in Culture," 149; Gifford, *Culture Element Distribution*, 64–65.

55. Opler, "The Theory of Themes in Culture," 148.

56. Ibid.

57. Ibid., 149–50; Opler, "The Apachean Culture Pattern and Its Origins," 371.

58. Opler, "The Theory of Themes in Culture," 159–60; Opler, "The Apachean Culture Pattern and Its Origins," 379.

59. Opler, "The Lipan Apache Death Complex and Its Extensions," *Southwestern Historical Quarterly* 1 (1945): 123; Opler, "Component, Assemblage, and Theme in Cultural Integration and Differentiation," *American Anthropologist* 61 (December 1959): 957–58; Opler, "The Apachean Culture Pattern and Its Origins," 379.

60. Opler, "The Lipan Apache Death Complex and Its Extensions," 123–25; Opler, "Component, Assemblage," 956–57; Gifford, *Culture Element Distribution*, 68–69; Sjoberg, "Lipan Apache Culture," 92; Richard J. Perry, "Proto-Athapaskan Culture: The Use of Ethnographic Reconstruction," *American Ethnologist* 10 (November 1983): 726; Opler, "The Apachean Culture and Its Origins," 377–78.

61. Boyer, "Stone as a Symbol in Apache Mythology," 18–19; Opler, "The Apachean Culture Pattern and Its Origins," 377–78; John J. Honigmann, "Northern and Southern Athapaskan Eschatology," *American Anthropologist* 47 (July–September 1945): 467–69; Opler, "The Lipan Apache Death Complex and Its Extensions," 125–26; Opler, "Component, Assemblage," 956–57; Gifford, *Culture Element Distribution*, 68–69; Sjoberg, "Lipan Apache Culture," 92; Opler, "The Theory of Themes in Culture," 160–61; Opler, "Problems in Apachean Cultural History," 185–86, 189.

62. Opler, "The Lipan Death Complex and Its Extensions," 137–39; Opler, "Component, Assemblage," 959.

63. Opler, "Component, Assemblage," 963.

64. Lourdes V. Lapuz, "Culture Change and Psychological Stress," *American Journal of Psychoanalysis* 36 (1976): 171–73.

65. Albert H. Schroeder, "Shifting for Survival in the Spanish Southwest," *New Mexico Historical Review* 43 (October 1968): 292; Lapuz, "Culture Change and Psychological Stress," 171–73.

66. Opler, "The Apachean Culture Pattern and Its Origins," 375.

67. Richard H. Lowie, *Indians of the Plains* (Lincoln: University of Nebraska Press, 1954), 5–7.

CHAPTER ONE

1. "The Emergence," in Morris E. Opler, *Myths and Legends of the Lipan Apache Indians*, 13–16.

2. Ibid.

3. Opler argues that Lipan and Jicarilla Apache creation stories are nearly identical. Ibid., 15n1; David French, "A Comparative Study of the Mythologies of the Jicarilla, Lipan, Mescalero, and Chiricahua Apache Indians" (master's thesis, Claremont College, 1940), 73.

4. The appellation "Na-Dene" is a composite term derived from the Athapaskan word for people. It combines the Haida word *na*, which means "to dwell" or "house," with the Tlingit word *dene*, meaning people. See John W. Ives, *A Theory of Northern Athapaskan Prehistory* (Boulder, CO: Westview Press, 1990), 66.

5. There are, of course, a multitude of opinions and estimates regarding the early peopling of the Americas. See Herbert S. Klein and Daniel C. Schiffner, "The Current Debate about the Origins of the PaleoIndians of America," *Journal of Social History* 37 (Winter 2003): 485–88; Joseph H. Greenberg, Christy G. Turner II, and Stephen L. Zegura, "The Settlement of the Americas: A Comparison of Linguistic, Dental, and Genetic Evidence," *Current Anthropology* 27 (December 1986): 479, 488; Merritt Ruhlen, "The Origin of the Na-Dene," *Proceedings of the National Academy of Sciences of the United States of America* 95 (November 10, 1998): 13995; Wendell H. Oswalt, *This Lands Was Theirs: A Study of North American Indians*, 4th ed. (Mountain View, CA: Mayfield Publishing Co., 1988), 14; J. Loring Haskell, *Southern Athapaskan Migration: 200–1750* (Tsaile, AZ: Navajo Community College Press, 1987), 11–12; William W. Newcomb Jr., *North American Indians: An Anthropological Perspective* (Pacific Palisades, CA: Goodyear Publishing Company, 1974), 105.

6. Richard J. Perry, *Western Apache Heritage: People of the Mountain Corridor* (Austin: University of Texas Press, 1991), 27, 54–58; Beryl C. Gillespie, "Major Fauna in the Traditional Economy," in *Handbook of North American Indians*, vol. 6, *The Subarctic*, ed. June Helm (Washington, DC: Smithsonian Institution Press, 1981), 15–18.

7. For a discussion of when the various Na-Dene groups separated from each other into distinct groups, see William R. Fowler, "Linguistic Evidence for Athapaskan Prehistory," in *Problems in the Prehistory of the North American Subarctic: The Athapaskan Question*, ed. J. W. Helmer et al. (Calgary, BC: University of Calgary Archeological Association, 1977).

8. Ruhlen, "The Origin of the Na-Dene," 13994; Michael E. Krauss and Victor K. Golla, "Northern Athapaskan Languages," in *Handbook of North American Indians*, vol. 6, ed. June Helm, 67; John P. Harrington,

"Southern Peripheral Athapaskawan Origins, Divisions, and Migrations," in *Essays in Historical Anthropology of North America* (Washington, DC: Smithsonian Institution, 1940), 506–7; Paul F. Donahue, "Concerning Athapaskan Prehistory in British Columbia," *Western Canadian Journal of Anthropology* 5 (1975): 21.

9. Shephard Krech III, "Disease, Starvation, and Northern Athapaskan Social Organization," *American Ethnologist* 5 (November 1978): 720.

10. Perry, "Proto-Athapaskan Culture: The Use of Ethnographic Reconstruction," 721–22; Ernest S. Burch Jr., "The Caribou/Wild Reindeer as a Human Resource," *American Antiquity* 37 (July 1972): 343, 362; James W. Vanstone, *Athapaskan Adaptations: Hunters and Fishermen of the Subarctic Forests* (Chicago: Aldine Publishing Co., 1974), 24–25, 38–40.

11. Richard J. Perry, "Matrilineal Descent in a Hunting Context: The Athapaskan Case," *Ethnology* 28 (1989): 34; Vanstone, *Athapaskan Adaptations*, 53, 78–79.

12. Perry, *Western Apache Heritage*, 23–24; Perry, "Matrilineal Descent in a Hunting Context," 34–36, 47.

13. Richard J. Perry, "The Apachean Transition from the Subarctic to the Southwest," *Plains Anthropologist* 25 (1980): 281, 284–85; Perry, *Western Apache Heritage*, 102–4; Burch, "The Caribou/Wild Reindeer as Human Resource," 356; Jane Hill, "Language Spread among Hunter-Gatherers," paper presented at the Second Conference on the Archaeology and Linguistics of Australia, Canberra, Australia, October 1–4, 2002, http://crlc.anu.edu.au/arcling2/Hill.htm.

14. D. Wayne Moodie et al., "Northern Athapaskan Oral Traditions and the White River Volcano," *Ethnohistory* 39 (Spring 1992): 148–72; Ives, *A Theory of Northern Athapaskan Prehistory*, 42–45; John W. Ives, Sally Rice, and Stephanie Heming, "On the Dispersal of the Apachean Peoples from Subarctic North America," paper presented at the Second Conference on the Archaeology and Linguistics of Australia, Canberra, Australia, October 1–4, 2002, http://crlc.anu.edu.au/arcling2/Ives2.htm; Hill, "Language Spread among Hunter-Gatherers." David Derry argues that the volcanic activity that triggered the Athapaskan migration occurred around 300 A.D.; see David E. Derry, "Later Athapaskan Prehistory: A Migration Hypothesis," *Western Canadian Journal of Anthropology* 5 (1975): 134, 138, 144.

15. Ives, *A Theory of Northern Athapaskan Prehistory*, 60–61; Hill, "Language Spread among Hunter-Gatherers"; Vanstone, *Athapaskan Adaptations*, 121–25; Haskell, *Southern Athapaskan Migration*, 25–26; John H. Blitz, "Adoption of the Bow in Prehistoric North America," *North American Archaeologist* 9 (1988): 127–30, 132–33, 135.

16. Krauss and Golla, "Northern Athapaskan Languages," 67–68; Duane Champagne, ed., *Chronology of Native North American History* (Detroit: Gale Research, 1994), 21; Perry, *Western Apache Heritage*, 20–22; Harrington, "Southern Peripheral Athapaskawan Origins, Divisions, and Migrations," 520; Colin G. Calloway, *One Vast Winter Count: The Native West before Lewis and Clark* (Lincoln: University of Nebraska Press, 2003), 57–58; Perry, "Proto-Athapaskan Culture," 715; Dean Snow, *The Archaeology of North America* (New York: Viking Press, 1976), 119, 152, 176; Newcomb, *North American Indians*, 107.

17. Champagne, *Chronology of Native North American History*, 21; Harrington, "Southern Peripheral Athapaskawan Origins, Divisions, and Migrations," 520; Snow, *The Archaeology of North America*, 119, 152, 176; Newcomb, *North American Indians*, 107; Perry, *Western Apache Heritage*, 24, 42–43; Thomas L. Jackson, "Reconstructing Migrations in California Prehistory," *American Indian Quarterly* 13 (Autumn 1989): 360.

18. Calloway, *One Vast Winter Count*, 57–58; Ripan S. Malhi et al., "Native American mtDNA Prehistory in the American Southwest," *American Journal of Physical Anthropology* 129 (2003): 122; Thomas F. Kehoe, "The Small Side-Notched Point System of the Northern Plains," *American Antiquity* 31 (October 1966): 839; Perry, "The Apachean Transition from the Subarctic to the Southwest," 286.

19. Proponents of an Avonlea-Athapaskan connection include Thomas F. Kehoe, Richard Perry, and J. Loring Haskell. David Meyer suggests an Algonquian association for Avonlea, while Leslie Davis questions the validity of the entire Avonlea construct. See Perry, *Western Apache Heritage*, 116–18, for a brief discussion of the debate. A more recent study by Dale Walde argues that ceramic wares associated with Avonlea have connections with Eastern Woodlands peoples, and that Avonlea points should not necessarily be linked to Athapaskans. See Walde, "Avonlea and Athabaskan Migrations: A Reconsideration," *Plains Anthropologist* 51 (2006): 185–98.

20. Kehoe, "The Small Side-Notched Point System of the Northern Plains," 839.

21. Ibid.; Haskell, *Southern Athapaskan Migration*, 23–34; Betty H. and Harold A. Huscher, "Athapaskan Migration via the Intermontane Region," *American Antiquity* 8 (July 1942): 88; David R. Wilcox, "The Entry of Athapaskans into the American Southwest: The Problem Today," in *The Protohistoric Period in the North American Southwest, A.D. 1450–1700*, ed. David R. Wilcox and W. Bruce Masse (Tempe: Arizona State University Anthropological Research Papers no. 24, 1981), 222.

22. Ives, *A Theory of Northern Athapaskan Prehistory*, 46–47, 50–52; John Upton Terrell, *American Indian Almanac* (New York: Barnes and Noble Books, 1971), 309; Huscher, "Athapaskan Migration via the Intermontane Region," 81–82, 88; Haskell, *Southern Athapaskan Migration*, 41–65;

James H. Gunnerson, "Plains-Promontory Relationships," *American Antiquity* 22 (1956): 69, 72; George E. Hyde, *Indians of the High Plains: From the Prehistoric Period to the Coming of Europeans* (Norman: University of Oklahoma Press, 1959), 4–5; Harrington, "Southern Peripheral Athapaskawan Origins, Divisions, and Migrations," 520–23; Karl H. Schlesier, ed., *Plains Indians, A.D. 500–1500: The Archaeological Past of Historic Groups* (Norman: University of Oklahoma Press, 1994), 326; Perry, "The Apachean Transition from the Subarctic to the Southwest," 281, 290; Wilcox, "The Entry of Athapaskans into the American Southwest," 213, 217–18.

23. Hill, "Language Spread among Hunter-Gatherers"; Calloway, *One Vast Winter Count*, 54–55; Peter B. deMenocal, "Cultural Responses to Climate Change during the Late Holocene," *Science* 292 (April 27, 2001): 667–68; William C. Foster, *Historic Native Peoples of Texas* (Austin: University of Texas Press, 2008), 107–8, 187–88; "Planning for the Drought," *Colorado Conservation Board* (May 2000): 4; Terry L. Jones et al., "Environmental Imperatives Reconsidered: Demographic Crises in Western North America during the Medieval Climatic Anomaly," *Current Anthropology* 40 (April 1999): 138–39; Marvin Kay, "The Great Plains Setting," in *Archaeology of the Great Plains*, ed. W. Raymond Wood (Lawrence: University of Kansas Press, 1998), 19–20, 38; Richard A. Krause, "A History of Great Plains Prehistory," in *Archaeology of the Great Plains*, ed. Wood, 68–69.

24. Kay, "The Great Plains Setting," 20; Foster, *Historic Native Peoples of Texas*, 107–8, 187–88; Krause, "A History of Great Plains Prehistory," 68–69; Waldo R. Wedel, "The Prehistoric Plains," in *Ancient Native Americans*, ed. Jesse D. Jennings (San Francisco: Freeman and Company, 1978), 210–11; Christopher Lintz, "Texas Panhandle–Pueblo Interactions from the Thirteenth through the Sixteenth Century," in Katherine A. Spielmann, *Farmers, Hunters, and Colonists: Interaction between the Southwest and the Southern Plains* (Tucson: University of Arizona Press, 1991), 92.

25. Lawrence A. Kingsbury and Loma H. Gabel, "Eastern Apache Campsites in Southeastern Colorado: A Hypothesis," *Plains Anthropologist* 28 (1983): 319, 324.

26. According to Tom Dillehay, bison populations on the southern plains increased from 1200–1550. See Dillehay, "Late Quaternary Bison Population Changes on the Southern Plains," *Plains Anthropologist* 19 (1974): 180–81.

27. Jack T. Hughes, "Prehistoric Cultural Developments on the High Plains," *Bulletin of the Texas Archeological Society* 60 (1989): 6–7; *Handbook of Texas Online*, s.v. "Panhandle," http://www.tsha.utexas.edu/handbook/online/articles/PP/ryp1.html (accessed June 16, 2006); *Handbook of Texas Online*, s.v. "Llano Estacado," http://www.tsha.utexas.edu/handbook/online/articles/LL/ry12.html (accessed June 16, 2006).

28. Wedel, "The Prehistoric Plains," 204–5; Paul H. Carlson, *Deep Time and the Texas High Plains* (Lubbock: Texas Tech University Press, 2005), 72–75; Hughes, "Prehistoric Cultural Developments on the High Plains," 31–33; *Handbook of Texas Online*, s.v. "Antelope Creek Phase," http://www.tsha.utexas.edu/handbook/online/articles/view/AA/bba7.html (accessed December 7, 2004); Calloway, *One Vast Winter Count*, 55–56; Christopher Lintz, "The Southwestern Periphery of the Plains Caddoan Area," *Nebraska History* 60 (1979): 163–74; Katherine A. Spielmann, Margaret J. Schoeninger, and Katherine Moore, "Plains-Pueblo Interdependence and Human Diet at Pecos Pueblo, New Mexico," *American Antiquity* 55 (October 1990): 746; Robert L. Stephenson, "Culture Chronology in Texas," *American Antiquity* 16 (October 1950): 153; James B. Schaeffer, "The Alibates Flint Quarry, Texas," *American Antiquity* 24 (October 1958): 189–90; Christopher Lintz, "The Historical Development of a Culture Complex: The Basis for Understanding Architectural Misconceptions of the Antelope Creek Focus," *Plains Anthropologist* 114 (1986): 112; Robert L. Brooks, "Southern Plains Cultural Complexes," in *Skeletal Biology of the Great Plains*, ed. Douglas W. Owsley and Richard L. Jantz (Washington, DC: Smithsonian Institution Press, 1994), 36–38; Lintz, "Texas Panhandle–Pueblo Interactions," 94–95, 100.

29. John D. Speth, "Some Unexplored Aspects of Mutualistic Plains-Pueblo Food Exchange," 18–28; Lintz, "Texas Panhandle–Pueblo Interactions," 101–2; Wilcox, "The Entry of Athapaskans into the American Southwest," 226, 228; James H. and Dolores A. Gunnerson, "Evidence of Apaches at Pecos," *El Palacio* 76 (1970): 1–3; Charles H. Lange, "Plains-Southwestern Inter-Cultural Relations during the Historic Period," *Ethnohistory* 4 (Spring 1957): 151–52; Katherine A. Spielmann, "Late Prehistoric Exchange between the Southwest and the Southern Plains," *Plains Anthropologist* 28 (November 1983): 257–69; Speilmann, Schoeninger, and Moore, "Plains-Pueblo Interdependence," 750, 760; Timothy G. Baugh and Fred W. Nelson Jr., "New Mexico Obsidian Sources and Exchange on the Southern Plains," *Journal of Field Archaeology* 14 (Autumn 1987): 326; Dolores A. Gunnerson, "The Southern Athabascans: Their Arrival in the Southwest," *El Palacio* 63 (November–December 1956): 346–48.

30. Timothy G. Baugh, "Ecology and Exchange: The Dynamics of Plains-Pueblo Interaction," in *Farmers, Hunters, and Colonists: Interaction between the Southwest and the Southern Plains*, ed. Katherine A. Spielmann (Tucson: University of Arizona Press, 1991), 114–15, 125; Foster, *Historic Native Peoples of Texas*, 186–188; Marjorie Ann Duncan, "Adaptation during the Antelope Creek Phase: A Diet Breadth and Site Catchment Analysis of the Subsistence Strategy at the Two Sisters Site" (Ph.D. diss., University of Oklahoma, 2002), xvi; Robert L. Brooks, "Warfare on the Southern Plains," in *Skeletal Biology in the Great Plains*, ed. Douglas W. Owsley and Richard L. Jantz (Washington, DC: Smithsonian Institution Press, 1994), 317–18, 321–22; Nancy P. Hickerson, "Jumano: The Missing

Link in South Plains History," *Journal of the West* 29 (1990): 6; Lintz, "The Southwestern Periphery of the Plains Caddoan Area," 171; Anderson, *The Indian Southwest, 1580–1830,* 4.

31. Alex D. Krieger, "The Eastward Extension of Puebloan Datings toward Cultures of the Mississippi Valley," *American Antiquity* 12 (January 1947): 143–44; Hughes, "Prehistoric Cultural Developments on the High Plains," 35, 43; Donald J. Blakeslee and David T. Hughes, "Southern Plains Archaeology, 1955–1995," *Panhandle-Plains Historical Review* 70 (1997): 25; Lintz, "The Southwestern Periphery of the Plains Caddoan Area," 178; Duncan, "Adaptation during the Antelope Creek Phase," 71; Schlesier, ed., *Plains Indians,* A.D. 500–1500, 35; Speth, "Some Unexplored Aspects of Mutualistic Plains-Pueblo Food Exchange," 25; Lintz, "Texas Panhandle–Pueblo Interactions," 93; Susan C. Vehik, "Conflict, Trade, and Political Development on the Southern Plains," *American Antiquity* 67 (January 2002): 42.

32. Hughes, "Prehistoric Cultural Developments on the High Plains," 35; Judith A. Habicht-Mauche, "Coronado's Querechos and Teyas in the Archeological Record of the Texas Panhandle," *Plains Anthropologist* 37 (August 1992): 251–53, 256–57; Enrique Gilbert-Maestas, "Culture and History of Native Peoples of South Texas" (Ph.D. diss., University of Texas at Austin, 2003), 36, 49–50.

33. Anderson, *The Indian Southwest,* 5, 13–15.

34. David LaVere, *The Texas Indians* (College Station: Texas A&M University Press, 2004), 68–71, 88–91; Anderson, *The Indian Southwest,* 5, 13–15; Hickerson, "Jumano: The Missing Link in South Plains History," 5–10; Reggie N. Wiseman, "The Jumano Diaspora: Some More Pieces to the Puzzle," *Journal of Big Bend Studies* 14 (2002): 97, 103–5; William B. Carter, "Indian Alliances in the Southwest, 1300–1706" (Ph.D. diss., Arizona State University, 2002), 109.

35. LaVere, *The Texas Indians,* 68–71, 88–91; Anderson, *The Indian Southwest,* 5, 13–15; Hickerson, "Jumano: The Missing Link in South Plains History," 5–10; Wiseman, "The Jumano Diaspora: Some More Pieces to the Puzzle," 97, 103–5; F. Todd Smith, *The Wichita Indians: Traders of Texas and the Southern Plains, 1540–1845* (College Station: Texas A&M University Press, 2000), 8; Carter, "Indian Alliances in the Southwest, 1300–1706," 109.

36. Wilcox, "The Entry of Athapaskans into the American Southwest," 226; Spielmann, "Late Prehistoric Exchange between the Southwest and Southern Plains," 269; Gunnerson, "The Southern Athabascans: Their Arrival in the Southwest," 348; John M. Miller, *El Llano Estacado: Exploration and Imagination on the High Plains of Texas and New Mexico, 1536–1860* (Austin: Texas State Historical Association, 1997), 144; LaVere, *The Texas Indians,* 88–91, 98–101; Baugh, "Ecology and Exchange," 121, 124–25; Vehik, "Conflict, Trade, and Political Development on the Southern Plains," 37, 41, 43; Anderson, *The Indian Southwest,* 48, 54–55, 63.

37. Schroeder, *A Study of the Apache Indians*, 34.

38. Herbert E. Bolton, *Coronado: Knight of Pueblos and Plains* (Albuquerque: University of New Mexico Press, 1949), 245–47; Habicht-Mauche, "Coronado's Querechos and Teyas," 248–54; Gunnerson, "The Southern Athabascans: Their Arrival in the Southwest," 346–48.

39. Anderson, *The Indian Southwest*, 106–7; Morris, *El Llano Estacado*, 135–38.

40. Schroeder, *A Study of the Apache Indians*, 479–80; Habicht-Mauche, "Coronado's Querechos and Teyas," 247–59; Hughes, "Prehistoric Cultural Developments on the High Plains," 35, 43; Carter, "Indian Alliances in the Southwest, 1300–1706," 109. Some anthropologists believe that the peoples that constituted the Garza complex of the lower Texas Panhandle were the Teyas, but are split over whether the Garza complex peoples were Plains Caddoan or Apachean. See Duncan, "Adaptation during the Antelope Creek Phase," 72–73.

41. James H. and Dolores A. Gunnerson, "Apachean Culture: A Study in Unity and Diversity," in *Apachean Culture History and Exchange*, ed. Keith H. Basso and Morris E. Opler (Tucson: University of Arizona Press, 1971), 19–21; Habicht-Mauche, Coronado's Querechos and Teyas," 255; John R. Swanton, *The Indian Tribes of North America* (Washington, DC: Smithsonian Institution Press, 1952), 322–23; Ralph A. Smith, ed. and trans., "Account of the Journey of Bénard de la Harpe: Discovery Made by Him of Several Nations Situated in the West," *Southwestern Historical Quarterly* 62 (1958): 375–79.

42. Habicht-Mauche, "Coronado's Querechos and Teyas," 255; Elizabeth A. H. John, *Storms Brewed in Other Men's Worlds: The Confrontation of Indians, Spanish, and French in the Southwest, 1540–1795* (College Station: Texas A&M University Press, 1975), 235–36.

43. Karl H. Schlesier, "Rethinking the Dismal River Aspect and Plains Athapaskans, A.D. 1692–1768," *Plains Anthropologist* 15 (1972): 110–12; Schroeder, *A Study of the Apache Indians*, 478–86, 495–502.

44. Carlisle, "Spanish Relations with the Apache Nations," 85; *Handbook of Texas Online*, s.v. "Posada, Alonso de," http://www.tsha.utexas.edu/handbook/online/articles/PP/fpo25.html (accessed March 28, 2006); *Handbook of Texas Online*, s.v. "Escanjaque Indians," http://www.tsha.utexas.edu/handbook/online/articles/EE/bme7.html (accessed March 28, 2006).

45. Dunn, "Apache Relations in Texas, 1718–1750," 263–69; Opler, "The Apachean Culture Pattern and Its Origins," 391; Maria F. Wade, *The Native Americans of the Texas Edwards Plateau, 1582–1799* (Austin: University of Texas Press, 2003), 172–73; Hodge, ed., *Handbook of American Indians North of Mexico*, 768–69; Anderson, *The Indian Southwest*, 112–13.

46. Hyde's full quote was: "Today, after the passage of two and a half centuries, how can we hope to unravel such an amazing tangle?"; see Hyde, *Indians of the High Plains*, 39.

47. John Torres-Nez, "Tracking the Apache," *El Palacio* 109 (2004): 15; Gunnerson, "Apachean Culture: A Study in Unity and Diversity," 7–12, 22; James H. Gunnerson, "Apache Archaeology in Northeastern New Mexico," *American Antiquity* 34 (January 1969): 23, 36.

48. Opler, "The Apachean Culture Pattern and Its Origins," 368; Opler, *Myths and Legends of the Lipan Apache Indians*, 6; Harry Hoijer, "The Southern Athapaskan Languages," *American Anthropologist* 40 (January–March 1938): 85–86; Hoijer, "The Position of the Apachean Languages in the Athapaskan Stock," in *Apachean Culture History and Ethnology*, ed. Basso and Opler, 3–5; James H. Gunnerson, "Southern Athapaskan Archeology," in *Handbook of North American Indians*, vol. 10, *The Southwest*, ed. Alfonso Ortiz (Washington, DC: Smithsonian Institution Press, 1983), 162; Mildred P. Mayhall, *The Kiowas*, 2nd ed. (Norman: University of Oklahoma Press, 1971), 12.

49. Martha A. Works, "Creating Trading Spaces on the New Mexican Frontier," *Geographical Review* 82 (July 1992): 273–74; F. Todd Smith, *From Dominance to Disappearance: The Indians of Texas and the Near Southwest, 1786–1859* (Lincoln: University of Nebraska Press, 2005), 8; Wiseman, "The Jumano Diaspora: Some More Pieces to the Puzzle," 97.

50. Smith, *The Wichita Indians*, 8; LaVere, *The Texas Indians*, 128; Newcomb, *The Indians of Texas*, 156–57; Smith, *From Dominance to Disappearance*, 12.

51. Newcomb, *The Indians of Texas*, 87–88; Hyde, *Indians of the High Plains*, 71.

52. Carlisle, "Spanish Relations with the Apache Nations East of the Rio Grande," 76–77.

CHAPTER TWO

1. Opler, "The Theory of Themes in Culture," 141; "The Moccasin Game for Day or Night between the Dangerous and the Harmless Birds and Animals," in Opler, *Myths and Legends of the Lipan Apache Indians*, 87–94; Haley, *Apaches: A History and Culture Portrait*, 4–5.

2. Opler, "The Apachean Culture Pattern and Its Origins," 385. According to David French, the tribe with the "closest mythological affiliation" with the Lipans was the Jicarilla Apaches. See French, "A Comparative Study of the Mythologies of the Jicarilla, Lipan, Mescalero, and Chiricahua Apache Indians," 72.

3. Anderson, *The Indian Southwest*, 95–96, 118.

4. John Francis Bannon, *The Spanish Borderlands Frontier, 1513–1821* (Albuquerque: University of New Mexico Press, 1974), 80–86; Thomas Nolan Campbell, *The Indians of Southern Texas and Northeastern Mexico* (Austin: Texas Archaeological Laboratory, 1988), 42; Works, "Creating Trading Spaces on the New Mexican Frontier," 272–73; Schilz, *Lipan Apaches in Texas*, 2.

5. Smith, *The Wichita Indians*, 16; Schroeder, *A Study of the Apache Indians*, 35–37, 497; Schlesier, "Rethinking the Dismal River Aspect," 113–14; Pekka Hämäläinen, *The Comanche Empire* (New Haven: Yale University Press, 2008), 28, 32–33; Gerald Betty, *Comanche Society before the Reservation* (College Station: Texas A&M University Press, 2002), 51; Morris F. Taylor, "Some Aspects of Historical Indian Occupation of Southeastern Colorado," *Great Plains Journal* 4 (1964): 19.

6. Schroeder, "Shifting for Survival in the Spanish Southwest," 302; Hyde, *Indians of the High Plains*, 65.

7. Dunn, "Apache Relations in Texas," 220; Sandra L. Myres, "The Lipan Apaches," in *The Indian Tribes of Texas*, ed. Dorman Winfrey (Waco: Texian Press, 1971), 133; Calloway, *One Vast Winter Count*, 285; Sherry Robinson, *Apache Voices: Their Stories of Survival as Told to Eve Ball* (Albuquerque: University of New Mexico Press, 2000), 131–34.

8. Schlesier, "Rethinking the Dismal River Aspect," 117; Opler, "Problems in Apachean Cultural History," 186–87.

9. *Handbook of Texas Online*, s.v. "Edwards Plateau," http://www.tsha.utexas. edu/handbook/online/articles/EE/rxe1.html (accessed July 7, 2006); *Handbook of Texas Online*, s.v. "Balcones Escarpment," http://www.tsha. utexas.edu/handbook/online/articles/BB/rxb1.html (accessed July 7, 2006).

10. LaVere, *The Texas Indians*, 68–71, 77–78; Hickerson, "Jumano: The Missing Link in South Plains History," 5–12; Newcomb, *The Indians of Texas*, 30–35. Jack D. Forbes argues that the Jumanos were Athapaskan speakers; see Jack D. Forbes, "Unknown Athapaskans: The Identification of the Jano, Jocome, Jumano, Manso, Suma, and other Indian Tribes of the Southwest," *Ethnohistory* 6 (April 1956): 105–28; Campbell, *The Indians of Southern Texas and Northeastern Mexico*, 42–43. Maria Wade's discussion of the Mendoza-Lopez Expedition of 1683–1684 mentions several other tribes that were displaced; see Wade, *The Native Americans of the Texas Edwards Plateau*, 107–14; Robert S. Weddle, *San Juan Bautista: Gateway to Spanish Texas* (Austin: University of Texas Press, 1968), 3; Schilz, *Lipan Apaches in Texas*, 6–7.

11. LaVere, *The Texas Indians*, 27, 80–81, 115–19; Hickerson, "Jumano: The Missing Link in South Plains History," 5–12; Wiseman, "The Jumano Diaspora," 97–98; Thomas R. Hester, "Historic Native American Populations," in *Ethnology of Texas Indians*, ed. Thomas R. Hester (New York: Garland Publishing, 1991), 1; Anderson, *The Indian Southwest*, 65–68;

Thomas N. Campbell, "Coahuiltecans and Their Neighbors," in *Ethnology of Texas Indians*, ed. Hester, 111–12; Campbell, *The Indians of Southern Texas and Northeastern Mexico*, 42–43; John, *Storms Brewed in Other Men's Worlds*, 153.

12. Schilz, *Lipan Apaches in Texas*, 2; Curtis D. Tunnell and W. W. Newcomb, *A Lipan Apache Mission: San Lorenzo de la Santa Cruz, 1762–1771* (Austin: Texas Memorial Museum, 1969), 149; Wade, *The Native Americans of the Texas Edwards Plateau*, 161; Testimony of Antonio de los Santos, August 21, 1733, BAT, reel 1, series 1, September 30, 1699–January 1, 1789, vol. 3, Hunter Room, UTB; Schlesier, "Rethinking the Dismal River Aspect," 111–12, 117; Dunn, "Apache Relations in Texas," 202–3.

13. Wade, *The Native Americans of the Texas Edwards Plateau*, 129–30; Campbell, *The Indians of Southern Texas and Northeastern Mexico*, 42.

14. Donald E. Worcester, "The Beginning of the Apache Menace of the Southwest," *New Mexico Historical Review* 16 (January 1941): 5; Jack D. Forbes, *Apache, Navajo, and Spaniard* (Norman: University of Oklahoma Press, 1960), 29–30, 37–38; William L. Merrill, "Cultural Creativity and Raiding Bands in Eighteenth Century Northern New Spain," in *Violence, Resistance, and Survival in the Americas: Native Americans and the Legacy of Conquest*, ed. William B. Taylor and Franklin Pease (Washington, DC: Smithsonian Institution Press, 1994), 124–25; Jeremy Adelman and Stephen Aron, "From Borderlands to Borders: Empires, Nation-States, and the Peoples in between in North American History," *American Historical Review* 104 (June 1999): 829.

15. Donald E. Chipman, *Spanish Texas, 1519–1821* (Austin: University of Texas Press, 1992), 78–83; Adelman and Aron, "From Borderlands to Borders," 832.

16. Dunn, "Apache Relations in Texas," 200; Chipman, *Spanish Texas*, 93–99; Juliana Barr, "A Diplomacy of Gender: Rituals of Contact in the Land of the Tejas," *William and Mary Quarterly* 61 (July 2004): 428–29.

17. Dunn, "Apache Relations in Texas," 200; Chipman, *Spanish Texas*, 106–7; Robert H. Jackson, "Ethnic Survival and Extinction on the Mission Frontiers of Spanish America: Cases from the Rio de la Plata Region, the Chiquitos Region of Bolivia, the Coahuila–Texas Frontier, and California," *Journal of South Texas* 19 (Spring 2006): 7–8.

18. Bannon, *The Spanish Borderland Frontier*, 112–15; Henri Folmer, "Contraband Trade between Louisiana and New Mexico in the Eighteenth Century," *New Mexico Historical Review* 16 (July 1941): 250–54; Dunn, "Apache Relations in Texas," 201; John, *Storms Brewed in Other Men's Worlds*, 203–8; Herbert E. Bolton, *Texas in the Middle Eighteenth Century* (Austin: University of Texas Press, 1970; reprint of 1915 edition), 4–5. The six missions were San Francisco de los Tejas, Purísima Concepción, Nuestra Señora de Guadalupe, San José de los Nazonis, Nuestra Señora de

los Dolores, and San Miguel de Linares. The presidio was called Nuestra Señora de los Dolores de los Tejas.

19. Bannon, *The Spanish Borderland Frontier*, 116–18; Barr, "A Diplomacy of Gender," 430; Bolton, *Texas in the Middle Eighteenth Century*, 5; Dunn, "Apache Relations in Texas," 201; Chipman, *Spanish Texas*, 116–17.

20. Wade, *The Native Americans of the Texas Edwards Plateau*, 160–61; Dunn, "Apache Relations in Texas," 203–4.

21. Diego Ramon to Viceroy Valero, May 2, 1717, BAT, reel 1, series 1, September 30, 1699–January 21, 1789, vol. 1, Hunter Room, UTB; John, *Storms Brewed in Other Men's Worlds*, 209.

22. Castañeda, *Our Catholic Heritage in Texas*, 2:188.

23. David LaVere, "Between Kinship and Capitalism: French and Spanish Rivalry in the Colonial Louisiana-Texas Indian Trade," *Journal of Southern History* 64 (May 1998): 203–7; Juliana Barr, "From Captives to Slaves: Commodifying Indian Women in the Borderlands," *Journal of American History* 92 (June 2005): 25; Martha McCollough, "Political Decentralization as a Strategy to Maintain Sovereignty: An Example from the Hasinais during the 1700s," *Plains Anthropologist* 46 (August 2001): 306, 315–16.

24. Thomas F. Schilz and Donald E. Worcester, "The Spread of Firearms among the Indian Tribes on the Northern Frontier of New Spain," *American Indian Quarterly* 11 (Winter 1987): 2; Works, "Creating Trading Spaces on the New Mexican Frontier," 276; Secoy, *Changing Military Patterns of the Great Plains Indians*, 83.

25. Chipman, *Spanish Texas*, 118–27; Dunn, "Apache Relations in Texas," 205–6; Wade, *The Native Americans of the Texas Edwards Plateau*, 161; Anderson, *The Indian Southwest*, 70, 80–81; Bannon, *The Spanish Borderlands Frontier*, 119–23. In 1719 the Spaniards had again abandoned their east Texas missions, fearing a French attack.

26. J. Villasana Haggard, "Spain's Indian Policy in Texas," *Southwestern Historical Quarterly* 43 (April 1940): 479–80; LaVere, "Between Kinship and Capitalism," 208–10; Adelman and Aron, "From Borderlands to Borders," 830–31.

27. Dunn, "Apache Relations in Texas," 207.

28. Castañeda, *Our Catholic Heritage in Texas*, 2:190–201; Tunnell and Newcomb, *A Lipan Apache Mission*, 154–55; Dunn, "Apache Relations in Texas," 207–9. Castañeda states that the Spaniards recovered 120 horses/mules, painted saddles, hats, knives, bridles, iron stirrups, spearheads, ribbons, sugar, corn, *pinole* (ground flour), salt, buffalo and deer hides, and beads. Jeffrey Carlisle maintains that the Apaches involved were Jicarillas or Faraones. See Carlisle, "Spanish Relations with the Apache Nations East of the Rio Grande," 219.

29. David J. Weber, *Bárbaros: Spaniards and Their Savages in the Age of Enlightenment* (New Haven: Yale University Press, 2005), 8–9.

30. Ibid., 9; Dunn, "Apache Relations in Texas," 209–16; Schilz, *Lipan Apaches in Texas*, 8–9; Castañeda, *Our Catholic Heritage in Texas*, 2:193–201.

31. Schilz and Worcester, "The Spread of Firearms among the Indian Tribes," 2–3; Calloway, *One Vast Winter Count*, 285. According to Martha W. Works, by the 1730s the Comanches had taken over trade at Taos; see Works, "Creating Trading Places on the New Mexico Frontier," 273.

32. Jesús De La Teja, *San Antonio de Béxar: A Community on New Spain's Northern Frontier* (Albuquerque: University of New Mexico Press, 1995), 9–10.

33. Dunn, "Apache Relations in Texas," 216–19; Schilz, *Lipan Apaches in Texas*, 8–9.

34. John, *Storms Brewed in Other Men's Worlds*, 261–63; Wade, *The Native Americans of the Texas Edwards Plateau*, 172; Bannon, *The Spanish Borderlands Frontier*, 123; Dunn, "Apache Relations in Texas," 223–24; Carlisle, "Spanish Relations with the Apache Nations East of the Rio Grande," 225.

35. Anderson, *The Indian Southwest*, 81; Jesús De La Teja, "Forgotten Founders: The Military Settlers of Eighteenth Century San Antonio de Béxar," in *Tejano Origins in Eighteenth Century San Antonio*, ed. Gerald E. Poyo and Gilberto M. Hinojosa (Austin: University of Texas Press, 1991), 34.

36. John, *Storms Brewed in Other Men's Worlds*, 263–64; Bannon, *The Spanish Borderlands Frontier*, 134; Schilz, *Lipan Apaches in Texas*, 9; Dunn, "Apache Relations in Texas," 223–28; Tunnell and Newcomb, *A Lipan Apache Mission*, 154; Castañeda, *Our Catholic Heritage in Texas*, 3:37–39; Charles Ramsdell, *San Antonio: A Historical and Pictorial Guide* (Austin: University of Texas Press, 1959), 23–24; De La Teja, *San Antonio de Béxar*, 10–11.

37. Dunn, "Apache Relations in Texas," 228–30; Roberto Mario Salmón, "A Thankless Job: Mexican Soldiers in the Spanish Borderlands of the Southwest," *Military History of the Southwest* 22 (Spring 1991): 1–2.

38. Dunn, "Apache Relations in Texas," 230–34; Schilz, *Lipan Apaches in Texas*, 10; Wade, *The Native Americans of the Texas Edwards Plateau*, 173; Robert S. Weddle, *The San Saba Mission: Spanish Pivot in Texas* (College Station: Texas A&M University Press, 1999), 13–15; Tunnell and Newcomb, *A Lipan Apache Mission*, 154–56.

39. One USDA website indicated that mules could carry 20 percent of their body weight. Thus, a 1,000 lb. mule could carry 200 lbs. See http://www.fs.fed.us/r2/psicc/spl/string.shtml.

40. Dunn, "Apache Relations in Texas," 234–37; Carlisle, "Spanish Relations with the Apache Nations East of the Rio Grande," 234–35; Don Juan de

Olivan Rebolledo to the Viceroy Marquis de Casafuerte, July 18, 1733, BAT, reel 1, series 1, September 30, 1699–January 31, 1789, vol. 3; Report of Texas Governor Prudenzio de Orobio Bastera regarding Apache Hostilities to Viceroy Juan Antonio Vizarron y Eguiarreta, Arzobishop de Mexico, 1738, BAT, reel 2, series 1, September 30, 1699–January 31, 1789, vol. 11, Hunter Room, UTB.

41. Castañeda, *Our Catholic Heritage in Texas*, 3:44–46; Report of Texas Governor Prudenzio de Orobio Basterra regarding Apache Hostilities, BAT.

42. Dunn, "Apache Relations in Texas," 238–44; Report of Texas Governor Prudenzio de Orobio Basterra regarding Apache Hostilities, BAT.

43. Report of Texas Governor Prudenzio de Orobio Basterra regarding Apache Hostilities, BAT, Hunter Room, UTB; Dunn, "Apache Relations in Texas," 244–47; Castañeda, *Our Catholic Heritage in Texas*, 3:46–47; Max L. Moorhead, "Spanish Deportation of Hostile Apaches: The Policy and the Practice," *Arizona and the West* 17 (1975): 206; Barr, "Commodifying Indian Women in the Borderlands," 36–38; Archer, "The Deportation of Barbarian Indians from the Internal Provinces of New Spain," 376–85.

44. Dunn, "Apache Relations in Texas," 248–49.

45. John, *Storms Brewed in Other Men's Worlds*, 273–74.

46. Tunnell and Newcomb, *A Lipan Apache Mission*, 156; Dunn, "Apache Relations in Texas," 249–50; Castañeda, *Our Catholic Heritage in Texas*, 3:46–47.

47. Tunnell and Newcomb, *A Lipan Apache Mission*, 157; Dunn, "Apache Relations in Texas," 250–54; Castañeda, *Our Catholic Heritage in Texas*, 3:47; De La Teja, *San Antonio de Béxar*, 123.

48. Dunn, "Apache Relations in Texas," 252–53.

49. Ibid.; John, *Storms Brewed in Other Men's Worlds*, 314–17; Smith, *The Wichita Indians*, 25–26; Smith, *From Dominance to Disappearance*, 13; Hämäläinen, *The Comanche Empire*, 42–43. Elizabeth A. Harper, "The Taovayas Indians in Frontier Trade and Diplomacy, 1719–1768," *Chronicles of Oklahoma* 31 (1953): 272; Captain Joachim de Orobio Bazterra, Report on the Tejas, October 1, 1745, BAT, reel 3, series 1, September 30, 1699–January 31, 1789, vol. 17, Hunter Room, UTB; Stan Hoig, *Tribal Wars of the Southern Plains* (Norman: University of Oklahoma Press, 1993), 62–63; Barr, "Commodifying Indian Women in the Borderlands," 28.

50. LaVere, *The Texas Indians*, 101; Philip Mantor, "The San Gabriel Mission," *Frontier Times* 3 (February 1926): 34; Anderson, *The Indian Southwest*, 85–86; Castañeda, *Our Catholic Heritage in Texas*, 3:245–51; Smith, *From Dominance to Disappearance*, 16; *Handbook of Texas Online*, s.v. "San Xavier Missions," http://www.tsha.utexas.edu/handbook/online/articles/SS/uqs34.html (accessed March 9, 2006).

51. Castañeda, *Our Catholic Heritage in Texas*, 3:255–63; Dunn, "Apache Relations in Texas," 254–55; Donald E. Chipman and Luis López Elizondo, "New Light on Felipe de Rábago y Terán," *Southwestern Historical Quarterly* 111 (October 2007): 162–70; Wade, *The Native Americans of the Texas Edwards Plateau*, 180; Anderson, *The Indian Southwest*, 85–86; Smith, *From Dominance to Disappearance*, 16–17.

52. Dunn, "Apache Relations in Texas," 255–57; Tunnell and Newcomb, *A Lipan Apache Mission*, 156.

53. Thomas Phelipe de Winthuysen, Report on Conditions and Missions in Texas, August 19, 1744, BAT, reel 3, series 1, September 30, 1699–January 31, 1789, vol. 15, Hunter Room, UTB.

54. Dunn, "Apache Relations in Texas," 260–61; Tunnell and Newcomb, *A Lipan Apache Mission*, 156–57.

55. Tunnell and Newcomb, *A Lipan Apache Mission: San Lorenzo de la Santa Cruz*, 157; Weddle, *The San Saba Mission*, 19; Dunn, "Apache Relations in Texas," 260–62; William Edward Dunn, "Missionary Activities among the Eastern Apaches Previous to the Founding of the San Saba Mission," *Southwestern Historical Quarterly* 15 (1912): note on page 189.

56. Dunn, "Apache Relations in Texas," 260–62; Weddle, *The San Saba Mission*, 19–20.

CHAPTER THREE

1. "Coyote Helps Lizard Hold Up the Sky," in Opler, *Myths and Legends of the Lipan Apache Indians*, 149–50.

2. LaVere, *The Texas Indians*, 140. Gary Clayton Anderson notes that apparent Indian willingness to enter mission life often stemmed from the creation of an obligation in which the Indians benefited from Spanish presents and wished to repay such generosity to continue the relationship. See Anderson, *The Indian Southwest*, 70.

3. Hämäläinen, *The Comanche Empire*, 47–48, 55–58.

4. Dunn, "Missionary Activities among the Eastern Apaches," 188; Weddle, *The San Sabá Mission*, 42; Schilz, *Lipan Apaches in Texas*, 12–13; Bolton, *Texas in the Middle Eighteenth Century*, 78–79.

5. Dunn, "Missionary Activities among the Eastern Apaches," 192–96; General Don Pedro de Barrio, July 1750, Béxar Archives Translations, reel 3, vol. 20, Hunter Room, UTB.

6. Weddle, *The San Sabá Mission*, 23; Dunn, "Missionary Activity among the Eastern Apaches," 196–99; Forbes, "Unknown Athapaskans," 136–37.

7. Weddle, *The San Sabá Mission*, 25–29; William E. Dunn, "The Apache Mission on the San Sabá River: Its Founding and Failure," *Southwestern Historical Quarterly* 17 (1914): 382–84; Chipman, *Spanish Texas*, 157–58; Dunn, "The Apache Mission on the San Sabá River," 384; Wade, *The Native Americans of the Texas Edwards Plateau*, 180.

8. José Manuel Serrano Álvarez and Allan J. Kuethe, "The San Sabá Presidio and Spain's Frontier Policy in North America," *West Texas Historical Association Year Book* 83 (October 2007): 12–13; Dunn, "The Apache Mission on the San Sabá River," 386–91; Chipman and Elizondo, "New Light on Felipe de Rábago y Terán," 170–71; Weddle, *The San Sabá Mission*, 34–37; Lesley Byrd Simpson, ed., *The San Sabá Papers: A Documentary Account of the Founding and Destruction of the San Sabá Mission*, trans. Paul D. Nathan, forward by Robert S. Weddle (Dallas: Southern Methodist University Press, 2000), xviii.

9. Dunn, "The Apache Mission on the San Sabá River," 389; Weddle, *The San Sabá Mission*, 38–39; Robert T. Hill, "Monumenting at the San Sabá Mission," *Frontier Times* 14 (September 1937): 510–11.

10. Lipan Interviews, *Opler Papers*.

11. Dunn, "The Apache Mission on the San Sabá River," 392–96; Weddle, *The San Sabá Mission*, 45–46.

12. Weddle, *The San Sabá Mission*, 53–57; Dunn, "The Apache Mission on the San Sabá," 395–99; Tunnell and Newcomb, *A Lipan Apache Mission*, 158–61; Schilz, *Lipan Apaches in Texas*, 14–15.

13. Weddle, *The San Sabá Mission*, 53–57; Dunn, "The Apache Mission on the San Sabá," 395–99; Tunnell and Newcomb, *A Lipan Apache Mission*, 158–61; Anderson, *The Indian Southwest*, 86–87.

14. Dunn, "The Apache Mission on the San Sabá River," 399–403; Weddle, *The San Sabá Mission*, 57–63.

15. Harper, "The Taovayas Indians in Frontier Trade and Diplomacy," 279–80.

16. George E. Hyde, *The Pawnee Indians* (Denver: University of Denver Press, 1951), 58–59; Weddle, *The San Sabá Mission*, 64–66.

17. Dunn, "The Apache Mission on the San Sabá River," 399–403; Weddle, *The San Sabá Mission*, 57–63.

18. The best full-length accounts remain Robert Weddle's *The San Sabá Mission: Spanish Pivot in Texas* (College Station: Texas A&M University Press, 1999) and Lesley Byrd Simpson's *The San Sabá Papers: A Documentary Account of the Founding and Destruction of the San Sabá Mission* (Dallas: Southern Methodist University Press, 2000), which is a revision of the earlier 1959 edition. William Edward Dunn's article "The Apache Mission on the San Sabá: Its Founding and Failure," *Southwestern Historical Quarterly* 17 (1914): 379–414, is dated but still useful.

19. Weddle, *The San Sabá Mission*, 70–86; Dunn, "The Apache Mission on the San Sabá River," 404–12; Hyde, *The Pawnee*, 59.

20. Weddle, *The San Sabá Mission*, 86–88; Dunn, "The Apache Mission on the San Sabá River," 407–12; Juan M. Romero de Terreros, "The Destruction of the San Sabá Apache Mission: A Discussion of the Casualties," *The Americas* 60 (April 2004): 618–26.

21. Weddle, *The San Sabá Mission*, 53.

22. Dunn, "The Apache Mission on the San Sabá," 414.

23. Dunn, "The Apache Mission on the San Sabá," 413; Wade, *The Native Americans of the Texas Edwards Plateau*, 187; Schilz and Worcester, "The Spread of Firearms among the Indian Tribes on the Northern Frontier of New Spain," 4; Chipman, *Spanish Texas*, 161.

24. Wade, *The Native Americans of the Texas Edwards Plateau*, 187.

25. Ibid., 183; Simpson, *The San Sabá Papers*, xx.

26. Weddle, *The San Sabá Mission*, 102–3.

27. Álvarez and Kuethe, "The San Sabá Presidio," 13; Sam D. Ratcliffe, "Escenas de Martirio: Notes on the Destruction of Mission San Sabá," *Southwestern Historical Quarterly* 94 (April 1991): 516–17; Simpson, *The San Sabá Papers*, 153.

28. Harper, "The Taovayas Indians in Frontier Trade and Diplomacy," 281; Simpson, *The San Sabá Papers*, 107–9, 144–47; Henry Easton Allen, "The Parrilla Expedition to the Red River in 1759," *Southwestern Historical Quarterly* 43 (July 1939): 55–57.

29. Simpson, *The San Sabá Papers*, 153–54; Anderson, *The Indian Southwest*, 124; Allen, "The Parrilla Expedition to the Red River," 58–60; Wade, *The Native Americans of the Texas Edwards Plateau*, 191; Harper, "The Taovayas Indians in Frontier Trade and Diplomacy," 281–82.

30. Wade, *The Native Americans of the Texas Edwards Plateau*, 191; Simpson, *The San Sabá Papers*, 154–55; Allen, "The Parrilla Expedition to the Red River," 60–61; Weddle, *The San Sabá Mission*, 118.

31. Simpson, *The San Sabá Papers*, 154–55; Allen, "The Parrilla Expedition to the Red River," 60–64; Weddle, *The San Sabá Mission*, 118–19; Robert S. Weddle, *After the Massacre: The Violent Legacy of the San Sabá Mission* (Lubbock: Texas Tech University Press, 2007), 12–13; Thomas W. Dunlay, "Indian Allies in the Armies of New Spain and the United States: A Comparative Study," *New Mexico Historical Review* 56 (July 1981): 239–41.

32. Weddle, *The San Sabá Mission*, 137; Weddle, *After the Massacre*, 25–27.

33. Ralph H. Vigil, Frances W. Kaye, and John R. Wunder, eds., *Spain and the Plains* (Niwot, CO: University of Colorado Press, 1994), 16; Harper, "The Taovayas Indians in Frontier Trade and Diplomacy," 282–83; Weddle, *After the Massacre*, 29–31.

34. Allen, "The Parrilla Expedition to the Red River," 64–69; Simpson, *The San Sabá Papers*, 155; LaVere, *The Texas Indians*, 143; Hoig, *Tribal Wars of the Southern Plains*, 67; Weddle, *The San Sabá Mission*, 119–23; Harper, "The Taovayas Indians in Frontier Trade and Diplomacy," 283; Weddle, *After the Massacre*, 29–33, 129.

35. Weddle argues that the Spaniards held their own against a numerically superior force, inflicted about fifty casualties on the enemy, and did not "flee" the area in panic. The Taovayas did not claim victory, furthermore, and put out peace-feelers to the Spaniards in 1760. See Weddle, *After the Massacre*, 33–34, 49.

36. This lesson was apparently lost on Parrilla. Upon reaching San Sabá on October 25, 1759, he sought to organize a new campaign against the Norteños and their allies. For a variety of reasons (the approach of winter and lack of horses), his officers demurred. See Chipman and Elizondo, "New Light on Felipe de Rábago y Terán," 173.

37. Allen, "The Parrilla Expedition to the Red River," 70–71; Weddle, *The San Sabá Mission*, 130–31; Chipman, *Spanish Texas*, 174; Harper, "The Taovayas Indians in Frontier Trade and Diplomacy," 285.

38. Tunnell and Newcomb, "A Lipan Apache Mission," 162. The Apaches suffered one man killed and one wounded. See Weddle, *After the Massacre*, 134.

39. Weddle, *The San Sabá Mission*, 132–33; Schlesier, "Rethinking the Dismal River Aspect and the Plains Athapaskans," 125–26. Quotes taken from Weddle.

40. Weddle, *The San Sabá Mission*, 137–42; Conrad Dunagan, "Spanish-Mexican Trails and Traces in the Pecos Plains of Texas," *Permian Historical Annual* 1 (1961): 52; Donald E. Chipman and Harriet D. Joseph, *Notable Men and Women of Spanish Texas* (Austin: University of Texas Press, 1999), 117–18; Weddle, *After the Massacre*, 40–45. For an excellent discussion of Felipe Rábago's career and his ability to gain official appointments, see Chipman and Elizondo, "New Light on Felipe de Rábago y Terán," *Southwestern Historical Quarterly* 111 (October 2007).

41. In 1760, the garrison consumed nearly 100,000 pesos, an impressive sum for such an isolated fort. See Álvarez and Kuethe, "The San Sabá Presidio," 14.

42. Weddle, *The San Sabá Mission*, 154–55; Tunnell and Newcomb, "A Lipan Apache Mission," 162–63; Chipman and Joseph, *Notable Men and Women of Spanish Texas*, 118–19; Rábago spent upwards of 12,000 pesos of his own money to purchase provisions, clothing, and livestock. See Chipman and Elizondo, "New Light on Felipe de Rábago y Terán," 177; Odie B. Faulk, "The Comanche Invasion of Texas, 1743–1836," *Great Plains Journal* 9 (Fall 1969): 18; Weddle, *After the Massacre*, 50.

43. Tunnell and Newcomb, "A Lipan Apache Mission," 163; LaVere, *The Texas Indians*, 144–45; Weddle, *After the Attack*, 50–51.

44. Tunnell and Newcomb, "A Lipan Apache Mission," 163–64; Weddle, *The San Sabá Mission*, 156–57; Schilz, *Lipan Apaches in Texas*, 16–17; John, *Storms Brewed in Other Men's Worlds*, 359–61; *Handbook of Texas Online*, s.v. "San Lorenzo de la Santa Cruz Mission," http://www.tsha.utexas.edu/handbook/online/articles/SS/uqs26.html (accessed February 19, 2006).

45. Tunnell and Newcomb, "A Lipan Apache Mission," 166–67; Weddle, *The San Sabá Mission*, 157–59; Chipman and Joseph, *Notable Men and Women of Spanish Texas*, 119–20; Weddle, *San Juan Bautista*, 274.

46. Tunnell and Newcomb, "A Lipan Apache Mission," 166–68; Weddle, *The San Sabá Mission*, 158–60.

47. Tunnell and Newcomb, "A Lipan Apache Mission," 166–68; John, *Storms Brewed in Other Men's Worlds*, 362; Weddle, *San Juan Bautista*, 275; Chipman and Elizondo, "New Light on Felipe de Rábago y Terán," 178.

48. Tunnell and Newcomb, "A Lipan Apache Mission," 169; Chipman and Joseph, *Notable Men and Women of Spanish Texas*, 120; Weddle, *San Juan Bautista*, 275.

49. Tunnell and Newcomb, "A Lipan Apache Mission," 169; Isaac Joslin Cox, "The Louisiana-Texas Frontier," *Quarterly of the Texas State Historical Association* 10 (July 1906): 27–28; Weddle, *The San Sabá Mission*, 160; Álvarez and Kuethe, "The San Sabá Presidio," 15.

50. Tunnell and Newcomb, "A Lipan Apache Mission," 168–69; Weddle, *San Juan Bautista*, 276.

51. John, *Storms Brewed in Other Men's Worlds*, 362–64; Dunn, *The San Sabá Mission*, 160–61; Tunnell and Newcomb, "A Lipan Apache Mission," 168; Chipman and Joseph, *Notable Men and Women of Spanish Texas*, 121; Schilz, *Lipan Apaches in Texas*, 17–18; Weddle, *San Juan Bautista*, 275–76.

52. Castañeda, *Our Catholic Heritage in Texas*, 4:187–90. Forrest Kirkland speculates that pictographs near Paint Rock, Texas, were probably the work of Lipans—perhaps Bigote's people? See Forrest Kirkland, *The Rock Art of Texas Indians*, text by W. W. Newcomb (Austin: University of Texas Press, 1967), 152–55.

53. Weddle, *The San Sabá Mission*, 162–63; John, *Storms Brewed in Other Men's Worlds*, 363, 367; Anderson, *The Indian Southwest*, 124; Chipman and Joseph, *Notable Men and Women of Spanish Texas*, 121.

54. Father Marino de los Dolores to Governor Martos, August 6, 1762, BAT, reel 5, series 1, vol. 35, Hunter Room, UTB.

55. Tunnell and Newcomb, "A Lipan Apache Mission," 171; Weddle, *San Juan Bautista*, 281; John C. Ewers, "The Influence of Epidemics on the Indian Populations and Cultures of Texas," *Plains Anthropologist* 18 (1973): 107–8.

56. Philleo Nash, "The Place of Religious Revivalism in the Formation of the Intercultural Community on the Klamath Reservation," in *Social Anthropology of North American Tribes: Essays in Social Organization, Law, and Religion*, ed. Fred Eggan (Chicago: University of Chicago Press, 1937), 441–42; Tunnell and Newcomb, "A Lipan Apache Mission," 171–72.

57. Anderson, *The Indian Southwest*, 125. Odie B. Faulk's study of Comanche warfare states that the Comanches attacked Mission San Lorenzo on January 22, 1766, and killed twenty-three Apaches; see Faulk, "The Comanche Invasion of Texas," 19.

58. Schilz, *Lipan Apaches in Texas*, 18; Tunnell and Newcomb, "A Lipan Apache Mission," 172–73. Gary Clayton Anderson refutes these accounts; see Anderson, *The Indian Southwest*, 305n77.

59. Anderson, *The Indian Southwest*, 126; Tunnell and Newcomb, "A Lipan Apache Mission," 173–74; Wade, *The Native Americans of the Texas Edwards Plateau*, 198–99; Weddle, *The San Sabá Mission*, 164; Weddle, *San Juan Bautista*, 283.

60. Anderson, *The Indian Southwest*, 126–27.

61. Sidney B. Brinckerhoff and Odie B. Faulk, *Lancers for the King: A Study of the Frontier Military System of Northern New Spain, with a Translation of the Royal Regulations of 1772*, with a forward by Kieran McCarty (Phoenix: Arizona Historical Foundation, 1965), 4–5; Weddle, *The San Sabá Mission*, 167–68; William C. Foster, *Spanish Expeditions into Texas, 1689–1768* (Austin: University of Texas Press, 1995); Weddle, *San Juan Bautista*, 282–83; Joseph K. Park, "Spanish Indian Policy in Northern Mexico, 1765–1810," in *New Spain's Far Northern Frontier: Essays on Spain in the American West, 1540–1821*, ed. David J. Weber (Dallas: Southern Methodist University Press, 1979), 219–21; Wade, *Native Americans of the Texas Edwards Plateau*, 199–202.

62. Odie B. Faulk, *The Last Years of Spanish Texas, 1778–1821* (London: Mouton & Co., 1964), 15–17; Park, "Spanish Indian Policy in Northern Mexico," 219–22.

63. Gary B. Starnes, "Juan de Ugalde and the Coahuila-Texas Frontier," *Texana* 10 (1972): 117; *Handbook of Texas Online*, s.v. "New Regulations for Presidios," http://www.tsha.utexas.edu/handbook/online/articles/NN/nfn1.html (accessed July 28, 2005); Lawrence Kinnaird, *The Frontiers of New Spain: Nicholas De Lafora's Description, 1766–1768* (Berkeley, CA: The Quivira Society, 1958), 38–39, 77; Brinckerhoff and Faulk, *Lancers for the King*, 5; Park, "Spanish Indian Policy in Northern Mexico," 220–21.

64. Kinnaird, *The Frontiers of New Spain*, 79.

65. Ibid., 214–17; Kieran McCarty, "Bernardo de Galvez on the Apache Frontier: The Education of a Future Viceroy," *Journal of the Southwest* 36 (1994): 107.

66. Weber, *Bárbaros: Spaniards and Their Savages*, 148; *Handbook of Texas Online*, s.v. "New Regulations for Presidios"; Lt. Don Antonio Bonilla, "A Brief Compendium of the Events Which Have Occurred in the Province of Texas from its Conquest, or Reduction, to the Present Date," *Texas State Historical Association Quarterly* 8 (July 1904): 60; Kinnaird, *The Frontiers of New Spain*, 216–17; Brinckerhoff and Faulk, *Lancers for the King*, 5.

67. Tunnell and Newcomb, "A Lipan Apache Mission," 176.

68. Anderson, *The Indian Southwest*, 126.

69. Lapuz, "Culture Change and Psychological Stress," 173.

CHAPTER FOUR

1. Robinson, *Apache Voices*, 140–42.

2. Faulk, "The Comanche Invasion of Texas," 21; Wade, *The Native Americans of the Texas Edwards Plateau*, 203; Schilz, *Lipan Apaches in Texas*, 19–20; Sjoberg, "Lipan Apache Culture in Historical Perspective," 78; Tunnell and Newcomb, "A Lipan Apache Mission," 176; Chipman and Joseph, *Notable Men and Women of Spanish Texas*, 160–62; Weddle, *San Juan Bautista*, 299. Morris Opler maintains, however, that the Lipans did not arrive on the Texas Gulf Coast until 1796; see Opler, *Myths and Legends of the Lipan Apache Indians*, 1.

3. Chipman, *Spanish Texas*, 184; Bannon, *The Spanish Borderlands Frontier*, 180; *Handbook of Texas Online*, s.v. "New Regulations for Presidios"; Faulk, *The Last Years of Spanish Texas*, 17–18; Weber, *Bárbaros: Spaniards and Their Savages*, 148–50; Verne Ray, "Ethnohistorical Analysis of Documents Relating to the Apache Indians of Texas," in *Apache Indians X* (New York: Garland Publishing, 1974), 34.

4. Bannon, *The Spanish Borderlands Frontier*, 180–81; Chipman, *Spanish Texas*, 184–85; David M. Vigness, "Don Hugo Oconor and New Spain's Northeastern Frontier, 1764–1776," *Journal of the West* 6 (1967): 28–31; Mary Lu Moore and Delmar L. Beene, "The Interior Provinces of New Spain: The Report of Hugo O'Conor, January 30, 1776," *Arizona and the West* 13 (1971): 267–68.

5. Chipman, *Spanish Texas*, 182; Chipman and Joseph, *Notable Men and Women of Spanish Texas*, 160–62; Smith, *From Dominance to Disappearance*, 20–21; Cox, "The Louisiana-Texas Frontier," 30–31; LaVere, *The Texas Indians*, 145–46; John, *Storms Brewed in Other Men's Worlds*, 397–99; Hoig, *Tribal Wars of the Southern Plains*, 68–69.

6. Chipman, *Spanish Texas*, 182; Chipman and Joseph, *Notable Men and Women of Spanish Texas*, 160–62; Viceroy Antonio de Bucareli to Governor Ripperda, October 31, 1771, BAT, reel 7, vol. 50, Hunter Room,

UTB; Cecile E. Carter, *Caddo Indians: Where We Come From* (Norman: University of Oklahoma Press, 1995), 191.

7. Chipman and Joseph, *Notable Men and Women of Spanish Texas*, 162; Carter, *Caddo Indians*, 191–92; McCollough, "Political Decentralization as a Strategy to Maintain Sovereignty: An Example from the Hasinais during the 1700s," 317–19.

8. Faulk, "The Comanche Invasion of Texas," 22–25; Wade, *The Native Americans of the Texas Edwards Plateau*, 204–5; Schilz, *Lipan Apaches in Texas*, 21; Hugo O'Connor, *The Defenses of Northern New Spain: Hugo O'Conor's Report to Teodoro de Croix, July 22, 1777*, trans. and ed. Donald C. Cutter (Dallas: Southern Methodist University Press, 1994), 73.

9. Bernard E. Bobb, *The Viceregency of Antonio María Bucareli in New Spain, 1771–1779* (Austin: University of Texas Press, 1962), 141–42; O'Connor, *The Defenses of Northern New Spain*, 7; Salmón, "A Thankless Job: Mexican Soldiers in the Spanish Borderlands," 4–6; Vigness, "Don Hugo Oconor and New Spain's Northeastern Frontier," 35–36; Frank C. Lockwood, *The Apache Indians* (Lincoln: University of Nebraska Press, 1939), 22–23.

10. Bobb, *The Viceregency of Antonio María Bucareli in New Spain*, 141–42; Robert S. Weddle, "Campaigning in Texas, 1775," *Texas Military History* 6 (Winter 1967): 257–58; Salmón, "A Thankless Job: Mexican Soldiers in the Spanish Borderlands," 7.

11. Weddle, "Campaigning in Texas, 1775," 257–60; Alfred B. Thomas, trans. and ed., *Forgotten Frontiers: A Study of the Spanish Indian Policy of Don Juan Bautista de Anza, Governor of New Mexico, 1777–1787* (Norman: University of Oklahoma Press, 1932), 10–11; Bobb, *The Viceregency of Antonio María Bucareli in New Spain*, 141–42; Moore and Beene, "The Interior Provinces of New Spain," 269; Calloway, *One Vast Winter Count*, 387; Wade, *The Native Americans of the Texas Edwards Plateau*, 205; Bernardo de Gálvez, *Instructions for Governing the Interior Provinces of New Spain, 1786*, trans. and ed. Donald E. Worcester (Berkeley, CA: The Quivira Society, 1951), 11–12.

12. The disappointing results of Ugarte's campaign made him skittish about using Lipans as guides and trackers, believing them to be "double agents." See Wade, *The Native Americans of the Texas Edwards Plateau*, 206.

13. On January 2, 1776, Ugarte's men captured an Apache couple who reported that Spanish soldiers to the west had "killed and captured all the Lipillanes," a Plains Apache people closely identified with the Lipans. This information seems to square with the oft-cited report that the Oconór campaign, in fifteen separate engagements, killed 138 warriors, captured 104 prisoners, and recovered nearly 2,000 animals. See Wade, *The Native Americans of the Texas Edwards Plateau*, 206; Weddle, "Campaigning in Texas, 1775," 267–69; *Handbook of Texas Online*, s.v. "Garza Falcon de la Alejo," http://www.tsha.utexas.edu/handbook/online/articles/GG/fgaae.

html (accessed August 15, 2005); Bobb, *The Viceregency of Antonio María Bucareli in New Spain*, 142; Calloway, *One Vast Winter Count*, 387; Gálvez, *Instructions for Governing the Interior Provinces*, 11–12.

14. In October 1776, Oconór wrote to Viceroy Bucareli that he had engaged the Apaches on five separate occasions, and had killed twenty-seven and captured eighteen. See Thomas, *Forgotten Frontiers*, 12–13.

15. Letter of Governor Ugarte to Viceroy Bucareli with Related Declaration and Draft Response, 7 November 1776, Archivo General de la Nación, Mexico City, Provincias Internas, vol. 024 FF. 268–72, microfilm copy, serial no. 041-00567, Arizona State Museum, University of Arizona, Tucson, Arizona. Translated by Rocio Chavarro.

16. Weddle, "Campaigning in Texas, 1775," 268–70; Salmón, "A Thankless Job: Mexican Soldiers in the Spanish Borderlands," 7–8; O'Connor, *The Defenses of Northern New Spain*, 94; Bobb, *The Viceregency of Antonio María de Bucareli in New Spain*, 143.

17. Chipman, *Spanish Texas*, 189–91; Bobb, *The Viceregency of Antonio María de Bucareli in New Spain*, 143–47; Weber, Bárbaros: *Spaniards and Their Savages*, 156–57; Faulk, *The Last Years of Spanish Texas*, 18; Schilz, *Lipan Apaches in Texas*, 23–24; Gálvez, *Instructions for Governing the Interior Provinces*, 13–17; Donald E. Worcester, "The Apaches in the History of the Southwest," *New Mexico Historical Review* 50 (1975): 28; Starnes, "Juan de Ugalde and the Coahuila-Texas Frontier," 118.

18. Commandant General Teodoro de Croix to Governor Ripperdá, July 9, 1777, BAT, reel 9, vol. 65, Hunter Room, UTB; Weber, *Bárbaros: Spaniards and Their Savages*, 156–57; Chipman, *Spanish Texas*, 191; Gálvez, *Instructions for Governing the Interior Provinces*, 17–18; Starnes, "Juan de Ugalde and the Coahuila-Texas Frontier," 120. Croix's policy foreshadowed by a decade that of Bernardo Gálvez, who in the 1780s recommended the establishment of *establecimientos de paz* (peace establishments) for Indians seeking peace. See William B. Griffen, *Apaches at War and Peace: The Janos Presidio, 1750–1858* (Norman: University of Oklahoma Press, 1988), 14, 119; John, *Storms Brewed in Other Men's Worlds*, 503–4, 507–8.

19. John, *Storms Brewed in Other Men's Worlds*, 509–19, 529–30; Chipman and Joseph, *Notable Men and Women of Spanish Texas*, 166–69; Hoig, *Tribal Wars of the Southern Plains*, 69; Faulk, "The Comanche Invasion of Texas," 26–27; Chipman, *Spanish Texas*, 192; O'Connor, *The Defenses of Northern New Spain*, 92; Weber, *Bárbaros: Spaniards and Their Savages*, 157–58; Catherine M. Price, "The Comanche Threat to Texas and New Mexico in the Eighteenth Century and the Development of Spanish Indian Policy," *Journal of the West* 24 (April 1989): 42–43; Max L. Moorhead, *The Apache Frontier: Jacobo Ugarte and Spanish-Indian Relations in Northern New Spain, 1769–1791* (Norman: University of Oklahoma Press, 1968), 127–28; Moorhead, "Spanish Deportation of Hostile Apaches," 207–8.

20. John, *Storms Brewed in Other Men's Worlds*, 529–30; Chipman, *Spanish Texas*, 192; O'Connor, *The Defenses of Northern New Spain*, 92; Weber, *Bárbaros: Spaniards and Their Savages*, 157–58; Price, "The Comanche Threat to Texas and New Mexico in the Eighteenth Century," 42–43; Moorhead, *The Apache Frontier*, 127–28; Moorhead, "Spanish Deportation of Hostile Apaches," 207–8.

21. Thomas, *Teodoro de Croix and the Northern Frontier of New Spain*, 82, 89, 96.

22. Chipman and Joseph, *Notable Men and Women of Spanish Texas*, 203–4.

23. Ibid., 204; John, *Storms Brewed in Other Men's Worlds*, 531–34.

24. John, *Storms Brewed in Other Men's Worlds*, 534; Governor Domingo Cabello to Teodoro de Croix, March 18, 1779, BAT, reel 10, vol. 80; Teodoro de Croix to Cabello, May 1779, BAT, reel 10, vol. 81, Hunter Room, UTB; Barr, "Commodifying Indian Women in the Borderlands," 44.

25. John, *Storms Brewed in Other Men's Worlds*, 501–3, 534–35; Governor Cabello to Croix, May 14, 1779, BAT, reel 10, vol. 81, Hunter Room, UTB; Moorhead, *The Apache Frontier*, 203–5.

26. John, *Storms Brewed in Other Men's Worlds*, 535; Teodoro Croix to Governor Cabello, August 16, 1779, BAT, reel 11, vol. 85, Hunter Room, UTB; Moorhead, *The Apache Frontier*, 203–5; Starnes, "Juan de Ugalde and the Coahuila-Texas Frontier," 120.

27. Governor Cabello to Croix, August 19, 1779, BAT, reel 11, vol. 86, Hunter Room, UTB; John, *Storms Brewed in Other Men's Worlds*, 535–36.

28. Governor Cabello to Croix, November 2, 1779, BAT, reel 11, vol. 89, Hunter Room, UTB.

29. Ibid.

30. Sjoberg, "Lipan Apache Culture," 78–79; Smith, *From Dominance to Disappearance*, 28.

31. Max Moorhead describes four major eastern Apache groups: Yntajen-ne (Faraones), Sejen-ne (Mescaleros), Cuelcajen-ne (Llaneros), and the Lipajen-ne (Lipans), who lived along the upper and lower banks of the Rio Grande River. See Moorhead, *The Apache Frontier*, 200–203; Dolores A. Gunnerson, *The Jicarilla Apaches: A Study in Survival* (Dekalb, IL: Northern Illinois University Press, 1974), 253–54, 277, 290. The general consensus is that bands of Faraones, Llaneros, Lipiyanes, and Natagés eventually merged with either the Mescaleros or the Lipans (or both).

32. Lipan Interviews, *Opler Papers*; Governor Cabello to Croix, February 12, 1780, BAT, reel 12, vol. 93, Hunter Room, UTB; John, *Storms Brewed in Other Men's Worlds*, 613.

33. Governor Cabello to Croix, November 20, 1780, BAT, reel 13, vol. 106. The Lipans estimated that more than four hundred of their people died from the smallpox epidemic. See Cabello to Croix, December 6, 1780, BAT, reel 13, vol. 106, Hunter Room, UTB; Ramsdell, *San Antonio*, 29.

34. Weber, *Bárbaros: Spaniards and Their Savages*, 151.

35. John, *Storms Brewed in Other Men's Worlds*, 629; Lipan Interviews, *Opler Papers*.

36. John, *Storms Brewed in Other Men's Worlds*, 633–34; Gálvez, *Instructions for Governing the Interior Provinces*, 18–19; Starnes, "Juan de Ugalde and the Coahuila-Texas Frontier," 121.

37. Schilz, *Lipan Apaches in Texas*, 28–29; John, *Storms Brewed in Other Men's Worlds*, 634–36; Smith, *From Dominance to Disappearance*, 30.

38. Status Report and Daily Record of the Cavalry Company at San Antonio de Bexar for April 1783, April 30, 1783, BAT, reel 14, vol. 118, Hunter Room, UTB.

39. Ibid.; John, *Storms Brewed in Other Men's Worlds*, 641–43; Status Report and Daily Record of the Cavalry Company at San Antonio de Bexar for May 1783, May 31, 1783, BAT, reel 14, vol. 119; Commandant-general Felipe de Neve to Governor Cabello, January 9, 1784, BAT, reel 14, vol. 121; Neve to Cabello, December 18, 1783, BAT, reel 14, vol. 121; Neve to Cabello, February 20, 1784, BAT, reel 14, vol. 122; Cabello to Neve, March 20, 1784, BAT, reel 14, vol. 123, Hunter Room, UTB.

40. Status Report and Daily Record of the Cavalry Company at San Antonio de Bexar for January 1784, January 31, 1784, BAT, reel 14, vol. 122; Status Report and Daily Record of the Cavalry Company at San Antonio de Bexar for February 1784, February 29, 1784, BAT, reel 14, vol. 122; Cabello to Neve, June 20, 1784, BAT, reel 15, vol. 126, Hunter Room, UTB; John, *Storms Brewed in Other Men's Worlds*, 647–48.

41. John, *Storms Brewed in Other Men's Worlds*, 661–65; Hämäläinen, *The Comanche Empire*, 113–26; Odie Faulk, "Spanish-Comanche Relations and the Treaty of 1785," *Texana* 2 (Spring 1964): 44–47; Thomas, *Forgotten Frontiers*, 329–32; Smith, *From Dominance to Disappearance*, 31–32; Betty, *Comanche Society before the Reservation*, 13, 29, 34.

42. Faulk, "Spanish-Comanche Relations and the Treaty of 1785," 48–49; Smith, *From Dominance to Disappearance*, 32; Governor Cabello to Rengel, November 25, 1785, BAT, reel 16, vol. 135, Hunter Room, UTB; Works, "Creating Trading Places on the New Mexican Frontier," 277.

43. Governor Cabello to Rengel, November 25, 1785, BAT, reel 16, vol. 135, Hunter Room, UTB.

44. John, *Storms Brewed in Other Men's Worlds*, 689–95; Elizabeth A. H. John, "Independent Indians and the San Antonio Community," in Poyo

and Hinojosa, eds., *Tejano Origins in Eighteenth Century San Antonio*, 127; Governor Cabello to Rengel, December 24, 1785, BAT, reel 16, vol. 135; Cabello to Rengel, January 10, 1786, BAT, reel 16, vol. 136; Cabello to Rengel, January 24, 1786, BAT, reel 16, vol. 136; Cabello to Rengel, January 31, 1786, BAT, reel 16, vol. 136, Hunter Room, UTB.

45. John, *Storms Brewed in Other Men's Worlds*, 699–700; Smith, *From Dominance to Disappearance*, 41; Governor Cabello to Commandant-General Jacobo de Ugarte, June 12, 1786, BAT, reel 16, vol. 138, Hunter Room, UTB; Commandant-General Ugarte to Governor Cabellos, August 3, 1786, Bexar Archives, reel 17, microfilm copy, Arnulfo Oliviera Library, Hunter Room, UTB.

46. Governor Cabello to Commandant-General Ugarte, June 12, 1786, Bexar Archives, reel 17, microfilm copy, Arnulfo Oliviera Library, Hunter Room, UTB; Status Report and Daily Record of the Cavalry Company at San Antonio de Bexar for June 1786, June 30, 1786, BAT, reel 16, vol. 138; Governor Cabello to Commandant-General Ugarte, July 2, 1786, BAT, reel 16, vol. 139, Hunter Room, UTB; Governor Cabello to Commandant-General Ugarte, August 3, 1786, Bexar Archives, reel 17, microfilm copy, Arnulfo Oliviera Library, Hunter Room, UTB.

47. According to Spanish observers who witnessed the Lipans departure for the Frío River, of the one thousand horses they took with them, two-thirds carried Spanish brands.

48. Governor Cabello to Commandant-General Ugarte, July 3, 1786, BAT, reel 16, vol. 139, Hunter Room, UTB.

49. On August 26, 1786, Spanish authorities divided the Provincias Internas into three sectors. The two easternmost sectors came under the oversight of Ugarte except in military matters. Juan de Ugalde received the title "commander in arms" of the easternmost sector, which included Texas, Coahuila, Nuevo León, and Nuevo Santander. This arrangement lasted fifteen months.

50. Commandant-General Ugarte to Governor Cabello, July 20, 1786, BAT, reel 16, vol. 139; Ugarte to Cabello, August 3, 1786, BAT, reel 16, vol. 140, Hunter Room, UTB.

51. Gálvez, *Instructions for Governing the Interior Provinces*, 34, 43–44, 47–49, 79–81; Weber, *Bárbaros: Spaniards and Their Savages*, 9, 160–61; Worcester, "The Apaches in the History of the Southwest," 28; Starnes, "Juan de Ugalde and the Coahuila-Texas Frontier," 122.

52. Worcester, "The Apaches in the History of the Southwest," 28–29.

53. Governor Cabello to Commandant-General Ugarte, September 10, 1786, BAT, reel 16, vol. 141; Cabello to Ugarte, September 11, 1786, BAT, reel 16, vol. 141, Hunter Room, UTB; Smith, *From Dominance to Disappearance*, 41–42.

54. Governor Cabello to Commandant-General Ugarte, September 25, 1786, BAT, reel 16, vol. 141, Hunter Room, UTB.

55. John, *Storms Brewed in Other Men's Worlds*, 722–23; *Handbook of Texas Online*, s.v. "Martinez Pacheco, Rafael," http://www.tsha.utexas.edu/handbook/online/articles/MM/fmadt.html (accessed September 13, 2005).

56. John, *Storms Brewed in Other Men's Worlds*, 722–25; Smith, *From Dominance to Disappearance*, 42.

57. Commandant-General Ugarte to Governor Pacheco, February 1, 1787, BAT, reel 17, vol. 144, Hunter Room, UTB.

58. Fray José Raphel Oliva to Governor Pacheco, February 11, 1787, BAT, reel 17, vol. 144, Hunter Room, UTB.

59. Governor Pacheco to Fray José Raphael Oliva, February 14, 1787, BAT, reel 17, vol. 144; Governor Pacheco to Commandant-General Ugarte, March 10, 1787, BAT, reel 17, vol. 144, Hunter Room, UTB; Starnes, "Juan de Ugalde and the Coahuila-Texas Frontier," 123.

60. Ugarte's account was news to Governor Pacheco, who immediately made an inquiry as to the soldiers involved. According to Lieutenant José Antonio Curvelo, who was an eyewitness, the Lipans received the Spanish escort cordially in late February. Chief Chiquito, in particular, was hospitable. On March 3, a Lipan named Casaca from mission La Concepción arrived and began spreading rumors that a large Spanish contingent was on the way to take them into captivity and to kill anyone who resisted. This caused a panic, and several Lipan families fled. Some Lipans later reported that "a Spaniard" had told them the soldiers were going to send the Lipans to Vera Cruz in shackles, to board them on ships, and to imprison them "in some dwellings which were located in the middle of the ocean" where they would become slaves. See Pacheco to Curvelo, September 19, 1787, and Curvelo's reply on September 25, 1787, BAT, reel 17, vol. 146. The testimony of Alférez Luis Cazorla substantiates Curvelo's testimony. See Pacheco to Cazorla, September 21, 1787, and Cazorla's reply on September 28, 1787, BAT, reel 17, vol. 146, Hunter Room, UTB.

61. Commandant-General Ugarte to Governor Pacheco, May 25, 1787, BAT, reel 17, vol. 145, Hunter Room, UTB.

62. Al B. Nelson, "Juan de Ugalde and Picax-Ande Ins-Tinsle, 1787–1788," *Southwestern Historical Quarterly* 43 (April 1940): 438–44; Moorhead, *The Apache Frontier*, 250–54; Al B. Nelson, "Campaigning in the Big Bend of the Rio Grande in 1787," *Southwestern Historical Quarterly* 39 (January 1936): 205; Wade, *The Native Americans of the Texas Edwards Plateau*, 209; Starnes, "Juan de Ugalde and the Coahuila-Texas Frontier," 123.

63. Governor Pacheco to Juan de Ugalde, September 29, 1787, BAT, reel 17, vol. 146; Captain Luis Cazorla to Governor Pacheco, September 20, 1787, BAT, reel 17, vol. 146; Cazorla to Pacheco, November 2, 1787, BAT, reel 17, vol. 148;

Juan de Ugalde to Governor Pacheco, September 29, 1787, BAT, reel 17, vol. 146; Governor Pacheco to Juan de Ugalde, January 7, 1788, BAT, reel 18, vol. 151; Pacheco to Ugalde, January 17, 1788, BAT, reel 18, vol. 151; Pacheco to Ugalde, February 3, 1788, BAT, reel 18, vol. 152, Hunter Room, UTB; Smith, *From Dominance to Disappearance*, 42.

64. Letter from Governor Concha to Commandant-General Ugarte, November 10, 1787; Ugarte's Order to Governor Concha, January 17, 1788, in Marc Simmons, "Governor Anza, the Lipan Apaches and Pecos Pueblo," *El Palacio* 77 (1970): 38–40.

65. Murial H. Wright, *A Guide to the Indian Tribes of Oklahoma* (Norman: University of Oklahoma Press, 1986), 181.

66. Nelson, "Juan de Ugalde and Picax-Ande Ins-Tinsle," 457–64; Wade, *The Native Americans of the Texas Edwards Plateau*, 209.

67. Wade, *The Native Americans of the Texas Edwards Plateau*, 209–11.

68. John, *Storms Brewed in Other Men's Worlds*, 755.

69. Faulk, "The Comanche Invasion of Texas," 32–33; Wade, *The Native Americans of the Texas Edwards Plateau*, 212–13; Smith, *From Domination to Disappearance*, 43–44; Haley, *Apaches: A History and Culture Portrait*, 40; Chipman, *Spanish Texas*, 200.

70. Wade, *The Native Americans of the Texas Edwards Plateau*, 213–14; Smith, *From Dominance to Disappearance*, 44–45; J. B. Wilkinson, *Laredo and the Rio Grande Frontier* (Austin: Jenkins Publishing Co., 1975), 57–58; Moorhead, *The Apache Frontier*, 264–67.

71. Smith, *From Dominance to Disappearance*, 45.

72. Faulk, "The Comanche Invasion of Texas," 33–34; Smith, *From Domination to Disappearance*, 45; Wilkinson, *Laredo and the Rio Grande Frontier*, 58–59; William H. Oberste, *History of Refugio Mission* (Refugio, TX: Refugio Timely Remarks, 1942), 55; Frank D. Reeve, "The Apache Indians in Texas," *Southwestern Historical Quarterly* 50 (October 1946): 200; Cordero, "Cordero's Description of the Apache—1796," 355–56.

73. Ramon de Castro to Revilla Gigedo, 3 April 1792, Archivo General de la Nación, Mexico City, Provincias Internas, vol. 170 FF. 239–53, microfilm copy, serial no. 041–04007, Arizona State Museum, University of Arizona, Tucson, Arizona. Translated by Raul Reyes.

74. Coleccion de Oficios y Documentos de los Commandante Generals sobre Paces de los Lipanes y Novedades de los Demas Apaches, 14 September 1792, Archivo General de la Nación, Mexico City, Provincias Internas, vol. 170 FF. 388–400, microfilm copy, serial no. 041–04014, Arizona State Museum, University of Arizona, Tucson, Arizona. Translated by Raul Reyes.

75. Smith, *From Dominance to Disappearance*, 45; Weddle, *San Juan Bautista*, 355–56; Cordero, "Cordero's Description of the Apache—1796," 355–56.

76. State of Affairs between Spaniards, Lipan Apaches and Northern Provincias Internas, July 23, 1799, Archivo General de la Nación, Mexico City, Provincias Internas, vol. 012 FF. 458–64, microfilm copy, serial no. 041–00184, Arizona State Museum, University of Arizona, Tucson, Arizona. Translated by Raul Reyes.

77. John, *Storms Brewed in Other Men's Worlds*, 729.

78. Faulk, *The Last Days of Spanish Texas*, 58–59. Wharton writes that "the Apache was a veritable Ishmael of the plains, for his hand was against every man, and every man's hand was against him"; see Clarence R. Wharton, *History of Texas* (Dallas: Turner Company, 1935), 346.

CHAPTER FIVE

1. "Coyote Tries to Lead Her Children like Turkey Hen and Kills Them," in Opler, *Myths and Legends of the Lipan Apache Indians*, 186.

2. The Spanish population of Texas in 1790 was 3,169. See Barr, "From Captives to Slaves," 32.

3. David J. Weber, *The Spanish Frontier in North America* (New Haven: Yale University Press, 1992), 295; *Handbook of Texas Online*, s.v. "Texas in the Age of Mexican Independence," http://www.tsha.utexas.edu/handbook/online/articles/TT/nptsd.html (accessed October 6, 2005).

4. Cortes, *Views from the Apache Frontier*, 30; Park, "Spanish Indian Policy in Northern Mexico, 230–31; William B. Griffen, *Utmost Good Faith: Patterns of Apache-Mexican Hostilities in Northern Chihuahua Border Warfare, 1824–1848* (Albuquerque: University of New Mexico Press, 1988), 15.

5. Elizabeth A. H. John, "Nurturing the Peace: Spanish and Comanche Cooperation in the Early Nineteenth Century," *New Mexico Historical Review* 59 (October 1984): 347–51.

6. Robert D. Wood, *Life in Laredo: A Documentary History from the Laredo Archives* (Denton: University of North Texas Press, 2004), 84.

7. John, "Nurturing the Peace," 356–57.

8. Félix D. Almaráz, *Tragic Cavalier: Governor Manuel Salcedo of Texas, 1808–1813* (College Station: Texas A&M University Press, 1991), 110–11.

9. *Handbook of Texas Online*, s.v. "Texas in the Age of Mexican Independence"; "Lipans," *The American Cyclopedia*, 10:516; John, "Independent Indians and the San Antonio Community," 129. Opler notes that an American member of the expedition—a "Captain McFarland"—also recruited many Lipans, and that the Lipans provided the rebels with buckskin, moccasins, and provisions; see Morris E. Opler, "The Lipan and Mescalero Apache in Texas," 258.

10. According to Elizabeth A. H. John, two hundred Lipans participated in the Magee-Gutierrez revolt due to their friendship with the José Menchaca family; see John, "Nurturing the Peace," 364–65.

11. Smith, *From Dominance to Disappearance*, 98; *Handbook of Texas Online*, s.v. "Castro, Cuelgas De," http://www.tsha.utexas.edu/handbook/online/articles/CC/fca92.html (accessed October 15, 2005).

12. Harry McCorry Henderson, "The Magee-Gutiérrez Expedition," *Southwestern Historical Quarterly* 55 (July 1951): 44–61; Schilz, *Lipan Apaches in Texas*, 35–37; *Handbook of Texas Online*, s.v. "Davenport, Peter Samuel," http://www.tsha.utexas.edu/handbook/online/articles/DD/fda23.html (accessed October 6, 2005); *Handbook of Texas Online*, s.v. "Rosillo, Battle of," http://www.tsha.utexas.edu/handbook/online/articles/RR/qfr2.html (accessed October 6, 2005); Ted Schwarz and Robert H. Thonhoff, *Forgotten Battlefield of the First Texas Revolution: The Battle of Medina, August 18, 1813* (Austin: Eakin Press, 1985), 28–29, 64, 147; Smith, *From Dominance to Disappearance*, 99; *Handbook of Texas Online*, s.v. "Medina, Battle of," http://www.tsha.utexas.edu/handbook/online/articles/MM/qfm1.html (accessed October 6, 2005); Castañeda, *Our Catholic Heritage in Texas*, 6:115.

13. Hubert Howe Bancroft, *The Works of Hubert Howe Bancroft*, vol. 16, *History of the North Mexican States and Texas* (San Francisco: The History Company, Publishers, 1889), 31–32; Berlandier, *The Indians of Texas in 1830*, 133.

14. Faulk, *The Last Years of Spanish Texas*, 71; Park, "Spanish Indian Policy in Northern Mexico," 231; Antonio Menchaca, *Memoirs* (San Antonio: Yanaguana Publications, 1937), 19–20; Smith, *From Dominance to Disappearance*, 101–7; Mattie Austin Hatcher, ed. and trans., "Letters of Antonio Martinez: Last Spanish Governor of Texas, 1817–1822," *Southwestern Historical Quarterly* 39 (April 1936): 327–31; Lockwood, *The Apache Indians*, 31; Schilz, *Lipan Apaches in Texas*, 38–39; Virginia H. Taylor and Juanita Hammons, eds. and trans., *The Letters of Antonio Martinez: Last Governor of Spanish Texas, 1817–1822* (Austin: Texas State Library, 1957), 22–23, 71; Hämäläinen, *The Comanche Empire*, 186.

15. H. Allen Anderson, "The Delaware and Shawnee Indians and the Republic of Texas, 1820–1845," *Southwestern Historical Quarterly* 94 (October 1990): 233–34, 243.

16. Smith, *From Dominance to Disappearance*, 102–3, 109; Taylor and Hammon, *The Letters of Antonio Martinez*, 150–51, 180, 217–18, 228, 308; Schilz, *Lipan Apaches in Texas*, 38–39; Jack Jackson, *Los Mesteños: Spanish Ranching in Texas, 1721–1821* (College Station: Texas A&M University Press, 1986), 547; David B. Adams, "Embattled Borderland: Northern Nuevo Leon and the Indios Bárbaros, 1686–1870," *Southwestern Historical Quarterly* 95 (1991): 214.

17. Charles A. Gulick Jr. et al., *The Papers of Mirabeau B. Lamar*, vol. 4, pt. 1 (Austin: The Pemberton Press, 1968), 191–92.

18. Lamar apparently bases this episode on a Spanish account written in 1820. If even half that number of Lipan warriors died, it would have ranked as one of the most successful campaigns against the Lipans in a century.

19. Population estimates are virtually impossible to nail down with any precision. Juan Antonio Padilla puts the total Lipan population at around 700; see Padilla, "Texas in 1820," 56. José Francisco Ruíz states that the Southern Lipans numbered about 150 families (or 600 people); see José Francisco Ruíz, *Report on the Indian Tribes of Texas in 1828*, ed. John C. Ewers and trans. Georgette Dorn (New Haven: Yale University Press, 1972), 6. Henry M. Morfit, who was sent by Andrew Jackson in 1836 to investigate the military, civil, and political condition of Texas, estimated that the Lipan population included 250 warriors and 900 people total. Anna Muckelroy argues that the total Texas Indian population in the 1830s was around 20,000; see Anna Muckelroy, "The Indian Policy of the Republic of Texas," *Southwestern Historical Quarterly* 25 (April 1922): 241–42.

20. Opler, "Component, Assemblage, and Theme in Cultural Integration and Differentiation," 956.

21. Smith, *From Dominance to Disappearance*, 104; Padilla, "Texas in 1820," 54–56.

22. David J. Weber, "Mexico's Far Northern Frontier, 1821–1854: Historiography Askew," *Western Historical Quarterly* 7 (July 1976): 290–91; Omar S. Valerio-Jiménez, "Neglected Citizens and Willing Traders: The Villas del Norte (Tamaulipas) in Mexico's Northern Borderlands, 1749–1846," *Mexican Studies* 18 (Summer 2002): 279–80; Ray, "Ethnohistorical Analysis of Documents Relating to the Apache Indians," 46–49; Kenneth F. Neighbors, "Government, Land, and Indian Policies Relative to the Lipan, Mescalero, and Tigua Indians," in *Apache Indians III* (New York: Garland Publishing, 1974), 283–91; Josefina Zoraida Vazquez, "The Mexican Declaration of Independence," *Journal of American History* 85 (March 1999): 1369.

23. Ruíz, *Report on the Indian Tribes of Texas in 1828*, 2; Joseph Carl McElhannon, "Imperial Mexico and Texas, 1821–1823," *Southwestern Historical Quarterly* 53 (October 1949): 123–30; Maestas, "Culture and History of Native Peoples of South Texas," 324; Schilz, *Lipan Apaches in Texas*, 40; Wood, *Life In Laredo*, 85; Betty, *Comanche Society before the Reservation*, 62; Smith, *From Dominance to Disappearance*, 117–18; Berlandier, *The Indians of Texas in 1830*, 133.

24. McElhannon, "Imperial Mexico and Texas," 138–50; Eugene C. Barker, *Mexico and Texas, 1821–1845* (Dallas: P. L. Turner Co., 1928), 14–17; Anderson, *The Conquest of Texas*, 3.

25. Andres Resendez, "National Identity on a Shifting Border: Texas and New Mexico in the Age of Transition, 1821–1845," *Journal of American History* 86 (September 1999): 670, 678–79; Adams, "Embattled Borderland: Northern Nuevo Leon and the Indios Bárbaros," 215–16; Kelly F. Himmel, *The Conquest of the Karankawas and Tonkawas, 1821–1859* (College Station: Texas A&M University Press, 1999), 29–30.

26. Betty, *Comanche Society before the Reservation*, 62; James F. Brooks, *Captives and Cousins: Slavery, Kinship, and Community in the Southwest Borderlands* (Chapel Hill: University of North Carolina Press, 2002), 184, 256–57.

27. Sjoberg, "Lipan Apache Culture in Historical Perspective," 79; Schilz, *Lipan Apaches in Texas*, 42–43; Dorman Winfrey, ed., *Texas Indian Papers, 1825–1843*, vol. 1 (Austin: Texas State Library, 1959), 1; William B. Gannett, "The American Invasion of Texas, 1820–1845: Patterns of Conflict between Settlers and Indians" (Ph.D. diss., Cornell University, 1984), 264–68; Smith, *From Dominance to Disappearance*, 132–33.

28. *Handbook of Texas Online*, s.v. "Mier y Teran, Manuel de," http://www.tsha.utexas.edu/handbook/online/articles/MM/fmi2.html (accessed October 25, 2005); Smith, *From Dominance to Disappearance*, 137; Anderson, *The Conquest of Texas*, 70–71.

29. *Handbook of Texas Online*, s.v. "Mier y Teran, Manuel de"; Manuel de Mier y Terán, *Texas by Terán: The Diary Kept by General Manuel de Mier y Terán on his 1828 Inspection of Texas*, trans. John Wheat and ed. Jack Jackson (Austin: University of Texas Press, 2000), 1–2, 92; Sanchez, "A Trip to Texas in 1828," 249–52; Berlandier, *The Indians of Texas in 1830*, 65, 85–86, 128–29, 132, 134. In July 1825, Laredo officials reported that sixty troops and fifty Lipans went out after Comanches who had attacked several ranches, killed seven people, and taken several captives. On the twenty-sixth, they found the Comanches and killed two, seized seventy-two animals, thirty saddles, and some booty—much of it turned over to the Lipans. See Wood, *Life in Laredo*, 85–86, 114.

30. Sánchez, "A Trip to Texas in 1828," 253, 256–58; Ruíz, *Report on the Indian Tribes of Texas in 1828*, 6–7; Lester G. Bugbee, "The Texas Frontier, 1800–1825," *Publications of the Southern History Association* 4 (March 1900): 119.

31. Sánchez, "A Trip to Texas in 1828," 266–83; *Handbook of Texas Online*, s.v. "Mier y Terán, Manuel de"; Barker, *Mexico and Texas, 1821–1845*, 56–57; Smith, *From Dominance to Disappearance*, 137.

32. Barker, *Mexico and Texas, 1821–1845*, 58–59; Leroy P. Graf, "Colonizing Projects in Texas South of the Nueces, 1820–1845," *Southwestern Historical Quarterly* 50 (April 1947): 435–36; Bethel Coopwood, "Route of Cabeza de Vaca," *Texas Historical Association Quarterly* 3 (April 1900): 237; Bugbee, "The Texas Frontier," 118–19; Weber, *The Mexican Frontier*, 89, 93–95, 104, 120; Daniel Tyler, "Mexican Indian Policy in New Mexico," *New Mexico Historical Review* 55 (April 1980): 107–9, 114.

33. Ralph A. Smith, "Apache Plunder Trails Southward, 1831–1840," *New Mexico Historical Review* 37 (1962): 20.

34. Ralph A. Smith, "Indians in American-Mexican Relations before the War of 1846," *Hispanic American Historical Review* 43 (February 1963): 42, 44, 46.

35. Griffen, *Utmost Good Faith*, 28–29; Weber, *The Mexican Frontier*, 86; W. D. Wood, "Sketch of the Early Settlement of Leon County, Its Organization, and Some of the Early Settlers," *Southwestern Historical Quarterly* 4 (October 1900): 205; Andrée F. Sjoberg, "The Culture of the Tonkawa, a Texas Indian Tribe," in *Ethnology of the Texas Indians*, ed. Thomas R. Hester (New York: Garland Publishing, 1991), 357–58; J. Marvin Hunter, "Bowie's Battle Ground on the San Saba," *Frontier Times* 16 (February 1939): 215–19; "Campaign Plan Drawn Up by Manuel Rudecindo Barragán, February 25, 1832," in *Papers Concerning Robertson's Colony in Texas*, ed. Malcolm D. McLean (Arlington: University of Texas at Arlington Press, 1980), 7: 134–37; Smith, *From Dominance to Disappearance*, 143–44.

36. Lipan Interviews, *Opler Papers*.

37. An article in the nineteenth-century periodical *Littell's Living Age* mentions that shortly after the Goliad massacre, the Mexican army—along with three hundred Lipan and Karankawa auxiliaries—attacked a Texan force and wounded several soldiers before artillery fire drove them away. See "A Campaign in Texas," *Littell's Living Age* 8 (February 1846): 417.

38. Schilz, *Lipan Apaches in Texas*, 47; Opler, "The Lipan and Mescalero Apaches in Texas," 259; John H. Jenkins, ed., *The Papers of the Texas Revolution, 1835–1836* (Austin: Presidial Press, 1973), 8:334–38. Jenkins maintains that Texas Indians favored Texas independence by a ratio of four to one. Gannett, "The American Invasion of Texas," 266; Sjoberg, "Lipan Apache Culture in Historical Perspective," 79; Maestas, "Culture and History of Native Peoples of South Texas," 326; Mary Margaret McAllen Amberson et al., *I Would Rather Sleep in Texas: A History of the Lower Rio Grande Valley and the People of the Santa Anita Land Grant* (Austin: Texas State Historical Association Press, 2003), 73; Don Vicente Filisola, *Memoirs for the History of the War in Texas*, vol. 2, trans. Wallace Woolsey (Austin: Eakin Press, 1987), 161.

39. Anna Muckelroy, "The Indian Policy of the Republic of Texas," *Southwestern Historical Quarterly* 26 (July 1922): 1–20; Neighbors, "Government, Land, and Indian Policies," 293–94; Amelia W. Williams and Eugene C. Barker, eds., *The Writings of Sam Houston*, vol. 1, *1813–1836* (Austin: University of Texas Press, 1938), 449; Anderson, *The Conquest of Texas*, 153–57; George D. Harmon, "The United States Indian Policy in Texas, 1845–1860," *Mississippi Valley Historical Review* 17 (December 1930): 377–78.

40. Anderson, *The Conquest of Texas*, 159–60; Winfrey, *Texas Indian Papers*, 1:24. The committee members may have been attempting to further establish that Indians were not citizens but "aliens" and were thus (under article 10 of the constitution's "General Provisions") ineligible to own land in Texas, except by titles emanating directly from the government. Another possible explanation is that the three tribes were living below the Nueces River, which Texans (at that time at least) may have recognized as Mexican territory.

41. Winfrey, *Texas Indian Papers*, 1:30–32.

42. Ibid., 32–43, 44; Frank X. Tolbert, "When Castro Came to the Texas Capital," *Dallas Morning News* (October 17, 1962), 7; Address of M. B. Lamar to General de Castro, March 6, 1838, in Gulick, *The Papers of Mirabeau B. Lamar*, 43–44; Andrew Forest Muir, ed., "Notes and Documents: Diary of a Young Man in Houston, 1838," *Southwestern Historical Quarterly* 53 (January 1950): 290–91; "Texas and Its Revolution," *Southern Literary Messenger* 7 (June 1841): 403. The Lipans took advantage of the Texans' hospitality more than once. A grocery receipt dated July 13, 1838, indicates that Castro ran up a $484 bill for flour, sugar, whiskey, and a large bucket. See Claim no. 1466, reel 17, *Republic Claims*, Texas State Library and Archives Commission Web site, http://www.tsl.state.tx.us/arc/repclaims.

43. Anna Muckelroy, "The Indian Policy of the Republic of Texas," *Southwestern Historical Quarterly* 26 (October 1922): 128–31; Anderson, *The Conquest of Texas*, 170–74; Harmon, "United States Indian Policy in Texas," 378–79.

44. Harmon, "The United States Indian Policy in Texas," 378–79.

45. Muckelroy, "The Indian Policy of the Republic of Texas" (October 1922): 134–39; Smith, *From Dominance to Disappearance*, 171–73; LaVere, *The Texas Indians*, 173–75. The exodus of various Indian peoples to Mexico is borne out in a January 1840 report by Daniel W. Smith, the U.S. consul at Matamoros. According to Smith, during the previous six months, small parties of Cherokees, Delawares, Kickapoos, and Caddos had entered Mexico from Texas. Daniel W. Smith to Secretary of State John Forsyth, January 1, 1840, *Dispatches from the U.S. Consulate in Matamoros, 1826–1906*, record group 59, roll 2, microfilm copy, Arnulfo Oliveira Library, University of Texas at Brownsville.

46. Letter from Joseph Baker to M. B. Lamar, January 2, 1839, in Gulick, *The Papers of Mirabeau B. Lamar*, 397–98; Ray, "Ethnohistorical Analysis of Documents Relating to the Apache Indians," 59.

47. John Henry Brown, *Indian Wars and Pioneers of Texas* (Austin: State House Press, 1988), 69; John H. Jenkins and Kenneth Kesselus, *Edward Burleson: Texas Frontier Leader* (Austin: Jenkins Publishing Company, 1990), 216–18. According to Jenkins and Kesselus, the mother, three children, and two sisters of John Bowles were among the captives. *Handbook of Texas Online,*

s.v. "Burleson, Edward," http://www.tsha.utexas.edu/handbook/online/articles/BB/fbu40.html (accessed November 8, 2005); Gerald S. Pierce, "Burleson's Northwestern Campaign," *Texas Military History* 6 (Fall 1967): 195–97.

48. Jenkins and Kesselus, *Edward Burleson: Texas Frontier Leader*, 169–70; "From Texas," *Atkinson's Saturday Evening Post* 18 (January 26, 1839).

49. Winfrey, *Texas Indian Papers*, 1: 57–59; Noah Smithwick, who also participated in the campaign, recollects that the battle took place on the San Sabá River; see Noah Smithwick, *The Evolution of a State or Recollections of Old Texas Days* (Austin: Steck-Vaughn Co., 1968), 215. According to J. M. Morphis, the battle took place at Wallace's Creek, located seven miles from San Sabá; see Morphis, *History of Texas*, 414. David Crosby maintains that the battle occurred in the valley of the San Sabá River near Spring Creek; see David F. Crosby, "Texas Rangers in the Battle of Brushy Creek," *Wild West* 10 (August 1997): 60–67; Brian Delay, "The Wider World of the Handsome Man: Southern Plains Indians Invade Mexico, 1830–1848," *Journal of the Early Republic* 27 (Spring 2007): 104.

50. Carl Coke Rister writes that the Lipans killed all Comanche prisoners; see Carl Coke Rister, *Border Captives: The Traffic in Prisoners by Southern Plains Indians, 1835–1875* (Norman: University of Oklahoma Press, 1940), 85; Crosby, "Texas Rangers in the Battle of Brushy Creek," 60–67; Maestas, "Culture and History of Native Peoples of South Texas," 327.

51. Moore's force lost one man killed and six wounded. See Crosby, "Texas Rangers in the Battle of Brushy Creek," 60–67; Winfrey, *Texas Indian Papers*, 1: 57–59; Smithwick, *The Evolution of a State or Recollections of Old Texas Days*, 215–20; "Moore's Defeat on the San Saba," *Frontier Times* 3 (February 1926): 1–2; Robert S. Reading, *Arrows over Texas* (San Antonio: The Naylor Company, 1960), 73–74; Smith, *From Dominance to Disappearance*, 174; James M. Smallwood, *The Indian Texans* (College Station: Texas A&M Press, 2004), 77. The Texan and Indian force boasted that they had killed or wounded eighty to one hundred Comanches, but downplayed the large number of women, children, and elderly noncombatants; see Delay, "The Wider World of the Handsome Man," 104. The payment of $1,140 was for services rendered in Burleson's Cherokee campaign and Moore's Comanche campaign; see voucher no. 13787, dated February 23, 1841, *Republic Claims*, reel 16, Texas State Library and Archives Commission Web site.

52. Muckelroy, "The Indian Policy of Texas" (October 1922): 141–45; *Handbook of Texas Online*, s.v. "Council House Fight," http://www.tsha.utexas.edu/handbook/online/articles/CC/btc1.html (accessed November 8, 2005); Smith, *From Dominance to Disappearance*, 175.

53. Muckelroy, "The Indian Policy of Texas" (October 1922): 141–45; *Handbook of Texas Online*, s.v. "Council House Fight," http://www.tsha.utexas.edu/

handbook/online/articles/CC/btc1.html (accessed November 8, 2005); *Handbook of Texas Online*, s.v. "Linnville Raid Of 1840," http://www.tsha. utexas.edu/handbook/online/articles/LL/bt11.html (accessed November 8, 2005); Mayhall, *Indian Wars of Texas*, 31–33; Daniel W. Smith to Sec. of State John Forsyth, May 21, 1840, *Dispatches from the U.S. Consulate in Matamoros, 1826–1906*, record group 59, roll 2, microfilm copy, Arnulfo Oliveira Library, University of Texas at Brownsville.

54. Muckelroy, "The Indian Policy of Texas" (October 1922): 145; Hoig, *Tribal Wars of the Southern Plains*, 161; Mayhall, *Indian Wars of Texas*, 39–40; Gary C. Anderson, *The Conquest of Texas: Ethnic Cleansing in the Promised Land, 1820–1875* (Norman: University of Oklahoma Press, 2005), 190–91; Brown, *Indian Wars and Pioneers of Texas*, 83–84.

55. In March 1841, Flacco and fifteen Lipan scouts received payments of $355 and $60 for scouting services provided for Generals Burleson and Edwin Morehouse. See receipts of vouchers no. 21688 (dated March 22, 1841) and no. 21687 (dated March 18, 1841), in *Republic Claims*, reel 31, Texas State Library and Archives Commission Web site.

56. Joseph M. Nance, *Attack and Counter-Attack: The Texas-Mexican Frontier, 1842* (Austin: University of Texas Press, 1964), 41–44, 67, 116; Anderson, *The Conquest of Texas*, 197; *Handbook of Texas Online*, s.v. "San Patricio Minute Men," http://www.tsha.utexas.edu/handbook/online/articles/SS/qjs2.html (accessed November 17, 2005).

57. "The Lipan Indian Tribe," *Frontier Times* 1 (October 1923): 22–23; Smith, *From Dominance to Disappearance*, 188; Dudley G. Wooten, ed., *A Comprehensive History of Texas, 1685–1897* (Austin: Texas State Historical Association, 1986), 737; Smithwick, *The Evolution of a State or Recollections of Old Texas Days*, 221–23. Several different accounts of the murder exist; one is that Mexican bandits who took the horses to Louisiana killed him. Another account stated that authorities found the bodies of six Cherokees next to him, implying that members of that tribe killed him. His father and others of the tribe who searched for him believed that whites killed him. *Handbook of Texas Online*, s.v. "Flacco," http://www.tsha.utexas.edu/ handbook/online/articles/FF/ff11.html (accessed November 8, 2005).

58. Wooten, ed., *A Comprehensive History of Texas, 1685–1897*, 737–38.

59. Smithwick was probably mistaken about Chief Flacco giving away all his son's possessions. According to the Lipan death ritual, the deceased's belongings were usually destroyed or buried with the body.

60. Letter from General Flacco to Sam Houston, March 24, 1843; A Testimonial of John Castro's Friendship for the People of Texas, March 28, 1843, in Williams and Barker, eds., *The Writings of Sam Houston*, vol. 1, *1813–1836*, 343–44; Letter to Flacco from Sam Houston, March 28, 1843, in Winfrey, ed., *Texas Indian Papers*, 1:164–65; Opler, "The Lipan and Mescalero Apache in Texas," 262; Schilz, *Lipan Apaches in Texas*, 49.

61. Muckelroy, "The Indian Policy of Texas" (January 1923): 184–87; Anderson, *The Conquest of Texas*, 199–201.

62. Muckelroy, "The Indian Policy of Texas" (January 1923): 199–201; Himmel, *The Conquest of the Karankawas and the Tonkawas*, 68. The proposed line of demarcation ran roughly from Dallas to Del Rio.

63. Those tribes in attendance included the Delawares, Chickasaws, Wacos, Tawakonis, Keechis, Caddos, Anadarkos, Ionies, Biloxis, and Cherokees. Notably absent were representatives from the Comanches and Lipans.

64. Anna Muckelroy, "The Indian Policy of Texas" (January 1923): 188–91; Anderson, *The Conquest of Texas*, 204–5; Elijah Hicks, "The Journal of Elijah Hicks," *Chronicles of Oklahoma* 13 (March 1935): 68.

65. Winfrey, ed., *Texas Indian Papers*, 2:38–41; Anderson, *The Conquest of Texas*, 208–10; Muckelroy, "The Indian Policy of Texas" (January 1923): 193–96; Winfrey, ed., *Texas Indian Papers*, 2:112–17.

66. Muckelroy, "The Indian Policy of Texas" (January 1923): 196.

67. An estimated one to two hundred warriors and five hundred people total. See Winfrey, ed., *Texas Indian Papers*, 3:108, 140; Smith, *From Dominance to Disappearance*, 189. The U.S. consul in Matamoros reported a smallpox epidemic in November 1840, and what medical authorities described as a "malignant fever of an infectious character" (yellow fever?) in November 1841. See Daniel W. Smith to Sec. of State John Forsyth, November 12, 1840, and Smith to Sec. of State Daniel Webster, November 5, 1841, in *Dispatches from the U.S. Consulate in Matamoros, 1826–1906*, record group 59, roll 2, microfilm copy, Arnulfo Oliveira Library, University of Texas at Brownsville.

68. Letter from V. R. Palmer to Mirabeau Lamar, November 25, 1838, in Gulick, *The Papers of Mirabeau B. Lamar*, 303–4. In the summer of 1841, the mayor of San Antonio also complained about the Lipans; see Maestas, "Culture and History of Native Peoples of South Texas," 328.

69. This provision had been discussed at a preliminary council at Tehuacana Creek in May 1844. "The Tonkawa and Lipan are our friends and live near us. They will be kept at home, and will not be permitted to steal from our red brothers, or to do them harm. We want all our red brothers to treat them as friends and not to steal their horses or make war against them. They will be kept as far from our other red brothers as they can." See Winfrey, ed., *Texas Indian Papers*, 2:38.

70. Cambridge Green to Western, January 14, 1845, in Winfrey, ed., *Texas Indian Papers*, 2:150.

71. Thomas Western to Benjamin Sloat, June 15, 1844, and Robert S. Neighbors to Western, January 14, 1845, in Winfrey, ed., *Texas Indian Papers*, 2:72, 167; W. Eugene Hollon and Ruth Lapham Butler, eds., *William Bollaert's Texas* (Norman: University of Oklahoma Press, 1956), 376.

72. Himmel, *The Conquest of the Karankawas and the Tonkawas*, 88.

73. Thomas Western to Robert S. Neighbors, February 15, 1845, and Western to Neighbors, March 2, 1845, in Winfrey, ed., *Texas Indian Papers*, 2:197–98, 206. This may have been Ramón Castro's band; see Smith, *From Dominance to Disappearance*, 189.

74. Neighbors, "Government, Land, and Indian Policies Relative to Lipan, Mescalero, and Tigua Indians," 321–22.

75. According to W. W. Newcomb, the Lipans encamped along Cibolo Creek also planted crops. See Newcomb, *German Artist on the Texas Frontier*, 49.

76. Thomas Western to Robert Neighbors, May 22, 1845, and July 8, 1845, in Winfrey, *Texas Indian Papers*, 2:254, 273; Wooten, ed., *A Comprehensive History of Texas*, 738.

77. Report of a Council Held with the Comanche Indians, November 23, 1845; Letter from William G. Cooke to Anson Jones, December 12, 1845; Letter from J. C. Neill, Thomas I. Smith, and E. Morehouse to Anson Jones, September 27, 1845, all in Winfrey, *Texas Indian Papers*, 2:336–38, 368–70, 411–12, 422–23.

CHAPTER SIX

1. "The Kickapoo Raid the Camps of the Lipan," in Opler, *Myths and Legends of the Lipan Apaches*, 227–29.

2. Neighbors to Western, February 4, 1846, in Winfrey, *Texas Indian Papers*, 3:13–14; Neighbors, "Government, Land, and Indian Policies Relative to Lipan, Mescalero, and Tigua Indians," 322; Anderson, *The Conquest of Texas*, 215; Roemer, *Texas*, 106. Roemer is the source for the Lipan population estimate. In September 1851, Lt. Col. W. H. Hardee estimated that the Lipans possessed 70 warriors and a total population of 350. See *Annual Report of the Secretary of War*, 32nd Cong., 1st sess. (1851), serial set 611, pp. 123–24.

3. Griffen, *Utmost Good Faith*, 28–38, 96; Worcester, "The Apaches in the History of the Southwest," 29–30.

4. Ray, "Ethnohistorical Analysis of Documents Relating to the Apache Indians," 71–72.

5. Anderson, *The Conquest of Texas*, 211; Harmon, "The United States Indian Policy in Texas," 381.

6. Ray, "Ethnohistorical Analysis of Documents Relating to the Apache Indians," 72–73; Anderson, *The Conquest of Texas*, 218–19; Kenneth F. Neighbors, *Robert Simpson Neighbors and the Texas Frontier, 1836–1859* (Waco: Texian Press, 1975), 29; Hicks, "Journal of Elijah Hicks," 72–89. See chapter three for an alternate wedding ceremony.

7. Hicks, "Journal of Elijah Hicks," 92.

8. Anderson, *The Conquest of Texas*, 218–19; Hicks, "Journal of Elijah Hicks," 95–96; Opler, *The Lipan and Mescalero Apache in Texas*, 275.

9. In the treaty's preamble, the commissioners list the Comanches, Ionis, Ana-darkos, Caddos, Lipans, Longwas, Keechis, Tawakonis, Wichitas, and Waco Tribes of Indians as signatories, although no Lipans, Longwas, Anadarkos, nor Ionis affixed their mark.

10. Hicks, "The Journal of Elijah Hicks," 98; Winfrey, *Texas Indian Papers*, 3:43–61; Lena Clara Koch, "The Federal Indian Policy in Texas, 1845–1860," *Southwestern Historical Quarterly* 28 (April 1925): 263–65.

11. Anderson, *The Conquest of Texas*, 220; Ray, "Ethnohistorical Analysis of Documents Relating to the Apache Indians," 82–83, 88; Richard M'Sherry, *El Puchero* (Philadelphia: Lippincott, Grambo and Co., 1850), 146; *Memoir of a Military Expedition from San Antonio to Saltillo, Mexico*, Senate Executive Document 31, 31st Cong., 1st sess. (1850), serial set 558, pp. 35, 48; John S. Jenkins, *History of the War between the United States and Mexico* (Auburn, TX: Derby and Miller, 1850), 319–20; Frederick Adolph Wislizenus, *Memoir of a Tour to Northern Mexico, Connected with Col. Doniphan's Expedition* (Washington, DC: Tippen & Streeper, 1848), 71–72; Newcomb, *German Artist on the Texas Frontier*, 62; Opler, *The Lipan and Mescalero Apache in Texas*, 275–76.

12. Anderson, *The Conquest of Texas*, 221–22; John C. Duval, *The Adventures of Big-Foot Wallace: The Texas Ranger and Hunter* (Georgia, TX: J. W. Burke and Co., 1870), 150–62; Charles Howard Shinn, "Tales of the Mexican Border," *New Peterson Magazine* 1 (June 1893): 600.

13. John Salmon Ford, *Rip Ford's Texas*, ed. and intro. Stephen B. Oates (Austin: University of Texas Press, 1963), 449–50; Neighbors, *Robert Simpson Neighbors and the Texas Frontier*, 43–48; John C. Cremony, *Life among the Apaches* (1868; Alexandria, VA: Time-Life Books, 1981), 18.

14. Harmon, "The United States Indian Policy in Texas," 383–87; Fred J. Rippy, "The Indians of the Southwest in the Diplomacy of the United States and Mexico, 1848–1853," *Hispanic American Historical Review* 2 (August 1919): 368–69, 395; William C. Holden, "Frontier Defense, 1846–1860," *West Texas Historical Association Year Book* 6 (June 1930): 46–48; Lena Clara Koch, "The Federal Indian Policy in Texas, 1845–1860," *Southwestern Historical Quarterly* 28 (January 1925): 231; Lena Clara Koch, "The Federal Indian Policy in Texas, 1845–1860," *Southwestern Historical Quarterly* 28 (April 1925): 268–69, 272–73; Koch, "The Federal Indian Policy in Texas," *Southwestern Historical Quarterly* 29 (October 1925): 98–108.

15. Reeve, "The Apache Indians in Texas," 202; Rollins to Brooke, September 25, 1850, in Winfrey, *Texas Indian Papers*, 3:124–26; Newcomb, *German Artist on the Texas Frontier*, 62–63. In 1849, William H. C. Whiting

reported a friendly encounter with Lipans encamped along the San Sabá and Pecos rivers. See A. B. Bender, "Opening Routes across West Texas, 1848–1850," *Southwestern Historical Quarterly* 37 (October 1933): 122.

16. *Reports of the Committee of Investigation Sent in 1873 by the Mexican Government to the Frontier of Texas* (New York: Baker and Godwin, Printers, 1875), 288–91. Hereafter cited as *Reports of the Mexican Committee of Investigation*.

17. "Treaty between the United States and the Comanche, Caddo, Lipan, Quapaw, Tawakoni, and Waco Tribes of Indians," in Winfrey, *Texas Indian Papers*, 3:130–37; *Handbook of Texas Online*, s.v. "Indian Relations," http://www.tsha.utexas.edu/handbook/online/articles/II/bzi1.html (accessed May 2, 2006).

18. Anderson, *The Conquest of Texas*, 240–41; *Claims Request of James Meyer*, Senate Report 175, 36th Cong., 1st sess. (1860), serial set 2502; *Reports of the Mexican Committee of Investigation*, 96; Thomas T. Smith, *Fort Inge: Sharps, Spurs, and Sabers on the Texas Frontier, 1849–1869* (Austin: Eakin Press, 1993), 34.

19. Anderson, *The Conquest of Texas*, 241–42; Rippy, "The Indians of the Southwest in the Diplomacy of the United States and Mexico," 376–77; "Negotiations between the United States and the Comanche, Lipan, and Mescalero Tribes of Indians," in Winfrey, *Texas Indian Papers*, 3:142–44.

20. "Treaty between the United States and the Comanche, Lipan, Mescalero and Other Tribes of Indians," in Winfrey, *Texas Indian Papers*, 3:149–54.

21. Ray, "Ethnohistorical Analysis of Documents Relating to the Apache Indians," 138–41; Rudolph L. Biesele, "The Relations between German Settlers and the Indians in Texas, 1844–1860," *Southwestern Historical Quarterly* 31 (October 1927): 127; "Later from Texas," *New York Daily Times*, June 24, 1852, 4; Newcomb, *German Artist on the Texas Frontier*, 84; Opler, *The Lipan and Mescalero Apache in Texas*, 278–79; *Annual Report of the Commissioner of Indian Affairs*, Senate Executive Document no. 1, 32nd Cong., 2nd sess. (1852), serial set 658, pp. 430–36.

22. Anderson, *The Conquest of Texas*, 254–55; Opler, *The Lipan and Mescalero Apache in Texas*, 279–80; Newcomb, *German Artist on the Texas Frontier*, 136–37; Ray, "Ethnohistorical Analysis of Documents Relating to the Apache Indians," 143–44.

23. Smith, *From Dominance to Disappearance*, 161.

24. Thomas T. Smith, "U.S. Army Combat Operations in the Indian Wars of Texas, 1849–1881," *Southwestern Historical Quarterly* 99 (April 1996): 503, 506, 512. Smith explains that the army lagged in cavalry troops, since it had fought most of its previous Indian wars in the old Northwest or Southeast in heavily wooded areas; see pp. 509–10.

25. Anderson, *The Conquest of Texas*, 261–62; "Later from Texas: Indian Depredations—The Whites Arming for Defense," *New York Daily Times*, April 6, 1854, 8; Opler, *The Lipan and Mescalero Apache in Texas*, 279–80; Ray, "Ethnohistorical Analysis of Documents Relating to the Apache Indians, 144–46; Newcomb, *German Artist on the Texas Frontier*, 147. Frank D. Reeve identifies the raiders near Fort Ewell as Lipans and Seminoles; see Reeve, "The Apache Indians in Texas," 205.

26. Newcomb, *German Artist on the Texas Frontier*, 146–47.

27. Ibid., 147; E. L. Deaton, "The Big Indian Council at Fort Chadbourne," *Frontier Times* 5 (February 1928): 198–99.

28. Olmstead, *A Journey through Texas*, 285–98.

29. Deaton, "The Big Indian Council at Fort Chadbourne," 198–99; "Monthly Summary," *Graham's American Monthly Magazine* 45 (December 1845): 579.

30. Anderson, *The Conquest of Texas*, 261–63; Reeve, "The Apache Indians in Texas," 204–5; Adams, "Embattled Borderland: Northern Nuevo Leon and the Indios Bárbaros," 218; Kenneth W. Porter, "The Seminole in Mexico, 1850–1861," *Hispanic American Historical Review* 31 (February 1951): 4, 16; Gibson, *The Kickapoos*, 153–58.

31. Porter, "The Seminole in Mexico," 22; *Reports of the Mexican Committee of Investigation*, 420; Edward H. Moseley, "Indians from the Eastern United States and the Defense of Northeastern Mexico: 1855–1864," *Southwestern Social Science Quarterly* 46 (December 1965): 275–77; "Massacre of Indians in Northern Mexico," *New York Daily Times*, April 15, 1856, 1; "News from the Rio Grande," *New York Daily Times*, May 1, 1856, 1; Reeve, "The Apache Indians in Texas," 205–6.

32. Smith, *Fort Inge*, 116–17; Schilz, *Lipan Apaches in Texas*, 56–59.

33. *Claims for Spoilations Committed by Indians and Mexicans*, House Report 535, 36th Cong., 1st sess. (May 18, 1860), serial set 2483, pp. 1–11.

34. Ray, "Ethnohistorical Analysis of Documents Relating to the Apache Indians," 162–63; Byrde Pearce Hamilton, "Albert Schwander, a Captive of the Lipans," *Frontier Times* 14 (June 1937): 403–5; T. H. Stribling and P. Smythe to President Johnson, October 14, 1865, and Governor J. W. Throckmorton to Commissioner D. M. Cooley, November 5, 1865, in *Texas Indian Papers*, ed. James M. Day and Dorman Winfrey, 4:87–88, 124–26.

35. Anna Lewis, "Camp Napoleon," *Chronicles of Oklahoma* 9 (December 1931): 359–64; "Compact between Confederate Indian Tribes and the Prairie Indian Tribes made at Camp Napoleon," in *The War of the Rebellion: A Compilation of the Official Records of the Union and Confederate Armies*, series 1, vol. 48 (Washington, DC: Government Printing Office, 1896), 1102–4.

36. *Handbook of Texas Online*, s.v. "Placido," http://www.tsha.utexas.edu/ handbook/online/articles/PP/fp11.html (accessed May 9, 2006); Gannett, "The American Invasion of Texas," 273–74; C. Ross Hume, "Historic Sites around Anadarko," *Chronicles of Oklahoma* 16 (December 1938): 414–15. Hume states that the Tonkawa survivors fled to Fort Arbuckle. Joseph B. Thoburn, "Horace P. Jones, Scout and Interpreter," *Chronicles of Oklahoma* 2 (December 1924): 380–90.

37. *Testimony Taken by the Committee on Military Affairs in Relation to the Texas Border Troubles*, House Miscellaneous Document 64, 45th Cong., 2nd sess. (1878), serial set 1820, p. 16 (hereafter cited as *Texas Border Troubles*); Arrell Morgan Gibson, *The Kickapoos: Lords of the Middle Border* (Norman: University of Oklahoma Press, 1963), 210. H. J. Richards to Governor Throckmorton, February 25, 1867; A. Vogt to Throckmorton, March 1, 1867; Richards to Throckmorton, March 19, 1867; Richards to Governor E. M. Pease, May 18, 1868, in *Texas Indian Papers*, ed. Day and Winfrey, 4:167–68, 173–74, 177–80, 262–64.

38. R. W. Black to Governor Throckmorton, January 6, 1867, in *Texas Indian Papers*, ed. Day and Winfrey, 4:138–39.

39. Letter from Stephen S. Brown to General J. J. Reynolds, April 23, 1868; Letter from Brown to Reynolds, September 1, 1868, in Letters Received by the Office of the Adjutant General, Main Series (1861–1870), record group 94, roll 642, microcopy 619, National Archives, Washington, DC (hereafter cited as Letters Received, RG 94).

40. Report upon Indians and tribal peoples pertaining to the territory of the United States now harbored by Mexicans in the state of Coahuila, Mexico, September 1, 1968, Statement C, Letters Received, RG 94; Kenneth W. Porter, *The Negro on the American Frontier* (New York: Arno Press, 1971), 474; Felipe A. Latorre and Dolores L. Latorre, *The Mexican Kickapoos*, foreword by William Madsden (Austin: University of Texas Press, 1976), 15–20.

41. Report upon Indians and tribal peoples pertaining to the territory of the United States now harbored by Mexicans in the state of Coahuila, Mexico, September 1, 1968, Statement C, Letters Received, RG 94; *Texas Frontier Troubles*, House Report 701, 45th Cong., 2nd sess. (1878), serial set 1824, p. 5; Latorre and Latorre, *The Mexican Kickapoos*, 15–20.

42. Report upon Indians and tribal peoples pertaining to the territory of the United States now harbored by Mexicans in the state of Coahuila, Mexico, September 1, 1968, Extracts from Official Mexican Papers, appendix E, Letters Received, RG 94.

43. Ibid.; *Handbook of Texas Online*, s.v. "Fort Griffin," http://www.tsha.utexas. edu/handbook/online/articles/FF/uef4.html (accessed May 10, 2006); Ty Cashion, *A Texas Frontier: The Clear Fork Country and Fort Griffin, 1849–1887* (Norman: University of Oklahoma Press, 1996), 144; Brevet Major General Edward R. S. Canby to Adjutant General of the Army, February 25, 1869, in Letters Received, RG 94.

44. *Kickapoo Indians*, House Executive Document 340, 40th Cong., 2nd sess. (July 20, 1868), serial set 1346; Report upon Indians and tribal peoples pertaining to the territory of the United States now harbored by Mexicans in the state of Coahuila, Mexico, September 1, 1968, Extracts from Official Mexican Papers, Explanatory Letter A, Letters Received, RG 94.

45. "The Lipan Come to Mescalero," in Opler, *Myths and Legends of the Lipan Apache Indians*, 260–73. According to Sherry Robinson's *Apache Voices*, a chief named Magoosh likely led the Lipan refugees. Agent A. J. Curtis counted 350 Lipans at Mescalero in 1871. This number is hugely exaggerated, or possibly a misprint—I think the number was probably closer to 35 rather than 350. See Robinson, *Apache Voices*, 135.

46. Opler, *The Lipan and Mescalero Apache in Texas*, 294; General J. J. Reynolds to the Adjutant General, June 21, 1869, Letters Received, RG 94; Colonel Ranald S. Mackenzie to Captain C. E. Morse, May 29, 1869, Letters Received, RG 94; Martha Buntin, "The Mexican Kickapoos," *Chronicles of Oklahoma* 11 (March 1933): 695–98.

47. Buntin, "The Mexican Kickapoos," 698–701; Report of W. T. Atkinson and T. G. Williams to E. P. Smith, Commissioner of Indian Affairs, October 8, 1873, *Report of the Commissioner of Indian Affairs, 1873*, 169–70.

48. Porter, *The Negro on the American Frontier*, 479; Robert G. Carter, "A Raid into Mexico," *Outing* 12 (April 1888): 1–9; Testimony of First Lieutenant John L. Bullis, *Texas Border Troubles*, 187–88; Opler, *The Lipan and Mescalero Apaches in Texas*, 297–98; Ernest Wallace, *Ranald S. Mackenzie on the Texas Frontier* (Lubbock: West Texas Museum Association, 1964), 103–4; *Handbook of Texas Online*, s.v. "Remolino Raid," http://www.tsha.utexas.edu/handbook/online/articles/RR/qfr3.html (accessed May 15, 2006).

49. Buntin, "The Mexican Kickapoos," 701–4; Report of W. T. Atkinson and T. G. Williams to E. P. Smith, 170–71; Opler, *The Lipan and Mescalero Apache in Texas*, 295–96.

50. Ray, "Ethnohistorical Analysis of Documents Relating to the Apache Indians," 166; Francis A. Walker, *The Indian Question* (Boston: James R. Osgood and Company, 1874), 233; Neighbors, "Government, Land, and Indian Policies Relative to Lipan, Mescalero, and Tigua Indians," 327–28; James Mooney, "Our Last Cannibal Tribe," *Harper's Monthly Magazine* 103 (June/November 1901): 554; Cashion, *A Texas Frontier*, 256; Smith to Secretary of the Interior, November 1, 1875, *Annual Report of the Commissioner of Indian Affairs for the Year 1875* (Washington, DC: Government Printing Office, 1875), 81–101; Schilz, *Lipan Apaches in Texas*, 60–61.

51. Mayhall, *Indian Wars of Texas*, 174; Porter, *The Negro on the American Frontier*, 489; *Depredations on the Texas Frontier*, House Miscellaneous Document 37, 44th Cong., 1st sess. (November 24, 1875), serial set 1698, pp. 1–3.

52. Steven M. Kerr, "Indian Depredations along Texas's Rio Grande and Trans-Pecos Frontiers, 1877–1882," *New Mexico Historical Review* 79 (Spring 2004): 189–213.

53. For a chronological listing of specific raids and military engagements in the mid to late 1870s, see *Texas Frontier Troubles*, 104–6; *Texas Border Troubles*, 17.

54. Testimony of General E. O. C. Ord and William Schuchardt, *Texas Frontier Troubles*, 3–5, 40–41.

55. *Mexican Border Troubles*, House Executive Document 13, 45th Cong., 1st sess. (1877), serial set 1773, pp. 171–72; Porter, *The Negro on the American Frontier*, 488; "Pursuit of Indians into Mexico," *New York Times*, July 10, 1877, 1.

56. William Schuchardt letter and Shafter letter, in *Mexican Border Troubles*, 208–10; "The Mexican Border Troubles," *New York Times*, August 17, 1877, 5.

57. It appears that the Mexican military also took part in a campaign against the Lipans in the fall of 1878; see Opler, *The Lipan and Mescalero Apache in Texas*, 306. In October 1878, the *New York Times* ran an article reporting that Mexican general F. Naranjo had recently completed a campaign against the Lipans. Two weeks later, the *New York Times* reported that two companies of infantry, one of cavalry, and two batteries of artillery had left Monterrey to take part in a campaign against the Lipans. See "The Mexican Border Cattle Thieves," *New York Times*, October 24, 1878, 1; "Late Advices from Mexico," *New York Times*, November 7, 1878, 8.

58. Letter of Moses E. Kelley to Bullis, *Mexican Border Troubles*, 241–42; Joseph A. Stout, *Apache Lightning: The Last Great Battles of the Ojo Calientes* (New York: Oxford University Press, 1974), 90–91; Reeve, "The Apache Indians of Texas," 208; *Report of the Secretary of War*, House Executive Document 1, part 2, 46th Cong., 2nd sess., 1879, serial set 1903–1908, p. 88.

59. Robert Wooster, "The Army and the Politics of Expansion: Texas and the Southwestern Borderlands, 1870–1886," *Southwestern Historical Quarterly* 93 (October 1989): 162; "Last Indian Raid in Southwest Texas," *Frontier Times* 4 (August 1927): 58–59; Porter, *The Negro on the American Frontier*, 489–90.

60. Opler, *The Lipan and Mescalero Apache in Texas*, 307; Cashion, *A Texas Frontier*, 144; Sjoberg, "Lipan Apache Culture in Historical Perspective," 80; Mooney, "Our Last Cannibal Tribe," 554; Berlin B. Chapman, "Establishment of the Iowa Reservation," *Chronicles of Oklahoma* 21 (December 1936): 376–77; Hodge, *Handbook of American Indians*, 768–69.

61. In 1892, Indian agent Hinman Rhodes reported the presence of a few Lipans at Mescalero who claimed to possess supernatural powers. According to Rhodes, the Lipans, "if not closely watched may sometime result in trouble." See *Annual Report of the Commission of Indian Affairs*, House Executive Document 13, 52nd Cong., 2nd sess., 1892, serial set 3088, p. 330.

62. Eve Ball, *Indeh: An Apache Odyssey* (Provo, UT: Brigham Young University Press, 1980), 267–72; Robinson, *Apache Voices*, 135–38; Hodge, *Handbook of American Indians*, 768–69.

63. *Report of the Mexican Committee of Investigation*, 420.

64. C. C. Rister, "Harmful Practices of Indian Traders of the Southwest, 1865–1876," *New Mexico Historical Review* 6 (July 1931): 232.

EPILOGUE

1. Sherry Robinson states that there were just twenty-eight Lipans in 1910; see Robinson, *Apache Voices*, 131. Frederick Hodge gives a grand total of about thirty-five; see Hodge, *Handbook of American Indians*, 769. Muriel H. Wright notes that in 1905, out of an estimated thirty-five members of the tribe living in the United States, ten were reported in Oklahoma and twenty-five on the Mescalero Reservation in New Mexico; see Muriel H. Wright, *A Guide to the Indian Tribes of Oklahoma*, 180.

2. M. L. Henderson, "Settlement Patterns on the Mescalero Apache Reservation since 1883," *Geographical Review* 80 (July 1990): 226–39. Exactly how many Lipans died because of the epidemic is unknown.

3. Ball, *Indeh: An Apache Odyssey*, 271–72.

4. *Mescalero Apache Information Pamphlet* (Mescalero, NM: Mescalero Cultural Center, 2005); *Constitution and Bylaws of the Apache Tribe of the Mescalero Reservation* (Washington, DC: Government Printing Office, 1936). Article 2, section 1 states that "The membership of the Apache Tribe of the Mescalero Reservation shall consist of all persons enrolled on the 1935 census of the tribe, all children of resident members, and all children of nonresident members who have resided on the reservation for 5 years." Article 2 of the April 1938 Tonkawa Tribal Constitution provides membership to "Any child born of a marriage between a member of the Tonkawa Tribe and a member of any other Indian tribe who chooses to affiliate with the Tonkawa Tribe," and that "Any Indian, one whose parent is an enrolled Tonkawa Indian on an official roll of any Indian agency jurisdiction, may be admitted to membership by the Tribal Council." See http://www.tonkawatribe.com/gov/constitution.htm (accessed May 17, 2006).

5. Reeve, "The Apache Indians in Texas," 208. In 1962, Wallace L. Chafe estimated that there were fewer than ten Lipan speakers remaining in the United States; see Wallace L. Chafe, "Estimates Regarding the Present Speakers of North American Indian Languages," *International Journal of American Linguistics* 28 (July 1962): 164.

6. *The Apache Tribe of the Mescalero Reservation vs. the United States*, Proceedings before the Indian Claims Commission, 36 ICC 7, Docket

no. 22-C, March 14, 1975; *Final Award in Apache Tribe of the Mescalero Reservation vs. the United States*, Proceedings before the Indian Claims Commission, 37 ICC 221, Docket no. 22-C, February 19, 1976.

7. Copy of Letter from the Lipan Apache Band of Texas, Inc. to the Assistant Secretary of Indian Affairs, May 8, 1999, in Maestas, "Culture and History of Native Peoples of South Texas," 345.

8. *Bylaws of the Lipan Apache Band of Texas*, http://hometown.aol.com/lipanapachetx/bylaws.html (accessed May 19, 2006).

9. This would make Daniel Castro Romero Jr. the great-great-great grandson of Chief Cuelgas de Castro. See Maestas, "Culture and History of Native Peoples of South Texas," 292. Today's Lipan Apaches, Romero believes, are the survivors of two bands—the Cúelcahén Ndé (People of the High Grass) and the Tú sìs Ndé (Big Water People).

10. The written historical record does not mention that the Castros were residing at Remolino at the time. The Castro Family Oral History, meanwhile, does not mention the capture of Lipan chief Costilietos—or even the chief's being present, for that matter.

11. The Castro family's oral traditions vary about where John Castro and the other survivors went after Remolino. Some of the places mentioned include San Juan, Texas; a ranch in Reynosa, Coahuila (Mexico); McAllen, Texas; Cerralvo, Nuevo León (Mexico); and Valle Hermosa (near Brownsville, Texas). See Maestas, "Culture and History of Native Peoples of South Texas," 324–35.

12. Daniel Castro Romero Jr. to Thomas A. Britten, December 10, 2005, transcript in the hand of Thomas A. Britten.

13. Maestas, "Culture and History of Native Peoples of South Texas," 344–49; Patrick Brendel, "Restoring Ancient Remains," *Victoria Advocate*, April 2, 2006; Daniel Castro Romero Jr. to Thomas A. Britten, May 9, 2005, transcript in the hand of Thomas A. Britten. The bill's author is Senator Eliot Shapleigh (D-El Paso). As of May 2005, the bill had been referred to the State Affairs Committee.

14. Dana Bowker Lee, "Cultural-Historical Background for the Apache-Choctaw of Ebarb," unpublished manuscript written in 1990, photocopy obtained from the Eugene P. Watson Memorial Library, Northwestern State University, Natchitoches, Louisiana, 1–13; Maestas, "Culture and History of Native Peoples of South Texas," 346–47; *Choctaw-Apache Tribe of Ebarb*, http://www.sabineparish.com/community/ebarbtribe.asp (accessed May 19, 2006).

15. Daniel Castro Romero Jr. to Thomas A. Britten, July 25, 2007, transcript in the author's possession; Victor Crayhon, BIA compliance officer for the Lipan Apache Tribe of Texas, telephone interview with author, September 2007.

BIBLIOGRAPHY

(

ARCHIVAL SOURCES

Archivo General de la Nación, Mexico City, Provincias Internas. Microfilm copy. Arizona State Museum, University of Arizona, Tucson, Arizona.

Bexar Archives. Microfilm copy, reel 17, 1785–1786. Arnulfo Oliveira Library, Hunter Room, University of Texas at Brownsville-Texas Southmost College.

Bexar Archives Translations. Microfilm copy, reels 1–26, series 1, September 30, 1699–January 31, 1789. Arnulfo Oliveira Library, Hunter Room, University of Texas at Brownsville-Texas Southmost College.

Dispatches from the U.S. Consulate in Matamoros, 1826–1906. Record group 59, roll 2, vols. 4–6, microfilm copy. Arnulfo Oliveira Library, Hunter Room, University of Texas at Brownsville-Texas Southmost College.

Letters Received by the Office of the Adjutant General. Main series (1861–1870). Record group 94, roll 642, microcopy 619. National Archives, Washington, DC.

Mooney, James. "Tribal Names and Divisions of the Jicarilla, Lipan, and Mescalero Apaches, 1897." Manuscript 3785. Smithsonian Institution National Anthropological Archives, Washington, DC.

Morris Edward Opler Papers. Collection 14–25–3238, subseries D, box 44. Division of Rare and Manuscript Collections, Cornell University Library, Ithaca, New York.

Reports of the Committee of Investigation Sent in 1873 by the Mexican Government to the Frontier of Texas. New York: Baker and Godwin, Printers, 1875.

Republic Claims. Texas State Library and Archives Commission Web site.

U.S. GOVERNMENT DOCUMENTS

Annual Report of the Commissioner of Indian Affairs. Senate Executive
Document 1. 32nd Congress, 2nd session, 1852. Serial set 658.

Annual Report of the Commissioner of Indian Affairs, 1873.
Washington, DC: Government Printing Office, 1874.

Annual Report of the Commissioner of Indian Affairs, 1875.
Washington, DC: Government Printing Office, 1875.

Annual Report of the Commissioner of Indian Affairs, 1892. House Executive
Document 13. 52nd Congress, 2nd session, 1892. Serial set 3088.

Annual Report of the Secretary of War. Senate Executive Document
1. 32nd Congress, 1st session, 1851. Serial set 611.

Annual Report of the Secretary of War. House Executive Document 1,
part 2. 46th Congress, 2nd session, 1879. Serial set 1903–1908.

Claims for Spoilations Committed by Indians and Mexicans. House Report
535. 36th Congress, 1st session, May 18, 1860. Serial set 2483, pp. 1–11.

Claims Request of James Meyer. Senate Report 175. 36th
Congress, 1st session, 1860. Serial set 2502.

Constitution and Bylaws of the Apache Tribe of the Mescalero Reservation.
Washington, DC: Government Printing Office, 1936.

Depredations on the Texas Frontier. House Miscellaneous Document 37. 44th
Congress, 1st session, November 24, 1875. Serial set 1698, pp. 1–5.

*Final Award in Apache Tribe of the Mescalero Reservation vs. the United
States.* Proceedings before the Indian Claims Commission.
37 ICC 221. Docket no. 22-C, February 19, 1976.

Kickapoo and Other Roaming Bands of Indians in Mexico. House Executive
Document 90. 43rd Congress, 1st session, 1874. Serial set 1607.

Kickapoo Indians, House Executive Document 340. 40th
Congress, 2nd session, July 20, 1868. Serial set 1346.

Memoir of a Military Expedition from San Antonio to Saltillo, Mexico. Senate
Executive Document 31. 31st Congress, 1st session, 1850. Serial set 558.

Mexican Border Troubles. House Executive Document 13.
45th Congress, 1st session, 1877. Serial set 1773.

Resolution of the Legislature of Texas. Senate Miscellaneous Document
37. 42nd Congress, 1st session, March 28, 1871. Serial set 1467.

*Testimony Taken by the Committee on Military Affairs in Relation
to the Texas Border Troubles.* House Miscellaneous Document
64. 45th Congress, 2nd session, 1878. Serial set 1820.

Texas Frontier Troubles. House Report 701. 45th Congress,
2nd session, 1878. Serial set 1824.

The Apache Tribe of the Mescalero Reservation vs. the United States. Proceedings before the Indian Claims Commission. 36 ICC 7. Docket no. 22-C, March 14, 1975.

The War of the Rebellion: A Compilation of the Official Records of the Union and Confederate Armies. Series 1, vol. 4. Washington, DC: Government Printing Office, 1882.

———. Series 1, vol. 48. Washington, DC: Government Printing Office, 1896.

BOOKS

Adovasio, J. M., and Jake Page. *The First Americans: In Pursuit of Archaeology's Greatest Mystery.* New York: Random House, 2002.

Almaráz, Félix D. *Tragic Cavalier: Governor Manuel Salcedo of Texas, 1808–1813.* College Station: Texas A&M University Press, 1991.

Amberson, Mary, Margaret McAllen et al. *I Would Rather Sleep in Texas: A History of the Lower Rio Grande Valley and the People of the Santa Anita Land Grant.* Austin: Texas State Historical Association Press, 2003.

American Cyclopedia, 1873 ed. s.v. "Athabascas."

American Cyclopedia, 1873–1876 ed. s.v. "Lipans."

Anderson, Edward F. *Peyote: The Divine Cactus.* 2nd ed. Tucson: University of Arizona Press, 1996.

Anderson, Gary Clayton. *The Conquest of Texas: Ethnic Cleansing in the Promised Land, 1820–1875.* Norman: University of Oklahoma Press, 2005.

———. *The Indian Southwest, 1580–1830: Ethnogenesis and Reinvention.* Norman: University of Oklahoma Press, 1999.

Ball, Eve. *Indeh: An Apache Odyssey.* Provo, UT: Brigham Young University Press, 1980.

Bancroft, Hubert Howe. *The Works of Hubert Howe Bancroft.* Vol. 16, *History of the North Mexican States and Texas.* San Francisco: The History Company, Publishers, 1889.

Bannon, John Francis. *The Spanish Borderlands Frontier, 1513–1821.* Albuquerque: University of New Mexico Press, 1974.

Banta, S. E. *Buckelew: The Indian Captive or The Life Story of F. M. Buckelew While a Captive among the Lipan Indians in the Western Wilds of Frontier Texas.* Mason, TX: The Mason Herald, 1911; reprint, New York: Garland Publishing, 1977.

Barker, Eugene C. *Mexico and Texas, 1821–1845.* Dallas: P. L. Turner Co., 1928.

Barnett, Roger W. *Asymmetrical Warfare: Today's Challenge to U.S. Military Power.* Washington, DC: Brassey's Inc., 2003.

Basehart, Harry W. "Mescalero Apache Band Organization and Leadership." In *Apachean Culture History and Ethnology,* ed. Keith H. Basso and Morris E. Opler, 35–49. Tucson: University of Arizona Press, 1971.

Baugh, Timothy G. "Ecology and Exchange: The Dynamics of Plains-Pueblo Interaction." In *Farmers, Hunters, and Colonists: Interaction between the Southwest and the Southern Plains,* ed. Katherine A. Spielmann, 114–25. Tucson: University of Arizona Press, 1991.

Berlandier, Jean Louis. *The Indians of Texas in 1830.* Edited and with an introduction by John C. Ewers. Washington, DC: Smithsonian Institution Press, 1969.

Betty, Gerald. *Comanche Society before the Reservation.* College Station: Texas A&M University Press, 2002.

Bobb, Bernard E. *The Viceregency of Antonio María Bucareli in New Spain, 1771–1779.* Austin: University of Texas Press, 1962.

Bolton, Herbert E. *Coronado: Knight of Pueblos and Plains.* Albuquerque: University of New Mexico Press, 1949.

———. *Texas in the Middle Eighteenth Century.* Austin: University of Texas Press, 1970. Reprint of 1915 edition.

Brinckerhoff, Sidney B., and Odie B. Faulk. *Lancers for the King: A Study of the Frontier Military System of Northern New Spain, with a Translation of the Royal Regulations of 1772.* With a forward by Kieran McCarty. Phoenix: Arizona Historical Foundation, 1965.

Brooks, James F. *Captives and Cousins: Slavery, Kinship, and Community in the Southwest Borderlands.* Chapel Hill: University of North Carolina Press, 2002.

Brooks, Robert L. "Southern Plains Cultural Complexes." In *Skeletal Biology of the Great Plains,* ed. Douglas W. Owsley and Richard L. Jantz, 33–50. Washington, DC: Smithsonian Institution Press, 1994.

———. "Warfare on the Southern Plains." In *Skeletal Biology in the Great Plains,* ed. Douglas W. Owsley and Richard L. Jantz, 317–23. Washington, DC: Smithsonian Institution Press, 1994.

Brown, John Henry. *Indian Wars and Pioneers of Texas.* Austin: State House Press, 1988.

Calloway, Colin G. *One Vast Winter Count: The Native American West before Lewis and Clark.* Lincoln: University of Nebraska Press, 2003.

Campbell, Thomas Nolan. "Coahuiltecans and Their Neighbors." In *Ethnology of Texas Indians,* ed. Thomas R. Hester, 109–26. New York: Garland Publishing, Inc., 1991.

———. *The Indians of Southern Texas and Northeastern Mexico.* Austin: Texas Archaeological Laboratory, 1988.

Carlson, Paul H. *Deep Time and the Texas High Plains.*
Lubbock: Texas Tech University Press, 2005.

———. *The Plains Indians.* College Station: Texas A&M University Press, 1998.

Carter, Cecile E. *Caddo Indians: Where We Come From.*
Norman: University of Oklahoma Press, 1995.

Cashion, Ty. *A Texas Frontier: The Clear Fork Country and Fort Griffin,
1849–1887.* Norman: University of Oklahoma Press, 1996.

Castañeda, Carlos E. *Our Catholic Heritage in Texas, 1519–1936.*
Vols. 1–6. Austin: Von Boeckmann-Jones Co., 1936.

Champagne, Duane, ed. *Chronology of Native North
American History.* Detroit: Gale Research, 1994.

Chipman, Donald E. *Spanish Texas, 1519–1821.* Austin:
University of Texas Press, 1992.

Chipman, Donald E., and Harriet D. Joseph. *Notable Men and Women
of Spanish Texas.* Austin: University of Texas Press, 1999.

Cornett, James W. *How Indians Used Desert Plants.* Palm
Springs, CA: Nature Trails Press, 2002.

Cortes, Jose. *Views from the Apache Frontier: Report on the Northern
Provinces of New Spain, 1799.* Edited by Elizabeth A. H.
John. Norman: University of Oklahoma Press, 1989.

Cremony, John C. *Life among the Apaches.* Alexandria, VA:
Time-Life Books, 1981. Reprint of the 1868 edition.

De La Teja, Jesús. "Forgotten Founders: The Military Settlers of
Eighteenth Century San Antonio de Béxar." In *Tejano Origins in
Eighteenth Century San Antonio,* ed. Gerald E. Poyo and Gilberto M.
Hinojosa, 27–38. Austin: University of Texas Press, 1991.

———. *San Antonio de Béxar: A Community on New Spain's Northern
Frontier.* Albuquerque: University of New Mexico Press, 1995.

Dennis, T. S. *Life of F. M. Buckelew: The Indian Captive.*
Bandera, TX: Hunter's Printing House, 1925.

Dollard, John, Leonard Doob et al. *Frustration and Aggression.*
New Haven: Yale University Press, 1939.

Duval, John C. *The Adventures of Big-Foot Wallace: The Texas Ranger
and Hunter.* Georgia, TX: J. W. Burke and Co., 1870.

Ewers, John C. "Women's Roles in Plains Indian Warfare." In *Skeletal
Biology in the Great Plains,* ed. Douglas W. Owsley and Richard L.
Jantz, 325–32. Washington, DC: Smithsonian Institution Press, 1994.

Faulk, Odie B. *The Last Years of Spanish Texas, 1778–
1821.* London: Mouton & Co., 1964.

Filisola, Don Vicente. *Memoirs for the History of the War in Texas.* Vol. 2. Translated by Wallace Woolsey. Austin: Eakin Press, 1987.

Forbes, Jack D. *Apache, Navajo, and Spaniard.* Norman: University of Oklahoma Press, 1960.

Ford, John Salmon. *Rip Ford's Texas.* Edited and with an introduction by Stephen B. Oates. Austin: University of Texas Press, 1963.

Foster, William C. *Historic Native Peoples of Texas.* Austin: University of Texas Press, 2008.

———. *Spanish Expeditions into Texas, 1689–1768.* Austin: University of Texas Press, 1995.

Fowler, William R. "Linguistic Evidence for Athapaskan Prehistory." In *Problems in the Prehistory of the North American Subarctic: The Athapaskan Question,* ed. J. W. Helmer et al., 102–5. Calgary: University of Calgary Archeological Association, 1977.

Galvez, Bernardo de. *Instructions for Governing the Interior Provinces of New Spain, 1786.* Translated and edited by Donald E. Worcester. Berkeley, CA: The Quivira Society, 1951.

Gibson, Arrell Morgan. *The Kickapoos: Lords of the Middle Border.* Norman: University of Oklahoma Press, 1963.

Gifford, Edward W. *Culture Element Distributions: Apache-Pueblo.* Volume 4 in University of California Anthropological Records, ed. A. L. Kroeber, R. H. Lowie, and R. L. Olson. Berkeley: University of California Press, 1940.

Gillespie, Beryl C. "Major Fauna in the Traditional Economy." In *Handbook of North American Indians,* vol. 6, *The Subarctic,* ed. June Helm, 15–18. Washington, DC: Smithsonian Institution Press, 1981.

Green, Stanley C. *The Mexican Republic: The First Decade, 1823–1832.* Pittsburgh: University of Pittsburgh Press, 1987.

Griffen, William B. *Apaches at War and Peace: The Janos Presidio, 1750–1858.* Norman: University of Oklahoma Press, 1988.

———. *Utmost Good Faith: Patterns of Apache-Mexican Hostilities in Northern Chihuahua Border Warfare, 1824–1848.* Albuquerque: University of New Mexico Press, 1988.

Gulick, Charles A., et al., ed. *The Papers of Mirabeau B. Lamar.* Vol. 4, part 1. Austin: The Pemberton Press, 1968.

Gunnerson, Dolores A. *The Jicarilla Apaches: A Study in Survival.* Dekalb, IL: Northern Illinois University Press, 1974.

Gunnerson, James H. "Southern Athapaskan Archeology." In *Handbook of North American Indians,* vol. 10, *The Southwest,* ed. Alfonso Ortiz, 162–69. Washington, DC: Smithsonian Institution Press, 1983.

Gunnerson, James H., and Dolores A. "Apachean Culture: A Study in Unity and Diversity." In *Apachean Culture History and Ethnology,* ed. Keith H. Basso and Morris E. Opler, 1–22. Tucson: The University of Arizona Press, 1971.

Haley, James L. *Apaches: A History and Culture Portrait.* Garden City, NY: Doubleday & Company, 1981.

Hämäläinen, Pekka. *The Comanche Empire.* New Haven: Yale University Press, 2008.

Harrington, John P. "Southern Peripheral Athapaskawan Origins, Divisions, and Migrations." In *Essays in Historical Anthropology of North America.* Washington, DC: Smithsonian Institution, 1940.

Haskell, J. Loring. *Southern Athapaskan Migration, 200–1750.* Tsaile, AZ: Navajo Community College Press, 1987.

Hester, Thomas R. "Historic Native American Populations." In *Ethnology of Texas Indians*, ed. Thomas R. Hester, 1–8. New York: Garland Publishing, 1991.

Himmel, Kelly F. *The Conquest of the Karankawas and Tonkawas, 1821–1859.* College Station: Texas A&M University Press, 1999.

Hodge, Frederick W., ed. *Handbook of American Indians North of Mexico.* Part 1. New York: Greenwood Press Publishers, 1907.

Hoig, Stan. *Tribal Wars of the Southern Plains.* Norman: University of Oklahoma Press, 1993.

Hoijer, Harry. "The Position of the Apachean Languages in the Athapaskan Stock." In *Apachean Culture History and Ethnology*, ed. Keith H. Basso and Morris E. Opler, 3–6. Tucson: University of Arizona Press, 1971.

Hollon, W. Eugene, and Ruth Lapham Butler, eds. *William Bollaert's Texas.* Norman: University of Oklahoma Press, 1956.

Hyde, George E. *Indians of the High Plains: From the Prehistoric Period to the Coming of Europeans.* Norman: University of Oklahoma Press, 1959.

———. *The Pawnee Indians.* Denver: University of Denver Press, 1951.

Ives, John W. *A Theory of Northern Athapaskan Prehistory.* Boulder, CO: Westview Press, 1990.

Jackson, Jack. *Los Mesteños: Spanish Ranching in Texas, 1721–1821.* College Station: Texas A&M University Press, 1986.

Jenkins, John H., ed. *The Papers of the Texas Revolution, 1835–1836.* Vol. 8. Austin: Presidial Press, 1973.

Jenkins, John H., and Kenneth Kesselus. *Edward Burleson: Texas Frontier Leader.* Austin: Jenkins Publishing Company, 1990.

Jenkins, John S. *History of the War between the United States and Mexico.* Auburn, TX: Derby and Miller, 1850.

John, Elizabeth A. H. "Independent Indians and the San Antonio Community." In *Tejano Origins in Eighteenth Century San Antonio*, ed. Gerald E. Poyo and Gilberto M. Hinojosa, 123–35. Austin: University of Texas Press, 1991.

———. *Storms Brewed in Other Men's Worlds: The Confrontation of Indians, Spanish, and French in the Southwest, 1540–1795.* College Station: Texas A&M University Press, 1975.

Kay, Marvin. "The Great Plains Setting." In *Archeology of the Great Plains*, ed. W. Raymond Wood, 16–47. Lawrence: University of Kansas Press, 1998.

Keeley, Lawrence H. *War before Civilization.* New York: Oxford University Press, 1996.

Kinnaird, Lawrence. *The Frontiers of New Spain: Nicholas De La Fora's Description, 1766–1768.* Berkeley, CA: The Quivira Society, 1958.

Kirkland, Forrest. *The Rock Art of Texas Indians.* Text by W. W. Newcomb. Austin: University of Texas Press, 1967.

Krause, Richard A. "A History of Great Plains Prehistory." In *Archeology of the Great Plains*, ed. W. Raymond Wood, 48–86. Lawrence: University of Kansas Press, 1998.

Krauss, Michael E., and Victor K. Golla. "Northern Athapaskan Languages." In *Handbook of North American Indians*, vol. 6, *The Subarctic*, ed. June Helm, 67–75. Washington, DC: Smithsonian Institution Press, 1981.

Latorre, Felipe A., and Dolores L. Latorre. *The Mexican Kickapoos.* With a foreword by William Madsden. Austin: University of Texas Press, 1976.

LaVere, David. *The Texas Indians.* College Station: Texas A&M University Press, 2004.

Lehmann, Hermann. *Nine Years among the Indians, 1870–1879.* Edited by J. Marvin Hunter. Von Boeckmann-Jones Company, 1927; reprint, Albuquerque: University of New Mexico Press, 2001.

Lintz, Christopher. "Texas Panhandle–Pueblo Interactions from the Thirteenth through the Sixteenth Century." In *Farmers, Hunters, and Colonists: Interaction between the Southwest and the Southern Plains*, ed. Katherine A. Spielmann, 89–106. Tucson: University of Arizona Press, 1991.

Lockwood, Frank C. *The Apache Indians.* Lincoln: University of Nebraska Press, 1939.

Lowie, Robert H. *Indians of the Plains.* Lincoln: University of Nebraska Press, 1954.

Mayhall, Mildred P. *Indian Wars of Texas.* Waco: Texian Press, 1965.

———. *The Kiowas.* 2nd ed. Norman: University of Oklahoma Press, 1971.

McConnel, J. L. *Western Characters or Types of Border Life in the Western States.* New York City: Redfield, 1853.

McLean, Malcolm D., ed. *Papers Concerning Robertson's Colony in Texas.* Vol. 2. Fort Worth: Texas Christian University Press, 1975.

———. *Papers Concerning Robertson's Colony in Texas.* Vol. 7. Arlington: University of Texas at Arlington Press, 1980.

Menchaca, Antonio. *Memoirs*. San Antonio: Yanaguana Publications, 1937.

Merrill, William L. "Cultural Creativity and Raiding Bands in Eighteenth Century Northern New Spain." In *Violence, Resistance, and Survival in the Americas: Native Americans and the Legacy of Conquest*, ed. William B. Taylor and Franklin Pease, 124–52. Washington DC: Smithsonian Institution Press, 1994.

Mier y Terán, Manuel. *Texas by Terán: The Diary Kept by General Manuel de Mier y Terán on His 1828 Inspection of Texas*. Translated by John Wheat and edited by Jack Jackson. Austin: University of Texas Press, 2000.

Miller, John M. *El Llano Estacado: Exploration and Imagination on the High Plains of Texas and New Mexico, 1536–1860*. Austin: Texas State Historical Association, 1997.

Moorhead, Max L. *The Apache Frontier: Jacobo Ugarte and Spanish-Indian Relations in Northern New Spain, 1769–1791*. Norman: University of Oklahoma Press, 1968.

Morphis, J. M. *History of Texas from Its Discovery and Settlement*. New York: United States Publishing Company, 1875.

Morris, John Miller. *El Llano Estacado: Exploration and Imagination on the High Plains of Texas and New Mexico, 1536–1860*. Austin: Texas State Historical Association, 1997.

M'Sherry, Richard. *El Puchero*. Philadelphia: Lippincott, Grambo and Co., 1850.

Myres, Sandra L. "The Lipan Apaches." In *The Indian Tribes of Texas*, ed. Dorman Winfrey, 129–45. Waco: Texian Press, 1971.

Nance, Joseph M. *Attack and Counter-Attack: The Texas-Mexican Frontier, 1842*. Austin: University of Texas Press, 1964.

Nash, Philleo. "The Place of Religious Revivalism in the Formation of the Intercultural Community on the Klamath Reservation." In *Social Anthropology of North American Tribes: Essays in Social Organization, Law, and Religion*, ed. Fred Eggan, 377–442. Chicago: University of Chicago Press, 1937.

Neighbors, Kenneth F. "Government, Land, and Indian Policies Relative to the Lipan, Mescalero, and Tigua Indians." In *Apache Indians III*, 277–358. New York: Garland Publishing, 1974.

———. *Robert Simpson Neighbors and the Texas Frontier, 1836–1859*. Waco: Texian Press, 1975.

Newcomb, William W. *A German Artist on the Texas Frontier: Friedrich Richard Petri*. Austin: University of Texas Press, 1978.

———. *The Indians of Texas: Prehistory to Present*. Austin: University of Texas Press, 1961.

———. *North American Indians: An Anthropological Perspective.* Pacific Palisades, CA: Goodyear Publishing Company, 1974.

Oberste, William H. *History of Refugio Mission.* Refugio, TX: Refugio Timely Remarks, 1942.

O'Connor, Hugo. *The Defenses of Northern New Spain: Hugo O'Conor's Report to Teodoro de Croix, July 22, 1777.* Translated and edited by Donald C. Cutter. Dallas: Southern Methodist University Press, 1994.

Olmstead, Frederick Law. *A Journey through Texas: Or a Saddle Trip on the Southwestern Frontier.* With a foreword by Larry McMurtry. Austin: University of Texas Press, 1978. Reprint of 1857 edition.

Opler, Morris E. *An Apache Life-Way: The Economic, Social, and Religious Institutions of the Chiricahua Apaches.* Chicago: University of Chicago Press, 1941.

———. "The Apachean Culture Pattern and Its Origins." In *Handbook of North American Indians*, vol. 10, *The Southwest*, ed. Alfonso Ortiz, 368–92. Washington, DC: Smithsonian Institution Press, 1983.

———. "The Lipan and Mescalero Apaches in Texas." In *Apache Indians X*, 199–369. New York: Garland Publishing, 1974.

———. *Myths and Legends of the Lipan Apache Indians.* Memoirs of the American Folk-Lore Society, vol. 36. New York: J. J. Augustin Publisher, 1940.

———. "An Outline of Chiricahua Apache Social Organization." In *Social Anthropology of North American Tribes: Essays in Social Organization, Law, and Religion*, ed. Fred Eggan, 172–239. Chicago: University of Chicago Press, 1937.

Oswalt, Wendell H. *This Land Was Theirs: A Study of North American Indians.* 4th ed. Mountain View, CA: Mayfield Publishing Co., 1988.

Park, Joseph F. "Spanish Indian Policy in Northern Mexico, 1765–1810." In *New Spain's Far Northern Frontier: Essays on Spain in the American West, 1540–1821*, ed. David J. Weber, 216–34. Dallas: Southern Methodist University Press, 1979.

Perry, Richard J. *Western Apache Heritage: People of the Mountain Corridor.* Austin: University of Texas Press, 1991.

Porter, Kenneth W. *The Negro on the American Frontier.* New York: Arno Press, 1971.

Ramsdell, Charles. *San Antonio: A Historical and Pictorial Guide.* Austin: University of Texas Press, 1959.

Ray, Verne F. "Ethnohistorical Analysis of Documents Relating to the Apache Indians." In *The Apache Indians X*, 13–198. New York: Garland Publishing, 1974.

Reading, Robert S. *Arrows over Texas*. San Antonio: The Naylor Company, 1960.

Rister, Carl Coke. *Border Captives: The Traffic in Prisoners by Southern Plains Indians, 1835–1875*. Norman: University of Oklahoma Press, 1940.

Robinson, Sherry. *Apache Voices: Their Stories of Survival As Told to Eve Ball*. Albuquerque: University of New Mexico Press, 2000.

Roe, Frank G. *The Indian and the Horse*. Norman: University of Oklahoma Press, 1955.

Roemer, Ferdinand. *Texas*. Translated by Oswald Mueller. San Antonio: Standard Printing Co., 1935.

Ruíz, José Francisco. *Report on the Indian Tribes of Texas in 1828*. Edited by John C. Ewers and translated by Georgette Dorn. New Haven: Yale University Press, 1972.

Schilz, Thomas. *The Lipan Apaches in Texas*. El Paso: Texas Western Press, 1987.

Schlesier, Karl H., ed. *Plains Indians, A.D. 500–1500: The Archeological Past of Historic Groups*. Norman: University of Oklahoma Press, 1994.

Schroeder, Albert H. *A Study of the Apache Indians*. New York: Garland Publishing, 1974.

Schwartz, Ted, and Robert H. Thonhoff. *Forgotten Battlefield of the First Texas Revolution: The Battle of Medina, August 18, 1813*. Austin: Eakin Press, 1985.

Schweinfurth, Kay Parker. *Prayer on Top of the Earth: The Spiritual Universe of the Plains Apache*. Boulder: University of Colorado Press, 2002.

Secoy, Frank R. *Changing Military Patterns of the Great Plains Indians*. With an introduction by John C. Ewers. Lincoln: University of Nebraska Press, 1992. Reprint of 1953 edition.

Sheridan, Philip H. *Personal Memoirs of P. H. Sheridan*. Vol. 1. New York: Charles L. Webster and Company, 1888.

Simpson, Lesley Byrd, ed. *The San Saba Papers: A Documentary Account of the Founding and Destruction of the San Saba Mission*. Translated by Paul D. Nathan. Dallas: Southern Methodist University Press, 2000. Reprint of 1959 edition.

Sjoberg, Andrée F. "The Culture of the Tonkawa, a Texas Indian Tribe." In *Ethnology of the Texas Indians*, ed. Thomas R. Hester, 354–78. New York: Garland Publishing, 1991.

Smallwood, James M. *The Indian Texans*. College Station: Texas A&M Press, 2004.

Smith, F. Todd. *From Dominance to Disappearance: The Indians of Texas and the Near Southwest, 1786–1859*. Lincoln: University of Nebraska Press, 2005.

——. *The Wichita Indians: Traders of Texas and the Southern Plains, 1540–1845*. College Station: Texas A&M University Press, 2000.

Smith, Thomas T. *Fort Inge: Sharps, Spurs, and Sabers on the Texas Frontier, 1849–1869.* Austin: Eakin Press, 1993.

Smithwick, Noah. *The Evolution of a State or Recollections of Old Texas Days.* Austin: Steck-Vaughn Co., 1968.

Snow, Dean. *The Archeology of North America.* New York: Viking Press, 1976.

Speth, John D. "Some Unexplored Aspects of Mutualistic Plains-Pueblo Food Exchange." In *Farmers, Hunters, and Colonists: Interaction between the Southwest and the Southern Plains*, ed. Katherine A. Spielmann, 18–35. Tucson: University of Arizona Press, 1991.

Stewart, Omer C. *Peyote Religion: A History.* Norman: University of Oklahoma Press, 1987.

Stout, Joseph A. *Apache Lightning: The Last Great Battles of the Ojo Calientes.* New York: Oxford University Press, 1974.

Swanton, John R. *The Indian Tribes of North America.* Washington, DC: Smithsonian Institution Press, 1952.

Taylor, Virginia H., and Juanita Hammons, eds. and trans. *The Letters of Antonio Martinez: Last Governor of Spanish Texas, 1817–1822.* Austin: Texas State Library, 1957.

Terrell, John Upton. *American Indian Almanac.* New York: Barnes and Noble Books, 1971.

———. *The Plains Apache.* New York: Thomas Y. Crowell Company, 1975.

Thomas, Alfred B. *Forgotten Frontiers: A Study of the Spanish Indian Policy of Don Juan Bautista de Anza, Governor of New Mexico, 1777–1787.* Norman: University of Oklahoma Press, 1932.

———. *Teodoro de Croix and the Northern Frontier of New Spain, 1776–1783.* Norman: University of Oklahoma Press, 1941.

Tunnell, Curtis D., and W. W. Newcomb. *A Lipan Apache Mission: San Lorenzo de la Santa Cruz, 1762–1771.* Austin: Texas Memorial Museum, 1969.

Turney-High, Harry Holbert. *Primitive War: Its Practice and Concepts.* Columbia: University of South Carolina Press, 1949.

Vanstone, James W. *Athapaskan Adaptations: Hunters and Fishermen of the Subarctic Forests.* Chicago: Aldine Publishing Company, 1974.

Vigil, Ralph H., Frances W. Kaye, and John R. Wunder, eds. *Spain and the Plains.* Niwot, CO: University of Colorado Press, 1994.

Wade, Maria F. *The Native Americans of the Texas Edwards Plateau, 1583–1799.* Austin: University of Texas Press, 2003.

Wadley, Reed L. "Treachery and Deceit: Parallels in Tribal and Terrorist Warfare." *Studies in Conflict and Terrorism.* New York: Taylor and Francis, 2003, 331–345.

Walker, Francis A. *The Indian Question*. Boston: James R. Osgood and Company, 1874.

Wallace, Ernest. *Ranald S. Mackenzie on the Texas Frontier*. Lubbock: West Texas Museum Association, 1964.

Weber, David J. *Bárbaros: Spaniards and Their Savages in the Age of Enlightenment*. New Haven: Yale University Press, 2005.

———. *The Spanish Frontier in North America*. New Haven: Yale University Press, 1992.

Weddle, Robert S. *After the Massacre: The Violent Legacy of the San Sabá Mission*. Lubbock: Texas Tech University Press, 2007.

———. *San Juan Bautista: Gateway to Spanish Texas*. Austin: University of Texas Press, 1968.

———. *The San Sabá Mission: Spanish Pivot in Texas*. College Station: Texas A&M University Press, 1999.

Wedel, Waldo R. "The Prehistoric Plains." In *Ancient Native Americans*, ed. Jesse D. Jennings, 183–219. San Francisco: Freeman and Company, 1978.

Wharton, Clarence R. *History of Texas*. Dallas: Turner Company, 1935.

Wilcox, David R. "The Entry of Athapaskans into the American Southwest: The Problem Today." In *The Protohistoric Period in the North American Southwest, A.D. 1450–1700*, ed. David R. Wilcox and W. Bruce Masse, 213–56. Tempe: Arizona State University Anthropological Research Papers no. 24, 1981.

Wilkinson, J. B. *Laredo and the Rio Grande Frontier*. Austin: Jenkins Publishing Co., 1975.

Williams, Amelia W., and Eugene C. Barker, eds. *The Writings of Sam Houston*. Vol. 1, *1813–1836*. Austin: University of Texas Press, 1938.

Winfrey, Dorman, et al. *The Indian Tribes of Texas*. Waco: Texian Press, 1971.

———. *Texas Indian Papers, 1825–1843*. 4 vols. Austin: Texas State Library, 1959.

Wislizenus, Frederick Adolph. *Memoir of a Tour to Northern Mexico, Connected with Col. Doniphan's Expedition*. Washington, DC: Tippen & Streeper, 1848.

Wood, Robert D. *Life in Laredo: A Documentary History from the Laredo Archives*. Denton: University of North Texas Press, 2004.

Wooten, Dudley G., ed. *A Comprehensive History of Texas, 1685–1897*. Austin: Texas State Historical Association, 1986.

Wright, Murial H. *A Guide to the Indian Tribes of Oklahoma*. Norman: University of Oklahoma Press, 1986.

Zesch, Scott. *The Captured: A True Story of Abduction by Indians on the Texas Frontier*. New York: St. Martin's Press, 2004.

JOURNALS AND MAGAZINES

"A Campaign in Texas." *Littell's Living Age* 8 (February 1846): 413–22.

Adams, David B. "Embattled Borderland: Northern Nuevo Leon and the Indios Barbaros, 1686–1870," *Southwestern Historical Quarterly* 95 (1991): 205–20.

Adelman, Jeremy, and Stephen Aron. "From Borderlands to Borders: Empires, Nation-States, and the Peoples In Between in North American History." *American Historical Review* 104 (June 1999): 814–41.

Allen, Henry Easton. "The Parrilla Expedition to the Red River in 1759." *Southwestern Historical Quarterly* 43 (July 1939): 53–71.

Álvarez, José Manuel Serrano, and Allan J. Kuethe. "The San Sabá Presidio and Spain's Frontier Policy in North America." *West Texas Historical Association Year Book* 83 (October 2007): 7–18.

Anderson, H. Allen. "The Delaware and Shawnee Indians and the Republic of Texas, 1820–1845." *Southwestern Historical Quarterly* 94 (October 1990): 231–60.

Archer, Christon I. "The Deportation of Barbarian Indians from the Internal Provinces of New Spain, 1789–1810." *The Americas* 29 (January 1973): 376–85.

Aschmann, Homer. "Athapaskan Expansion in the Southwest." *Yearbook of the Association of Pacific Coast Geographers* 32 (1970): 79–97.

Barr, Juliana. "A Diplomacy of Gender: Rituals of First Contact in the 'Land of the Tejas.'" *William and Mary Quarterly* 61 (July 2004): 393–434.

———. "From Captives to Slaves: Commodifying Indian Women in the Borderlands." *Journal of American History* 92 (June 2005): 19–46.

Baugh, Timothy G., and Fred W. Nelson Jr. "New Mexico Obsidian Sources and Exchange on the Southern Plains." *Journal of Field Archaeology* 14 (Autumn 1987): 313–29.

Bender, A. B. "Opening Routes across West Texas, 1848–1850." *Southwestern Historical Quarterly* 37 (October 1933): 116–35.

Bender, Susan J., and Gary A. Wright. "High-Altitude Occupations, Cultural Processes, and High Plains Prehistory: Retrospect and Prospect." *American Anthropologist* 90 (September 1988): 619–39.

Berry, Jane M. "The Indian Policy of Spain in the Southwest, 1783–1795." *Mississippi Valley Historical Review* 3 (March 1917): 462–77.

Biesele, Rudolph L. "Early Times in New Braunfels and Comal County." *Southwestern Historical Quarterly* 50 (July 1946): 75–92.

———. "The Relations between German Settlers and Indians in Texas, 1844–1860." *Southwestern Historical Quarterly* 31 (October 1927): 116–29.

Blakeslee, Donald J., and David T. Hughes. "Southern Plains Archaeology, 1955–1995." *Panhandle-Plains Historical Review* 70 (1997): 19–25.

Blitz, John H. "Adoption of the Bow in Prehistoric North America." *North American Archaeologist* 9 (1988): 123–45.

Bollaert, William. "Observations of the Indian Tribes in Texas." *Journal of the Ethnological Society of London* 2 (1850): 262–83.

Bonilla, Lt. Don Antonio. "A Brief Compendium of the Events Which Have Occurred in the Province of Texas from its Conquest, or Reduction, to the Present Date." *Texas State Historical Association Quarterly* 8 (July 1904): 9–78.

Bourke, John G. "Notes upon the Religion of the Apache Indians." *Folklore* 2 (December 1891): 419–54.

Boyer, L. Bryce. "Stone as a Symbol in Apache Mythology." *American Imago* 22 (Spring–Summer 1965): 14–39.

Brant, Charles S. "The Cultural Position of the Kiowa Apache." *Southwestern Journal of Anthropology* 5 (1949): 56–61.

Brasser, Ted J. "The Tipi as an Element in the Emergence of Historic Plains Indian Nomadism." *Plains Anthropologist* 27 (1982): 309–21.

Bugbee, Lester G. "The Texas Frontier, 1800–1825." *Publications of the Southern History Association* 4 (March 1900): 102–17.

Buntin, Martha. "The Mexican Kickapoos." *Chronicles of Oklahoma* 11 (March 1933): 691–708.

Burch, Ernest S. "The Caribou/Wild Reindeer as a Human Resource." *American Antiquity* 37 (July 1972): 339–68.

Carter, Robert G. "A Raid into Mexico." *Outing* 12 (April 1888): 1–9.

Chafe, Wallace L. "Estimates Regarding the Present Speakers of North American Indian Languages." *International Journal of American Linguistics* 28 (July 1962): 162–71.

Chapman, Berlin B. "Establishment of the Iowa Reservation." *Chronicles of Oklahoma* 21 (December 1936): 366–77.

Chipman, Donald E., and Luis López Elizondo. "New Light on Felipe de Rábago y Terán." *Southwestern Historical Quarterly* 111 (October 2007): 161–81.

Coopwood, Bethel. "Route of Cabeza de Vaca." *Texas Historical Association Quarterly* 3 (April 1900): 229–64.

Cordero, Don Antonio. "Cordero's Description of the Apache—1796." Edited by Daniel S. Matson and Albert H. Schroeder. *New Mexico Historical Review* 32 (October 1957): 335–56.

Cox, Isaac Joslin. "The Louisiana-Texas Frontier." *Quarterly of the Texas State Historical Association* 10 (July 1906): 1–75.

Crosby, David F. "Texas Rangers in the Battle of Brushy
    Creek." *Wild West* 10 (August 1997): 60–67.

Deaton, E. L. "The Big Indian Council at Fort Chadbourne."
    Frontier Times 5 (February 1928): 198–99.

deMenocal, Peter D. "Cultural Responses to Climate Change during
    the Late Holocene." *Science* 292 (April 27, 2001): 667–73.

Delay, Brian. "The Wider World of the Handsome Man: Southern
    Plains Indians Invade Mexico, 1830–1848." *Journal of
    the Early Republic* 27 (Spring 2007): 83–113.

Derry, David E. "Later Athapaskan Prehistory: A Migration Hypothesis."
    Western Canadian Journal of Anthropology 5 (1975): 134–47.

Dillehay, Tom D. "Late Quaternary Bison Population Changes on the
    Southern Plains." *Plains Anthropologist* 19 (1974): 180–96.

Donahue, Paul F. "Concerning Athapaskan Prehistory in British Columbia."
    Western Canadian Journal of Anthropology 5 (1975): 21–63.

Dumond, D. E. "Toward a Prehistory of the Na-Dene, with a General
    Comment on Population Movements among Nomadic Hunters."
    American Anthropologist 71 (October 1969): 857–63.

Dunagan, Conrad. "Spanish-Mexican Trails and Traces in the Pecos
    Plains of Texas." *Permian Historical Annual* 1 (1961): 43–65.

Dunlay, Thomas W. "Indian Allies in the Armies of New
    Spain and the United States: A Comparative Study." *New
    Mexico Historical Review* 56 (July 1981): 239–58.

Dunn, William E. "The Apache Mission on the San Saba River: Its Founding
    and Failure." *Southwestern Historical Quarterly* 17 (1914): 379–414.

———. "Apache Relations in Texas, 1718–1750." *Texas State
    Historical Association Quarterly* 14 (1911): 198–274.

———. "Missionary Activities among the Eastern Apaches
    Previous to the Founding of the San Saba Mission."
    Southwestern Historical Quarterly 15 (1912): 186–200.

Ewers, John C. "The Influence of Epidemics on the Indian Populations
    and Cultures of Texas." *Plains Anthropologist* 18 (1973): 104–15.

Faulk, Odie B. "The Comanche Invasion of Texas, 1743–1836." *Great Plains
    Journal* 9 (Fall 1969): 10–50.

———. "Spanish-Comanche Relations and the Treaty of 1785." *Texana* 2
    (Spring 1964): 44–53.

Fiedel, Stuart J. "The Peopling of the New World: Present Evidence, New
    Theories, and Future Directions." *Journal of Archaeological Research* 8
    (2000): 39–103.

Flores, Dan. "Bison Ecology and Bison Diplomacy: The Southern Plains from 1800–1850." *Journal of American History* 78 (September 1991): 465–85.

Folmer, Henri. "Contraband Trade between Louisiana and New Mexico in the Eighteenth Century." *New Mexico Historical Review* 16 (July 1941): 249–74.

Forbes, Jack D. "The Appearance of Mounted Indians in Northern Mexico and the Southwest, to 1680." *Southwestern Journal of Anthropology* 15 (1959): 189–211.

———. "Unknown Athapaskans: The Identification of the Jano, Jocome, Jumano, Manso, Suma, and other Indian Tribes of the Southwest." *Ethnohistory* 6 (Spring 1956): 97–159.

Gat, Azar. "The Pattern of Fighting in Simple, Small-Scale, Prestate Societies." *Journal of Anthropological Research* 55 (1999): 563–83.

Goodwin, Grenville. "The Characteristics and Function of Clan in a Southern Athapaskan Culture." *American Anthropologist* 39 (July–September 1937): 394–407.

Graf, Leroy P. "Colonizing Projects in Texas South of the Nueces, 1820–1845." *Southwestern Historical Quarterly* 50 (April 1947): 431–48.

Greenberg, Joseph H., Christy G. Turner II, and Stephen L. Zegura. "The Settlement of the Americas: A Comparison of Linguistic, Dental, and Genetic Evidence." *Current Anthropology* 27 (December 1986): 477–97.

Gunnerson, Dolores A. "The Southern Athabascans: Their Arrival in the Southwest." *El Palacio* 63 (November–December 1956): 346–65.

Gunnerson, James H. "Apache Archaeology in Northeastern New Mexico." *American Antiquity* 34 (January 1969): 23–39.

———. "Plains Apache Archeology: A Review." *Plains Anthropologist* 13 (August 1968): 167–89.

———. "Plains-Promontory Relationships." *American Antiquity* 22 (1956): 69–72.

Gunnerson, James H., and Dolores A. Gunnerson. "Evidence of Apaches at Pecos." *El Palacio* 76 (1970): 1–6.

Habicht-Mauche, Judith A. "Coronado's Querechos and Teyas in the Archeological Record of the Texas Panhandle." *Plains Anthropologist* 37 (August 1992): 247–59.

Haggard, J. Villasana. "Spain's Indian Policy in Texas." *Southwestern Historical Quarterly* 43 (April 1940): 479–82.

Hamilton, Byrde Pearce. "Albert Schwander, a Captive of the Lipans." *Frontier Times* 14 (June 1937): 403–5.

Harmon, George D. "The United States Indian Policy in Texas, 1845–1860." *Mississippi Valley Historical Review* 17 (December 1930): 377–403.

Harper, Elizabeth Ann. "The Taovayas Indians in Frontier Trade and Diplomacy, 1719–1768." *Chronicles of Oklahoma* 31 (1953): 268–89.

Hatcher, Mattie Austin, ed. and trans. "Letters of Antonio Martinez: Last Spanish Governor of Texas, 1817–1822." *Southwestern Historical Quarterly* 39 (April 1936): 327–32.

Henderson, Harry McCorry. "The Magee-Gutiérrez Expedition." *Southwestern Historical Quarterly* 55 (July 1951): 43–61.

Henderson, M. L. "Settlement Patterns on the Mescalero Apache Reservation since 1883." *Geographical Review* 80 (July 1990): 226–39.

Hester, Thomas Roy. "Aboriginal Watercraft on the Lower Rio Grande of Texas." *The Masterkey* 46, no. 3 (1972): 108–9.

Hickerson, Nancy P. "Jumano: The Missing Link in South Plains History." *Journal of the West* 29 (1990): 5–12.

Hicks, Elijah. "The Journal of Elijah Hicks." *Chronicles of Oklahoma* 13 (March 1935): 68–99.

Hill, Robert T. "Monumenting at the San Saba Mission." *Frontier Times* 14 (September 1937): 509–16.

Hoijer, Harry. "The History and Customs of the Lipan, As Told by Augustina Zuazua." *Linguistics* 161 (1975): 5–38.

———. "The Southern Athapaskan Languages." *American Anthropologist* 40 (January–March 1938): 75–87.

Holden, William C. "Frontier Defense, 1846–1860." *West Texas Historical Association Year Book* 6 (June 1930): 39–71.

Honigmann, John J. "Northern and Southern Athapaskan Eschatology." *American Anthropologist* 47 (July–September 1945): 467–469.

———. "Parallels in the Development of Shamanism among the Northern and Southern Athapaskans." *American Anthropologist* 51 (July–September 1949): 512–14.

Hughes, Jack T. "Prehistoric Cultural Developments on the High Plains." *Bulletin of the Texas Archeological Society* 60 (1989): 1–55.

Hume, C. Ross. "Historic Sites around Anadarko." *Chronicles of Oklahoma* 16 (December 1938): 410–24.

Hunter, J. Marvin. "Bowie's Battle Ground on the San Saba." *Frontier Times* 16 (February 1939): 213–20.

Huscher, Betty H., and Harold A. Huscher. "Athapaskan Migration via the Intermontane Region." *American Antiquity* 8 (July 1942): 80–88.

Jackson, Robert H. "Ethnic Survival and Extinction on the Mission Frontiers of Spanish America: Cases from the Rio de la Plata Region, the Chiquitos Region of Bolivia, the Coahuila–Texas Frontier, and California." *Journal of South Texas* 19 (Spring 2006): 5–31.

Jackson, Thomas L. "Reconstructing Migrations in California Prehistory." *American Indian Quarterly* 13 (Autumn 1989): 359–68.

John, Elizabeth A. H., ed. "A Cautionary Exercise in Apache Historiography." *Journal of Arizona History* 25 (1984): 301–15.

———. "Nurturing the Peace: Spanish and Comanche Cooperation in the Early Nineteenth Century." *New Mexico Historical Review* 59 (October 1984): 345–69.

———. "Views from a Desk in Chihuahua: Manuel Merino's Reports on Apaches and Neighboring Nations, ca. 1804." *Southwestern Historical Quarterly* 95 (1991): 139–75.

Jones, Terry L., et al. "Environmental Imperatives Reconsidered: Demographic Crises in Western North America during the Medieval Climatic Anomaly." *Current Anthropology* 40 (April 1999): 137–70.

Kehoe, Thomas F. "The Small Side-Notched Point System of the Northern Plains." *American Antiquity* 31 (October 1966): 827–41.

Kerr, Steven M. "Indian Depredations along Texas's Rio Grande and Trans-Pecos Frontiers, 1877–1882." *New Mexico Historical Review* 79 (Spring 2004): 189–213.

Kingsbury, Lawrence A., and Loma H. Gabel. "Eastern Apache Campsites in Southeastern Colorado: A Hypothesis." *Plains Anthropologist* 28 (1983): 319–25.

Klein, Herbert S., and Daniel C. Schiffner. "The Current Debate about the Origins of the PaleoIndians of America." *Journal of Social History* 37 (Winter 2003): 483–92.

Knowles, Nathaniel. "The Torture of Captives by the Indians of Eastern North America." *Proceedings of the American Philosophical Society* 82 (March 22, 1940): 151–225.

Koch, Lena Clara. "The Federal Indian Policy in Texas, 1845–1860." *Southwestern Historical Quarterly* 28 (January 1925): 223–24.

———. "The Federal Indian Policy in Texas, 1845–1860." *Southwestern Historical Quarterly* 28 (April 1925): 259–86.

———. "The Federal Indian Policy in Texas, 1845–1860." *Southwestern Historical Quarterly* 29 (July 1925): 19–35.

———. "The Federal Indian Policy in Texas, 1845–1860." *Southwestern Historical Quarterly* 29 (October 1925): 98–126.

Krech, Shephard, III. "Disease, Starvation, and Northern Athapaskan Social Organization." *American Ethnologist* 5 (November 1978): 710–32.

Krieger, Alex D. "The Eastward Extension of Puebloan Datings toward Cultures of the Mississippi Valley." *American Antiquity* 12 (January 1947): 141–48.

Kroeber, Alfred L. "Athabascan Kin Term Systems." *American Anthropologist* 39 (October–December 1937): 602–8.

LaBarre, Weston. "Twenty Years of Peyote Studies." *Current Anthropology* 1 (January 1960): 45–60.

Lange, Charles H. "Plains-Southwestern Inter-Cultural Relations during the Historic Period." *Ethnohistory* 4 (Spring 1957): 150–73.

Lapuz, Lourdes V. "Culture Change and Psychological Stress." *American Journal of Psychoanalysis* 36 (1976): 171–76.

"Last Indian Raid in Southwest Texas." *Frontier Times* 4 (August 1927): 58–59.

LaVere, David. "Between Kinship and Capitalism: French and Spanish Rivalry in the Colonial Louisiana-Texas Indian Trade," *Journal of Southern History* 64 (May 1998): 197–218.

Lewis, Anna. "Camp Napoleon." *Chronicles of Oklahoma* 9 (December 1931): 359–64.

Lintz, Christopher. "The Historical Development of a Culture Complex: The Basis for Understanding Architectural Misconceptions of the Antelope Creek Focus." *Plains Anthropologist* 114 (1986): 111–28.

———. "The Southwestern Periphery of the Plains Caddoan Area." *Nebraska History* 60 (1979): 161–82.

Malhi, Ripan, et al. "Native American mtDNA Prehistory in the American Southwest." *American Journal of Physical Anthropology* 129 (2003): 108–24.

Mantor, Phillip. "The San Gabriel Mission." *Frontier Times* 3 (February 1926): 34–35.

McCarty, Kieran. "Bernardo de Galvez on the Apache Frontier: The Education of a Future Viceroy." *Journal of the Southwest* 36 (1994): 103–30.

McCollough, Martha. "Political Decentralization as a Strategy to Maintain Sovereignty: An Example from the Hasinais during the 1700s." *Plains Anthropologist* 46 (August 2001): 305–22.

McElhannon, Joseph Carl. "Imperial Mexico and Texas, 1821–1823." *Southwestern Historical Quarterly* 53 (October 1949): 123–30.

"Monthly Summary." *Graham's American Monthly Magazine* 45 (December 1845): 579.

Moodie, D. Wayne, et al. "Northern Athapaskan Oral Traditions and the White River Volcano." *Ethnohistory* 39 (Spring 1992): 148–71.

Mooney, James. "Our Last Cannibal Tribe." *Harper's Monthly Magazine* 103 (June/November 1901): 550–55.

Moore, Mary Lu, and Delmar L. Beene. "The Interior Provinces of New Spain: The Report of Hugo O'Conor, January 30, 1776." *Arizona and the West* 13 (1971): 265–82.

"Moore's Defeat on the San Saba." *Frontier Times* 3 (February 1926): 1–2.

Moorhead, Max L. "Spanish Deportation of Hostile Apaches: The Policy and the Practice." *Arizona and the West* 17 (1975): 205–20.

Moseley, Edward H. "Indians from the Eastern United States and the Defense of Northeastern Mexico: 1855–1864." *Southwestern Social Science Quarterly* 46 (December 1965): 273–80.

Muckelroy, Anna. "The Indian Policy of the Republic of Texas." *Southwestern Historical Quarterly* 25 (April 1922): 229–60.

———. "The Indian Policy of the Republic of Texas." *Southwestern Historical Quarterly* 26 (July 1922): 1–29.

———. "The Indian Policy of the Republic of Texas." *Southwestern Historical Quarterly* 26 (October 1922): 128–48.

———. "The Indian Policy of the Republic of Texas." *Southwestern Historical Quarterly* 26 (January 1923): 184–205.

Muir, Andrew Forest, ed. "Notes and Documents: Diary of a Young Man in Houston, 1838." *Southwestern Historical Quarterly* 53 (January 1950): 276–307.

Nelson, Al B. "Campaigning in the Big Bend of the Rio Grande in 1787." *Southwestern Historical Quarterly* 39 (January 1936): 200–227.

———. "Juan de Ugalde and Picax-Ande Ins-Tinsle, 1787–1788." *Southwestern Historical Quarterly* 43 (April 1940): 438–60.

Newcomb, W. W. "A Re-Examination of the Causes of Plains Warfare." *American Anthropologist* 52 (July–September 1950): 317–30.

Opler, Morris E. "Apache Data Concerning the Relation of Kinship Terminology to Social Classification." *American Anthropologist* 39 (April–June 1937): 201–12.

———. "An Application of the Theory of Themes in Culture." *Journal of the Washington Academy of Sciences* 36 (May 15, 1946): 137–66.

———. "Cause and Effect in Apachean Agriculture, Division of Labor, Residence Patterns, and Girls' Puberty Rites." *American Anthropologist* 74 (October 1972): 1133–46.

———. "Component, Assemblage, and Theme in Cultural Integration and Differentiation." *American Anthropologist* 61 (December 1959): 955–64.

———. "The Kinship Systems of the Southern Athabaskan-Speaking Tribes." *American Anthropologist* 38 (October–December 1936): 620–33.

———. "The Lipan Apache Death Complex and Its Extensions." *Southwestern Historical Quarterly* 1 (1945): 122–41.

———. "Lipan Apache Navigation." *The Masterkey* 49, no. 2 (1975): 70–72.

———. "A Note on the Cultural Affiliations of Northern Mexican Nomads." *American Anthropologist* 37 (1935): 702–6.

———. "Problems in Apachean Cultural History, with Special Reference to the Lipan Apache." *Anthropological Quarterly* 48 (July 1975): 182–92.

———. "Remuneration to Supernaturals and Man in Apache
Ceremonialism." *Ethnology* 7 (October 1968): 356–93.

———. "A Summary of Jicarilla Apache Culture." *American
Anthropologist* 38 (April–June 1936): 202–23.

———. "The Use of Peyote by the Carrizo and Lipan Apache Tribes."
American Anthropologist 40 (April–June 1938): 271–85.

Padilla, Juan Antonio. "Texas in 1820." Translated by Mattie Austin
Hatcher. *Southwestern Historical Quarterly* 23 (July 1919): 47–68.

Perry, Richard J. "The Apachean Transition from the Subarctic to
the Southwest." *Plains Anthropologist* 25 (1980): 279–96.

———. "Matrilineal Descent in a Hunting Context: The
Athapaskan Case." *Ethnology* 28 (1989): 33–51.

———. "Proto-Athapaskan Culture: The Use of Ethnographic
Reconstruction." *American Ethnologist* 10 (November 1983): 715–33.

Pierce, Gerald S. "Burleson's Northwestern Campaign."
Texas Military History 6 (Fall 1967): 191–201.

Porter, Kenneth W. "The Seminole in Mexico, 1850–1861." *Hispanic
American Historical Review* 31 (February 1951): 1–36.

Price, Catherine M. "The Comanche Threat to Texas and New Mexico
in the Eighteenth Century and the Development of Spanish
Indian Policy." *Journal of the West* 24 (April 1989): 34–45.

Ratcliffe, Sam D. "Escenas de Martirio: Notes on the Destruction of Mission
San Sabá." *Southwestern Historical Quarterly* 94 (April 1991): 507–34.

Reeve, Frank D. "The Apache Indians in Texas." *Southwestern
Historical Quarterly* 50 (October 1946): 187–219.

Resendez, Andres. "National Identity on a Shifting Border: Texas
and New Mexico in the Age of Transition, 1821–1845." *Journal
of American History* 86 (September 1999): 668–88.

Rippy, Fred J. "The Indians of the Southwest in the Diplomacy
of the United States and Mexico, 1848–1853." *Hispanic
American Historical Review* 2 (August 1919): 363–96.

Rister, Carl Coke. "Harmful Practices of Indian Traders of the Southwest,
1865–1876." *New Mexico Historical Review* 6 (July 1931): 231–48.

Ruhlen, Merritt. "The Origin of the Na-Dene." *Proceedings
of the National Academy of Sciences of the United States
of America* 95 (November 10, 1998): 13994–96.

Salmón, Roberto Mario. "A Thankless Job: Mexican Soldiers
in the Spanish Borderlands of the Southwest." *Military
History of the Southwest* 22 (Spring 1991): 1–19.

Sánchez, José María. "A Trip to Texas in 1828." Translated by Carlos E. Castañeda. *Southwestern Historical Quarterly* 29 (April 1926): 249–88.

Schaefer, Stacy B. "The Peyote Religion and Mescalero Apache: An Ethnohistorical View from West Texas." *Journal of Big Bend Studies* 12 (2000): 51–70.

Schaeffer, James B. "The Alibates Flint Quarry, Texas." *American Antiquity* 24 (October 1958): 189–91.

Schilz, Thomas F., and Donald E. Worcester. "The Spread of Firearms among the Indian Tribes on the Northern Frontier of New Spain." *American Indian Quarterly* 11 (Winter 1987): 1–10.

Schlesier, Karl H. "Rethinking the Dismal River Aspect and the Plains Athapaskans, A.D. 1692–1768," *Plains Anthropologist* 15 (1972): 101–33.

Schroeder, Albert H. "Shifting for Survival in the Spanish Southwest." *New Mexico Historical Review* 43 (October 1968): 291–310.

Shapiro, Anne Dhu, and Ines Talamantez. "The Mescalero Apache Girls' Puberty Ceremony: The Role of Music in Structuring Ritual Time." *Yearbook for Traditional Music* 18 (1986): 77–90.

Shinn, Charles Howard. "Tales of the Mexican Border." *New Peterson Magazine* 1 (June 1893): 600.

Shover, Merle. "Apache Fiddles." *Indians at Work* 4 (1937): 46–47.

Simmons, Marc, ed. and trans. "Governor Anza, the Lipan Apaches and Pecos Pueblo." *El Palacio* 77 (1970): 35–40.

Sjoberg, Andrée F. "Lipan Apache Culture in Historical Perspective." *Southwestern Journal of Anthropology* 9 (1953): 76–98.

Slotkin, J .S. "Peyotism, 1521–1891." *American Anthropologist* 57 (April 1955): 202–30.

Smith, Ralph A. "Apache Plunder Trails Southward, 1831–1840." *New Mexico Historical Review* 37 (1962): 20–42.

———. "Indians in American-Mexican Relations before the War of 1846." *Hispanic American Historical Review* 43 (February 1963): 34–64.

———, ed. and trans. "Account of the Journey of Bénard de la Harpe: Discovery Made by Him of Several Nations Situated in the West." *Southwestern Historical Quarterly* 62 (1958): 371–85.

Smith, Thomas T. "U.S. Army Combat Operations in the Indian Wars of Texas, 1849–1881." *Southwestern Historical Quarterly* 99 (April 1996): 501–31.

Spielmann, Katherine A. "Late Prehistoric Exchange between the Southwest and Southern Plains." *Plains Anthropologist* 28 (November 1983): 257–72.

———, Margaret J. Schoeninger, and Katherine Moore. "Plains-Pueblo Interdependence and Human Diet at Pecos Pueblo, New Mexico." *American Antiquity* 55 (October 1990): 745–65.

Starnes, Gary B. "Juan de Ugalde and the Coahuila-Texas Frontier." *Texana* 10 (1972): 116–28.

Stephenson, Robert L. "Culture Chronology in Texas." *American Antiquity* 16 (October 1950): 151–57.

Stewart, Omer C. "Origin of the Peyote Religion in the United States," *Plains Anthropologist* 19 (1974): 211–23.

Taylor, Morris F. "Some Aspects of Historical Indian Occupation of Southeastern Colorado." *Great Plains Journal* 4 (1964): 17–28.

Terreros, Juan M. Romero. "The Destruction of the San Sabá Apache Mission: A Discussion of the Casualties." *The Americas* 60 (April 2004): 617–27.

"Texas and Its Revolution." *Southern Literary Messenger* 7 (June 1841): 398–421.

"The Lipan Indian Tribe." *Frontier Times* 1 (October 1923): 22–23.

Thoburn, Joseph B. "Horace P. Jones, Scout and Interpreter." *Chronicles of Oklahoma* 2 (December 1924): 380–90.

Torres-Nez, John. "Tracking the Apache." *El Palacio* 109 (2004): 14–17.

Tweedie, M. Jean. "Notes on the History and Adaptation of the Apache Tribe," *American Anthropologist* 70, no. 6 (December 1968): 1132–42.

Tyler, Daniel. "Mexican Indian Policy in New Mexico." *New Mexico Historical Review* 55 (April 1980): 101–20.

Valerio-Jiménez, Omar S. "Neglected Citizens and Willing Traders: The Villas del Norte (Tamaulipas) in Mexico's Northern Borderlands, 1749–1846." *Mexican Studies* 18 (Summer 2002): 251–96.

Vazquez, Josefina Zoraida. "The Mexican Declaration of Independence." *Journal of American History* 85 (March 1999): 1362–69.

Vehik, Susan C. "Conflict, Trade, and Political Development on the Southern Plains." *American Antiquity* 67 (January 2002): 37–64.

Vigness, David M. "Don Hugo Oconor and New Spain's Northeastern Frontier, 1764–1776." *Journal of the West* 6 (1967): 27–39.

Walde, Dale. "Avonlea and Athabaskan Migrations: A Reconsideration." *Plains Anthropologist* 51 (2006): 185–98.

Wayland, Virginia. "Apache Playing Cards." *Expedition* 4 (Spring 1962): 34–39.

Weber, David J. "Mexico's Far Northern Frontier, 1821–1854: Historiography Askew." *Western Historical Quarterly* 7 (July 1976): 279–93.

Weddle, Robert S. "Campaigning in Texas, 1775." *Texas Military History* 6 (Winter 1967): 254–70.

Wedel, Waldo R. "Some Aspects of Human Ecology in the Central Plains." *American Anthropologist* 55 (October 1953): 499–514.

Wiseman, Reggie N. "The Jumano Diaspora: Some More Pieces to the Puzzle." *Journal of Big Bend Studies* 14 (2002): 97–107.

Wissler, Clark. "Culture of the North American Indian Occupying the Caribou Area and Its Relation to Other Types of Culture." *Proceedings of the National Academy of Sciences of the United States of America* 1, no. 1 (January 15, 1915): 51–54.

Wood, W. D. "Sketch of the Early Settlement of Leon County, Its Organization, and Some of the Early Settlers." *Southwestern Historical Quarterly* 4 (October 1900): 203–17.

Wooster, Robert. "The Army and the Politics of Expansion: Texas and the Southwestern Borderlands, 1870–1886." *Southwestern Historical Quarterly* 93 (October 1989): 151–67.

Worcester, Donald E. "The Apaches in the History of the Southwest." *New Mexico Historical Review* 50 (1975): 25–43.

———. "The Beginnings of the Apache Menace of the Southwest." *New Mexico Historical Review* 16 (January 1941): 1–14.

———. "The Spread of Spanish Horses in the Southwest." *New Mexico Historical Review* 19 (1944): 225–32.

———. "The Spread of Spanish Horses in the Southwest, 1700–1800." *New Mexico Historical Review* 20 (January 1945): 1–12.

Works, Martha A. "Creating Trading Spaces on the New Mexican Frontier." *Geographical Review* 82 (July 1992): 268–81.

NEWSPAPERS

Brendel, Patrick. "Restoring Ancient Remains." *Victoria Advocate.* April 2, 2006.

"From Texas." *Atkinson's Saturday Evening Post.* January 26, 1839.

"Late Advices from Mexico." *New York Times.* November 7, 1878, 8.

"Later from Texas." *New York Daily Times.* June 24, 1852, 4.

"Later from Texas: Indian Depredations—The Whites Arming for Defense." *New York Daily Times.* April 6, 1854, 8.

"Massacre of Indians in Northern Mexico." *New York Daily Times.* April 15, 1856, 1.

"News from the Rio Grande." *New York Daily Times.* May 1, 1856, 1.

"Pursuit of Indians into Mexico." *New York Times.* July 10, 1877, 1.

"The Mexican Border Cattle Thieves." *New York Times.* October 24, 1878, 1.

"The Mexican Border Troubles." *New York Times.* August 17, 1877, 5.

Tolbert, Frank X. "When Castro Came to the Texas Capital." *Dallas Morning News.* October 17, 1962, 7.

WEB SITES

Bylaws of the Lipan Apache Band of Texas. http://hometown.aol. com/lipanapachetx/bylaws.html (accessed May 19, 2006).

Choctaw-Apache Tribe of Ebarb. http://www.sabineparish.com/ community/ebarbtribe.asp (accessed May 19, 2006).

Constitution and By-Laws of the Tonkawa Tribe of Indians of Oklahoma. http:// www.tonkawatribe.com/gov/constitution.htm (accessed May 17, 2006).

Handbook of Texas Online. S.v. "Antelope Creek Phase." http:// www.tsha.utexas.edu/handbook/online/articles/view/ AA/bba7.html (accessed December 7, 2004).

————. S.v. "Burleson, Edward." http://www.tsha.utexas.edu/handbook/ online/articles/BB/fbu40.html (accessed November 8, 2005).

————. S.v. "Castro, Cuelgas De." http://www.tsha.utexas.edu/handbook/ online/articles/CC/fca92.html (accessed October 15, 2005).

————. S.v. "Council House Fight." http://www.tsha.utexas.edu/handbook/ online/articles/CC/btc1.html (accessed November 8, 2005).

————. S.v. "Davenport, Peter Samuel." http://www.tsha.utexas.edu/ handbook/online/articles/DD/fda23.html (accessed October 6, 2005).

————. S.v. "Edwards Plateau." http://www.tsha.utexas.edu/handbook/ online/articles/EE/rxe1.html (accessed July 7, 2006).

————. S.v. "Escanjaque Indians." http://www.tsha.utexas.edu/handbook/ online/articles/EE/bme7.html (accessed March 28, 2006).

————.S.v. "Flacco." http://www.tsha.utexas.edu/handbook/online/ articles/FF/ff11.html (accessed November 8, 2005).

————. S.v. "Fort Griffin." http://www.tsha.utexas.edu/handbook/ online/articles/FF/uef4.html (accessed May 10, 2006).

————. S.v. "Garza Falcón, Aljedo de la." http://www.tsha.utexas.edu/ handbook/online/articles/GG/fgaae.html (accessed August 15, 2005).

————. S.v. "Indian Relations." http://www.tsha.utexas.edu/handbook/ online/articles/II/bzi1.html (accessed May 2, 2006).

————. S.v. "Linnville Raid of 1840." http://www.tsha.utexas.edu/handbook/ online/articles/LL/bt11.html (accessed November 8, 2005).

————. S.v. "Llano Estacado." http://www.tsha.utexas.edu/handbook/ online/articles/LL/ry12.html (accessed June 16, 2006).

————. S.v. "New Regulations for Presidios." http://www.tsha.utexas.edu/ handbook/online/articles/NN/nfn1.html (accessed July 28, 2005).

————. S.v. "Martiniz Pacheco, Rafael." http://www.tsha.utexas.edu/handbook/ online/articles/MM/fmadt.html (accessed September 13, 2005).

———. S.v. "Medina, Battle of." http://www.tsha.utexas.edu/handbook/
online/articles/MM/qfm1.html (accessed October 6, 2005).

———. S.v. "Mier y Terán, Manuel De." http://www.tsha.utexas.edu/
handbook/online/articles/MM/fmi2.html (accessed October 25, 2005).

———. S.v. "Panhandle." http://www.tsha.utexas.edu/handbook/
online/articles/PP/ryp1.html (accessed June 16, 2006).

———. S.v. "Placido." http://www.tsha.utexas.edu/handbook/
online/articles/PP/fp11.html (accessed May 9, 2006).

———. S.v. "Posada, Alonso de." http://www.tsha.utexas.edu/handbook/
online/articles/PP/fp025.html (accessed March 28, 2006).

———. S.v. "Remolino Raid." http://www.tsha.utexas.edu/handbook/
online/articles/RR/qfr3.html (accessed May 15, 2006).

———. S.v. "Rosillo, Battle of." http://www.tsha.utexas.edu/handbook/
online/articles/RR/qfr2.html (accessed October 6, 2005).

———. S.v. "San Lorenzo de la Santa Cruz Mission." http://www.tsha.utexas.edu/
handbook/online/articles/SS/uqs26.html (accessed February 19, 2006).

———. S.v. "San Patricio Minute Men." http://www.tsha.utexas.edu/
handbook/online/articles/SS/qjs2.html (accessed November 17, 2005).

———. S.v. "San Xavier Missions." http://www.tsha.utexas.edu/handbook/
online/articles/SS/uqs34.html (accessed March 9, 2006).

———. S.v. "Texas in the Age of Mexican Independence." http://www.tsha.utexas.
edu/handbook/online/articles/TT/nptsd.html (accessed October 6, 2005).

THESES, DISSERTATIONS, INTERVIEWS,
AND OTHER UNPUBLISHED PAPERS

Carlisle, Jeffrey D. "Spanish Relations with the Apache Nations East of
the Rio Grande." Ph.D. diss., University of North Texas, 2001.

Carter, William B. "Indian Alliances in the Southwest, 1300–
1706." Ph.D. diss., Arizona State University, 2002.

Crayhon, Victor, BIA Compliance Officer for the Lipan Apache Tribe
of Texas. Telephone interview with author. September 2007.

Duncan, Marjorie Ann. "Adaptation during the Antelope Creek Phase: A
Diet Breadth and Site Catchment Analysis of the Subsistence Strategy
at the Two Sisters Site." Ph.D. diss., University of Oklahoma, 2002.

French, David H. "A Comparative Study of the Mythologies of
the Jicarilla, Lipan, Mescalero, and Chiricahua Apache
Indians." Master's thesis, Claremont College, 1940.

Gannett, William B. "The American Invasion of Texas, 1820–1845: Patterns of Conflict between Settlers and Indians." Ph.D. diss., Cornell University, 1984.

Hill, Jane. "Language Spread among Hunter-Gatherers." Paper presented at the Second Conference on the Archeology and Linguistics of Australia. Canberra, Australia, October 1–4, 2002.

Ives, John W., Sally Rice, and Stephanie Heming. "On the Dispersal of the Apachean Peoples from the Subarctic North America." Paper presented at the Second Conference on the Archeology and Linguistics of Australia. Canberra, Australia, October 1–4, 2002.

Lee, Dana Bowker. "Cultural-Historical Background for the Apache-Choctaw of Ebarb." Unpublished manuscript written in 1990. Photocopy obtained from Eugene P. Watson Memorial Library, Northwestern State University, Natchitoches, Louisiana.

Maestas, Enrique Gilbert-Michael. "Culture and History of Native Peoples of South Texas." Ph.D. diss., University of Texas, 2003.

Mescalero Apache Information Pamphlet. Mescalero, NM: Mescalero Cultural Center, 2005.

"Planning for the Drought." Colorado Conservation Board. May 2000.

Romero, Jr., Daniel Castro to Thomas A. Britten. December 10, 2005. Transcript in the hand of Thomas A. Britten.

———. May 9, 2005. Transcript in the hand of Thomas A. Britten.

INDEX

☾